This text provides an introduction to mass communication, a somewhat versatile course and a contemporary player in the world's globalisation. The book collects numerous terminologies and jargons used in the various components of the media ranging from journalism, advertising, public relations, communication research, broadcasting etc. The marriage of these terms seeks to make easy the understanding of the field mass communication which is complex in its own.

**OBINNA CHARLES OKWELUME** studied Mass Communication in Madonna University, Okija, Nigeria, graduating with an honours degree in 2003. He also has a Masters degree in International Relations from London Metropolitan University. In 2001 he received the Nigerian Institute of Public Relations award for his contributions to literary writing. He worked briefly with Nigerian National Petroleum Corporation in the Group Public Affairs Division, Abuja and the Federal Ministry of Information and National Orientation, Abuja, Nigeria in the Public Relations Unit. He founded the Dynamics Choir and Dynamites Theatre in 1997. Through his works, he founded and is Coordinator, Save Africa Project, a project that aims to immortalise African culture via literature. Okwelume is a member of the Association of Nigerian Authors and a Graduate Member of the Nigerian Institute of Management and Nigerian Institute of Public Relations. He was Editor-in-Chief of the NYSC FCT Editorial Board and was a member of the Editorial Board of the Catholic Corpers Organisation. His other published works include *Ogurigwe*, *Arrow of Vengeance*, *Three Plays*, *Babel of Voices* and *Drumbeats of Black Africa*.

Okwelume is a play director; at his leisure he directs music performances and cultural displays. He is presently at the University of Birmingham.

In a generalised sense, Mass Communication has been used to designate features of disparate phenomena as broadcast television, cable, video-playback, theatre projection, recorded songs, radio talk, advertising, newspaper and magazine publications, etc. The sheer diversity of the field has given rise to complex and specialised use of words and terminologies that underscore a need for a reference material that would enhance familiarity and understanding of the appropriate usage of these words...This work is an impressive presentation that seeks to meet the purpose identified above. It is also a demonstration of the meaningful contribution that our young scholars are capable of making in their chosen field of endeavour. The Author has devoted immense effort to this work and I trust that Journalists, Broadcasters, Public Relations and Advertising Practitioners as well as Mass Communication Scholars will find it a useful reference material.

**Chukwuemeka Chikelu**, *Minister, Information and National Orientation, Nigeria, 2004.*

Two people cannot make even the simplest house if they don't know what to build, how to build and why they are building – information and communication is a key ingredient that makes this possible. Okwelume's *Dictionary of Mass Communication* has provided the platform for understanding and applying appropriate terms in our various information and communication processes. This book is an invaluable reference hub for PR Practitioners and others in related fields of communication ...from a brilliant author who knows his onions.

**Joe Itah**, *Chapter Chairman- Nigerian Institute of Public Relations, Abuja 2006.*

We live in an era not only of mass communications, but of massive communications. Wherever we live in the world, and whatever work we do, we communicate. We communicate in increasingly varied and complicated ways, and we receive information from huge range of courses. This book is a valuable resource; a guide through the jargon and terminology of the world of media and mass communication. The book provides students, professionals and academics alike with a way to comprehend the world of mass communications, and to ensure that they are clear and precise in their understanding of the world around them. Okwelume is an amazing and inspiring person, committed to seeing the world in a clearer way, with the perspective that comes from an interest in, yet at times a detached awareness of, our lives.

**Mark Bickerton**, *Director, Student Recruitment, Marketing and Communications, London Metropolitan University*

# DICTIONARY OF
# MASS COMMUNICATION

O. Charles Okwelume Jnr.

Published 2006 by arima publishing

www.arimapublishing.com

ISBN 1 84549 142 4
ISBN 978 1 84549 142 10

Printed and bound in the United Kingdom

Typeset in Century Gothic

arima publishing
ASK House, Northgate Avenue
Bury St Edmunds, Suffolk IP32 6BB
t: (+44) 01284 700321

www.arimapublishing.com

*For Madonna University Mass Communication
graduating class of 2003*

# Preface

More than half a century ago, the talk of communication was compared to the irrelevance of a child's hiss. The succeeding one-half, up till now has been submerged all over with the discuss of mass communication. When Marshall McLuhan's influential work on 'global village' in 1964 stormed the world, he anticipated only then, some of the main themes of globalisation, a somewhat indefinite and vague concept, focusing primarily on the communications revolution. Mass communication in many ways has become a strapping, yet imperative force in this era of globalisation.

Mass communication, undoubtedly, is significant to all societies, our daily life, socio-economic relations and especially in all development trends and circles. As a subject of study, it is an omnibus field espousing diverse but closely related facets of human communication. It is becoming one of the world's most holistic and influential courses because of its sway in the development and globalisation of the world. The subject, as may be noticed in this text, comprehends such spheres of study as: advertising, journalism- broadcast and print, marketing and research, photo-graphics and public relations. As well, teaching the subject has stretched lately to include other subjects as sociology and psychology, even more recently economics, politics and international relations. Hence, the usefulness of an overture text as this is necessary particularly for beginners, students and practitioners of fields in this cone.

My emphasis is to offer a general reference to mass communication. This title is an introductory text targeted to all parts of the society particularly journalists, broadcasters, printers and photojournalists, public relations and advertising practitioners and especially mass communication scholars. All students in these fields will find it very useful. It is written primarily as a modest and conscious effort to ease the teaching and learning process of mass communication which is largely extensive, technical and usually specialised.

The book is organised alphabetically for easy reference, collecting the various explanations or description of terms with more than one meaning, to keep readers far from being confused with what the differences are. The definitions are apt and straight to the point to give precise understanding. The structure is also perfect in the sense that a definition might lead a reader to another description, particularly where it may be necessary to see another term to understand their differences, similarities or otherwise as intended by the reader.

Worthy to note is that mass communication terminologies may often vary from one media to another, country to country and maybe continent to continent, but most of them are universal in context. Nevertheless, all irrespective of any differences can use it. Most of the terms in this book may be found in other books whose authors professionally narrowed the subject to a particular aspect say PR or Advertising. This book presents a general approach and also gives relevant examples to some terms for easy understanding and appreciation.

A number of persons have helped me refine my thinking along the long, unusually tortuous path to the publication of this book. None has been more helpful than Dr. A. Tom Adaba, even more in my career of theatre production and script writing. He became my astute mentor from my days in university up until my graduation even after postgraduate studies. His oratory gift and academic comport enticed me fully to the academic profession. I think of Tom more as a colleague with shared interests than a lecturer.

Special thanks should also go to members of the NYSC FCT Editorial Board especially during my tenure as Editor-in-Chief. The Coordinators Olanipekun Alao, Egbeyemi Oluwakemi and Carol Embu were wonderful, the members indescribable in brilliance. My experience while on the board was a major start of my academic hurtle, teaching and learning from those I considered wiser and elderly in almost if not all ramifications. I must especially thank my deputy and erstwhile editor-in-chief, Toyin Ajao for reading through the manuscript and making useful suggestions. Also, I cannot not mention my boss and editor before me, a stunning lady, beautiful in character and intelligent to a fault, Angeline Anya, who gave me the biggest surprise in June 2004, not minding my quietness and simplicity then.

Experience taught me that gratitude to an unknown mentor is necessary, even when one is not known or has never met his mentor. One man I have not met, but hear his name everyday, maybe because of my looks or career is our own Wole Soyinka. I have grown to admire his consistency especially in his criticisms and lifestyle. I am grateful to him in more ways than this for his works and availability to young ones, especially Nigerians.

I am grateful to the following persons for the encouragement which they gave me during the preparation of this book: my colleagues in the Department of Mass Communication, Madonna University, especially Lucy Ozongwu, Dumebi Unabor, Solomon Falade, Ester Ibeh and Ngozi Omeligwe; also in the same Department, Professor Anthony U. John-Kamen, Tony Ibe, Emeka Okpala, Gabriel Ezeuku, Peter Ossai, Nnadiuku and Victor Alozie. I am also indebted to Professor Romanus Unegbu, Vice Chancellor of Madonna University, Nigeria for his regular criticisms and advice; officials of Federal Ministry of Information and National Orientation, Nigerian Television Authority and Federal Radio Corporation of Nigeria who gave me useful information and suggestions. Also to Ndubisi Obi and Taiwo Hassan of the Federal Ministry of Information and National Orientation for their support and incessant lectures.

Chukwuemeka Chikelu, my brother and boss, the former minister for information and national orientation is beyond doubt a vernal guru, his chaste intelligence and career strengthened my vision and prospects. I remain grateful to him especially for his apposite review and comment on this apropos text. Also to Dr. Okey Ikechukwu, formerly of the same ministry, for his advice, criticisms and assistance.

Mark Bickerton of London Metropolitan University was my yardstick for excellence, thank you. Professor Olu Obafemi, Dr. Wale Okediran, Professor Saint Gbilekaa, Nduka Otiono and Denja Abdullahi: all of the Association of Nigerian Authors; Ndu Ughamadu, Levi Ajuonuma, Abdullahi Idris, Jones Uwazie and Nyong Nyong: my instructors during my PR experience; Emmanuel Igwenwanne, Bursary Meture and Anthony Njoku: my noisy friends who usually spat criticisms each time I set out on an academic project; Victor Njoku, Samson Nwakanma, Malvis Idenekpoma, Andyson Ololo, Ofeoritse Atiwe and Omo Atafo: my friends who saw me sail in the international relations ferry, my contact with you is cum laude.

As always, my parents Charles and Mary Okwelume were there whenever needed, providing wise and practical counsel. Even though both of them where not trained in this field, they taught me more than I learnt from my text books and classrooms, thank you for giving me life. I also could not have completed this without the love and support of my siblings Sandra, Rose and Anthony; and a host of relatives and friends who kept me going and believing through challenges, large and small, public and private.

Rukevwe, you missed this dedication for a good reason, even though by a hair's breathe; to Cecilia Egbele, Tekena Harry, Ogo Ezenwa and

Louis Ezeonyim, thank you. My publishers and editors of my plays, Spectrum Books Nigeria, thank you for your continued projection of my publications and ideas. Then to my Father in heaven, thank you God for my life and work, you only came last because you are first.


*O. Charles Okwelume Jnr.*
Abuja, 2006.

# Selected Abbreviations

| | |
|---|---|
| **AA** | Advertising Association; Average Audience |
| **AAP** | Australian Associated Press |
| **ABA** | Australian Broadcasting Authority |
| **ABE** | Association of British Editors |
| **ABS** | Association of Broadcasting and Allied Staffs |
| **ACTT** | Association of Cinematography, Television & Allied Technicians |
| **ADP** | Association of Directors and Producers |
| **AEJMC** | Association for Education in Journalism and Mass Communication |
| **AFDC** | Automatic Data Processing |
| **AFP** | Agence France Presse |
| **AIT** | African Independent Television |
| **ALCS** | Author's Lending & Copyright Society |
| **ANA** | Association of Nigerian Authors |
| **AP** | Associated Press |
| **APCON** | Advertising Practitioners Council of Nigeria |
| **AR** | Audience Research |
| **ASA** | Advertising Standards Authority |
| **ASCAP** | American Society of Composers, Authors and Publishers |
| **ATV** | Associated Television (Associated Broadcasting Company) |
| | |
| **BAFTA** | British Academy of Film and Television Arts |
| **BAPLA** | British Association of Picture Libraries and Agencies |
| **BARB** | Broadcasting Audience Research Board |
| **BBC** | British Broadcasting Corporation |
| **BBFC** | British Board of Film Classification |
| **BBS** | Bulletin Board System |
| **BCC** | Broadcasting Complaints Commission |
| **BEA** | Broadcast Education Association |
| **BFI** | British Film Institute |
| **bit** | binary digit |
| **BJA** | Black Journalists' Association |
| **BMWA** | Black Media Workers Association |
| **BON** | Broadcasting Organisation of Nigeria |
| **bps** | bits per second |
| **BSB** | British Satellite Broadcasting |
| **BSC** | British Society of Cinematography |
| **BSC** | Broadcasting Standards Council |
| **BT** | British Telecom |

| | |
|---|---|
| **CACI** | Campaign Against Censorship of the Internet |
| **CAM** | Communications Advertising and Marketing Educational Foundation |
| **CAP** | Code of Advertising Practice |
| **CAP** | Campaign Against Pornography |
| **CAR** | Computer Assisted Reporting |
| **CARM** | Campaign Against Racism in the Media |
| **CATV** | Cable Antenna Television System |
| **CAV** | Constant Angular Velocity |
| **CBS** | Columbia Broadcasting System |
| **CCCS** | Centre for Contemporary Culture Studies (University of Birmingham) |
| **CCD** | Charge-Coupled Device |
| **CCN** | Cable News Network |
| **CCTV** | Closed Circuit Television |
| **CD** | Compact Disc |
| **CDV** | Compact Disc Video |
| **CMCS** | Computer Mediated Communication System |
| **CNN** | Cable News Network |
| **COI** | Central Office of Information |
| **CPBF** | Campaign for Press & Broadcasting Freedom |
| **CPJ** | Committee to Protect Journalist (US) |
| **CPU** | Central Processing Unit |
| **CRA** | Community Radio Association |
| **CRT** | Cathode Ray Tube |
| **CSI** | Crime Scene Investigation |
| | |
| **DAB** | Digital Audio Broadcasting |
| **DBS** | Direct Broadcasting Satellite |
| **DIT** | Digital Imaging Technology |
| **DJ** | Disc Jockey |
| **DOS** | Disc Operating System |
| **DP** | Data Processing |
| **DTP** | Desk Top Publishing |
| **DTT** | Digital Terrestrial Television |
| **DVD** | Digital Video Disc |
| | |
| **EBU** | European Broadcasting Union |
| **EDP** | Electronic Data Processing |
| **ENG** | Electronic News Gathering |
| **ENS** | Electronic Newsroom System |
| **ESM** | Experience Sampling Method |

| | |
|---|---|
| **FAIR** | Fairness and Accuracy in Reporting |
| **FAPRA** | Federation of African Public Relations Associations |
| **fax** | facsimile |
| **FFE** | Fund for Free Expression (US) |
| **FM** | Frequency Modulation |
| **FNC** | Fox News Channel |
| **FOIA** | Freedom of Information Act |
| **FRCN** | Federal Radio Corporation of Nigeria |
| | |
| **GBNE** | Guild of British Newspaper Editors |
| **GCHQ** | Government Communications Headquarters |
| **GIGO** | Garbage In, Garbage Out (computer operator's acronym) |
| **GII** | Global Information Infrastructure |
| | |
| **HDTV** | High-Definition Television |
| **HDVS** | High Definition Video System |
| **HF** | High Frequency |
| **HMD** | Head Mounted Display |
| **HMSO** | Her Majesty's Stationary Office |
| | |
| **IAD** | Internet Addiction Disorder |
| **IAMCR** | International Association of Mass Communication Research |
| **IARP** | Independent Association of Radio Producers |
| **IBA** | Independent Broadcasting Authority (succeeded by ITC in 1991) |
| **IBM** | International Business Machines |
| **IBT** | International Broadcasting Trust |
| **IFEX** | International Freedom of Expression Exchange |
| **IFFI** | International Foundation for Freedom of Information |
| **IFJ** | International Federation of Journalists |
| **IFVA** | Independent Film and Video Markers Association |
| **IGC** | Institute for Global Communications |
| **ILR** | Independent Local Radio |
| **INR** | Independent National Radio |
| **In-tel-sat** | International Telecommunications Satellite (Consortium) |
| **IOJ** | International Organisation of Journalists |
| **IPA** | Institute of Practitioners in Advertising |
| **IPA** | International Publishers Association |
| **IPC** | International Publishing Corporation |
| **IPDC** | International Programme for the Development of Communication |
| **IPI** | International Press Institute |
| **IPR** | Institute of Public Relations |

SELECTED ABBREVIATIONS

| | |
|---|---|
| **Iras** | Infra-red astronomy satellite |
| **IRL** | In Real Life |
| **ISBN** | International Standard Book Number |
| **ISDN** | Integrated Services Digital Networks |
| **ISN** | International Services Digital Network |
| **ISOC** | Internet Society |
| **ISSN** | International Standard Serial Number |
| **IT** | Information Technology |
| **ITC** | Independent Television Commission |
| **ITCA** | Independent Television Companies Association |
| **ITU** | International Telecommunications Union |
| **ITV** | Independent Television |
| **IV** | Interactive Video |
| **IWF** | Internet Watch Foundation |
| | |
| **JICNAR** | Joint Industrial Council for Newspaper Audience Research |
| **JICPAR** | Joint Industrial Council for Poster Audience Research |
| **JICRAR** | Joint Industrial Committee for Radio Audience Research (succeeded by RAJAR in 1992) |
| **JICTAR** | Joint Independent Committee for Television Advertising Research |
| | |
| **LAN** | Local Area Network |
| **Laser** | Light amplification by stimulated emission radiation |
| **LED** | Light Emitting Diode |
| **LOP** | Least Objectionable Programme |
| | |
| **MBS** | Mutual Broadcasting System |
| **MDC** | More Developed Country |
| **MIS** | Management Information System |
| **MO** | Mass Observation |
| **modem** | modulator-demodulator |
| **MOMI** | Museum of the Moving Image |
| **MMX** | Multi-Media Extensions |
| **MPAA** | Motion Picture Association of America |
| **MR** | Motivation Research |
| **MTV** | Music Television |
| | |
| **NAHBO** | National Association of Hospital Broadcasting Organisations |
| **NAN** | News Agency of Nigeria |
| **NANAP** | Non-Aligned News Agencies Pool |
| **NASB** | National Association of Student Broadcasting |
| **NBC** | National Broadcasting Commission (Nigeria) |

| | |
|---|---|
| **NBC** | National Broadcasting Company (US) |
| **NCC** | Nigerian Copyright Commission; National Communications Commission (Nigeria) |
| **NCU** | National Communications Union |
| **NFA** | National Film Archive |
| **NFC** | Nigerian Film Corporation |
| **NFT** | National Film Theatre |
| **NGO** | Non Government Agency |
| **NIC** | Newly Industrialised Country |
| **NIIA** | Nigerian Institute of International Affairs |
| **NIIO** | New International Information Order |
| **NIJ** | Nigerian Institute of Journalism |
| **NIPOST** | Nigerian Postal Services |
| **NIPR** | Nigerian Institute of Public Relations |
| **NITEL** | Nigerian Telecommunications |
| **NMMA** | National Media Merit Award (Nigeria) |
| **NOA** | National Orientation Agency (Nigeria) |
| **NPA** | Newspaper Proprietors Association (UK) |
| **NPAN** | Newspaper Proprietors Association of Nigeria |
| **NPO** | Nigerian Press Organisation |
| **NTA** | Nigerian Television Authority |
| **NUJ** | Nigerian Union of Journalists |
| **NUJ** | National Union of Journalists |
| **NVLA** | National Viewers and Listeners Association |
| **NWICO** | New World Information and Communication Order |
| | |
| **OB** | Outside Broadcast |
| **OCR** | Optical Character Recognition |
| **OFTEL** | Office of Telecommunications |
| | |
| **PA** | Press Association |
| **PANA** | Pan African News Agency |
| **PBS** | Public Broadcasting System |
| **PC** | Personal Computer; Politically Correct |
| **PCC** | Press Complaints Commission |
| **PCC** | Public Complaints Commission (Nigeria) |
| **PEN** | Poets/Playwrights/Editors/Essayists/Novelists: PEN International |
| **PII** | Public Interest Immunity |
| **PLR** | Public Lending Rights |
| **PR** | Public Relations |
| **PRISA** | Public Relations Institute of Southern Africa |
| **PRSA** | Public Relations Society of America |
| **PSI** | Para-Social Interaction |

| | |
|---|---|
| **PSN** | Public Switched Network |
| **RA** | Radio Authority |
| **RAJAR** | Radio Joint Audience Research (succeeded by JICRAR in 1992) |
| **RATTAWU** | Radio, Television and Theatre Workers' Union (Nigeria) |
| **RCA** | Radio Corporation of America |
| **RDS** | Radio Data System |
| **RI** | Reaction Index |
| **RMB** | Radio Marketing Bureau |
| **RP** | Received Pronunciation |
| **rpm** | revolutions per minute |
| **RSF** | Reporters Sans Frontieres |
| **RSI** | Repetitive Strain Injury |
| **RTS** | Royal Television Society |
| **SCA** | Speech Communication Association (US) |
| **SEFT** | Society for Education in Film and Television |
| **SIGINT** | Signals Intelligence |
| **SLR** | Single Lens Reflex |
| **STD** | Subscriber Trunk Dialling |
| **STV** | Straight-To-Video |
| **SYNCOM** | Synchronous Communication Satellite |
| **TAM** | Television Audience Management |
| **T & SG** | Television and Screen Writers Guild |
| **TASS** | Telegraph Agency of the Soviet Union |
| **TBDF** | Trans-Border Data Flow |
| **THESIS** | Times Higher Education Supplement Internet Service |
| **TNAUK** | Talking Newspaper Association of the United Kingdom |
| **TNC** | Transnational Corporation |
| **TTL** | Through the Lens |
| **UDHR** | Universal Declaration of Human Rights |
| **UHF** | Ultra High Frequency |
| **UNESCO** | United Nations Educational Scientific and Cultural Organisation |
| **UNO** | United Nations Organisation |
| **UPI** | United Press International |
| **USB** | Universal Serial Bus |
| **USP** | Unique Selling Point/Property |
| **VDU** | Visual Display Unit |
| **VES** | Video Encoding Standard |

| | |
|---|---|
| **VHD** | Video High Density |
| **VHF** | Very High Frequency |
| **VHS** | Video Home System |
| **VLV** | Voice of the Listener and Viewer |
| **VOA** | Voice of America |
| **VON** | Voice of Nigeria |
| **VR** | Virtual Reality |
| | |
| **WELL** | Whole Earth Lectronic Link (US) |
| **WP** | Word Processing |
| **WPFC** | World Press Freedom Committee |
| **wpm** | words per minute |
| **WSET** | Writers and Scholars Educational Trust |
| **WSJ** | Wall Street Journal |
| **WWW** | World Wide Web |

# A

**A/B Roll Editing.** A complex videotape editing method that makes full use of computerised editing controllers. The AB roll method permits dissolves, wipes, superimpositions, and other special effects between scenes and sequences. One scene on a pre-recorded tape from machine A and another scene from a tape on machine B are played back simultaneously, along with a blank tape on a third machine. The computer determines the edit points on A and B, and the result ends up on the third tape. This technique is usually used with online editing.

**A/B Split Method.** Another name for split run media testing, a control and a test advertisement appearing in different editions of a paper on the same day and in the same position. Similarly, different advertisements can be exposed on different radio or TV stations or different transmitters of the same station. Response or recall can be measured to decide the most effective advertisement.

**A/B Switch.** A mechanical switch that is used to conveniently select between two electronic input signals. It enables the cable input to the television set to be bypassed and the reception switched to the incoming signal from a broadcast receiving antenna on the roof or mast.

**ABC.** (1) Abbreviation for Audit Bureau of Circulation, an organisation that compiles statistics on circulation. Or American Broadcasting Company, a radio and television broadcast network company currently owned by Disney. (2) In photojournalism, abbreviation for Auto Backlighting Control, metering feature that automatically recognises a subject in back lighting condition and increase the exposure to balance.

**Aberration.** Failing in the ability of a lens to produce a true image. There are many forms of aberration and the lens designer may often correct some only by allowing others to remain. Generally, the more expensive the lens, the less its aberrations. It affects the ideal performance in an optical system and can be divided into six basic faults (a) spherical aberration- basically, a beam of light passing through a lens parallel to the optical axis converges to form three focused image on the film. This kind of optical fault is caused by the spherical form of a lens that produces different focus points along the axis for central and marginal rays; (b) curvature of field- this optical defect causes points on an object plane vertical to the lens axis to focus on a curved surface rather than a plane; (c) astigmatism- rays of light from a single point of an object which is not on the axis of a lens and fails to meet in a single focus, hence causing the image of a point to be drawn out into two sharp lines, one radial to the optical axis and another perpendicular to this line, in two different planes near the curvature of field; (d) coma- this optical defect causes the image of an off-axis point of light to appear as a comet-shaped blur of light. This as well as curvature of field and astigmatism, degenerate the image forming ability of the lens at the rims of the picture; (e) distortion.- even if the first four aberrations were totally eliminated, images could result that still have a distorted appearance. For instance, a rectangle may appear as a barrel or pin cushion-shaped object; (f) chromatic aberration- this aberration is caused by light rays of different wavelengths coming to focus at different distances from the lens. Blue will focus at the shortest distance and red at the greatest distance. Since the natural rays of light are a mixture of colours, each aberration will give a different value corresponding to each colour thus producing blurred images.

**Above-the-line.** Sometimes called media advertising. Press, TV, radio, cinema and outdoor which traditionally pay recognised agencies commission on purchases.

**Abstract.** Concise written summary of a research article. Often appearing at the beginning of full-length articles published in academic journals, abstracts are also used in conference programs and research literature indexes.

**AC.** (1) Adult Contemporary. A soft rock music format aired by radio stations. This type of format is typically targeted for the 25-54 year-old groups. (2) Alternating Current. Standard 120-volt, 60-Hz (cycle) household electricity. Also called line voltage.

**Academic Journal.** Publication that contains primarily research articles. Almost all well-respected academic journals are blind peer reviewed; that is, articles are accepted or rejected based on the opinions of research-reviewers who do not know the authors.

**Accelerated Motion.** The apparently increased speed of movement obtained by projecting at normal speed a film that has been taken at less than normal speed when shooting.

**Accent.** The entire pattern of pronunciation typical of a particular region or social group. It is a feature of dialect. The use of most languages is marked by differing dialects and their accompanying accents. This is why when one speaks, we can really tell or guess what part of the world he comes from.

**Access.** In the context of newsgathering, the legal right a news reporter has to go onto a private property to obtain information or videotape footage. In a communication process or system, it can refer either to the possibility for a sender to reach a chosen audience or for an audience to receive certain messages or channels. In practice it mainly relates to the degree of openness of media channels to a wide range of voices, especially those with little power or limited resources. An example is a 'public access' channel provided in a cable system for community or non-profit purposes. As a general principle it is related to media diversity.

**Access Provider.** An internet service provider (ISP); a company selling Internet connections, such as AOL, NTL, Bulldog and British telecommunications (BT).

**Account.** (1) In sales, an invoice. (2) In advertising, a client of an advertising, PR or other agency, that is to say, an organisation providing a service in consideration of which an income is derived; hence, the term account.

**Account Controller, Executive Handler.** A person who acts as liaison between an agency or consultancy and clients. Once known as 'contact man' or 'middle man'. He presents client needs to the agency, proposals to the client, and generally maintains the agency-client relationship and supervision progress of a campaign.

**Account Executive.** An executive in an advertising agency, or other such organisation, responsible for the overall managing of a client's requirements. Sometimes known as Account Supervisor,

Manager, or Director, the different titles only indicate degrees of responsibility or of choice of organisation. He also sells broadcast time or space for a station or media organisation.

**Account Planner.** In an advertising agency the person who incorporates the work of departments and personnel, planning a creative brief, and working closely with the Account Controller. He is concerned with research, marketing, promotional strategy and the day-to-day direction of the campaign. Not all agencies actually have an account planner.

**Acculturation.** Process of becoming adapted to a new culture, partially by adopting its value system. Immigrants become acculturated to the culture of their new nation.

**A.C.E. or Ace.** Assistant City Editor. This person performs such functions as heading an editorial team of creative journalists and professionals that cover events in and around a particular city or more. The functions may differ in various media organisations, but the traditional editorial function of the media is the core of the position.

**Acetate.** Thin plastic transparent sheet, originally cellulose acetate, used in graphics as an overlay on layouts or artwork.

**Acousmatic Sound.** A sound which one hears without seeing its source. E.g. seagull cries, traffic outside the window, a bomb in the distance.

**Acoustics.** The science of sound. Also a consideration of the environment for sound recording. Usually in broadcast or recording studios, acoustics are fixed to the walls of the studio to absorb sound. They are foam-like materials that prevents sound from going out of the studio and prevents unwanted sounds from coming in to ensure smooth and clear recording.

**Acrobat.** Adobe software that allows PDF files to be produced and read on any computer.

**Acronym.** Short attractive name usually derived from the initial letters of a long business name, or a wordy description. For example, Fiat is derived from Fabbrica Italiana di Automobili Torino, meaning Italian car factory in Turin, AIT meaning African Independent Television or more popularly used CNN, Cable News Network.

**Across the Board.** A type of programme scheduling strategy in which individual programmes in a series are scheduled at the same time each weekday. The programmes are said to run "across the board" and the technique is designed to foster tune-in loyalty in various dayparts. The phrase is often used synonymously with stripping.

**Act.** A section of a television programme that is part of the organisation and construction of the show. Half-hour sitcoms are often divided into three segments, with the first act establishing the problem, the second complicating it, and the third resolving it.

**Action Research.** A kind of research that aims not only to collect and analyse information but also to bring about practical social change. Most social science research in this regard is motivated by the desire to alter and improve a social situation, for instance a bad culture as apartheid.

**Active Audience.** The term arose in the context of revised ideas about the mass audience. Research established early on that media audiences are in varying degrees selective, motivated and resistant to influence. The kind and degree of audience activity is very relevant to the possibility of any effect from media. Audience activity has been studied in more detail within the tradition of uses and gratifications research as well as reception analysis. In the latter case, activity is mainly found to reside in differential interpretation.

**Active Light Lock Door.** A lock on the Advanced Photo System film cassette that allows unexposed or partially exposed film to be advanced only when the cassette is properly loaded into any of the system's equipment, including cameras and photofinishing devices.

**Activity Sampling.** An observational technique, using discontinuous tests to estimate the incidence of any defined activity.

**Actual Malice.** Broadcasting or publishing something that is either known to be false or with reckless disregard for its truth or accuracy.

**Actuality.** A term used in radio news to refer to a report featuring someone other than broadcast personnel (politician, police inspector, athlete or eye witness) who provides an actual statement rather than one paraphrased and spoken by a reporter.

**A/D Conversion.** A process that converts an analogue communications signal into its equivalent in digital communications terms. A converter measures the amplitude (voltage) of an incoming analogue electronic signal thousands of times each second and stores each of the measurements as a number.

**Ad.** Short for advertisement, classified or displayed.

**Ad hoc Survey.** Single, one-off research survey, complete in itself, as distinct from a continuous research such as Consumer Panel or Dealer Audit.

**Ad impression.** A term used to depict the number of times an advert is seen. Advertisers typically sell space based on the exposure per thousand impressions (CPM).

**Adaptation.** Use of a basic idea, as in an advertisement, for other media, e.g. posters, point of sale, literature. Also different version of original advertisement to fit different size or shape space.

**Adaption.** Variation of basic advertisement layout and copy to fit different spaces, shapes and sizes.

**Add.** Written or copy to be added marked with ad-placings and sizes of advertisements. Sometimes called the scheme, could be used in editing to indicate a material to be added to a write up or piece.

**Address Line.** Part of advertisement or promotional material, which contains the address of the advertiser, or the address to which any inquiries should be sent. See base line.

**Addressable Converter.** A small box containing a microcomputer that is placed on the television set. The subscriber uses a keypad connected to the converter and by punching buttons, orders a particular channel from the cable head end. Such converters are addressable because they can be individually accessed by the computer at the head end.

**Adequate Distribution.** Ensuring that stocks of a product are available in shops to meet demand created by advertising. It is necessary to co-ordinate selling-in delivery to retailers.

**Adjacency.** A period of commercial time that precedes or follows a network programme. About two minutes in length, it is offered to advertisers for spot announcements.

**Adjustable Camera.** Commonly called the manual camera. It functions with manually adjustable settings for distance, lens openings, and shutter speeds. E.g. Nikon FM series, Carl Zeiss S2, Pentax K1000, etc.

**Adjustable-Focus Lens.** A lens that has adjustable distance settings.

**Admap.** Founded in the United Kingdom in 1964, it covers media, advertising research and marketing areas. They also publish the Admap international quarterly which was launched in 1984. It usually holds annual conferences and has high level attendance recorded yearly.

**ADR.** Automatic Dialogue Replacement. A process during feature film production, also known as 'looping', which allows actors to rerecord dialogue for greater clarity while watching themselves on screen.

**Adult Contemporary.** Descriptive of a format or type of music played on some stations consisting of soft to moderate rock, ballads and current hits.

**Adult Videos.** An euphemistic term used to identify films in the pre-recorded home video industry whose content is primarily sexual, horror, etc. and cannot be viewed by children under the age of 18.

**Ad Valorem.** According to value. Usually applied to rates, taxes, duty and levies etc.

**Advance.** A story that delineates a future event. Could also mean to raise the priority of a story. (1) It could be announcing an event that is to occur, such as a speech or government meeting, (2) or could be written and made available to an editor days before its publication date. Typically, such stories are features that do not have to appear immediately.

**Advanced Photo System.** A new standard in photography developed by Kodak and four other companies- Canon, Fuji, Minolta and Nikon - based on a new film format and innovative film, camera and photofinishing technologies. Generally, APS cameras are more compact in size, weight and embodied with most of the latest and most advance technologies available. There are options in various sizes of print out and it could provide thumbnail prints (contact sheet) for one to select or preview prior to actual printing. They usually have different series of lenses and some of the 35mm format AF lenses can be shared with limitation or effective focal length increased.

**Advanced Television (ATV).** A broad term that refers to the technical systems that will eventually improve television image and sound.

**Adversarial Situation.** State of conflict which exists between journalists and PR practitioners, due to different reasons for publishing or seeking publication of information.

**Advertisement Analysis.** MEAL service giving description of every press and television advertisement placed during the month for each brand. Every advertisement is listed by data within brand and shows details of: date of appearance; TV station and channel or publication; spot length or size; time-on, special position, use of colour; rate card cost; whether it is a Range Advertisement in which case the costs are divided equally between products in the range; whether it is a co-operative advertisement (in which case the total cost is given to the prime advertiser, and the secondary advertiser is listed); whether it is a Dealer advertisement (pre-fixed 'T'). Total expenditure and sub-totals for press and television are shown for each brand and the product group.

**Advertisement Department.** Part of a publishing outfit or other organisation in the communications business concerned with selling advertising space or time, either to an agency or direct to a client. It could also be a department in another organisation that buys space and time on behalf of its organisation.

**Advertisement Manager.** A sales manager who controls the sales force and who sell advertising media. Not to be confused with Advertising Manager because more often than not they are different positions.

**Advertising.** Use of paid-for space in a publication, for instance, or time on television, radio or cinema, usually as a means of persuading people to take a particular course of action, or to reach a point of view by creating awareness, making brand images, forming positive associations and encouraging consumer behaviour. It may also be taken to include posters and other outdoor advertising. Advertising recently is done more often on the internet on big websites especially, like the Yahoo and Google sites. There are many different classes of advertising, which are linked to different media forms (classified, display, personal, etc.). For some major media, advertising provides the greater part of income. All advertising content shares the fact of being paid for by its source. Advertising has been controversial for several reasons, especially the following. It is not generally wanted by its receivers; it has a propagandist character and is suspected of deception and manipulation; it has a distorting effect on the relation between media and audience; its content is usually stereotyped and misleading; the presence of advertising influences other non-advertising content. The general effectiveness of advertising for its purposes is more or less accepted, but certain evidence of success or of reasons for success is hard to come by. Advertising is integrated into a very large industry of market research, public relations and marketing.

**Advertising Age**. A weekly newspaper/magazine covering the advertising industry.

**Advertising Agency.** An independent company that creates and manages advertising for other firms. In addition to creating and producing commercials, ad agencies conduct product and consumer research and buy commercial time for clients on television and cable operations, radio, newspapers and magazines. The film *What Women Want* literally shows what advertising agencies do.

**Advertising Agency Review.** The procedure followed when an account is opened to competition from other advertising agencies. When a contract between an agency and a client expires, it is often renewed for another period. On occasion, however, the client believes there is need for a change and undertakes an agency review. While the incumbent is usually also encouraged to make a presentation, other agencies are contacted to pitch the account.

**Advertising Awareness Research.** As conducted on the London Underground with pre-research and post-research into the brand awareness as a result of advertising. In one survey conducted by

Survey and Fieldwork, 600 Underground travellers were interviewed regarding the Tube Car Panel campaign run for two months. Spontaneous brand awareness rose from 1% to 14%, prompted brand awareness from 2% to 30%.

**Advertising Boycotts.** The reliance of the press and of commercial television upon advertising for revenue indicates the important influence advertisers and their clients can wield over the media. This presents a situation where a newspaper may be deemed to be publishing material or expressing views which might be detrimental to consumerist interest, as a result companies normally pull out their high-priced advertisement, or at times threaten to do so.

**Advertising Budget.** Sum of money set aside for spending on an advertising campaign. Sometimes represents total sum available to cover all advertising expenditure including overheads. Alternatively referred to as 'Advertising appropriation'.

**Advertising Funded.** A publication that partly or totally depends on advertisement revenue. However, much income is today derived from the cover price if there is one, and few publications depend solely on advertising for their income. Unlike pre-war 'penny' newspapers that were subsidised by advertisers, post-war newsprint, labour and distribution costs required extra income via cover or selling price. It is noticeable that many Controlled Circulation journals have developed a cover price or subscription sales, e.g. Marketing, Marketing Week, PR Week.

**Advertising Manager.** In-house buyer and controller of advertising and person who liaises with the account executive of an advertising agency. Now largely absorbed in the duties of Brand or Product Manager.

**Advertising Medium.** Vehicle of communication that provides for some form of advertising, e.g. the press, television, radio and transport services. Alternatively, a communication channel designed specially for the purpose of advertising, e.g. direct mail, internet, exhibitions, poster site, and some printed publications, e.g. catalogues.

**Advertising Regulations.** Conditions imposed upon advertising by media owners, trade associations, or government. It could be laws concerning a particular type of product. For instance, in advertising tobacco, publishing that smokers a liable to die young.

**Advertising Schedule.** Programme of planned advertisement insertions, showing detailed costs, timing, nature of media and the bookings to be reserved.

**Advertising Spiral.** The stages through which a product-class advertising passes, including: Pioneering, Competitive and Retentive.

**Advertising Strategy.** The overall plan of an advertising campaign.

**Advertorial.** Combination of the words advertisement and editorial. Form of advertising on controversial issues, as used by politicians and political parties or groups in Nigeria, when space is taken on a leader page to position an organisation regarding an economic, social or political issue. Can also be used to promote a case against media bias or misreporting.

**Advocacy Advertising.** Advertising championing preventive action against conditions affecting the public welfare.

**AE.** Automatic Exposure.

**AEJMC.** Association for Education in Journalism and Mass Communication. This is a major international membership organisation for academics in the field, offering regional and national conferences and refereed publications. It has numerous membership divisions, interest groups, publications and websites. Its major journal, *Journalism & Mass Communication Quarterly* was formerly titled *Journalism Quarterly*. The association is also involved in accrediting schools, colleges and departments of mass communication and journalism in the United States of America through its Accrediting Council on Education in Journalism and Mass Communication.

**Aerial Advertising.** Different types of advertising in the sky depending on legislation which may ban low flying aircraft or the use of a single engine aircraft over towns. Forms include skywriting with smoke; trailed banners; illuminated messages on wings of night-flying aircraft; advertisements projected onto clouds and two or three aircrafts linked together with banners. Goodyear airships with illuminated public announcements; tethered balloons; Hot Air Balloons are more recent examples. Fuji films have used an airship painted in their green and red house colours, making it very eye-catching. Airship Industries normally hire airships to advertisers.

**Aesthetics.** Activities which try to understand or evaluate the sense of beauty, or of form in a text or art work.

**Affidavit**. A sworn statement given to a client to verify that a commercial appearing on an invoice aired or was printed as claimed.

**Affiliate.** A station that airs network programming is said to be an 'affiliate' of that network. An affiliated station usually receives more than 70 percent of their programming from their network. The networks provide the programmes at no cost to their affiliates in exchange for commercial time.

**Affiliation Contract.** The formal statement of the relationship between an affiliated station and its network. The station is compensated for the carriage of the programmes according to the terms of its affiliation contract.

**'Affordable' Method.** One of a variety of ways of arriving at an advertising budget, on the basis of what a company can afford, rather than what task has to be achieved.

**Afghanistanism.** A journalistic word for avoiding home front controversy by focusing news coverage on obscure, distant lands. It describes media tendency of giving much critical attention to faraway issues and ignoring local conflicts. A good example of this tendency is where the Nigerian media leaves its home issues as education, political democracy and other topical and contemporary matters to report or focus on subjects in far away America. The neglect of its home concerns or conflicts close to home is disparaging because proximity is a major consideration for writing and reporting.

**African Communication System.** This covers the entire traditional system of communication, especially those typical of Africa before the introduction of modern technology and communication advancement. The use of metal gongs, smoke, gossips, drums and other traditional means numerously used by different villages and tribes are occurrences of this system used to spread messages as the birth of a child, the death of a person, war, etc. Also see Oramedia.

**After Market.** After a product or service has been sold, all those means of satisfying the customer, maintaining goodwill, encouraging recommendations, and achieving repeat or renewal sales, including sales of accessories. Includes guarantees, promise of good performance, service manuals, servicing, spare parts, and special PR effort such as customer magazines and clubs. Having back up services may be an important part of advertising.

**Agate.** Small type often used for statistical data on sports and stock pages. It is a type size of approximately 5 1/2 points tall, a point being 1/72nd of an inch.

**Agate Line.** Newspaper advertising space, one column wide by one-fourteenth of an inch deep; often referred to simply as "line"; somewhat obsolete because most newspapers now use "column inch" measurements of advertising space, especially for national advertising.

**AGC.** Automatic Gain Control. An electronic circuit that attempts to automatically regulate and control the audio or video levels when recorded or replayed.

**AGE Buyer Ratings.** Research system which can reduce advertising expenditure. It improves Targeting of TV commercials by helping buyers to choose Airtime according to the audience's purchases instead of their social grades. The performance of a commercial can be checked against desired audience. It guides a buyer's prediction of programmes and day-parts that are most likely to have the highest proportion of purchasers of particular products. Data is continuous.

**Age Profile.** The audience for a particular media text, classified according to age group.

**Agence France Presse (AFP).** A news agency belonging to France. Founded in 1835 by Charles-Louis Havas as *Agence Havas*, it is the oldest news agency in the world. It is also the largest French agency and the third largest news agency in the world, behind the Associated Press and Reuters. The agency is based in Paris, with regional centres in Washington, Hong Kong, Nicosia and Montevideo and Bureaus in 110 countries. It sends out news in French, English, Arabic, Spanish, German, Portuguese and Russian. The principal client of AFP is the French government, which purchases subscriptions for its various services. In practice, those subscriptions are somewhat a subsidy to AFP. AFP statutes prohibit direct government subsidies.

**Agency Commission.** Usually 15 percent, allowed to advertising agencies by media on the agencies' purchase of media space or time.

**Agency of Record.** Advertising agency that coordinates an advertiser's promotion of several products handled by more than a single agency (see Blanket Contract).

**Agency Recognition.** Acknowledgment by media owners that certain advertising agencies are responsible for placing advertisements on specific mass media outlets, thus qualifying for a commission.

**Agenda.** Prioritised list of items dealt with by a media text, especially in news- hence the term agenda setting.

**Agenda Setting.** Closely related to public opinion generation, it is a basic function of the mass media to set agenda and raise issues of public importance. For instance, when a media focuses its reports on an aspect say human rights, it draws government ears to the issues at hand.

**Agent.** Person or organisation with express or implied authority to act for another (the principal) in order to establish a contractual relationship between the principal and any third party. Also can act as legal representative. Advertising agencies are an important exception to this role, acting as principals for the services they purchase on behalf of their clients. Term may be used in a general sense indicating the person or organisation representing another.

**Agent's Lien.** Where the agent legally possesses goods still owned by its principal, it is said to have a lien for monies due from the principal.

**Agents Torts.** Principal is jointly and severally liable for his agent's torts where the agent has been acting for him in the normal course of its agency or upon the instructions of the principal. An advertising agency is an exception.

**Agitation.** In photojournalism, keeping the developer or fixer in a gentle uniform motion while processing film or paper. It helps to speed and achieve even development and prevent spotting or staining.

**AH.** Accent height of a typeface, which may vary from one type-founder to another according to the amount of white space above and below the character.

**AIDA.** Well known formula standing for attention, interest, desire, action to which a fifth element, conviction, is sometimes inserted after 'desire'. This is a historical model of how advertising works, by first getting the consumer's attention, then their interests, etc. These elements may be achieved by a combination of contributory factors such as headline, selling points, text copy, illustration(s), layout, typography, size, shape or position of space and colour or choice of medium.

**Aided Recall.** A research technique that uses prompting questions or materials to aid a respondent's memory and a means of obtaining answers from respondents such as cards bearing Mastheads of publications during a Readership Survey. For example, a researcher shows a respondent an advertisement in a magazine then asks if he/she has seen the ad before. Unaided recall technique would have the researcher asking the respondent to identify the advertisement that impressed him or her most in the recent issue of a specific magazine.

**Air Brush.** Mechanical device which sprays atomised dye or paint in a controlled manner. Used for retouching photographs and for producing artwork or shaded effect.

**Air Check.** (1) An audition tape, usually a portion of an actual broadcast. Also made at the direction of an advertising agency to verify that a commercial has been aired. (2) Recording a broadcast to serve as an archival or file copy. Also used frequently by air talent to help potential employers evaluate his or her skills and on-air abilities.

**Air Date.** Date when TV or radio commercial is to be broadcast.

**Air Quality.** Program material that meets technical (generally FCC, could be the NBC for Nigeria) standards for quality.

**Airport Corridors.** Approach roads to airports which offer prime sites for posters such as 64 sheets and Bulletin Boards.

**Airtime.** Advertisement time on commercial radio or TV. Generally the length of a particular broadcast. It is also used to mean available talk time on mobile phones.

**Aisle Arch.** Advertising display above the aisle in supermarkets.

**A la Carte Agency.** An agency that offers creative services on a negotiated fee basis, but does not plan or buy media and consequently does not require recognition, making small firms viable and not dependent on volume of billings.

**Align.** Correction on proof to strengthen irregular lines of type or characters.

**Alignment.** Arrangement of type and or illustrations in a layout to justify horizontally or vertically.

**Allocations.** (1) The blocks of frequencies apportioned to specific communications services to avoid interference with other transmissions. The electromagnetic spectrum is divided into groups of frequencies and these are then allocated to specific communication services, such as AM and FM radio and UHF and VHF television. (2) Division of advertising appropriation for different above-the-line and below-the-line purposes plus production costs.

**Allocation Table**. A listing of potential and actual frequency assignments from the FCC.

**Allonge.** Attachment to a bill of lading allowing for the inclusion of extra endorsement.

**Alternate Sponsorship.** The practice of two or more companies alternating as sponsors on a day-by-day basis. This technique has been traditionally used for programme series and soap operas or for programmes in syndication that are transmitted on regular basis during the week.

**Alternate Weeks Sponsorship.** An advertising practice, in which a commercial on a television or cable operation is scheduled for one week, then dropped for a week, and resumed the third week. This technique is usually used in small or limited campaigns.

**Alternate Television.** A type of television that in its earliest manifestation, was called underground or guerrilla TV. It referred to the activist, radical movement television production which often had a political purpose. In Nigeria for instance, the Radio Kudirat which was initially launched as Radio Democrat International and run by a London-based group called UDFN functioned as an alternate television. It opposed the dictatorship of General Sani Abacha in Nigeria. The programs were well funded by Worldview Rights, a media non-governmental organisation, and used commercial airtime on South African transmitters. In 1999, after broadcasting for 3 years, it closed down.

**AM.** Amplitude Modulation. A process by which the amplitude of an otherwise constant signal is altered. The amplitude modulation produces a signal that occupies a little more than twice the bandwidth of the modulating signal. For the most part, the quality of AM signals is less than that of FM signals and AM signals tend to be heard further, especially at night.

**Amateur Radio.** People who operate transmission equipment (both radio and television) as a hobby. Radio amateurs (sometimes called hams) must pass an exam covering electronics, broadcast theory, and noise code before receiving an amateur license.

**Ambient Light.** The available natural light completely surrounding a subject. The light already exists in an indoor or outdoor setting and is not caused by any illumination supplied by a photographer, that is, not by artificial light source.

**Ambient Sounds.** Normal background sounds at a specific time or location that do not detract from the recording of a program and may even add to the excitement of the broadcast.

**American Research Bureau (ARB).** One of several national firms engaged in radio and television research in the United States of America.

**Amp / Ampere.** A measure of electrical current volume. Fuses are rated in terms of the maximum amps they are designed to carry. It is named after André-Marie Ampère, one of the main discoverers of electromagnetism. The ampere technically is that constant current which, if maintained in two straight parallel conductors of infinite length, of negligible circular cross-section, and placed 1 metre apart in vacuum, would produce between these conductors a force equal to $2\times10^{-7}$ newton per metre of length. Electric current is the time rate of change or displacement of electric charge. One ampere represents the rate of 1 coulomb of charge per second (A= C/s). The ampere is defined first (it is a base unit, along with the metre, the second, and the gram), without reference to the quantity of charge. The unit of charge, the coulomb, is defined to be the amount of charge displaced by a one ampere current in the time of one second.

**Ampersand.** G-ligative representing 'and' formed from the Latin 'et'.

**Amplifier.** A device used to make electronic signals stronger by increasing the amplitude or level of an electronic signal. In the process of amplification, signal strength is increased to provide greater power for subsequent use. Some amplifiers increase the voltage, while others amplify the power of the signal.

**Amplitude.** A description of the level of an electronic signal. Amplitude is the strength or magnitude of waveform or voltage. In audio, this intensity governs the loudness of the sound; in video, the brightness of the image.

**Amongst Matter.** Position of an advertisement, where it is situated amongst editorial material.

**Amortising.** A hot type term for excising part of a picture and replacing the excision with something else- type of art. Sometimes it involves cutting a rectangular piece away from a corner to make room for another picture or as a place to put a caption, or even a headline.

**Analogue.** As opposed to a digital signal, a signal that varies smoothly between certain ranges. An analogue signal bears an exact, continuous relationship to the original information. This is also any device that represents a quality or value by a physical change in a measuring agent, e.g. the silver nitrate on photographic film which changes colour in response to light.

**Analogue to Digital Conversion (ADC).** The process of converting an analogue signal to digital data.

**Analogue Editor.** Linear editor. An editing approach that requires you to make edits in a set progression like adding links on a chain, as opposed to non-linear, digital editing which is based on digitised information that can be accessed in a random order.

**Analysis.** Resolution into simple elements, e.g. summary of data into tabulated form. May take the form of a chart or diagram

**Anamorphic Lens.** Distorting lens on a movie camera which 'squeezes' a wide picture on to standard film. In a projector it 'un-squeezes' the image to fill a widescreen.

**Anchoring.** Written or spoken text (e.g. caption, voice over) used to control or select a specific reading of a visual image.

**Anecdote.** A short narrative, usually of a personal nature, used to illustrate a general issue. It is often used in media coverage to heighten the emotional aspect of an issue. It could be a brief tale narrating an interesting or amusing personal incident. It is usually based on real life, involving actual persons, whether famous or not, in real places. Modification in reuse may convert a particular anecdote to a fictional piece, one that is retold but is "too good to be true". Sometimes humorous, anecdotes are not jokes, because their primary purpose is not simply to evoke laughter, but to reveal a truth more general than the brief tale itself, or to delineate a character trait or the workings of an institution in such a light that it strikes in a flash of insight to their very essence.

**Angle.** Aspect of point of approach or focus in a story; play up this angle- give it emphasis, stress. The angle of a story concerning the graduation of the pioneer students of a University may differ, for instance, depending on the writer or media. A writer may hub on the aspect of the university's growth, another may choose the aspect of the university graduating only one first class student. These angles all carry the main ingredients of the convocation story but only choose to highlight a certain point that is considered catchy or interesting.

**Angle of View.** In photojournalism, the area of a scene that a lens covers or sees. It is determined by the focal length of the lens. A wide-angle lens (short-focal-length) includes more of the scene- a wider angle of view- than a normal (normal-focal-length) or telephoto (long-focal-length) lens. Currently, the widest view available is 220 degree (achieved by Nikon's Nikkor 6mm F2.8 fisheye lens - 220 degree; while the narrowest is Nikon, 2000mm F11 Reflex Nikkor, only slightly over 1 degree of view. It also can be explained as the extent of the view taken in by a lens. For any particular film size, it varies with the focal length of the lens. Usually expressed on the diagonal of the image spot. Basically, there are three types of angles which can be measured (based on horizontal, vertical and diagonals of the film frame), the lens must be designed to cover the widest angle in the diagonal direction. Consequently, the angle of view is the angle between imaginary lines drawn from the opposite ends of the film plane to the second nodal point of the lens. All objects within this angle is recorded by the lens on the film.

**Animated Bulletin Boards.** Specially constructed solus outdoor advertising site which has stand-out three dimensional effects, such as a replica of a product.

**Animatic.** A rough draft of a TV commercial which is developed by taking photographs of individual storyboard sketches and assembling them into a film strip. The audio portion is recorded on tape and synchronised to the visual images, resulting in an animatic.

**Animation.** Movement added to static objects, especially in relation to cartoons. Slides may also be used. The human eye makes the static item or graphic to come alive with movement.

**Announcement**. An advertising message that is broadcast between programs, or an advertisement within a syndicated program or feature film; any broadcast commercial regardless of time length, within or between programs, that presents an advertiser's message or a public service message.

**Annual Billings.** Money billed advertisers for commercials carried in a medium over one-year period.

**Annual Rebate**. See Rebate.

**Annuals.** Periodicals which are published once a year, usually in the form of reference books.

**Anomie.** Gotten from Greek, namely the prefix *a-*: "without", and *nomos*: "law", it is a condition or malaise in individuals, characterised by an absence or diminution of standards or values. As used by Émile Durkheim (1858-1917), a French socioloist and later theorists, it is a reaction against, or a retreat from, the regulatory social controls of society, and is a completely separate concept from a situation of anarchy which is an absence of effective rulers or leaders.

**Anonymous Sources.** Sources of news that are cited generically but are not named in a news account or story.

**ANOVA.** Methodological shorthand for *analysis of variance*. ANOVA distinguishes among independent variables in terms of the strength of their contributions to the variance in a dependent variable.

**Answer Print.** A stage in the technical production of a filmed programme or commercial in which the audio and video portions are combined with all of the optical effects into a nearly finished version. The term is derived from the process of sending a work print to the film laboratory and receiving an answer print back, which is then reviewed and approved before final print is ordered.

**Antenna.** A device used for transmitting or receiving electromagnetic signals. In television broadcasting, a transmitting antenna is a metallic device mounted on a tower that is located on high ground or on the top of a tall building. Receiving antennas on the top of a television set or rooftop, or simple monopole metal units 12 inches in height.

**Anthology Programming.** Self-contained programmes that begin and end during the period of time they are on air and do not carry over to subsequent shows. Although the anthology technique is used in all subject areas from music to comedy, it is most commonly applied to drama programmes.

**Anthropology.** Study of the human species- applied in audience studies. Derived from the Greek word "human" or "person", it consists of the study of humanity (genus Homo). It is holistic in two senses: it is concerned with all humans at all times and with all dimensions of humanity. Anthropology is typically distinguished from other disciplines by its emphasis on cultural relativity, in-depth examination of context, and cross-cultural comparisons.

**Anti-aliasing.** Smoothing jagged effect around curved and diagonal lines in electronic graphics through the use of filters.

**Anti-realism.** An aesthetic based on denying any attempt to represent surface reality.

**Anti-trust Legislation.** US government action taken to break up the monopoly of large producers, e.g. the Paramount decision in 1948 forcing Hollywood studios to sell their cinema chains.

**AOR**. Album Oriented Rock. A rock music format that tends to appeal to primarily male ages of 18-34. The radio format features usually three cuts from recent popular recordings plus relies heavily on "old" or music from the past decade.

**APCON.** Advertising Practitioners Council of Nigeria. Nigeria's body for advertising practitioners and organisations, it was born as the industry's main regulatory organ. Under Act 55 of 1988, the council was established to regulate advertising practice in all its ramifications. See APPN.

**A-PEN.** Annealed polyethylene naphthalate-a polyester material used as the base on Advanced Photo System film. It is thinner, stronger and flatter than the acetate base traditionally used in consumer photographic roll films.

**Aperture.** (Aperture setting) F-stop. Lens opening based on a ratio between focal length and the diameter of the lens opening that determines how much light will pass through the lens. The size of aperture is either fixed or adjustable and is usually calibrated in f-numbers- the larger the number, the smaller the lens opening. Aperture affects depth of field, the smaller the aperture, the greater is the zone of sharpness, the bigger the aperture, the zone of sharpness is reduced. The hole or opening formed by the metal leaf diaphragm inside the lens; controls amount of light and depth of field, preventing vignetting and reducing lens aberrations. The size of the aperture is indicated by its f-number, that is, the ratio of the diameter of the opening to the focal length of the lens; a large aperture is indicated by a small numerical f-number.

**Aperture Priority.** An exposure mode on an automatic or auto-focus camera that allows one set the aperture while the camera sets the shutter speed for proper exposure. If the aperture is changed, or the light level changes, the shutter speed changes automatically. Apart from the sport or action arena, aperture priority is the most common and effective automatic preference in photojournalism. It can be used in the stop-down mode with any lens that does not interfere with the metering system.

**Aperture Ring.** A ring located on the outside of the lens usually behind the focusing ring. It is linked mechanically to the diaphragm to control the size of the aperture and engraved with a set of numbers called f-numbers or f- stops.

**Apochromatic (APO).** Simply, having the ability to bring all colours of the visible spectrum to a common plane of focus, within close tolerances, usually refer to a lens with such superior colour correction.

**Appeal.** Basis of a selling proposition or advertising message designed to match a 'customers want', i.e. the appeal identifies what customers desire and what the product or service concerned can supply.

**Appendix.** Attachments in a book which contain certain information that cannot be included in the main text. Examples are research questionnaires, decrees, laws, glossary, statistical data, diagrams, etc.

**Applied.** Research done primarily to answer a question of immediate practical significance. Good applied research uses theory; its main purpose, however, is solving immediate problems rather than understanding theoretical issues. See Basic research.

**APPN.** The umbrella association for advertising practitioners of Nigeria. The organisation which comprises of all advertising agencies in Nigeria represents the organised sector of the advertising industry in Nigeria. The Association was born in 1972 and presently has membership of over 70 advertising agencies. See APCON.

**Appreciation of the Situation.** Assessment of the current situation, using observation, experience or scientific research, in order to identify communication strengths and weaknesses before making recommendations for a PR campaign.

**Approach.** (1) Treatment of advertisement copy, e.g. factual, hard sell, soft sell, emotional, bargains, humorous. (2)Outdoor. The distance measured along the line of travel from the point where the outdoor billboard first becomes fully visible to a point where the copy ceases to be readable. There is a long approach, medium

43

approach, short approach and flash approach in outdoor advertising.

**Appropriation.** The budget of an advertising/PR campaign, covering all production and media costs.

**Aquatint.** Intaglio printing process that give reproduction of even or graded tones.

**A&R.** 'Artists and Repertoire' represent the main assets of companies in the music industry. Performers are signed on contract and rights are held on recordings.

**Arbitrary Method.** Way of deciding advertising appropriation without making serious calculation. What the advertiser thinks he can afford.

**Arbitrary Signifiers.** Term used in semiotics; signifiers with no resemblance to the referent or the signified; see iconic, indexical and symbolic.

**Arc.** A camera movement in which the mount and camera are moved in curving path to the right or left of the subject. The movement is a combination of a dolly in and a truck shot. The term is also used as shorthand for the arc light or carbon-arc light, the high intensity lighting instrument used to provide light over vast areas and in large auditoriums and areas.

**Archer, Frederick Scott.** (1813-1857) The inventor of the photographic collodion process which preceded the modern gelatin emulsion. He was born in Bishop's Stortford in the UK and is remembered mainly for this single achievement which greatly increased the accessibility of photography in everyday life. See Camera.

**Archive.** Long-term, off-line electronic storage, generally on some form of disc or magnetic tape. If stored properly, the expected lifetime of a video tape should be anywhere from 10 years to beyond 30 years. Tapes should resist shedding and layer-to-layer adhesion; remain flexible; and retain the recorded signals with little loss. Poor performance tape may start shedding over time especially if exposed to extreme temperature. Also they may develop sticky substances as a result of high humidity exposure and the breakdown of the vinyl binders used to hold the magnetic particles onto the base film.

**Area of Dominant Influence (ADI).** Arbitron measurement area that comprises those counties in which stations of a single originating market account for a greater share of the viewing households than those from any other market; similar to Nielsen's Designated Market Area.

**Area Sample.** Number of people or organisations, part of a research study, situated in any particular geographical area.

**Arena Advertising.** Display panels around perimeter of sports arena, visible to both spectators and TV viewers. Also called perimeter advertising.

**Array.** Organised display of a set of observations in statistical analysis.

**Art Buyer.** Person responsible for purchasing artwork or photography, usually in advertising agency.

**Art Director.** Individual charged with the task of overseeing the transformation of a creative idea into visual form. May also control copy, visuals, layouts and typography.

**Art Paper.** High grade coated and polished paper. Sometimes called enamelled or cast coated. The best quality is made from esparto grass with china clay coating. Can be one-sided for decorating packages such as chocolate boxes.

**Artefacts.** Things made by human workmanship; in communication sense, the adornments worn which say something about the wearer: dress, hairstyles, jewellery, make-up; or objects which we possess- such as vehicles or media artefacts as CDs, newspaper or video. In cultural studies sculptures of all kinds are called artefacts.

**Article Number Association.** Body which promotes the use of Bar Coding, and has a code of practice for use of bar codes manufacturers and distributors.

**Article Works, Advertising of.** Under section 63 of the Copyright, Designs and Patents Act 1988, it is not an infringement of copyright in an artistic work to copy it, or to issue copies to the public, for the purpose of advertising the sale of the work.

**Artificial Light.** Light from an artificial source- manmade, usually restricted to studio photo lamp and domestic lighting. When used to describe film (also known as Type A or Type B) regularly means these types of lighting.

**Artists' Medium.** Materials used by an artist for his particular visual expression, e.g. pencil, ink, paint, photography.

**Artwork.** Pictorial or illustrative part of an advertisement, or publication, in its finished form ready for block making or production, e.g. a retouched and masked photograph.

**ASA.** (1) Advertising Standards Authority. An independent body set up and paid for by the advertising industry to ensure that its system of self-regulation work is in the public interest. The Authority has an independent chairman. Its members are appointed by him to serve as individuals and not as representatives of any section or interest. Half of its members must be from outside advertising. The Authority maintains close contact with central and local government departments, consumer organisational and trade associations and deals with complaints received through them or direct from the public. (2) Film speed. Denotes the level of film sensitivity, defined by the American National Standards Institution. For example, ASA 400 film is twice the speed of ASA 200 film. ASA has largely replaced by ISO index, which is roughly the same thing.

**ASCAP.** The American Society of Composers, Authors and Publishers. It has a membership of over 240,000 U.S. composers, songwriters, lyricists, and music publishers of every kind of music. Through agreements with affiliated international societies, ASCAP also represents hundreds of thousands of music creators worldwide. ASCAP is the only U.S. performing rights organisation created and controlled by composers, songwriters and music publishers, with a Board of Directors elected by and from the membership. It protects the rights of its members by licensing and distributing royalties for the non-dramatic public performances of their copyrighted works. It's licensees encompass all who want to perform copyrighted music publicly and it makes giving and obtaining permission to perform music simple for both creators and users of music.

**Ascenders.** Stroke, in typography, rising above the x-height of a lower case letter in a face, e.g. h, b, d, f, k, l.

**Ashcanning.** Inferring in an advertisement that a rival product is inferior and only worth discarding. Knocking copy. Denigration is an offence against the Code of Advertising Practice.

**Aspect Ratio.** The numerical ratio of picture width to height in photographic prints - 2:3 in 35 mm pictures to produce pictures most commonly measuring 3.5 x 5 inches or 4 x 6 inches. The standard broadcast aspect ratio is 4X3. Advanced Photo System cameras deliver three aspect ratios as selected by the user.

**Aspherical Lens.** A lens whose curved surface does not conform to the shape of a sphere; lenses are generally ground or moulded with spherical surfaces; because a spherical surface lens has difficulty in correcting distortion in ultra-wide-angle lenses, or coma in large-aperture lenses brought about by spherical aberration, an aspherical lens is used.

**Assemble Editing.** In contrast to insert editing, an editing process whereby a new video or audio sequence is consecutively added to a previously edited scene, complete with the associated control track.

**Assembled Negative.** Combination of line and halftone copy for making litho plate.

**Assignment.** A particular job given to reporters by editors or a senior reporter or officer. Sometimes reporters suggest their own assignments, but they usually get an editor's approval before beginning work.

**Assignment Editor.** The individual in a broadcast newsroom who has the responsibility of assigning news and ENG stories to specific reporters.

**Associated Press (AP).** A news agency founded in 1948 belonging to USA. This news gathering agency sells both audio and teletype news stories to broadcast stations.

**Association for Business Sponsorship of the Arts.** Advertises members who seek sponsors and encourages commercial sponsorship of the arts. Encourages media to give credit to sponsorships. The ABSA has achieved considerable increase in arts sponsorship.

**Association of Business Advertising Agencies.** Trade association representing business-to-business advertising agencies. Aims to protect such agencies from competition by general consumer agencies, to increase awareness of specialist business agencies, and to raise their creative standards.

**Association of Exhibition Organisers.** Trade association which aims to maintain standards of exhibition management. Promotes development of exhibitions as a major advertising medium.

**Association of Free Newspapers.** Uphold and promotes standards of free newspapers and their proprietors, and effectiveness of free newspapers as an advertising medium.

**Association Test.** Measures correct identification of brand names, slogans, and advertising themes.

**Asymmetrical Balance.** Composition arrangement in which a significant object placed close to the centre of the picture is balanced by a smaller object some distance from the middle.

**Asynchronous.** A technical term that describes signals that are not synchronised to one another, such as the sound with the picture or two video signals of the same scanning standard that are not in sync with each other.

**ATA.** The camera that supports the electrical interface standard, defined by the PC Card Association (formerly PCMCIA), known as ATA (AT Attachment). This is the mobile computing equivalent of the IDE standard for desktop computers. Most computers have ATA support built-in. It is supported by most operating systems like Microsoft Windows 3.1, Windows '95, Windows CE, IBM OS/2, Apple System 7, etc. It is also supported by most computer manufacturers including IBM, Compaq, Packard Bell, Dell, etc.

**Atex.** Kodak direct import computerised typesetting system widely used in modern newspaper offices, replacing foundry for letterpress printed newspapers. Combines text, graphics, display ads, classified in single full-page electronic production.

**Atmosphere.** Qualitative or subjective value of a medium or publication for advertising purposes.

**Atomistic Evaluation.** Evaluation of specific elements or steps in advertising, particularly using indices of advertising effectiveness.

**Attention Value.** In recall tests and Tracking Studies a measure of respondent's memory of advertisements.

**Attenuation.** The loss in electrical power between a signal's original transmission and its reception. The loss can result from the length of the transmission through the air or via wire or coaxial cable. Attenuation may also be caused by the quality or type of equipment used in transmitting or receiving signals. To attenuate is to decrease the level or loudness of a signal. The loss of power is expressed in decibels (DB).

**Attitude.** State of mind reflecting a negative or positive personal view about an object or concept; a state of indifference indicates a mid-point between these opportunities.

**Attitude Battery.** Study in which respondents are given statements and asked with which they agree or disagree. An analysis shows attitude patterns and motives.

**Attitude Change.** Extent to which an attitude varies, usually as a result of external stimuli.

**Attitude Research.** An investigation, often by personal interview or group discussion, into the attitude of people towards an organisation or its products. This could be done as a result of PR activity.

**Attribution.** To give someone the proper credit for what he or she has said or written.

**Attribution Theory.** This is a field of social psychology born out of the theoritical models of Fritz Heider, Harold Kelley, Edward E. Jones, and Lee Ross. It is concerned with how individuals interpret events and how this relates to their thinking and behaviour. The theory assumes that people try to determine why people do what they do, i.e., attribute causes to behaviour. A person seeking to understand why another person did something may attribute one or more causes to that behaviour. A three-stage process underlies an attribution: (1) the person must perceive or observe the behaviour, (2) then the person must believe that the behaviour was intentionally performed, and (3) then the person must determine if they believe the other person was forced to perform the behaviour- in which case the cause is attributed to the situation- or not- in which case the cause is attributed to the other person. The theory divides the way people attribute causes to events into two types: external or situational attribution assigns causality to an outside factor, such as the weather, whereas internal or dispositional attribution assigns causality to factors within the person, such as their own level of intelligence or other variables that make the individual responsible for the event. The theory is very relevant in doing mass communication research involving behavioural change or attitudes.

**Audience.** Group of people exposed to any of the media, but more usually associated with television, radio, or cinema. Thus, persons who receive an advertisement; individuals who read a newspaper or magazine, listen to a radio broadcast, view a television broadcast, and so on. The audience can also exist as an imagined 'target' or intended group of receivers. It may coincide with a real social group or public. Audiences can be defined according to the relevant media and content or in terms of their social composition, location or time of day. Media audiences are not fixed entities and may only be known after the event as statistical abstractions (e.g. 'the ratings'), with a known probability of recurrence. This is typically the view 'from the media', but there is an equally valid alternative perspective on the audience as a collective social cultural entity. Audience however, is a passive word and does not necessarily imply 'attention' to an advertisement.

**Audience Accumulation**. The total number of different persons or households exposed to a single media vehicle over a period of time (see Cumulative audience).

**Audience Composition.** Classification of audiences by particular characteristics, usually demographic.

**Audience Differentiation.** This is a process that works from the assumption that analysis of audience response to media messages can only be purposeful if it recognises that the mass is a complex of individuals, differentiated by gender, age, social class, profession, education and culture.

**Audience Duplication**. Those persons or households who see an advertisement more than once in a single media vehicle or in a combination of vehicles.

**Audience Date.** Information relating to size and/or nature of an audience.

**Audience Ethnographies.** Research using ethnographic approaches; joining a specific audience group and working 'from the inside'.

**Audience Flow.** Gain or loss of audience during a programme. This could be by movement of a broadcast audience's attention from one station to another when the program changes, and is measured against the audience that stays tuned to the same station or network to view the new program. An audience could be inherited from a previous programme. See Holdover audience.

**Audience Loyalty.** As achieved by a popular radio or TV programme. Can be valuable to an advertiser who wishes to reach a larger audience.

**Audience Profile.** The minute-by-minute viewing pattern for a program; a description of the characteristics of the people who are exposed to a medium or vehicle. See Profile.

**Audience Share.** Proportion of viewer's total viewing time devoted over a period to a particular channel. As the number of channels increases via satellite and cable, the audience share lessens as viewing becomes more fragmented. This is one aspect of the De-Massification of the media.

**Audience Turnover.** That part of a broadcast audience that changes over time. See Audience flow.

**Audile Technique, Techniques of Listening.** A set of practices of listening that were articulated to science, reason, and instrumentality and that encouraged the coding and rationalisation of what was heard.

**Audiometre.** A.C. Nielsen Company's automatic audio audience-measuring device that was adapted to measure television viewing in 1950. The device is usually attached to a radio or television receiving sets to record usage and station information. See People metre.

**Audio.** Written description on storyboard of script, sound effects, music in proposed programme. Sound that can be heard by the human ear.

**Audio Actuality.** The recording of the 'actual sounds' in the news for incorporation into radio newscasts.

**Audio Board; Audio Console.** A basic desktop control centre used to switch, mix and control audio levels for a variety of audio sources.

**Audio Booth.** An area-often a separate room-in a production facility where audio signals are controlled and mixed.

**Audio Channel.** A single audio circuit, generally consisting of an amplifier and one of more audio controls.

**Audio Compressor.** Audio-processing circuit that reduces dynamic range by simultaneously raising low audio levels and lowering high levels so that a higher average level is achieved.

**Audio Console.** An electronic mixing and switching device that controls audio sources during a production.

**Audio Control Booth.** Small room where all audio is controlled and mixed.

**Audio Dub.** Making a copy of an audiotape. In television, the recording of sound only, without disturbing the picture.

**Audio Expander.** An electrical circuit which increases the dynamic range of an audio signal.

**Audio-follow-video.** A switch that simultaneously switches both video and audio.

**Audio Frequency Response.** This is the measure of relative loudness of high frequencies compared to the playback level of the lower frequencies. It is measured at 7 KHz.

**Audio Limiter.** An electronic device intended to restrict the maximum amplitude of a signal.

**Audio Mix.** Audio track created through combining multiple sound sources.

**Audio Mixer.** A device that allows the simultaneous combining and blending of several sound inputs into one or two outputs.

**Audio Monitor.** An audio amplifier and speaker system used to check and listen to audio during a production.

**Audio Sensitivity.** The playback output level of the audio signal at lower frequencies (measured at 1 KHz). This represents the loudness of the audio signal on playback from conventional linear audio (not hi-fi VCRs).

**Audio Sweetening.** A postproduction process designed to correct problems in audio as well as to enhance and supplement audio tracks.

**Audio Track.** The portion of the audio videotape that records sound.

**Audiographics.** An interactive distance education tool that uses computers to transmit graphics and audio simultaneously over common television lines.

**Audiovisual.** Any form of combination of visual (cine film, transparency or video) and sound (record, type, cassette, optical or magnetic sound track). Usually portable.

**Audiovisual Sales Aids.** Equipment incorporating facilities for communicating by sight and sound, used by salesmen to stimulate an actual demonstration.

**Audit.** Formal examination of accounts or management resources.

**Audited Net Sale.** Average net sale of a newspaper/magazine excluding free copies.

**Audition.** A critical hearing that is scheduled before casting a television show or film production. A performer tries out for a part by demonstrating talent or suitability in a brief trial presentation. Also used to describe a distinct, separate, audio circuit that allows an engineer to preview or audition sound before using it in a production.

**Audition Channel.** An audio monitor circuit enabling a technician to listen to, preview, and cue audio sources before sending them through the audio console.

Aura.

**Aura.** That which gives art its distinctive individuality, its uniqueness, and its social separatedness.

**Auteur.** French term for author, used in 'la politique des auteurs', a debate from 1950s-60s film theory. See authorship.

**Authoritarian.** Characterised by media that are either 'private or public' and are chiefly instruments for effecting government policy, though not necessarily government owned.

**Authorship.** Approach originating in film studies which places emphasis on an individual author (usually the director) rather than the collective and collaborative nature of production.

**Autocue.** Device that projects the words of a script on to a screen just below the lens of the TV camera. It uses angled mirrors to perform this function which enables a presenter to read a script without looking down. Also known as teleprompt.

**Auto Exposure Bracketing.** In photojournalism, this performs automatic exposure bracketing with varied shutter speed and/or aperture.

**Auto Focus (AF).** Electronic system in some cameras that attempts with varying degrees of success to automatically focus subject matter. The autofocus camera revolution was first popularised with the launch of Minolta's Maxxium. Currently, most cameras are autofocus based.

**Auto Iris.** A system that automatically adjusts a lens aperture to compensate for the brightness of a scene. See automatic exposure control.

**Auto Kerning.** In phototypesetting, automatic closing of space where Ascenders overlap X-Height of next character.

**Automated Inserting.** Mechanical method of placing inserts into newspapers and magazines as introduced by the Mirror Group and the Financial Times.

**Automated Videocassette Systems.** Videocassette systems that are computer controlled to play back videotapes of commercials and programmes all day and night, in the proper sequence. May be called library management systems.

**Automatic Camera.** A camera with a built-in exposure metre that automatically adjusts the lens opening, shutter speed, or both (programme) for proper exposure.

**Automatic Exposure Lock (AEL).** Metering feature used to hold the exposure setting of a camera when used in automatic mode. It is used most commonly in situation where off centring of the subject in composition and wish to retain the exposure setting of the subject. It is also used when the level of exposure reading both the subject of interest and the background exposure reading is different e.g. back lighting. May be used to hold an automatically controlled shutter speed and/or aperture. Recommended when the photographer wants to control an exposure based on a scene's particular brightness area with Centre Weighted or Spot Metering.

**Automatic Fine Tuning (AFT).** An electronic circuit that automatically tracks a particular frequency. A common part of videocassette recorders and other electronic equipment, it corrects slight drifts and maintains signal strength at a minimum level.

**Automatic Gain Control (AGC).** An electronic circuit for audio or video that automatically controls the operating level in an amplifier by increasing or decreasing (as needed) the strength of the incoming sound or picture to maintain optimum signal strength. It monitors the output of an amplifier, ensuring that the outgoing signal is consistent, regardless of any variations in the level of the input.

**Automatic Iris Control.** Electronic device that automatically alters the lens diaphragm in response to the level of light. The automatic iris is controlled by a mechanism in the camera body coupled to the shutter release. The diaphragm closes to any preset value before the shutter opens and returns to the fully open position when it closes.

**Autonomy.** Immunity from arbitrary exercise of authority: political or personal independence. The term can be applied to individuals, groups or institutions. More often media autonomy is argued in areas where the media is controlled by the government.

**Autopage.** In litho printing, computer positioning of headlines, sub-heads, text and rules.

**AV.** The Aperture value, usually refer to aperture settings.

**Availability.** The commercial time periods that have not yet been sold by television or cable operations and is open for reservation by an advertiser in response to an advertiser's or agency's initial inquiry. An advertiser or advertising agency will query the station to determine which time slots are available for purchase from the inventory of the operation. (slang "avail").

**Available Light.** The naturally existing light which illuminates a scene.

**Avant Garde.** An artistic movement which is 'ahead of the mainstream' and usually experimental.

**Average Audience (AA).** A measurement of the television and radio audience. Familiarly known as the AA rating, it is an estimate of a programme's average audience on minute-by-minute basis.

**Average Cost Pricing.** Pricing policy where an average price is established over a product range based on average cost.

**Average Exposure**. The average (mean) number of times that each audience member has been exposed to an advertisement.

**Average Frequency.** (1) In commercial TV, average number of exposures/impacts per unit of a defined audience group covered. (2) Average opportunities to see a commercial announcement among those who are reached at all, i.e. gross reach divided by net reach.

**Average Hours.** Average length of time spent listening to radio or a particular station.
Total Hours/Reach = Average Hours.

**Average Net Paid Circulation**. Average (mean) number of copies that a publication distributes per issue.

**Average Propensity to Consume.** That part of national income devoted, on average, by the nation's individuals to consumption of goods and services.

**AVID.** Name of the market leader in provision of non-linear editing equipment. Often used as a generic term for computer editing of video or film.

**Awareness Level.** The percentage of the target market that knows about the existence of a product, services or company; it is different from Familiarity.

**Awareness Survey.** Similar to attitude survey and opinion poll, method of researching familiarity with subject, including increased awareness as a result of PR activity.

**Azerty.** Keyboard arrangement with accents used in French speaking countries, unlike the standard Qwerty keyboard.

# B

**B-copy.** This is when the background of a story is outlined first without having the specific or major details of the story. Also called A matter.

**'B' Picture.** In the studio era, the shorter and less important feature in a cinematic double bill.

**B-Roll.** See A/ B Roll Editing.

**B (Bulb) Setting.** A shutter-speed setting on an adjustable camera that allows for time exposures. When set on B, the shutter will stay open as long as the shutter release button remains depressed. Another similar option is the "T" setting, where it never drains the battery power on automatic camera body.

**B Series/Sizes.** ISO range of paper sizes for large print jobs such as posters.

**B Title.** A motion picture within the home video industry that features less-than-name actors but has had a reasonably successful theatrical run. The designation is applied to indicate the anticipated retail demand for the film and is distinct from the term B movie, which is a measure of relative quality.

**Baby Boom.** Small suspension device for holding a microphone.

**Back Bench.** A journalistic slang term for senior editorial executives in a newspaper usually consisting of assistant editors, a night editor, and the chief sub-editor. This group of editors is closest to the finished product, thus this gives them an upper hand in shaping the news.

**Back Cover.** (1) The backside of a book or any published material. (2) In advertising, the back cover of a magazine usually available at premium rates for advertising. Special rates apply to both inside and outside back covers.

**Back Focus.** Adjusting the distance between the back of a lens and the camera target to achieve the sharpest image possible of an object at infinity. Back focus adjustment determines whether a zoom lens will stay in focus when moved through its focal length range.

**Back Selling.** Promotion of goods of secondary suppliers to those who incorporate them in finished goods. Their identity is often unknown to the final buyer. Advertising may be aimed at the final buyer to encourage specification of a component or ingredient.

**Back Timing.** See backtime.

**Back-to-back Coupons.** Disaster situation when couponed ads are printed on seceding pages so that they cancel each other out. Can involve more than 7% of ads. The publisher is unaware of eventual copy when space orders are accepted and pages made up.

**Back-to-back Scheduling.** A type of TV programming strategy that involves the scheduling of similar shows consecutively. Two programmes appealing to the same demographics are aired successfully to encourage the audience to stay tuned.

**Background.** (1) Information given to a journalist or reporter to explain more about the situation and details of a story. It is understood that the information is not intended for publication. Could also be given in a marketing campaign or research. (2) Remoter part of an illustration or advertisement layout. (3) The part of the scene that appears behind the principal subject of a picture. The sharpness of the background can be influenced by apertures and shuttle set. In the flash mode, bulb setting usually is set for absorbing more ambience light (background information), so the end result of the exposure won't be pitch dark. (4) Also sound effect or musical strain in a broadcast or film.

**Background Lighting.** Lights that illuminate the walls of a room or set and generally separate them from the subject in a TV or film production. These types of lights provide flat lighting, usually controlled by a dimmer that enhances the visibility of a cyclorama or background. Scoop lights and soft lights are used to provide the overall light.

**Background Noise.** Signal path voltages that are not related to the signal. These usually random fluctuations in voltage mix with the desired signal and are amplified with it, emerging as 'hiss' in audio circuits and 'snow' in video.

**Backlight.** A TV and film lighting technique that directs light onto a performer, object, or scene from behind rather than from the front. The effect causes the subject to stand out vividly against the background. Sometimes produces a silhouette effect. It is advisable to always use something- a hand or a lens shade to avoid the light falls onto the lens- lens flares.

**Backlight Compensator (BLC).** A camera control that opens up the lens aperture two-to-three f-stops. Used to compensate for the error made by automatic iris circuits when shooting into light or against a bright background.

**Back-Printing.** Information printed on the back of a picture by the photofinisher. The system standard requires the printing of frame number, film cassette number and processing date automatically on the back of each Advanced Photo System print. It may also include more detailed information, such as customised titles and time and date of picture-taking.

**Backtime.** The process of calculating when to start a broadcast program by subtracting program length (or music length) from the clock time of when the program must end.

**Back to Back**. Two broadcast programs or commercials in succession.

**Bag.** Open ended container for wrapping goods usually at the point of sale. Made from paper or plastic, and some time including paperboard for added protection. Often bearing distinctive printing indicating origin, and advertising goods or services.

**Bait Advertising**. An alluring but insincere retail offer to sell a product that the advertiser in truth does not intend or want to sell. Its purpose is to switch a buyer from buying the advertised merchandise to buying something more expensive.

**Balance.** (1) The concept of making a news story or article flow with all the vital or must ingredients as the 5 W's and a H. (2) In photojournalism, placement of colours, light and dark masses, or large and small objects in a picture to create harmony and equilibrium. Description applied to colour films to indicate their ability to produce acceptable colour response in various types of lighting. The films normally available are balanced for daylight (550~6000K photo lamps (3400K) or studio lamps (3200K).

**Balanced Fill-Flash.** A type of TTL auto flash operation which uses the camera's exposure metre to control ambient light exposure settings, integrated with flash exposure control. Explicitly, flash output level is automatically compensated to balance with ambient light, resulting in a better exposure for both subject and background.

**Bandwagon Effect.** Literally, a bandwagon is a wagon that carries the band in a parade. It is an observation that people often do or believe things because many other people do or believe the same. The effect is often pejoratively referred to as herd instinct, particularly as applied to adolescents. Without examining the merits of the particular thing, people tend to "follow the crowd." Media wise, this effect usually occurs when audiences are urged to support a cause, purchase a product, engage in certain behaviour, or "jump on the bandwagon" because everybody else is doing so. For instance- a commercial urges children to buy particular toys because all of the children have one.

**Bandwidth.** A range of frequencies in a section of the electromagnetic spectrum that is expressed in terms of the lowest and highest signal in a frequency band. Bandwidths are normally narrow or wide, depending on the difference between the highest and lowest frequency in them. Used in internet connection.

**Bangtail Envelopes.** Envelopes with extra large perforated deep flap or stub which may serve as an order form, to give extra information, provide a competition entry form, or means of giving addresses of friends. Used in Direct Mail.

**Banner.** (1) Large headline across all or most of top of page. (2) Relating to an advertisement headline stretching across open space. Also large board or piece of fabric held or towed aloft bearing some slogan or symbol.

**BARB.** Broadcasters' Audience Research Board, the body in Britain which produces television viewing figures.

**Barbarism.** A blunder in speech similar to solecism.

**Bargain.** (1) To negotiate for terms. (2) An offer providing unusual value, e.g. a reduction in price. The benefits may be largely illusory but are found to have a motivating influence.

**Barn Doors.** Metal appurtenances that are attached to lighting instruments and act as extensions of them. They consist of four rectangular flaps, one on each side and on the top and bottom of the instrument. They can be adjusted, like a shutter, to focus and direct the beam of light and cut it off where it is not desired. Commonly used with a Fresnel light.

**Barrel Distortion.** Straight lines bowed in at the edges of a picture frame resembling the sides of a barrel; present in small amounts in some wide-angle or wide angle-zoom lenses, but uncorrected in fisheye lenses.

**BART.** Brief Affect Recognition Test. A test that was carried out by Paul Ekman and W.V. Friesen in 1978 to assess accuracy in decoding of, and individual differences in, sensitivity to facial expressions.

**Barter.** An advertising medium that sells time or space in return for merchandise or other non-monetary returns.

**Barter Syndication.** The method whereby programmes are traded for commercial time.

**Base Artwork.** Artwork that needs extra elements such as halftone positives before a litho plate can be made.

**Base Film.** Basic material for contact film in litho plate making to which film positives are stripped.

**Baseline.** (1) Imaginary line on which the majority of the characters in a typeface rest. (2) Signatory slogan or strap line at the foot of an advertisement. It may be a standard slogan for all campaigns, or different ones for different campaigns.

**Base-Superstructure.** Critical term from early Marxism referring to the economic base on which is built the 'superstructure' of cultural and ideological institutions and assumptions.

**Basic.** Research done primarily to answer a theoretical question. Good basic research addresses important questions; its main purpose, however, is understanding theoretical issues rather than solving immediate problems. See applied research.

**Basic Cable.** Normally refers to cable-only channels with advertising, supplied to subscribers at no extra cost to the basic monthly connection charge. Cable operators pay the basic cable networks a small fee per subscriber.

**Basic Rate.** See Open rate.

**Bastard.** A setting of type or size of block involving a fraction of a column e.g. 8½ems or block 2 ½ columns wide.

**Batch File Technique.** Variations on original shape of a bodytext face, e.g. bold, shadow, outline, contour, achieved by running options through a digital typesetter.

**Battery Letter.** Typeface which has been damaged or is in some way faulty; shows up in printing as an indistinct letter.

**Bayes Theorem (Bayesian Theorem).** Recently acquired sample information combined with prior personal probabilities, so producing revised probabilities in order to embark on new courses of action which may then, repeatedly, be subjected to further inputs of information and revised. It is close to the process of elimination with the use of probability theory.

**BBC.** British Broadcasting Corporation. This is the largest broadcasting corporation in the world, founded in 1922. It produces programmes and information services, broadcasting on television, radio, and the Internet. The mission of the BBC is to inform, educate and entertain, and the motto of the corporation is *Nation Shall Speak Peace Unto Nation*. Its domestic programming and broadcasts are primarily funded by levying television licence fees (under the Wireless & Telegraphy Act 1947), although there is also money raised through commercial activities such as sale of merchandise. In order to justify the licence fee the BBC is expected to produce a number of high-rating shows in addition to programmes that commercial broadcasters would not normally broadcast.

**BBFC.** British Board of Film Classification. The BBFC was set up in 1912 by the film industry as an independent non-governmental body to bring a degree of uniformity to the classification of film nationally.

It has classified cinema films since it was set up and videos since the passing of the Video Recordings Act in 1984. Statutory powers on film still remain with the local councils, which may overrule any of the Board's decisions, passing films BBFC reject, banning films they have passed, and even waiving cuts, instituting new ones, or altering categories for films exhibited under their own licensing jurisdiction.

**BEA.** Broadcast Education Association. This is the professional association for professors, industry professionals and graduate students who are interested in teaching and research related to electronic media and multimedia enterprises. There are currently more than 1,400 individual and institutional members. The association publishes the *Journal of Broadcasting*. This is considered one of the leading publications in the communication field, the Journal contains timely articles about new developments, trends and research in electronic media written by academicians, researchers and other electronic media professionals.

**Beam Separation.** Separates the transmission impulses of a satellite increasing its information.

**Beamwidth.** The angular width of a radio or radar beam.

**Beanstalk.** Point of Sale display consisting of stack of trays or shelves.

**Beard.** The part of type which accommodates the descenders in the letters g, j, p, q, y.

**Beat.** A reporters area or subject which he covers regularly. A reporter who checks the police daily and writes stories about crime and accidents is said to be assigned to the police beat. It could be Legislature, education, transport, business, culture, telecommunications or any sector where a reporter may be assigned to follow up reports. Think of reporters covering their areas as a cop might walk a beat.

**Beautiful Music.** A radio station format that features gentle or restful music ranging from motion picture sound tracks to instrumental arrangements of old standards and some stage musicals and operates.

**Bedroom Culture.** A phenomenon which greatly implies a situation where children and young people spend significant proportions of their leisure time at home with the mass media, increasingly screen media, in their own private space rather than communal or family space. This provokes concerns about children leading increasingly isolated lives, and about parents' ability to regulate and monitor media consumption.

**Behavioural Research.** Research into human behaviour, singly or in groups, particularly in connection with consuming or buying habits but also concerned with wider aspects of social and organisational conduct.

**Behavioural Sciences.** Sciences concerning psychology, sociology and anthropology. These are closely related to communication research.

**Behaviourism/Behaviourist.** Movement in psychology which sees human behaviour as something which can be moulded by punishment and reward. A behaviourist is a researcher characterised by an emphasis on readily observable behaviours rather than internal thoughts and feelings.

**Behaviouristic.** A method of describing a purchase decision-making influence using product usage and criteria of purchasing habits.

**Bell Curve.** Well known so-called normal distribution. Many naturally occurring variables, such as height or weight, follow this curve; some artificially created variables such as intelligence, are made to approximate the same shape.

**Bellows.** The folding portion in some cameras that connects the lens to the camera body. Also a camera accessory that, when inserted between lens and camera body, extends the lens-to-film distance for close focusing or macro photography. Some retain the automatic functions where some have to stop down the lens for manual exposure reading.

**Below-the-line Advertising.** Advertising activities which do not normally make provision for a commission to be payable to an advertising agency. These include direct mail, exhibitions, demonstrations, point-of-sale material, sometimes referred to as scheme advertising. This is often confused with sales promotion.

**Below the Fold.** When a newspaper is bent, the section that is below. Few people read a whole page at a time but fold it in the middle. The lead headline should not sink below the fold otherwise the "read-me" appeal may be lost, though perhaps unintentionally.

**Bending the Needle.** Causing the swinging of the Vu or VI on an audio console to hit the extreme right of its calibrated scale, indicating to the operator that the volume of the sound being sent through the console is too high.

**Benefits**. The rewards to be realised from the use of the product or service.

**Betacam.** A broadcast-quality format developed by the Sony Corporation and used in several types of camcorders.

**Betamax.** A consumer-quality 1/2-inch videocassette format developed by the Sony Corporation which eventually was supplanted by VHS.

**Between-the-Lens Shutter.** A shutter whose blades operate between two elements of the lens. Most medium format cameras like the Hasselblad have one family of lens with shuttle and another without. Most lenses in this family have a smaller maximum aperture than the other family.

**BG.** Script symbol for "background" referring most often to background music.

**Bias.** One sided point of view. Inaccuracy in response to a survey due to a sample not corresponding with the universe. An interviewer who allows his views to influence answers or his reporting has also introduced a bias. Normally, the tendency exist in a news report to deviate from an accurate, neutral, balanced and impartial representation of the reality of events and social world according to stated criteria, this represents bias. The former notwithstanding, stems mainly from partisanship, advocacy and the ideological standpoint of the media or source. The latter is generally attributed to organisational and routine factors in selection and processing of news. See also objectivity.

**Bibliotherapy.** This signifies assistance with human problems by means of books. It is a family of technique for structuring interaction between a facilitator and a participant based on mutual sharing of literature. Used chiefly with young people, it has also successfully been introduced to the elderly in long-stay hospital wards or other institutions. The idea of healing through books may not necessarily be new- it can be traced far back in history, from the days of the first libraries in Greece. The use of books in healing, however, has been interpreted differently by classical scholars, physicians, psychologists, social workers, nurses, parents, teachers, librarians, and counsellors. There is, in fact, confusion in determining the dividing line between reading guidance and Bibliotherapy. Even with diverse literature of the effects of bibliotherapy, empirical data shows mixed results for the efficacy of bibliotherapy as a separate treatment for the solving of problems. These literatures however indicate that bibliotherapy generally appears to be more successful as an adjunctive therapy. It is also called book therapy.

**Bicycling.** The shipment of videotape recordings of TV programmes from one transmitting entity to another. In order to save film and videotape costs, the programmes are sent to a station when they are needed for the station's schedule. After a programme is broadcast, that station or system sends it on to the next operation.

**Bi-directional Microphone.** A type of mike that is sensitive to sounds from front and back, but not from the sides. Sounds coming from sides cancel one another out, leaving only the front and rear sounds. The mike is sometimes called figure eight or pressure gradient.

**Bigotry.** This term signifies a situation where one, called a bigot, is prejudiced and intolerant of opinions, lifestyles or identities differing from their own. The origin of the word in English dates back to at least 1598, via Middle French, and started with the sense of religious hypocrite, especially a woman. It is often argued in mass communication that bigotry is the cause of noise within interpersonal communication process.

**Billboard.** (1) A wire service feed listing all the pre-recorded stories in the wire service's current audio file or a six to eight second radio commercial. (2) A major publication of the recording industry. (3) A slang term for outdoor advertising bulletin or outdoor poster. (4) A cast and production information that follows a broadcast program. (5) Could also be a short commercial announcement, usually eight or ten seconds in length, announcing the name of the sponsor, at the start and close of a program.

**Billing.** (1) Total value of business handled by an advertising agency in a given period. Gross turnover (often called "billings"). (2) The process of issuing invoices for media space and time that have been purchased; (3) Name credits of talent in order of importance.

**Bi-media Journalism.** A BBC policy to train journalists for television and radio under the same scheme.

**Binary.** (1) Of, or appertaining to, two (BS 3527). (2) Variable which can have one of two values only (0 or 1). It replaces the normal counting system of 1, 2, 3, 4, 5...n, by the values of 0 and 1 only. The basis for rapid computing in electronic data processing system.

**Binary Oppositions.** Sets of opposite values said to reveal the structure of cultures and, by extension, media texts; see structuralism.

**Binding.** Process of joining together pages of a book or other publication by means of stitches, staples, canvas, plastic, glue, or other such devices.

**Bingo Card.** Enquiry card bound into a magazine and containing matrix of numbers or letters which correlate with similar keys in advertisements or editorial items. Facilitates reader enquiries and is usually prepaid for return to publisher. May also be referred to as readers' enquiry card.

**Biopics.** 'Biographical pictures'- a traditional Hollywood film genre.

**Bipolar Scale.** A question that asks respondents to choose a numbered point on a line connecting two opposite poles, labelled with adjective pairs. The point chosen corresponds to the respondent's thoughts or feelings about an object, person, or data.

**Birmingham School.** Name often used to denote a number of authors associated with the Centre for Contemporary Cultural Studies (CCCS) at the sociology department of the University of Birmingham, England, established in the mid-1960s. Original founder was Richard Hoggart, in association with Stuart Hall. The work of the school was a major influence in the development of critical cultural studies, including reception research and feminist media studies.

**Bit.** (1) Corruption of 'binary digit', the '0' or '1' in a stream of binary data. Often used as an indicator of 'quality' or 'resolution', e.g. '24 bit colour image' implies a palette of millions of colours described by different combinations of primary colours. Whereas a '1 bit' image can be only black and white. (2) Also a show-business term that refers to a short piece of comedic business in a sketch or a routine in a stage or TV show. It may consist of a brief exchange with another performer or an abbreviated and succinct solo phrase, action, gesture or sound.

**Bitmap.** An image stored on a computer in the form of a matrix of 'bits'. Bitmaps cannot be enlarged without losing quality.

**Black.** Carbon copy of a reporter's story or feature; bold face type.

**Black Balancing.** Electronically setting the black level of a camera to correspond to TV black.

**Black Clipping.** A circuit used to limit the black level of video so that it does not intrude into the sync pulse.

**Black Level.** The darkest portion of the video picture. Reference black.

**Blanked Tape.** A videotape intended for insert editing onto which black (or colour bars) and a control track have been recorded. Also called a crystal tape.

**Blanket.** In Offset-Litho printing, a rubber blanket covering the blanket cylinder which receives the inked image from plate cylinder and offsets it on to paper introduced from impression cylinder.

**Blanket Contract.** A special rate or discount that is granted by an advertising medium to an advertiser who promotes several products or services through more than one agency.

**Blanket Coverage.** Advertising without prior selection of specific target audience.

**Blanket-to-blanket Press.** Offset-litho printing press in which paper is printed on both sides at the same time by feeding it between two blanket cylinders.

**Blanking.** The brief period during the scanning lines process in which the video signal is suppressed. The electron beam in a TV cathode ray tube travels constantly across and up-and-down the screen, but there is a regular period when the scanning beam returns from right to left and from bottom to top. This brief pause is known respectively as horizontal and vertical blanking. During this period the video signal is suppressed and invisible.

**Blanking a Tape.** Recording black, sync and a control track on a videotape. The process of creating a blanked tape. Also called blacking a tape.

**Blanking Areas.** White border or edge of poster for standard-size sites.

**Blanking Interval.** The retrace interval of 10.5 microseconds in which the effect of the electron beam is extinguished so that it can return from the right to the left side of the screen. Also the 1.3 millisecond interval in which the effect of the electronic beam is extinguished so that it can move from the bottom of one field to start scanning the top of the next field.

**Blanking Pulse.** Video signal which blacks out a video image between successive scanning lines, fields and frames.

**Bleach-out.** Photograph from which grey middle tones have been removed to create dramatic black and white effect. A drop-out.

**Bleed.** Printing illustrations or type area to extreme edge of page (or poster) by trimming with no margin or border to give bled-off effect. Artwork and print has to be larger than space or sheet size to permit trimming. Done more often in magazines.

**Blimp.** A sound-proof cover fixed over a camera during shooting, to absorb running noise.

**Blind Advertisement.** An advertisement which is anonymous, i.e. it omits the name of the sponsor as in 'situations vacant' where the company does not wish to disclose its identity and uses a box number or similar device instead.

**Blind Interview.** An interview with an unidentified source.

**Blind Product Test.** Product Pre-Test in which respondents compare two or more similar but unidentified products (media).

**Blind Review.** Process through which articles describing research projects are evaluated by reviewers who do not know who wrote the paper. The goal is a review unaffected by personal friendships or the reputations of either authors or their institutions.

**Blink Metre.** Used in advertising research to ensure the frequency of a person's blinking, so giving indications of interest or arousal.

**Blip Culture.** Information age culture consisting of conflict between conventional concepts and baffling flood of new ideas.

**Blobs/Bullets.** Black circles (properly, full face circles), useful for another adding colour to a page by itemising or setting out a series of points in a story, article or documents basically for emphasis.

**Block.** (1) A procedure that designs the movement of performers and cameras during the course of the rehearsal of a TV programme. (2) A set of consecutive broadcast time periods. (3) Plate of metal, rubber or plastic engraved, moulded, or cast for printing purposes (other than body type), e.g. of photographs or drawings.

**Block Programming.** A technique of scheduling similar TV programmes on a station, network, or cable system within a relatively brief period of time. The programmes which have a common appeal are scheduled during a two or three-hour block in a day part.

**Block Pull.** Carefully printed proof from a block to enable the accuracy and quality of reproduction to be checked before printing order is executed.

**Blocking-out.** In retouching, painting out or airbrushing unwanted parts of a photograph such as an untidy or obtrusive background.

**Blooming Effect.** A technical aberration in a TV picture. The defect consists of a very small distortion in the size of an image. It resembles a halo and the picture is also slightly out of focus.

**Blow-up.** An enlargement; a print that is made larger than the negative or slide.

**Blue Key.** Way of enhancing halftone effects in mono press advertisements. Produces pure black and white plus mid-tones, using separate overlays for black and white areas.

**Blurb.** Preliminary paragraph set up distinctly to introduce a feature or news story. Brief, written, description usually having the connotation of bias. Originally associated with details of a book printed on the cover- behind the book.

**BMI**. Broadcast Music Inc. Similar to ASCAP in that BMI is an organisation that protects the copyrights of its members and collects royalties on their behalf.

**Board.** Pasteboard, cardboard, strawboard, heavyweight paper or card, either one-sheet or made up of layers of paper.

**Board It Up.** An advertising agency slang term that is a directive for an artist to sketch out an idea for a commercial on poster board. To board it up implies that the concept is regarded seriously by the agency.

**Body Copy.** Main copy in advertisement, the text of the print ad, not including the headline, logo or subscript material.

**Body Language.** See Communication, Intrapersonal communication.

**Body Matter.** Text or reading matter as distinct from display lines.

**Body Type.** Type measured between 6 and 14 points, used to set the main body of text.

**Bold.** Same as black. To highlight a character or word(s) giving the type or words heavy weight for extra emphasis.

**Boldface.** A typeface which has been enhanced by rendering it in darker, thicker strokes so that it will stand out on the page. Headlines that need emphasis should be boldface. Italics are preferable for emphasis in body text.

**Bolt-on Promotion.** Sales Promotion scheme that is ready made e.g. Scratch card, bingo game, Be a millionaire, can be bought from a supplier and associated with a product for a special short-term promotion.

**BON.** Broadcasting Organisation of Nigeria. An organisation for all broadcast media in Nigeria.

**Bonus Pack.** Extra large container, e.g. toothpaste tube, cereal pack, aerosol with '10%' or so 'extra' printed on it to promote the product.

**Bonus Payment.** An incentive payment to salesmen for above-the-norm achievement; often ex gratia rather than contractual.

**Book.** A collection of sheets of paper, parchment or other material or data with a piece of text written on them, bound together along one edge within covers. A book is also a literary work or a main division of such a work. When produced in electronic format it is known as an e-book. In library and information science, a book is called a monograph to distinguish it from serial publications such as magazines, journals or newspapers. Publishers may produce low-cost, pre-proof editions known as galleys for promotional purposes, such as generating reviews in advance of publication. Galleys are usually made as cheaply as possible, since they are not intended for sale. A lover of books is usually referred to as a bibliophile, a bibliophilist, or a philobiblist, or, more informally, a bookworm. A book may be studied by students in the form of a book report. It may also be covered by a professional writer as a book review to introduce a new book. Some belong to a book club.

**Book Face.** Typeface used for text of editorial, books. Usually a serif face since easier to read in the mass than sans serif type. Examples: Times, Plantin, Platino.

**Booklet.** Small book containing up to fifty or so pages.

**Book Style.** Traditional and most legible way of typing and setting text matter. Arrangement of paragraphs as found in most books, newspapers and magazines and as opposed to secretarial letter-typing style. The first paragraph of each chapter of article, and first paragraph following a sub-heading, is set Full-Out, i.e. not indented. All other paragraphs are indented. Applies to all copy for printing. Achieves legibility and readability. Originated with handwritten Bibles which had decorated Drop Capitals for full-out paragraphs. This is still retained when initial drop capitals, or first word or two set in capitals are used in print.

**Book Matches, Box Matches.** As given away in clubs, restaurants and hotels, bearing sponsor's name and advertisement. Both advertising and PR medium.

**Booking**. Scheduling a broadcast program or commercial.

**Boom.** An adjustable and portable stand for a microphone that is used in both studio and remote TV productions. It supports a mike and keeps it out of sight of the camera, usually above and in front of the performer.

**Boom Issue.** Special and often seasonal issue of a magazine used to boost sales and advertising revenue.

**Boomerang Effect.** A situation where a message falls within ones' latitude of rejection, i.e. the known views on a given issue or subject which one do not accept.

**Boomerang Response.** Effect of mass media message which, in terms of audience reaction, proves to be the reverse of that which was intended.

**Booster Station.** A low-power repeater of a full power TV station that simply amplifies the signal of the parent station and rebroadcasts it on the same channel to an immediate area. Boosters always broadcast on the same channel as the parent and thus differ from translator stations that convert an incoming signal from a parent station and rebroadcast it on another channel.

**Booth.** Stall or stand at an exhibition. Most face-to-face contact sales marketers use booth during their sales. It is used as a shield or preservation area for staff and usually has the organisation's name or the product being marketed designed all over it. In most shopping malls in the UK, one will find booths of organisations like Sky, Barclaycard, NTL, AA and so on scattered all over the shopping area with the aim of increasing the number of customers they have.

**Bounce-back Card.** Way of calculating response to advertising by asking the enquirer questions about his or her job, use of product, other decision makers, etc.

**Bounce Lighting**. Flash or tungsten light bounced off a reflector such as the ceiling or walls; or attachment that fits on the flash to give the effect of natural or available light.

**Boutique Agency.** A service specialising in creating advertisements rather than a full range of facilities. Often calls in independent artists and writers. This is a term usually applied to small groups. Larger groups generally refer to themselves as creative services and they may develop into full-service advertising agencies.

**Bowdlerise.** To extract or copy from a text what is deemed offensive; to shorten or expurgate.

**Bowl.** Enclosed part of letter as in 'b' or 'd'.

**Box.** A sidebar or extra information. Also type matter enclosed by rules on all four sides.

**Box House.** A large volume, high discount dealer that sells TV sets, videocassettes recorders and other electronic gear to consumers from a large store. Derived from the practice by the retailer of selling devices in the manufacturer's original packing box.

**Bracket Flash.** Often called handle mount flash. It comprise of one arm of the L-shaped bracket which extends under the camera body and uses the camera's tripod socket to mount the camera on the bracket. The vertical arm of the bracket serves as a handle and mounts a flash unit in an accessory shoe often on top of the handle portion, though other methods exists. Flash mounted in a bracket usually requires a separate electrical cord to make the electrical connection between the camera body and flash unit.

**Bracketed Type.** Type in which Serif is linked to the main stem in an unbroken curve.

**Bracketing.** Taking a series of photographs of the same subject at different exposures to insure the "correct" exposure. More useful when shooting in situations where a normal metering reading is difficult to obtain. Some good cameras have provision for automatic bracketing, while manually you can bracket by the use of, say, adjust apertures or shuttle speeds setting or both, manually adjust the ASA setting or even reset the flash output power.

**Brainstorming.** An intensive group discussion to stimulate creative ideas and to solve business problems ranging from new product concepts to improved sales performance, brand names to co-operative strategies, advertising slogans to PR events. The essence of a brainstorming session is that no idea, no matter how apparently irrelevant, should be discarded without adequate consideration and debate, the intention being to repel normal inhibitions and stimulate every kind of suggestion.

**Brainwashing.** Concerted effort to change a persons beliefs or attitudes using a wide rage of techniques. It may involve forcible indoctrination into a new set of attitudes and beliefs, complete persuasion, or otherwise with an aim of washing out certain beliefs and replacing them with the beliefs of the brainwasher which could be a movement, group, party or nation.

**Brakelight Function.** A signal to an audience that a speaker is about to conclude his or her speech. It could be a word, phrase, sentence, gesture or movement.

**Brand.** Originates from cattle branding. Distinctive name for a product or service. If something has a brand name it is possible to advertise it using this name. It is difficult to advertise a nameless Generic. Brand names are a problem in overseas markets where there can be different and sometimes unfortunate meanings such as Mist meaning 'during' in German. Euro branding coupled with cross-frontier satellite TV means that brands have to be acceptable throughout the EC and others like the ECOWAS.

**Brand Activity Reports.** Data on advertising activity, giving a record of each press, TV or radio advertisement, available any time from Meal. Advertisements may be sorted/listed to show: name of advertiser and agency, date of appearance; TV station and channel, radio contractors and publication; spot length or size; time on, special position, use of colour, page number; rate card, cost; copy line. Reports are produced as required or as complete analysis on microfiche.

**Brand Awareness.** Percentage of consumers who express awareness of a brand as revealed by opinion poll.

**Brand Character Profile.** Human characteristics attributed to products but customers, induced either by personal experience or by advertising. Is it a feminine or masculine product, one for young or old, rich or poor, outdoor life or town dwelling? Is it associated with a particular class, or with those with special interest?

**Brand Development Index (BDI).** A comparative measure of a brand's sale in one market, compared with other markets, used to decide the relative sales value of one market versus another. See Category Development Index.

**Brand Image.** Character or style that identifies a product and distinguishes it from others. This may be based on a Unique Selling Proposition, on price or market segments with certain makes of motorcar, particular hotels, brands of perfume, or sort of wrist watches. For instance Glo mobile pioneering per second billing of the GSM in Nigeria.

**Brand Loyalty Ladder.** Sequence of customer acceptance which advertising can influence in achievement of eventual brand loyalty. Stages or 'rungs' include brand awareness, brand preference.

**Brand Name.** Name used to distinguish one product from its competitors. It can apply to a single product, an entire product line, or even a company.

**Brand Preference.** Preference for one brand over others which manufacturers try to obtain through advertising and sales promotion.

**Branded Goods.** Goods identified with a proprietary name, normally pre-packed by the manufacturer, for promotional, security or trading purposes. Branded goods offer some protection to the retailer or the distributor.

**Breadth and Depth.** The extent of the number of titles (breadth) and the number of copies of those titles (depth) in a video retail store.

**Break.** (1) Time period in television or radio when commercials are to be transmitted. Often referred to as commercial break. Or when a story is first published. (2) The part of a story that is continued on another page. Sometimes several breaks are gathered together on a "break page." Also called jumps.

**Breakdown.** Detailed assembly of data within defined categories. An advertising breakdown, for instance, would show the nature, medium and cost of each item within the campaign.

**Breakline.** A mid-sentence or paragraph that continues the story on the following page. Sometimes used to mean turnline.

Breakout (highlighted text box).

**Breakout (highlighted text box).** The synopsis of the story. Key highlights of the story that stand out.

**Bricolage.** French term for 'putting together different articles', as in pink fashion.

**Bridging Amplifier.** A device that boosts cable TV signals. Bridging amplifiers amplify the signals in a system and send them on.

**Brief.** (1) Short news of about one-two paragraph length each. (2) Summary of facts, objectives and instructions relating to the requirements for the creation of a campaign, an advertisement, or any other element of a marketing operation.

**Bristol Board.** Smooth finished paperboard used for commercial art.

**Brite/Bright.** A funny, short story.

**Broad Scale.** Full scale such as nationally, as when a product is marketed nationally following Test Marketing, or after a zoned launch in a limited area of the market.

**Broadband.** Common term for high speed internet access. In general electronics and telecommunications the term refers to a signal or circuit which includes or handles a relatively wide range of frequencies. Broadband is always a relative term, understood according to its context. The wider the bandwidth, the more information can be carried. In radio, for example, a very narrowband signal will carry Morse code; a broader band will carry speech; a yet broader band is required to carry music without losing the high audio frequencies required for realistic sound reproduction. A television antenna described as "normal" may be capable of receiving a certain range of channels; one described as "broadband" will receive more channels. In data communications a modem will transmit a bandwidth of 64 kilobits per seconds (kbit/s) over a telephone line; over the same telephone line a bandwidth of several megabits per second can be handled by ADSL, which is described as broadband- relative to a modem over a telephone line, although much less than can be achieved over a fibre optic circuit, for instance.

**Broadband Cable.** Modern telecommunications and television cable which allows more separate signals (channels) to be transmitted.

**Broadcast(ing).** This is the most pervasive machinery or channel of communication that uses electromagnetic impulses to reach the public instantly, without the connection of wires. In the process, radio and television signals are transmitted over air from fixed terrestrial transmitters and with limited range, before the advent of cable and satellite systems from the 1970s onwards. Broadcasting was intended for open reception by all within the transmission range and was mainly financed either by advertising or by receiver set/household licences. It was and remains governed by legal and regulatory regimes designed to allocate licences and supervise performance. It is virtually the only major medium in public or government ownership in non-socialist societies. See public service broadcasting.

**Broadcast Advertisers Report (BAR).** A commercial broadcast monitoring service that is available on a network and market-by-market basis.

**Broadcast Chain.** A process through which signals originating from a source or sources are made to pass through myriads of equipment that are linked together like a chain before they are transmitted.

**Broads.** Lighting instruments designed to generally illuminate a TV set in a studio by throwing soft light over a large area.

**Broadsheet.** A large page newspaper format folded in half as compared with a Tabloid, printed across the breadth of the web of newsprint. In direct mail, a large sheet which folds down to a smaller size like a map. It is also called blanket- an oversize newspaper.

**Brochure.** Stitched booklet, usually having eight or more pages, often with a prestige connotation.

**Bromide.** Photographic print on bromide paper, or a proof from photocomposition on paper instead of film. Used for sticking on to page in photoset newspapers. Bromide prints are normally 12000dpi or more.

**Brown Envelope.** Usually means any thing or 'gift' given to a journalist or reporter to twist his arm during the reportage of an event or situation. Sometimes referred to as bribe.

Browser.

**Browser.** A piece of software that allows users to view internet pages on the World Wide Web.

**Brute.** A high-intensity spot lamp.

**BSC.** Broadcasting Standards Commission. A UK body for both standards and fairness in broadcasting. It is the only organisation within the regulatory framework of UK broadcasting to cover all television and radio, both terrestrial and satellite. This includes text, cable and digital services. It has three main tasks, as established by the Broadcasting Act, 1996. These are: to produce codes of conduct relating to standards and fairness; to consider and adjudicate on complaints; to monitor, research and report on standards and fairness in broadcasting.

**BTA.** (in reference to scheduling). Best Time Available.

**Budget.** Estimate of future sources of income and expenditure including statement of intentions within a given period of time. Can relate to individual parts of the marketing mix, when it may include expenses only, or to the total marketing operation. Can also be the various news departments' proposals for what they want to put in the newspaper.

**Budgetary Control.** Methodical monitoring of planned income and expenditure by issuing sales targets, placing orders and authorising payments within the context of a previously approved and detailed budget. Provision is made for continuous feedback which relates to all financial commitments and projected surpluses or over-expenditures.

**Bug.** A short bit of type, such as (AP). In this case, it would signify that the story is from the Associated Press.

**Build-up.** Period before an exhibition when exhibits arrive and stands are erected, decorated and laid out.

**Build-up-method.** Assembly of advertising appropriation by making allocations to different media and so building up the total budget.

**Bulb, Flashbulb.** A special flashbulb that can be used at certain shutter speeds is called "FP" where the initials stand for Focal Plane. Designed for use with focal-plane shutters, these bulbs make a nearly uniform amount of light for a relatively long time. The idea is to turn on the light before the focal-plane shutter starts to open and keep the light on until the shutter is completely closed. Firing delay for flashbulbs is indicated by code letters: "F"- fast; "M"- medium; "MF" - medium fast; "S" – slow.

**Bulk Discount.** Reduction on standard price in consideration of purchasing a large quantity of goods or services, or, in the case of advertising, space or time. See Quantity discount.

**Bulk Rate.** See Bulk discount.

**Bulkhead.** In buses, advertisement position above windows of interior.

**Bulldog Edition.** A morning newspaper's early edition, printed on the preceding evening and sent to out-of-town readers on delivery trucks, trains or planes. Bulldog could be the city editor.

**Bullet.** Large or small decorative dot, arrows or squares used in layouts to draw attention to, say, selling points, useful for adding emphasis to lists.

**Bullet Theory.** Theory that suggests the mass audience is an unidentifiable group of people affected by messages received from the mass media and independent of an interpersonal influence. For the most part, replaced by the two-step flow theory, taking into consideration the role of interpersonal communication in the dissemination and influence of media messages. Another term for this theory is hypodermic needle model.

**Bulletin.** (1) Important news usually disseminated as an interruption in normal broadcast programming. (2) Wire service (audio or video) feed to subscribers. (3) Painted outdoor sign or display.

**Bulletin Board.** (1) Poster, illuminated outdoor sign, or transparency, size forty-eight sheet or even larger. Often found in city centres or on trunk roads. (2) Notice board- where information is put for a particular public.

**Bump.** To move the position or timing of a story.

**Bumper.** A brief announcement in TV or radio programming or station logo designed to separate the programme content from a commercial.

**Burden of Representation.** The problem posed for media worker when a previously under- or misrepresented group begins to be imaged in the media, and a few characters and producers have to bear the burden of being seen to represent the whole group- as 'positive role model' etc.

**Buried Advertisement.** An ad in a publication that is surrounded by other advertisements.

**Buried Offer.** An offer for a booklet, sample or information made by means of a statement within the text of an advertisement without use of a coupon or typographical emphasis.

**Burn.** A slang expression that refers to the image that remains on a camera tube when it has been focused on a subject too long or exposed to bright light.

**Burning-In.** Sometimes called printing-in, it is a darkroom process that gives additional exposure to part of the image projected on an enlarger easel to make that area of the print darker. This is accomplished after the basic exposure by extending the exposure time to allow additional image-forming light to strike the areas in the print one want to darken while holding back the image-forming light from the rest of the image.

**Burst.** Sort advertising campaign as distinct from regular Drip.

**Business and Advertisement.** Small ad resembling business card.

**Business-to-business Advertising.** Advertising which sells business services and equipment to businesses. Has specialist agencies with own trade association, Association of Business Advertising Agencies. Media may include trade and business press, trade exhibitions and direct, response mailings.

**Business Card.** A small print advertisement, announcing a business, that does not change over time. See Rate holder.

**Business Magazine/Paper.** Category of magazines or publications targeted to readers in business and industry. Subcategories include such areas as professional and trade magazines.

**Business Press.** Newspapers and magazines read mostly by businessmen, e.g. The Economists and Financial Times but also serious newspapers with considerable business sections such as THIS DAY.

**Buster.** A headline which has too many characters to fit the space allocated to it.

**Butterfly.** In films, a net stretched over an outdoor scene to soften the sunlight.

**Button Apathy.** A situation where a TV viewer is not bothered to switch off a programme, or to switch from one channel to another. This viewer can be said to be suffering from button apathy.

**Buy.** (1) The process of negotiating, ordering, and confirming the selection of a mass media advertising schedule. (2) The advertising that is purchased from a mass medium.

**Buyer.** See Media buyer and Media planner.

**Buying Influences.** All the individuals who have a say in the decision or the selection of a product or service.

**Buying Service.** A company primarily engaged in the purchase of media for advertising purposes; it supplants part of the advertising media function; also called "media buying specialist" or "time/space buying specialist/service."

**Buy Sheet.** The form used by a media buyer to keep track of the data on a media selection "buy."

**Buyout.** A compensation practice by which the talent in a pre-recorded commercial or programme receives a one-time payment and waives the rights to remuneration for all future transmissions of that appearance. Buyouts are different from residuals, which pay the performer each time a commercial or programme is aired.

**Buzz Words.** Contemporary expressions that represent current trends and situations, but may be short-lived. Also, in advertising. Clichés which may seem banal but which work in copy, e.g. now, at last, unique, free.

**By-line.** Name of journalist or writer credited with a newspaper (journal or magazine) report, and printed above or below headline. It simply tells who wrote the article. Artists and photographers typically get credits. When the reporter's name appears at the end, it often is preceded by a dash and is called a signer.

**Byte.** Computer term (not the same as bit), referring to the basic unit of data storage for characters. File sizes and the capacity of computer memory are measured in kilobytes (a thousand bytes-KB), megabytes (MB) or gigabytes (GB).

# C

**C-Band.** "Compromise" band, the original and most widely-used band of frequencies for satellite transponders. It is a portion of electromagnetic spectrum in the microwave range of frequencies ranging from 4 to 6 GHz. For military use, by North Atlantic Treaty Organisation (NATO) designation, "C band" is the frequency range between 0.5 and 1 GHz. This usage should not be confused with the "c band" in optical communications, which refers to near infrared wavelengths ranging from about 1525 nm to 1565 nm. C band in NATO definition is used in weather radars in many countries. Otherwise, it is primarily used for satellite communications, normally downlink 3.7 – 4.2 GHz, uplink 5.9 – 6.4 GHz, usually via twenty-four 36MHz-wide transponders on board a satellite. Most C band satellites serving North America use linear polarisation, while most of those serving other continents particularly Intelsat satellites use circular polarisation. The 802.11a wireless networking standard operates in the 5GHz area, and some recent-model cordless telephones use frequencies in the 5.8GHz vicinity. The applications include full-time satellite TV networks or raw satellite feeds, although subscription programming also exists. There are over thirty C band satellites in Geosynchronous orbit serving North America, which provide more than 1,000 video channels and countless audio services. In the past, direct C band reception was the only satellite television option available to consumers. Since the introduction of high-powered direct broadcast satellite systems, which normally used small 18-inch (45-cm) stationary dishes (in contrast to the large dishes and motors required by C band systems) in the middle 1990s, the number of homes using C band satellite systems in the United States for general reception has vastly declined while small-dish systems enjoyed unprecedented success. Despite this, C band satellites continue to be a key important distribution method for cable networks in the United States (to cable head-ends and mini-dish DBS services) and other network/broadcast users. For example, most satellite-distributed syndicated and network television shows are pre-aired for affiliate and Canadian pick-up by C band. Radio stations picking up satellite-fed programming also constitute an important American user of C band, with a major American radio "neighbourhood" located on the AMC 8 satellite at the 139° W orbital position. Compared to the Ku-band, the C-band has both advantages and disadvantages. Its usage is less common in Europe, where the Ku band has traditionally dominated. In many parts of the world, C band is often used to cover a very broad area, for example all of Africa or China. Indeed, many C band satellites have "global" beams with gigantic coverage areas. For instance, the global beam of the Thaicom 3 satellite, positioned at the 78.5° E orbital slot over the Indian Ocean, has a coverage range extending over most of Europe, Asia, Africa, and Australia. C band direct-to-home reception contrasts with the newer and now more common direct broadcast satellite, which is a completely closed system used to deliver subscription programming to small satellite dishes connected to proprietary receiving equipment. The band is highly associated with television receive-only (TVRO) satellite reception systems or "big dish" systems, larger antennas and more expensive receivers. It usually provides better video quality and is less affected by rain attenuation than the Ku band.

**C Clamp.** A metal device shaped like the letter C, used to connect lighting instruments to a pipe grid above a television studio. A version of the C clamp is used to temporarily hold flats together or pieces of scenery in place.

**C 41.** Kodak's standard chemical process for developing colour negative film, an industrial reference standard.

**C Format.** 'Classic' format - one of the three selectable Advanced Photo System print formats; identical to the 2:3 aspect ratio used in 35 mm photography and suitable for most general-purpose shots.

**C Mount.** A type of connection used to attach a lens to a TV or film camera. The connection is standardised so the threads, the hole, and the base are all compatible. Nearly all 16mm cameras and most TV cameras use the ubiquitous C mounts.

**C Type.** The term used for the Kodak photographic colour print made directly from negative.

**Cabalese, Cablese.** Set forms of words and abbreviations used in cabled copy to reduce expense transmission.

**Cable Drop.** The last connecting element of a cable system in a three network configuration. The cable drop consists of a small coaxial cable that connects the feeder cable to the distribution system to the subscriber's home and then to the converter or TV set.

**Cable Net.** Cable TV services in various countries which receive satellite TV programmes.

**Cable Spot Advertising.** The sale of commercial spots by cable companies to advertisers.

**Cable Television.** TV programmes delivered to homes by fibre-optic cable that is lain in the road. Offers a variety of programmes including the ones received by satellite. Popular because the system offered better programmes.

**Calendar.** Advertising/PR medium which keep the company name in a prominent place. Some companies print their own (e.g. Pirelli, Government Agencies and Organisations), others have their names overprinted on beautiful stock calendars supplied by firms such as Vigeo in Nigeria.

**Call Back.** The second phase of the auditioning process in which a performer is called back to perform or audition again or for a discussion of the role.

**Call Letters.** Combinations of alphabet characters that are used to identify radio and TV broadcasting stations. For example, Raypower-FM are the call letters assigned to Raypower radio station.

**Call Offs.** In an advertisement, copy which describes parts of an illustration. It is usually set around illustration and connected by lines to the parts described.

**Call Rate.** Number of personal contracts made with customers or prospects within a given period of time.

**Call Report.** Summary, usually in writing of visit by salesman to a customer, account executive to client, or similar business meetings.

**Calligraphy.** Handwriting, or lettering as an art form.

Calotype.

**Calotype.** An early photographic process introduced in 1841 by William Henry Fox Talbot (1800-77), using paper sheets covered with silver chloride. The image was fixed in strong salt solution - potassium iodide or hypo. The method produced negatives on coated paper from which any number of paper prints could be made. Talbot celebrated his invention in his book *The Pencil of Light* (1844). See Talbot, William Henry Fox.

**Camcorder.** Videotape recording units and TV cameras in one package. Battery-operated, they are lightweight and portable.

**Camera.** Generally a device used to input media into recording. Usually a lightproof box fitted with a lens though which the image of an object is recorded on a material sensitive to light. The name is derived from camera obscura, Latin for "dark chamber", an early mechanism for projecting images in which an entire room functioned much as the internal workings of a modern photographic camera, except there was no way at this time to record the image. The Camera Obscura was a dark box or room with a hole in one end. If the hole was small enough, an inverted image would be seen on the opposite wall. Such a principle was known by thinkers as early as Aristotle (c. 300 BC). It is said that Roger Bacon invented the camera obscura just before the year 1300, but this has never been accepted by scholars; more plausible is the claim that he used one to observe solar eclipses. In fact, the Arabian scholar Hassan ibn Hassan (also known as Ibn al Haitam), in the 10th century, described what can be called a camera obscura in his writings; manuscripts of his observations can be found in the India Office Library in London. Joseph Nicéphore Niépce made the first permanent photograph in 1826 using a sliding wooden box camera made by Charles and Vincent Chevalier in Paris. This was a big breakthrough. However, while this was the birth of photography, the camera itself can be traced back much further. Before the invention of photography, there was no way to preserve the images produced by these cameras apart from manually tracing them. The first camera that was small and portable enough to be practical for photography was built by Johann Zahn in 1685, though it would be almost 150 years before technology caught up to the point where this was possible. Early photographic cameras were essentially similar to Zahn's model, though normally with the addition of sliding boxes for focusing. Before each exposure a sensitised plate would be inserted in front of the viewing screen to record the image. Jacques Daguerre's popular daguerreotype process utilised copper plates, while the calotype process invented by William Fox Talbot recorded images on paper. Another feat in photography was the development of the collodion wet plate process by Frederick Scott Archer in 1850 which cut exposure times dramatically. It required photographers to prepare and develop their glass plates on the spot, usually in a mobile darkroom. Despite their complexity, the wet-plate ambrotype and tintype processes were in widespread use in the latter half of the 19th century. Wet plate cameras were little different from previous designs, though there were some models such as the sophisticated Dubroni of 1864 where the sensitising and developing of the plates could be carried out inside the camera itself rather than in a separate darkroom. Other cameras were fitted with multiple lenses for making cartes de visite. It was during this wet plate era that the use of bellows for focusing became widespread. The camera is however, analogous to a physical camera in the real world. It has a position from which a scene can be viewed and rendered. Like most objects, the camera has properties such as its rotation, depth of field, field of view, and clipping planes. In television, the device uses an optical system and a light-sensitive pickup tube or chip to convert visual signals into electrical impulses.

**Camera Angle.** The perspective from which a TV or film camera photographs a scene or subject. The camera angle could reflect various positions of the camera (high, medium, or low; and left, right, or straight on) with respect to the subject, each giving a different viewpoint, perspective or visual effect. Camera angles are usually measured from the camera operator's eyepiece. From that point there can be high or low angles or angles from the right or left of a subject.

**Camera Chain.** A complete camera system: camera, cables, video controls and power supply.

**Camera Control Unit, CCU.** A device containing electronics and controls used for setting up and adjusting the video from one or more cameras.

**Camera Cue Light.** Tally light. A red light on the camera that indicates when it is on-the-air or being recorded.

**Camera Head.** The actual television camera which is at the "head" of a chain of camera-related electronics.

**Camera Lucida.** 'Lucy' means of drawing layouts, permitting picture to be drawn in different sizes.

**Camera Obscura.** Literally a 'dark room', the precursor of the modern camera.

**Camera-ready Copy, CRC.** Line artwork and typesetting arranged as complete artwork ready to be photographed for litho plate making. It is the final version of the layout ready for printing.

**Camera Shake.** Movement of camera caused by unsteady hold or support, vibration, etc., leading, particularly at slower shutter speeds, to a blurred image on the film. It is a major cause of un-sharp pictures, especially with long focus lenses.

**Camp.** A sensibility, emerging from male gay culture, which revels in surface, style, theatricality, and exaggeration or parody of 'straight' forms of life.

**Campaign.** Organised course of action or coordinated advertising effort, planned carefully on behalf of a particular product or service to achieve predefined objectives that extends for a specified period of time. Can relate to advertising, sales, public relations, or any part of the promotional mix. This planned attempt is to influence public opinion, behaviour, attitudes and knowledge on behalf of some cause, person, institution or topic, using different media over a specific period of time. The main types of campaign are: advertising; political; public informational; fundraising. Public campaigns are usually directed towards socially approved goals. They are often based on research and subject to evaluation of success.

**Campaign Plan.** Formal documentation of a campaign, beginning with campaign objectives and finishing with campaign monitoring proposals.

**Cancel.** Anything deleted. Delete, spike.

**Candid Pictures.** Unposed pictures of people, often taken without the subject's knowledge. These usually appear more natural and relaxed than posed pictures.

**Cans.** Headphones worn by TV and radio production personnel. It is also used to refer to the circular metal containers in which a film is stored, leading to the industry use of the phrase, 'in the can,' for a completed motion picture or TV programme.

**Capacitor.** A central part of a condenser microphone. The device stores energy in the electric field created between a pair of conductors on which electric charges of equal magnitude, but opposite sign, have been placed. It is occasionally referred to using the older term condenser.

**Capital Letters.** Known as caps, should be used sparingly in editorial material and restricted to names of organisations, people's names, geographical place names, registered names, but only for a very few top people's names and not business or job titles. Whole words or brand names should not be spelt entirely in caps.

**Capitalism.** A competitive social system, emerging in the seventeenth century in Europe, based on commodification and the drive of the owners of the means of production to maximise the profits of their companies.

**Capstan.** A motor-driver roller and rotating shaft in the VTR that pulls the tape over the heads.

**Caption, Photo.** The text accompanying an illustration or photograph. All photographs should have a caption fixed to the back, usually with sellotape. Wording should state what the picture cannot say for itself, and include name, address and telephone number of sender (not the photographer). Pictures should be pasted on sheet of paper or on news release. Flapped captions liable to become detached. On printed papers, it is the description of the event on the photograph, noting some of the following: who, where, what, why and how. Also known as a cut line.

**Caption Board.** Artwork used when making titles for video tapes.

**Caption or Legend.** Description wording to explain an illustration.

**Captive Audience.** Audience which, by virtue of its particular situation, is likely to be exposed to advertising messages into to, e.g. a cinema or conference audience.

**Car Card.** Advertisement displayed in compartment of underground train, usually above the windows, in or on a bus, subway, or commuter train car.

**Card Rate**. The cost of time or space on a rate card.

**Cardboard.** Popular term for paperboard, often come in scores of colours.

**Cardioid Microphone.** A mike named after its pick up pattern, which is shaped like a heart. The device is unidirectional and is sensitive to sounds from both sides but especially from the front.

**Caricature.** A distorted representation of a person, type or action that is exaggerated for comic effect.

**Carrier Wave.** An electromagnetic wave modulated with audio or video information used to broadcast radio and television signals.

**Carryover Effect**. The residual level of awareness or recall after a flight or campaign period, used to plan the timing of schedules.

**Carry-through Rate.** Charging the higher time segment rate when a broadcast programme spans two segments.

**Cart, Cartridge.** A plastic container with audio or videotape that threads automatically when inserted into a record or playback machine. In contrast to a cassette, the tape is commonly in a continuous loop.

**Cartel.** A group of organisations in an industry which secretly agree on maintaining high prices and effectively killing competition; see also oligopoly.

**Cartoons.** Drawings of sequence of actions to produce a movie effect for films or TV commercials. Also, for press advertisements or instructions with products, cartoons strip demonstrating stage by stage how to use a product or criticising/appraising a political situation. Cartoons are also put on newspapers, magazines and other print materials to normally amuse readers or pass an important message in a funny way.

**Case Study.** This is a research design that focuses on one or more specific institutions or events (cases). Case studies are carried out with the intention of shedding light on general processes, but the results are not generalisable in the statistical sense. For instance one could be doing a research of the mass media as an effective tool for democratisation, a case study of Nigeria or South Africa may be used. Or in the case of researching the level of first degree university drop outs, a case study of London Metropolitan University or other university may be studied in carrying out this research.

**Cash/Barter Syndication.** A type of syndication that involves elements of full barter syndication and cash syndication in sale of TV programming. In this transaction the local station or cable operation pays a lower cash fee to license the program but gives up some of the available commercial time within the show to advertisers. The local operation retains the remainder of the time for its sale.

**Cash Discount.** A discount, usually 2 percent, by media to advertisers who pay promptly.

**Cash Syndication.** A method of syndication in which a TV or cable operation pays the syndicator or distributor a flat fee to license a programme for transmission. In this transaction the local station or system purchasing the right to air the programme(s) a number of times over a specified period. The operation assumes all of the risk in purchasing the show and must sell the commercial time locally or spots nationally.

**Cassette.** Light-trapped film container used with 35 mm cameras. It is elliptically shaped and designed especially for the Advanced Photo System that serves as the sealed, leaderless container for all System film whether unexposed, exposed or processed.

**Cast.** (1) The characters for a film, drama or production. In film making, the names of the cast is always provided at the end of the film with the entire crew. In drama or script writing, it is at the introductory pages of the script to know the roles of each dramatis personae. (2) Abnormal colouring of an image produced by departure from recommended exposure or processing conditions with a transparency film, or when making a colour print. Can also be caused by reflection within the subject as from a hat on to the face.

**Casting Off.** Estimating space in printing required to accommodate a given number of words of a certain typeface and size.

**Catalogue.** Publication containing descriptions or details of a number or range of products.

**Catalogue Product.** Titles listed in the catalogue or sales list of a program supplier in the pre-recorded video industry. The catalogue titles usually sell regularly and steadily throughout the year and are the equivalent of the backlist in the book industry.

**Catalyst Effect.** When a medium, say book, newspaper, magazine, film, TV or radio programme has the effect of modifying a situation, or taking a mediating role.

**Catch Phrase.** An advertising Slogan or Jingle which becomes so familiar that it becomes part of the language as a popular saying. "Nice one, Cyril" has been used in TV commercials for a baker and a banker. A very good example is 'MTN- your best connection'.

**Catch line.** Slogan, signature slogan, strap line, or tagline. Identifying word on copy or proofs enabling related material to be identified quickly and brought or kept together. Usually a single word at the top right hand side.

**Categorical.** Data that can be arranged in categories, like colour, shape, or name. However, the categories cannot be arranged in a logical rank order, as would be the case for ordinal data.

**Category Development Index (CDI).** A comparative market-by-market measure of a market's total sales of all brands of a single product category, used to evaluate the sales potential of a market for a product category or a brand See Brand Development Index.

**Catharsis.** A type of effect of tragic or violent fiction and drama that leaves the audience purged of emotion and released of any urge to be affected by the actions portrayed. Originally suggested by Aristotle and taken up by researchers into media violence to account for seeming lack of behavioural effects. Although theoretically plausible, it does not seem to have been specifically demonstrated or measured.

**Catharsis Hypothesis.** A psychodynamic principle that, in its most basic sense, is simply an emotional release. The hypothesis maintains that aggressive or sexual urges are relieved by "releasing" aggressive or sexual energy, usually through action or fantasy. For instance, a young male may watch a film in which an attractive woman engages in sexual behaviour. The young male may become sexually aroused from this and subsequently frustrated because of his inability to act out his sexual desires. To release this sexual tension, the young male may go outside and play sports or engage in fantasies about himself and the woman. In media language, this means the belief that violence and aggression on films and TV has a therapeutic effect.

**Cathode Ray Tube (CRT).** One version of an electric vacuum tube designed for the display of images. There are two types of cathode ray TV tubes, one for black-and-white TV and the other for colour.

**CATV.** Community Antenna Television, or cable TV. It is a system of providing television, FM radio programming and other services to consumers via radio frequency signals transmitted directly to people's televisions through fixed optical fibres or coaxial cables as opposed to the over-the-air method used in traditional television broadcasting via radio waves, in which a television antenna is required. It is most commonplace in North America, Europe, Australia and East Asia, though it is present in many other countries, mainly in South America and the Middle East. In Africa, cable TV has had little success, as it is not cost-effective to lay cables in sparsely populated areas, and although so-called "wireless cable" or microwave-based systems are used, "direct-to-home" satellite television is far more popular, especially in South Africa. Technically, both cable TV and CATV involve distributing a number of television channels collected at a central location (called a headend) to subscribers within a community by means of a network of optical fibres and/or coaxial cables and broadband amplifiers. As in the case of radio broadcasting, the use of different frequencies allows many channels to be distributed through the same cable, without separate wires for each. The tuner of the TV, VCR or radio selects one channel from this mixed signal. The same program is often simultaneously broadcast by radio and distributed by cable, usually at different frequencies. Other programs may be distributed by cable only; rules restricting content (e.g. regarding nudity and pornography) are often more relaxed for cable than for over-the-air TV. Traditional cable TV systems worked strictly by way of analogue signals (i.e. using standard radio waves) but many modern cable TV systems also employ the use of digital cable technology, which uses compressed digital signals, allowing them to provide many more channels than they could with analogue alone. Many cable television systems were formerly known as Community Antenna Television (CATV) systems as they were originally composed simply of a shared antenna located in a high location to which multiple households could have their TVs connected via coaxial cable. This was designed to provide access to television signals in areas where reception was traditionally poor. As cable-only networks began to appear on CATV systems, picked up via satellite rather than by antenna, the use of the term CATV has largely faded and the term cable television has taken its place.

**CAV.** Constant Angular Velocity. This depicts the motion of a body rotating at a constant velocity, because as it rotates it moves through a constant angle per unit time. CAV is one method of writing or reading information from a rotating data disk. An LP record spins at an angular rate (CAV) of 33⅓ rpm. Because the linear distance travelled by the phonograph stylus per revolution of the record decreases as it moves closer to the centre of the disk, the data rate increases and the data becomes more compressed. When LPs were introduced in 1948, motor speed control was not nearly as accurate as it is today, and the more desirable constant linear velocity (CLV) would have been more difficult to achieve. Thus a record cut and replayed with CLV would have suffered increased wow and flutter distortions. A compact disc (CD) employs CLV to maintain a constant data rate. The motor speed decreases from 495 to 212 rpm as the read head moves away from the centre to keep the disc moving past the read head at a constant linear velocity.

**CBS.** Columbia Broadcasting System. It is one of the largest television networks, and formerly one of the largest radio networks, in the United States of America. One of the pioneer radio networks, from its earliest days CBS established a reputation for quality; prior to the fracturing of the market under cable television, CBS's television network was one of three which dominated broadcasting in the United States.

**CCCS.** Centre for Contemporary Cultural Studies at Birmingham University, 1964-2002. It was a research centre at the University of Birmingham and was founded in 1964 by Richard Hoggart, its first director. Its object of study was the then new field of cultural studies. The Centre was the locus for what became known as the Birmingham School of Cultural Studies, or, more generally, British cultural studies. Birmingham School theorists such as Stuart Hall emphasised the reciprocity in how cultural texts, even mass-produced products are used, questioning the valorised division between "producers" and "consumers" that was evident in cultural theory such as that of Theodor Adorno and the Frankfurt School.

**CCD.** Electronic sensor used by all autofocus cameras, capable of detecting subject contrast; also an image-receiving device for video camera.

**CCM.** Column centimetre. Unit of measuring depth of column in press advertising, minimum space usually 3ccm.

**CD+G.** initials that stand for compact disc + graphics. It is a standard musical compact disc that also contains graphics such as the lyrics to a song or other related textual material. The visual material is encoded in some of the empty space on the CD and can only be displayed on a TV set by using a special player. See compact disc.

**CD ROM.** Initials that stand for compact disc read-only memory. It is a compatible CD player that plugs into the back of the computer or other electronic device. Computer CDs can carry large amounts of information for the computer to read. See compact disc.

**Cds.** Cadmium Sulfide (Cell). A battery powered, current-modulating light-sensing cell that is quite popular with lots of cameras exposure metering system and external metering devices. It is a photo conductive material used in exposure metres as alternative to selenium-based or silicon blue photocells. Its electrical resistance decreases as the light falling on it increases. Cds metres use current from an external power source, such as a battery.

**Cel.** Abbreviation of cellulose acetate. Transparent sheet used for drawing cartoons.

**Celebrity.** A figure understood as having the same access to fame as stars, but not always as closely associated with specific areas of achievement especially in cinema.

**Celebrity Journalism.** The preoccupation in modern print journalism with recording the activities, words, scandals and other events by celebs, known or influential persons.

**Cell.** For a frequency distribution involving two or more variables, a category defined by particular values of each of those variables.

The total number of cells is the product of the possible values of the total number of variables.

**Cellular Radio.** A mobile radiotelephone, often in an automobile, that uses a network of short-range transmitters located in overlapping cells throughout a region, with a central station making connections to regular telephone lines. The communications systems divide a geographic region into sections, called *cells*. The purpose of this division is to make the most use out of a limited number of transmission frequencies. Each connection, or conversation, requires its own dedicated frequency, and the total number of available frequencies is about 1,000. To support more than 1,000 simultaneous conversations, cellular systems allocate a set number of frequencies for each cell. Two cells can use the same frequency for different conversations so long as the cells are not adjacent to each other.

**Celluloid.** A transparent, colourless synthetic plastic made by treating cellulose nitrate with camphor and alcohol. It was the first important synthetic plastic and was widely used as a substitute for more expensive substances, such as ivory, amber, horn, and tortoiseshell. It is highly flammable and has been largely superseded by newer plastics with more desirable properties. It has been used for combs, brush handles, billiard balls, knife handles, buttons, and other useful objects. Most importantly it provides an ideal medium for carrying images.

**Censorship.** The practice of suppressing anything perceived as objectionable. It forbids or prevents publication or distribution of media products, or parts of those products by those with the power, either economic or legislative, to do so.

**Census.** Complete count of population. Where a survey is based on a partial count, or sample, a census tries to include all members.

**Census Sample.** Apparently contradictory term but meaning a sample drawn from compiled census data.

**Centre.** Typographical or proof correction instruction to place or move copy to middle of space.

**Centrefold Spread (or centre spread).** Middle pages of a publication which open flat as in wire-stitched magazine and can be printed right across. Also called Naturals. Facing pages in middle of a

Signature. It permits large pictures and headlines. Adverts are usually spread on these middle pages. (see Double Truck).

**Centre/Ceuline Spread.** Double page spread at the centre of a periodical. Usually regarded as desirable position since it occupies one continuous sheet of paper, enjoying the advantages both of extra size and a solus position. See Centrefold spread.

**Certification of Films.** Until December 1982, the British Board of Film censors had the following system of certification: *X*, denoting films with high sex and violence content or other disturbing subject matter to which those under 18 were not permitted; *AA* films from which children under 14 were barred; *A* films to which children were admitted if accompanied by an adult, and *U*-certificate films admitting all. The new 1982 categories are 18- permitting admission for those 18 and over; 15- replacing AA, and raising the admission age from 14 to 15; PG- Parental Guidance, a symbol used in the US especially, and intended to show that a film contains some scenes which individual parents may feel unsuitable for children; and U remaining as before.

**CG.** (1) Computergraphics. Using the computer for graphic designs and presentations. (2) Character generator. A device that electrically creates letters and symbols for TV titles and other graphic displays.

**CGI.** (1) Computer Generated Imagery, a term sometimes used for digital special effects; (2) Common Gateway Interface, an agreed standard that defines how a web page can allow users interactivity with an external program, e.g. using a search engine or shopping over the internet.

**Chain.** A broadcast network; also, a newspaper or magazine group of single ownership or control.

**Channel.** A narrow band of frequencies wide enough for one-way communication. Usually assigned geographically and specifies certain frequencies for use by AM and FM radio and UHF and VHF television stations.

**Channel Capacity.** Amount of information that a channel of communication can hold.

**Channel 4.** A public-service television broadcaster in the United Kingdom. Created by an Act of Parliament, it began regular broadcasts on 2 November 1982. Like the nation's long-established public-service broadcaster, the BBC, it has gifted broadcasting frequencies, but it does not receive funding from the television licence income. All programming is financed through its commercial activities, which include the sale of on-air advertising.

**Channel 5.** UK's fifth terrestrial channel. Offers programme information, multi channel TV listings, weather guide, news updates, competitions and games.

**Channel of Communication.** Any particular link between a communicator, e.g. an advertiser, and a receiver, e.g. potential customer.

**Character.** A single printing letter, digit or symbol in typesetting.

**Character Count.** Total number of type characters and spaces in copy to be printed.

**Character Generator (CG).** Computer based storage of letters and numbers that can be typed electronically onto a television

**Character Merchandising.** Use of celebrities for promotional purposes.

**Character Per Inch.** Measurement unit of type in a line or column width.

**Character Per Pica.** Methods of Copy fitting or Casting Off by average number of characters per pica, a pica being 12 points (point system consists of 72 points to the inch).

**Character per Second.** Speed of a phototypesetter.

**Charge-coupled Devices (CCD).** Devices that change light into electronic signals. They consist of one to three chips, which break down the TV picture into thousand of pixels. The horizontal and vertical photosensitive elements cross within the tiny device and create the image. The number of pixels determines the definition and quality of the picture.

**Chargeback System.** A method of accounting to calculate the funds used in producing media for other departments within an organisation. The basic overhead for the media centre is covered by the parent institution, but the centre charges a service fee to any department or division borrowing videocassettes or requesting graphics or TV production and an interdepartmental transfer of funds is made.

**Chart.** Clearest and most effective method of interpreting and presenting a subject visually. A chart is an information graphic that can be used to clarify complex problems, reveal hidden facts, or to detect mistakes in statistical work. They are often used to make it easier to understand large quantities of data and the relationship between different parts of the data. Charts can usually be read more quickly than the raw data that they come from. They are used in a wide variety of fields, and can be created by hand or by computer using a charting application. Certain types of charts are more useful for presenting a given data set than others. For example, data that presents percentages of different groups (such as "satisfied, not satisfied, unsure") might be best represented as a pie chart, allowing the viewer to compare the size of each sector slice. On the other hand, data that represents numbers that change over a period of time (such as "satisfaction between 1990 and 2000") might be best shown as a bar chart or histogram. The various types of chat include- (a) scatterplot used with Cartesian coordinates to show the relation of two or more quantitative variables, (b) histogram typically used to show the quantity of points that fall within various numeric ranges (or bins), (c) bar chart used by bars to show frequencies or values, (d) pie chart usually used to show percentage values as a slice of a pie, (e) a line chart horozontally used to depict non-cumulative data over, say, time, (f) box plot used to show information about the distribution (minimum, maximum, mean average, etc.) along a single axis, and (g)Polar area diagram developed by Florence Nightingale, and is same as a pie chat only an enhanced form.

**Charter 88.** A British human rights movement that advocates constitutional and electoral reform and owes its origins to the lack of a written constitution in the United Kingdom. It began as a letter to the New Statesman magazine in 1988 and it took its name from Charter 77 - the Czech dissident movement co-founded by Václav Havel. It also has a faint echo of the far more popular mid-19th Century Chartist Movement of England that resulted in an unsuccessful campaign for a People's Charter. Much of the original drive behind the organisation has been drained and rendered moot by a parallel movement to enact a written constitution for a United Europe. Generally they call for a new constitutional settlement which will:- enshrine, by means of a Bill of Rights, such civil liberties as the right to peaceful assembly, to freedom of association, to freedom from discrimination, to freedom from detention without trial, to trial by jury, to privacy and to freedom of expression; subject executive powers and prerogatives, by whomsoever exercised, to the rule of law; establish freedom of information and open government; create a fair electoral system of proportional representation; reform the Upper House to establish a democratic, non-hereditary Second Chamber; place the Executive under the power of a democratically renewed Parliament and all agencies of the state under the rule of law; ensure the independence of a reformed judiciary; provide legal remedies for all abuses of power by the state and by officials of central and local government; guarantee an equitable distribution of power between the nations of the United Kingdom and between local, regional and central government; draw up a written constitution anchored in the ideal of universal citizenship, that incorporates these reforms. The organisation is not a membership one so it costs nothing to add one's name to the Charter but they rely on the generosity of supporters for funding.

**Charts.** A term for record charts where songs are listed in order of popularity.

**Chase.** Metal frame in which page of a type is made up.

**Chaser.** A late edition of the newspaper for which the presses are not stopped until the plates are ready. Those pages, then, are said to be "chasing" a running press. The longer it takes for them to get there, the more papers are missed.

**Chat Rooms.** An interactive part of a website where guests can write messages to other people immediately. Also known as forums and message boards, popular chat rooms include yahoo and msn chat rooms.

**Checked Copy.** Typed or printed matter that has been proofread for accuracy, authenticity, or merit.

**Checkerboarding.** A programme scheduling strategy whereby individual programmes from a series are transmitted at the same time on alternate days of the week. The technique differs from stripping programmes or running them across the board each day of the week.

**Checking Copy.** A copy of a publication that is supplied by the medium to show that an advertisement appeared as specified.

**Cherry Picking.** A programme acquisition practice that involves the selection of programmes from a variety of sources. The objective is to pick and choose the best programmes for scheduling on a cable system or TV station. It is often used by independent stations that are free to choose from a number of distributors in acquiring the programmes that make up their broadcast schedules.

**Cheshire Labels.** Specially prepared paper used to print names and addresses that can be mechanically fixed singly to mailing pieces.

**Chi-square.** In probability theory and statistics, the chi-square distribution (also chi-squared or $\chi^2$ distribution) is one of the theoretical probability distributions most widely used in inferential statistics, i.e. in statistical significance tests. It is useful because, under reasonable assumptions, easily calculated quantities can be proven to have distributions that approximate to the chi-square distribution if the null hypothesis is true. The data for a chi-square test can be nominal or ordinal rather than a higher level of measurement.

**Chipboard.** Cheap quality of cardboard made from wastepaper. Most common form is what lined chip, in which a higher quality lining of white wood pulp is applied during manufacture. This provides a good printing surface and is used widely in packaging, e.g. of cereals, toothpaste, games and hardware.

**CHR.** Contemporary Hit Radio. A radio format that plays the most popular rock music but uses a playlist longer than 40 songs (Top 40).

**Chrétien, Henri.** (February 1, 1879 – February 6, 1956) A French astronomer and an inventor. His most famous invention is the anamorphic widescreen process, that resulted in CinemaScope, and the co-invention with George Willis Ritchey of the Ritchey-Chrétien type of astronomical telescope. See CinemaScope.

**Chroma.** Purity of colour.

**Chroma Copy.** Colour print made without negative.

**Chroma Key Slides.** Slides with picture outlined by black mask that allows viewers to see the picture as a background behind the TV studio announcer or presenter.

**Chromakey.** An electronic matting effect that keys out or removes a portion of video of a specific colour. Another video source is then substituted for the removed area. Generally, a deep, saturated blue is used as a keying colour.

**Chromatic Aberration.** A lens aberration producing an overall blurred image; the inability of a lens to bring all wavelengths of light (especially red and blue) into the same plane of focus; usually present in regular large-aperture telephoto and super-telephoto lenses. It does not improve by stopping down the lens and correctable through the use of low Dispersion (ED, LD SD) glass. Fundamentally, this aberration is caused by light rays of different wavelengths coming to focus at different distances from the lens. Blue will focus at the shortest distance and red at the greatest distance. Since the natural rays of light are a mixture of colours, each aberration will give a different value corresponding to each colour thus producing blurred images. See aberration.

**Chromo Paper.** Very heavily coated paper, superior to art paper. Dull or glazed for colour litho.

**Chromolithography.** Many coloured litho printing as distinct from the four colour process so that special colours may be printed. Used for poster printing when more than four inks are used.

**Chronology.** An arrangement of events in a news story. The record of these events in the order of their occurrence may be determined by the author or editor. But it has a low priority in the construction of news stories to the point where the audience has to be highly news-literate to follow happenings.

**Churn.** The rate of turnover of customers who do not renew their subscriptions to a cable TV operation that offer a scrambled signal.

**Churnalism.** Bad journalism: journalists who churn out rewrites of press releases and other materials.

**CI.** (1) Copy instruction when placing press advertisements. (2) Contrast Index. In photojournalism, numeric rating indicating the optimum development contrast for negative materials.

**Cibachrome Print.** High quality colour print from transparency.

**Cinema.** Theatre where motion pictures are shown; usually provides also an outlet for advertising films. In some cinemas, there is more than one theatre with different films showing in each theatre. A very good cinema is the Silverbird Cinema in Nigeria, Odeon Cinema in the UK and I-Max also in UK.

**Cinema Verite.** Literally cinema truth- an approach to documentary film-making aiming to get as close to events as possible, often producing very high shooting ratios of footage shot to that used in the final edit. Sometimes describes fiction narratives which attempt to resemble documentaries through use of hand-held cameras etc.

**Cinemacy.** A word coined by Thorold Dickinson to equate with literacy. In this process he thought that education sadly neglects the cinema as a serious area of study.

**CinemaScope.** Widescreen process copyrighted by 20th Century Fox in 1953 but invented much earlier by Henri Chrétien. Anamorphic lenses allowed the process to project film up to a 2.66:1 aspect ratio, twice as wide as the conventional format of 1.33:1. Although the lens system that CinemaScope employed was quickly made obsolete by technological developments, the anamorphic presentation of films that CinemaScope initiated in the 1950s has continued to this day.

**Cinematography.** A discipline that involves making lighting and camera choices when recording photographic images for the cinema. Etymologically, it means "writing in the movement", from the Greek words "Kinema" meaning movement and "grapho", a verb meaning I am writing. Put together it is *cinématographe*, the camera invented by the Lumière brothers in the 1890s. It is closely related to the art of still photography, though many additional issues arise when both the camera and elements of the scene may be in motion.

Circular.

**Circular.** Piece of printed matter distributed, or circularised, to a defined group of people.

**Circulation.** (1) In print, number of copies of a journal or publications sold or distributed. Average audited net scale of a publication, as certified in many countries by an Audit Bureau of Circulations which issues ABC figures at regular intervals. (2) In broadcast, the number of households within a signal area that have receiving sets. (3) In outdoor, the number of people who have a reasonable opportunity to see a billboard.

**Circulation Waste.** Circulation for which an advertiser pays, but it does not reach the type of prospect desired.

**Citizen Journalism.** Also known as 'participatory journalism,' it is the act of citizens 'playing an active role in the process of collecting, reporting, analysing and disseminating news and information' according to the seminal report *We Media: How Audiences are Shaping the Future of News and Information,* by Shayne Bowman and Chris Willis. They say, "The intent of this participation is to provide independent, reliable, accurate, wide-ranging and relevant information that a democracy requires." It should not be confused with Civic Journalism, which is practiced by professional journalists. It usually involves empowering ordinary citizens including traditionally marginalised members of society.

**City Editor or Business Editor.** Edits the financial section of a newspaper or magazine. In some countries the chief editor or news editor may be called the city editor.

**City Zone.** A central city and the contiguous areas that cannot be distinguished from it.

**City Zone Circulation.** The number of newspapers that are distributed within a city, rather than in outlying areas.

**Civil Society.** Usually refers to an intermediate zone between private life and the state, where relatively independent organisations are able to operate and circulate information relatively autonomously. This term is usually thought to offer a different understanding of the media to one which refers to control by the state or the market.

**Clapstick.** A small chalkboard with a hinged top used in film productions. The title of the programme, scene number and the take are written on it along with other information that identifies the scene been shot. Before the scene is undertaken, a production assistant claps the hinged top against the base of the board as the camera shoots it. Because the sound is usually recorded separately in film production, the sharp noise of the clap of the board is later used to synchronize the picture and sound. In TV productions, a clapstick or poster board card is used to visually identify the scene but the clap sound is not needed.

**Classifieds/Classified Advertisements.** In the press, 'small ads' with copy run on and classified under headings, sometimes with box numbers. Many publications have phone-in service. Journals like Exchange and Mart specialise in classifieds. Usually has a separate advertisement manager, set in small type and arranged according to categories or interests.

**Classified Display Advertising.** Compromise between display and classified advertising whereby a classified advertisement is presented in a display size and format of a larger size than most other classified advertising, possibly with headlines, illustrations, and so on; classified advertising with some of the characteristics of display advertising. See Display advertising.

**Class Magazine.** Periodical intended for readership by people having a particular common or specialised interest or desirable upscale audiences. In practice, usually applies to consumer, rather than business and professional magazines.

**Clean Proof.** Proof with few if any errors needing correction.

**Clear Channel.** An AM radio frequency that has only a few stations assigned on it. Usually, only one or two stations may transmit on this frequency at night. Primary stations on a clear channel may transmit with up to 50,000 watts.

**Clear Time.** The process of reserving time or time periods with a station or network; checking on available advertising time.

**Clearance.** Coverage of national television households by the number of stations (or markets) accepting a network program for airing; also, gaining available time on stations to carry a program or commercial.

**Clearance Ratio.** The proportion of affiliate stations that clear a network for airing.

**Clearing Agent.** In photojournalism, a chemical that neutralises hypo in film or paper, reducing wash time and helping to provide a more stable image.

**Clichés.** Word or phrases that writers have heard and copied over and over. Most of them are 200 or 300 years old- so old and overused that they have lost their original meaning and impact. Clichés no longer startle, amuse or interest the public, because they eliminate the need for thought, clichés have been called the greatest labour-saving devices ever invented. Journalists employ clichés when they lack the time or talent to find words more specific, descriptive or original. So a reporter under deadline pressure may say that a fire "swept through" a building, an explosion "rocked" a city, police officers gave a suspect a "spirited chase" or protesters were an "angry mob." Such phrases as this should be avoided when writing for the media. There are thousands of clichés and slang phrases reporters must learn to recognise and avoid. Some of the most common are listed below:

a close brush with
a keen mind
a step in the right
 direction
ambulance rushed
around the clock
arrived at the
 scene
at long last
at this point in time
baptism by fire
bare minimum
beginning a new
 life
behind the wheel
benefit of the
 doubt
bigger and better
blanket of snow
blessing in disguise
called to the
 scene

calm before the
 storm
came to their
 rescue
came to rest
came under
 attack
came under fire
cast aside
caught red-
 handed
clear-cut issue
colourful scene
complete stranger
complete success
coveted title
crystal clear
dead and buried
decide the fate
devoured by
 flames
dime a dozen
doomed to failure

dread disease
dream come true
drop in the bucket
dying breed
erupted in violence
escaped death
evidence of foul play
exchanged gunfire
faced an uphill battle
fell on deaf ears
few and far between
foreseeable future
gained ground
gave it their blessing
get a good look
go to the polls
got off to a good start
grief-stricken
ground to a halt
hail of bullets
heated argument
heed the warning
high-speed chase

hits the spot
in his new position
in the mix
in the wake of
landed the job
last but not least
last-ditch stand
left their mark
levelled an attack
light as feather
limped into port
line of fire
lingering illness
lodge a complaint
lucky to be alive
lying in a pool of
  blood
made off with
made their
  escape
made their way
  home
miraculous escape
Mother Nature
necessary evil
never a dull
  moment
no relief in sight
notified next of kin

once in a lifetime
one step closer
opened fire
paved the way
pillar of strength
pinpointed the
  cause
pitched battle
police dragnet
pose a challenge
proud parents
proves
  conclusively
pushed for
  legislation
quick thinking
real challenge
reign of terror
see-saw battle
set to work
smell a rat
sped to the scene
spread like wildfire
start their mission
still at large
stranger than
  fiction
strike a nerve
sudden death

sweep under the
  rug
take it easy
talk is cheap
tempers flared
thin as a rail
time will tell
tip of the iceberg
tipped the scales
took its toll
too late to turn
  back
tower of strength
tracked down
travelled the
  globe
tried their luck
under siege
under their noses
undertaking a
  study
up in the air
view with alarm
went to great
  lengths
won a reputation
word of caution
words of wisdom
word to the wise

**Click Stop.** In photojournalism, ball bearing and recess or similar construction used to enable shutter speeds, aperture values, etc. to be set by touch.

**Client.** Person or organisation, for whom a service is performed, such as advertising, market research or public relations. Sometimes used to refer to a customer.

**Clip.** (1) Shot or sequence of shots cut or clipped from complete film. (2) Fastener for retaining connection documentation on movements or transactions.

**Clipping.** A practice of cutting away from a programme transmitted by a network to insert and transmit local commercials. Clipping usually occurs at the end of a programme while the credits are being showed. It is unethical.

**Clipping Bureau/Service.** (1) An organisation that aids in checking print advertising by clipping the advertisements from print media. (2) An agency which will extract relevant news items or advertisements concerning a product or company in return for a monetary consideration.

**Close Up.** Proofreading instructions to delete space between characters or words. Different from close-up. See below, close-up.

**Closed Captioning.** The process of encoding written words into a TV or video programme. The captions are printed lines keyed on the bottom of the screen to explain the plot or to condense the dialogue for the benefit of the hearing impaired. It uses vertical blanking interval in TV scanning line process to transmit and display the writing.

**Closed Circuit Television (CCTV).** Narrow casting. TV is confined to location where shot, and not broadcast, or played back on videotape recorder, or delivered by private landline. Can be used as advertising medium in shops, hotels, in airlines or on board ship, or at showrooms and exhibitions. CCTV is often used for surveillance in areas where there is an increased need for security, such as banks, casinos, and airports. They may also have military uses. The use of CCTVs in public places has increased, causing debate over security versus privacy. It was developed as a means of increasing security in banks. Today it has developed to the point where it is simple and inexpensive enough to be used in home security systems, and for surveillance.

**Closed-ended Question.** In a research questionnaire, a question which requires a definite answer such as yes, no, don't know, choice from a list, or agreement or disagreement with a statement. Not an open-ended question where the informant may answer freely.

**Close-up (CU).** A TV or film shot where the subject dominates the screen. Sometimes called a tight shot, a CU often shows only the head of the person in the picture. An even closer view called an extreme close-up (ECU) with less space around the subject such as a shot of the eyes is sometimes used for dramatic effect. Different from close up. See above, close up.

**Close-Up Lens.** A lens attachment placed in front of a camera lens to permit taking pictures at a closer distance than the camera lens alone will allow.

**Closing Date.** The final deadline set by print media for advertising material to appear in a certain issue; in broadcast, the term "closing hour" may be used.

**Closure.** A sale resulting from following up on an inquiry from direct mail advertising.

**Club Line.** First line of a paragraph at foot of page, rest of paragraph running on to next page. Can look unattractive and is best avoided.

**Cluster Analysis.** A method of statistical geodemographic research and analysis used to identify a group of people with common characteristics in order to provide goods or services to these groups or other reasons.

**Cluster Sampling.** Basically used in communication research. Sample units devised in local groups often chosen geographically to reduce interview travelling costs.

**Clutter.** Excessive display of advertisements such as shop signs or estate agency boards. Each unit competes for the viewer's attention and within the mass of information, the impact of any single message is usually lost in the clutter.

**CNN.** American based international satellite TV news service Cable News Network, which provides live news of world events. It pioneered 24 hours news reporting and was founded in 1980 by Ted Turner.

**CNN Effect.** A theory in political science and media studies that contends that the development of popular 24-hour international television news channels has had a major impact on the conduct of states' foreign policy in both the late Cold War period and the post-Cold War era. While the free press has, in its role as the "Fourth Estate", always had an influence on policy-making in representative democracies, proponents of the CNN effect argue that 'the extent, depth, and speed of the new global media have created a new species of effects' qualitatively different from those which preceded them historically. The term's coinage reflects the pioneering role played by the network CNN in the field, whose "saturation coverage" of events like the Tiananmen Square protests of 1989, the fall of Communism in eastern Europe, the first Gulf War, and the Battle of Mogadishu was viewed as being strongly influential in bringing images and issues to the immediate forefront of American political consciousness and beyond. Despite these origins, the term as used generally refers to a broad range of real time modern media, and is not exclusive to CNN or even 24-hour broadcast cable news.

**Coarse Screen.** Printing block having larger than usual screen to facilitate its use on lower quality paper e.g. newsprint.

**Coated Lens.** A lens covered with a very thin layer of transparent material that reduces the amount of light reflected by the surface of the lens. A coated lens is faster (transmits more light) than an uncoated lens.

**Coaxial Cable.** Heavy cable consisting of an inner wire core surrounded by a layer of plastic, metal-webbed insulation, and a third layer of a plastic.

**Cobra Flash.** In photojournalism, also called Flip-up Flash. Kodak's patented flip-up flash mechanism that creates distance between the flash and the lens to reduce red-eye. The flash is located on the end of a hinged lever that covers the lens when closed, and flips up to switch on the camera and deploy the flash.

**Code of Ethics.** Set of rules specifying appropriate behaviour. Many professions including journalists, medical doctors, attorneys, and researchers in a variety of fields have their own codes of ethics.

**Coding.** (1) Keying of an advertisement to enable the origin of an enquiry to be traced. (2) Use of numbers or letters in a questionnaire against specific questions in order to facilitate analysis. Microsoft excel is often used for this exercise. Generally involves assigning numerical codes to raw data for purposes of analysis. Values of nominal variables can be assigned numbers so that computers can be used to process the data, even though the particular values assigned are arbitrary.

**Coding (or Encoding) and Decoding.** Broad terms for the production and 'reading' of texts of all kinds. The reference is less to the use of specific language (verbal or visual) than to structures of meaning embedded in or extracted from texts. The terms were popularised by Stuart Hall and incorporated in a much cited model of the relationship between media and audience. An important feature of the associated theory is that meaning is 'decoded' according to the social and cultural position of the receiver'. Most texts 'as sent' are also held to carry some 'preferred reading', that is essentially ideological, but we can usually expect alternative readings. In the case of news, Stuart Hall suggested that interpretations could either take up the preferred 'hegemonic' meanings, follow some more distanced 'negotiated' variant or reverse the intended meaning in an 'oppositional' reading. See also coding, polysemy and ideology.

**Coding and Tabulation.** In communication research, translation of survey replies into numerical order for automatic or computerised data processing.

**Coding Frame.** When compiling communication research questionnaire, a pattern of likely answers which can be aggregated in categories.

**Coefficient of Correlation.** Measure of the interdependence between two variables. Perfect positive correlation may be indicated by a measure of +1, whereas perfect negative correlations may be indicated by a measure of -1. No correlation at all may be inferred by a measure of zero or close to zero.

**Coefficient of Determination.** Amount of variability (or variance) in one variable that can be predicted based on knowledge of the values of another variable. The coefficient of determination is the square of the correlation coefficient.

**Coefficient of Variation.** Standard deviation of a distribution of values divided by its arithmetic mean. It is used to compare frequency distributions and their variability.

**Cognition/Cognitive.** Process which uses all human senses to observe the outside world and to form perceptions, attitudes, comprehension and memory. Loosely used as a synonym for Perception. In comparison to other branches of psychology, cognitive psychology is less concerned with emotions and observable behaviours and more concerned with thinking, including information processing.

**Coincidental Calls.** Carefully timed survey interviews- usually face-to-face or by phone- asking whether and what channel the informant and/or others in the household are watching at the moment the interviewer calls.

**Cold Colour.** Blue or one colour containing blue.

**Cold Composition.** Computerised typesetting, which does not use hot metal.

**Cold Lists.** Direct mail mailing lists that have no affinity with advertiser.

**Cold-set.** Drying of print on the machine without heat. Achieved by printing one colour at a time and feeding in sheets again for other colours, or because paper is absorbent, or with wet-on-wet printing of colours.

**Cold Type.** Type that is set photographically on paper, an advancement from type that was set in hot lead.

**Collage.** Abstract are form, pictures being scattered over a surface and fixed to it.

**Collaretic.** Card with a hole for attaching to the neck of a bottle as price tag, or to a sales promotion offer.

**Collate.** Putting together individual pages in a pre-determined order.

**Collating.** Collecting pages of print in page order.

**Collective Behaviour.** Behaviour that is characteristic of groups, such as crowd behaviour, rumour transmission, or public opinion formation. Collective behaviour cannot be reduced to the actions of individuals considered in isolation.

**Collotype.** Screenless gelatine printing process used for reproducing illustrations, especially fine art.

**Colophon.** Publishing inscription at front of publication stating details of author, publisher, printer copyright, ISBN, date and edition.

**Colour Balance.** To adjust the chroma channels in a video camera so that whites in a scene will be reproduced as true white. Colour films are made to be exposed by light of a certain colour quality such as daylight or tungsten. It also refers to the reproduction of colours in colour prints, which can be altered during the printing process.

**Colour Bars.** Vertical bars of different colours used to test and adjust brightness, contrast, colour intensity, and colour balance in TV cameras, videotape machines and other production gear. They consist of seven (sometimes eight) bars of pure white, yellow, blue-green, green, reddish purple, red and blue (and sometimes black). They can be created electronically or by focusing a camera at a cardboard test or colour chip poster board containing the bars.

**Colour Bar Generator.** Device that creates colour bar test signal.

**Colour Burst.** The colour timing information contained in the TV signal. A 3.58 MHz sub-carrier frequency timed to a quarter millionth of a second is used to synchronise colour information to the luminance signal.

**Colour Compatibility.** The ability of different colour subject matter to translate into a black and white picture and maintain adequate tonal contrast and separation.

**Colour Conversion Filter.** A camera filter used to convert light from indoor to outdoor colour temperature.

**Colour Correction.** Adjustment of colour values to obtain a correct colour printing and correct tonal and colour qualities of video.

**Colour Harmony.** Four principles. (a) order – colour harmony depends on colour being chosen according to a logical plan; (b) familiarity – colour combinations most familiar to observer will seem to be most harmonious. They are often based on colour combinations in nature; (c) similarity – related colours will have an harmonious effect; (d) contrast – good colour combination are very evident when contrasted with poor or odd ones.

**Colour Negative.** In photojournalism, film designed to produce colour image with both tones and colours reversed for subsequent printing to a positive image, usually on paper.

**Colour Noise.** Better known as chrominance signal-to-noise ratio. A measure of how accurately the colour signals are reproduced. Poor chroma signal-to-noise ratios are evidenced in colour fringing on edges of objects and what appears to be thousands of moving dots in large areas of highly saturated colours (especially red).

**Colour Output.** The playback output level of a colour (chrominance) signal after it is separated from the luminance signal. As with RF output, a low performing tape can lose colour resolution due to increased percentage of noise.

**Colour Phase.** As shown on a vectorscope, the electronic phase difference in degrees between the colour standard and specific colours reproduced by video equipment.

**Colour Positive.** Set of halftone screened positive colour separations.

**Colour Proof.** An early full-colour print of a finished advertisement, used to evaluate the ad's final appearance.

**Colour Resolution .**The degree to which the combined colour channels in a system can reproduce fine details.

**Colour Reversal.** In photojournalism, film designed to produce a normal colour positive image on the film exposed in the camera for subsequent viewing by transmitted light or projection on to a screen.

**Colour Separation.** Using computer or optical filters, separation of full colour pictures into four process colours to give four films for plate making. The four separate colours include: cyan, magenta, yellow and black. It consists of four separate screens; one for each of those four colours.

**Colour Separation Overlay.** TV method which enables pictures to be projected electronically to create super imposed pictures in constant electronic mural. Provides simultaneous movements or pictorial effects for TV presenters.

**Colour Sequence.** Printing order of colours: yellow, magenta (red), cyan (blue), black.

**Colour Standard.** A colour criterion or reference used to set-up colour video equipment.

**Colour Temperature.** The ratio between the six main colours (ranging from red to blue) in the colour spectrum of a light source for a TV picture. It is usually measured in degrees Kelvin (K). In photography, this describes the colour of a light-source by comparing it with the colour of light emitted by a (theoretical) perfect radiator at a particular temperature also expressed in Kelvin. Thus "photographic daylight" has a colour temperature of about 5500K. Photographic tungsten lights have colour temperatures of either 3400K or 3200K depending on their construction.

**Coloured Filter.** A glass or plastic material placed either in back or in front of a camera lens to subtract certain colours of light. Used to alter the colours in a scene.

**Colours, Legibility of Lettering/Type.** Coloured characters on coloured backgrounds are decreasingly effective in this order: black on yellow, green on white, blue on white, white on blue, black on white, yellow on black, white on red, white on orange, white on black, red on yellow, green on red, red on green, blue on red.

**Column.** A vertical text block. Also an article that appears regularly in a publication. It is written by one writer or about a special subject. See columnist.

**Column Inch, Centimetre.** Measure of depth of column space as used when measuring press media coverage. However, this volume is only one possible assessment. Tone and quality of coverage is also important. In advertising, unit for calculating and selling space.

**Column Inches.** Measurement of area derived from the width of a column of type in a publication, multiplied by its depth. Column centimetres now apply under metrication and is replacing column inches in practice.

**Columnist.** Journalist who writes a regular feature with by-line. This journalist produces a specific form of writing for publication called a "column". Columns appear in newspapers, magazines and the Internet. Some Internet columns are called blogs or Weblogs. What differentiates a column from other forms of journalism is that it is a regular feature in a publication personality-driven by the author and explicitly contain an opinion or point of view.

**Column Rule.** In printing, light rule for separating adjoining columns.

**Coma.** A lens aberration restricted to off axis image points; the inability of a lens to render point sources of light near the edges of the frame as circular. The points of light appear as comet-shaped blurs (hence the name coma) with the tails flaring toward the centre of the image. This aberration is very difficult to eliminate in wide-angle lenses with large maximum apertures. It improves by stopping down the lens.

**Combination.** Printing block which combines both line and screen (half-tone) etching.

**Combination Rate.** Special discounted space rate for inserting advertisement in more than one publication owned by the same publisher or interests.

**Combination Shot.** A TV and film camera shot that is a combination of a long shot and a close-up. Usually called combo for short, it is used in dramatic or musical variety shows where one person is in the foreground while another or others are seen behind the main action.

**Commentator.** Broadcasters who use spoken narrative language both on TV and radio to describe the event taking place to the listener or viewer. This individual could discuss social, political or cultural issues or events, typically in a public context; synonyms include pundit. Social commentator may refer to anything from a preacher to a columnist to a cultural critic. A live broadcast of a major public event, such as inauguration, funeral of a public figure, space flight or sporting occasion, is almost invariably accompanied by the thoughts of a commentator. This may be on television, accompanied by relevant images, or on radio. The technique involved differs between the two media, with radio broadcasters needing to be more explicit and descriptive because of the absence of pictures. Sports and other commentators usually broadcast live during events, in an essentially unscripted way, though they may refer to prepared materials, for example on sports statistics. Spontaneity, and even enthusiasm and partisan comments, are sometimes valued by those watching or listening to sports.

**Commercial.** Advertisement paid (could be unpaid) message in television (or radio) either in colour or monochrome. It combines motion, sight, sound and words and is designed to persuade or entice the viewer.

**Commercial Break.** Break in a television or radio programme in order to transmit an advertising message or commercial.

**Commercial Clutter.** Excessive advertising which looks untidy and offends the public.

**Commercial Impressions.** The total audience, including duplication, for all commercial announcements in an advertiser's schedule. See Gross impressions.

**Commercial Protection.** The practice of segregating commercials for similar products or services of different companies. Either as a requirement of a spot or through standard industry practices, spot for competing products like MTN and Globacom are scheduled at least 10 minutes apart from one another.

**Commercial Slot/Time.** Time between TV programmes, or Natural Break in programme, when commercials are transmitted.

**Commercialisation.** A process by which media structures and contents come to reflect the profit seeking goals of media industries and are governed by market considerations. The main reference is usually to cultural consequences, and these always have a negative connotation. Commercialised media content is believed to be in varying degrees 'inauthentic', standardised and stereotypical, given to sensationalism and personalisation. It promotes values of materialism and consumerism. It is also thought to be less creative and trustworthy. Commercial media are suspected of lacking full independence from their owners and advertisers. In some contexts the process is also referred to as 'Americanisation', on the grounds that imports of American content are involved, usually coupled with American production standards and values. See advertising, tabliodisation, commodification, sensationalism.

**Commission.** (1) Agreed financial share of a transaction accruing to a salesman or selling agent responsible for initiating or introducing business. (2) To hire or brief another concern to undertake a defined assignment. (3) Term used to describe discount allowed to an advertising agency by media owners in consideration of its space/time purchases on behalf of clients.

**Commitment (in Advertising).** Action whereby advertising space or time becomes chargeable at the full fee, whether cancelled or fulfilled. This occurs automatically to all bookings at a given time prior to scheduled appearance.

**Commodification.** Refers to the extent to which media messages and symbolic goods have become products to be bought and sold on the market.

**Common Carrier.** The types of communication services licensed by an authority or regulated by public agencies that do not maintain editorial control over the content of any transmissions. Organisations in this category will lease communication facilities to anyone willing to pay the fee. Long distance companies are examples of common carriers.

**Communication.** Gotten from the Latin word 'communicare', which means to make common. It is a social interaction and the act of transmitting information, ideas and attitudes from one person to another, which could be human or technological. Though the term has different meanings and definitions, the central idea is of a process of increased commonality or sharing between participants, on the basis of sending and receiving 'messages'. Theoretical disagreement exists about whether we should count as communication the transmission or expression of some message, on its own, without evidence of reception or effect or completion of a sequence. The most important dimensions of communication concern two points: the degree of response or feedback (one-way versus interactive process); and the degree to which a communication relationship is also a social relationship. In general, modern technologies increase the possibility and likelihood of detaching communication (message transmission or exchange) from any social basis.

**Communications Act of 1934, As Amended.** The Act of Congress (USA) that authorised broadcasting and the FCC.

**Communications Media.** Vehicles used to carry messages- informative, educational, or entertaining, to large groups of people; e.g. television cinema, or radio.

**Communication Mix.** Combination of different media in a specific promotional campaign to reach a pre-determined target audience.

**Communications Planner.** Media planner who evaluates comparative benefits of Media Advertising, Sponsorship, Sales Promotion, PR, etc. Introduced by Saatchi and Saatchi.

**Compact Disc (CD).** A small round disc usually three or five-and-quarter inches in diameter used for recording information. The digital information is embedded in small pits on the disc and is read by a laser while the disc rotates rapidly in a counter-clockwise direction. Introduced in 1982, it is the standard playback format for commercial audio recordings as of mid-2006. An audio compact disc consists of one or more stereo tracks stored using 16-bit PCM coding at a sampling rate of 44.1 kHz. Standard compact discs have a diameter of 120 mm or 80 mm. The 120 mm discs can hold approximately 80 minutes of audio. The 80 mm discs, sometimes used for CD singles, hold approximately 20 minutes of audio. Compact disc technology was later adapted for use as a data storage device, known as a CD-ROM, and to include record once and re-writable media (CD-R and CD-RW). CD-ROMs and CD-Rs remain widely used technologies in the personal-computer industry as of 2006. The CD and its extensions have been extremely successful: in 2004, the annual worldwide sales of CD-Audio, CD-ROM, and CD-R reached about 30 billion discs. See CD-ROM.

**CompactFlash.** A storage technology used by most digital cameras with PC Card interfaces. Standard supported by the CompactFlash Association. CompactFlash is ATA compatible and will fit into any Type II or Type III slot when used with a passive adapter.

**Comparative Advertising.** Drawing attention to one's own product's performance against those of particular competitors, in a recognisable form of measurement such as miles per gallon or usable space. See Comparison advertising.

**Comparative Analysis.** Comparison of quantitative factors relevant to different advertising media or vehicle based usually on cost factors taking into account demographic penetration of different publications.

**Comparison Advertising.** Used interchangeably with the term comparative advertising. It directly contrasts an advertiser's product with other named or identified products. Admissible when similar items are compared, such as motor-cars in the same price band. It must not contain derogatory "Knocking Copy".

**Compensation (in Advertising).** Money negotiated as a refund by the agency, media or production departments for advertising which has appeared incorrectly, the fault lying, at least in part, with the publisher or contractor.

**Competitions.** Promotional device, whereby prospects are invited to compete for prizes by submitting solutions to problems along with a required number of 'evidences of purchase'. Nearly always involve tiebreakers in the form of apt descriptions or advertising slogans in order to limit number of applicants for prizes, though some competitions offer a multitude of small prizes. Strictly controlled by gaming legislation.

**Competitive Claims.** Particular benefits or values promoted by manufacturers or advertisers.

**Competitor's Advertising Method.** Way of deciding advertising Appropriation according to expenditure by rivals. Can be used for a new product when promotion costs are uncertain, or to match a competitor.

**Component.** Part of a compound lens consisting of one element (single lens) or more than one element cemented or otherwise joined together. A lens may therefore be described as 4-element, 3-component when two of the elements are cemented together.

**Component Video System/Recording.** A method of processing, recording and playing back a video signal. The process involves the separate recording of the chrominance (colour) and luminance (black-and-white brightness) aspects of a TV signal. The colour video signals are recorded separately from black-and-white signals on two separate tracks prior to combining them. This reduces the loss of detail in the image and the result is a much superior picture in terms of sharpness and resolution.

**Composite Method.** A method of calculating the advertising appropriation by combining various factors and influences. There are many methods of arriving at appropriation, many of which can be combined.

**Composite Pages.** In a newspaper or magazine, those pages devoted to ads on particular subjects such as holidays, mail order offers, gardening or houses for sale. Makes small spaces viable because of market place appeal.

**Composite Print.** Commercial TV film or video with both sound and picture combined.

**Composite Signal.** A video signal that contains all of the necessary synchronising pulses. A video signal in which the luminance and chrominance information have been combined using a standard such as NTSC, PAL or SECAM. The composite video format is also used for consumer video recording systems.

**Composite Sizes.** Body or Text Type smaller than 14 point.

**Composite Video System/Recording.** An initial method of handling TV signals that is used in processing a video signal, recording it, and playing it back. In black-and-white TV, composite video consists of the picture signal as well as the synchronisation and blank pulses all combined into one signal. In colour TV additional colour picture and synchronising information is added.

**Composition.** The pleasing arrangement of the elements within a scene- the main subject, the foreground and background, and supporting subjects.

**Compositor.** Printing term, originally meaning one who composed type by hand, placing individual metal type characters in a hand held 'stick'. In computerised printing it refers to one who composes pages (either as paste up or on screen) prior to photography and plate making. Abbreviated as comp.

**Computer Graphics.** Post-production technique of drawing layouts or other designs by computer for taping and transferring to videotape. Also used for making slides. Input using keyboard, graphics tablet and VDU, and transmission to the computer. Image stored on disc, operator selecting colours, typefaces, shapes, and symbols using keyboard or touching VDU screen with electronic 'pen'. Final image transferred into camera which shoots picture of high definition TV screen.

**Computerised Flash.** In photojournalism, electronic flash guns which sense the light reflected from the subject, and cut off their output when they have received sufficient light for correct exposure. Most units must be used on or close to the camera for direct lighting only. And the camera lens must be set to a specific aperture (or a small range of apertures) determined by the speed of the film in use.

**Concepts.** The whole advertisement, headline, text, illustrations, coupon.

**Concept Testing.** Method of testing new products to estimate consumers' attitude to it before it is fully developed. Simple description, possibly drawn, and a questionnaire with assessment of intention to buy, supplied to sample. Studies may be repeated.

**Conceptual Differences.** Reasons why responses to advertising vary. Is a mailshot better received at home or workplace? Will readers or viewers respond differently according to their understanding of the subject, or the influence of the media, or the Copy Platform? All these make conceptual differences.

**Condensed.** Narrow version of a typeface, allowing more characters to the line. Useful for small spaces like boxes or coupons. Can also be generated by computerised typesetting software.

**Condenser.** Generally in photography, a simple lens used to collect light and concentrate it on a particular area, as in enlarger or projector. Frequently in the form of two planoconvex lenses in a metal housing. A condenser, normally of the fresnel type, is used to ensure even illumination of the viewing screens on SLR cameras.

**Condenser Enlarger.** In photojournalism, an enlarger with a sharp, undiffused light that produces high contrast and high definition in a print. Scratches and blemishes in the negative are emphasised.

**Condenser Microphone.** The most common microphone used in TV production. Often built into portable cameras and is also used as a lapel and tie clip mike for newscasters and interviewers. It detects sound by amplifying changes in electrical capacitance between two, closely spaced plates. Sometimes called an electrostatic or capacitor mike. See microphone.

**Confidence Interval.** Range of possible values that we believe a variable might reasonably be expected to have in the population, based on results from measuring that value in a sample.

**Confidence Level.** Probability to be achieved that the results observed did not occur by chance. The researcher chooses an acceptable level in advance; it is usually 95% or 99%; 90% is acceptable for exploratory research on new problems.

**Confirmation.** A broadcast media statement that a specific time is still open for purchase by an advertiser who is preparing a broadcast advertising schedule.

**Conflict Theorist.** Social scientist who emphasises the existence of conflict and competition in society, as opposed to one who emphasises stability and harmony.

**Confounding Variable.** Variable that has not been included among those measured in an experiment, or otherwise controlled, but has an influence on the dependent variables. Confounding variables make the interpretation of results difficult or misleading.

**Constant Comparative Method.** Method for developing categories from the data in a qualitative study rather than defining them in advance based on the researcher's preconceptions. As new data are analysed, the categories are continuously reviewed.

**Constraint.** Any limiting factor involved with the development of an idea or venture.

**Consumer Advertising.** Loosing relating to all advertising of goods or services to the mass markets of individuals or families. Used in contrast to industrial or capital goods advertising.

**Consumer Electronics.** A broad term encompassing the personal electronics products that bring education, information and entertainment to the public. These products include video devices such as TV sets, videocassette and videodisc machines, camcorders, electronic games, personal computers, etc.

**Consumer Magazines.** Periodic publications promoted and sold to members of the population as individuals, as opposed to trades, professions, or industries or to people having a common involvement in such working areas.

**Consumer Profile.** A demographic description of the people or households that are prospects for a product or service. See Target group.

**Consumption.** Rate at which a product or commodity is consumed or used.

**Contact Print.** Reproduction on photosensitive paper of the image from a negative by direct contact exposure which produces a print of the same size.

**Contact Printer.** A device used for contact-printing that consists of a light tight box with an internal light source and a printing frame to position the negative against the photographic paper in front of the light. See contact print.

**Contact Report.** Written by account executive after meeting with a client. It states decisions taken, with right-hand column giving initials of those responsible for next action. Distributed to all relevant parties on consultancy and client sides. Also known as call report. File of reports called the facts book.

**Contagion Effect.** Power of the media to create a craze or even an epidemic.

**Content Analysis.** A technique for the systematic, quantitative and objective description of media texts, that is useful for certain purposes of classifying output, looking for effects and making comparisons between media and over time or between content and 'reality'. Content analysis is not well suited to uncovering the underlying meaning of content, although it can provide certain indicators of 'quality' of media. No single method or technique for content analysis exists; it can be quantitative or qualitative, theoretical or applied.

**Content Page.** A very important part of a book that contains the chapter headings with the required page numbers against them.

**Contiguity Rate.** A reduced broadcast advertising rate for sponsoring two or more programs in succession; for example, an advertiser participating in two programs running from 7:00 p.m. - 7:30 p.m., and then 7:30 p.m. - 8:00 p.m., may qualify for a contiguity rate.

**Contingency Table.** Table or series of tables giving frequency distributions for two or more variables simultaneously, such as age and gender. Each category defined by particular values of the variables such as middle-aged women is called a cell.

**Continuity.** Repeated use of a theme, medium, script, or idea over a period of time, typically associated with the script of a commercial.

**Continuous.** Data that result from measurements on a continuous scale, as opposed to categorical data. Interval and ratio level measurements yield continuous data.

**Continuous Servo AF Focus.** Autofocus term used by Nikon, the AF sensor detection continues as long as the shutter release button is lightly pressed and the reflex mirror is in the viewing position. Useful when the camera-to-subject distance is likely to change.

**Contones.** Four-colour continuous tone colour separations made by camera fitted with colour filters.

**Contour.** The geographical area covered by a broadcast station's transmitted signal.

**Contour Setting.** Production of text which follows a shape or contour, this being possible with digital typesetting. While this presents a type mass which is visibly attractive, it can seriously detract from the readability of the text. Too clever design may destroy copy.

**Contract of Service.** Legally binding document or agreement between an advertiser and agency which states conditions of service such as method of remuneration, required notice of termination, and conditions regarding assignment of copyright. A contract could be signed or agreed between two or more parties.

**Contrast.** Ratio of light and dark on a scene. In black and white pictures, the difference between black and white which can create dramatic effect. In typography, contrast can be achieved by use of large and small type, or by bold headlines and subheadings contrasted against lighter text areas.

**Contrast Grade.** Numbers (usually 1-5) and names (soft, medium, hard, extra-hard, and ultra hard) of the contrast grades of photographic papers, to enable one get good prints from negatives of different contrasts. Use a low-numbered or soft contrast paper with a high contrast negative to get a print that most closely resembles the original scene. Use a high-numbered or an extra-hard paper with a low-contrast negative to get a normal contrast paper.

**Contrasty.** Higher-than-normal contrast including very bright and dark areas. The range of density in a negative or print is higher than it was in the original scene.

**Control Group.** In an experimental design, a group of subjects to whom no treatment is applied. Control group measurements tell the researcher what the values of dependent variables might have been if no experimental manipulation of an independent variable had taken place.

**Control Room.** A room where programmes director and his crew work together to produce a programme. The audio and video consoles are manipulated here during production. A control room can be the master control room or production control room. The master control is the technical hub of a broadcast operation common among most over-the-air television stations and TV networks. It is distinct from production control rooms in television studios where the activities such as switching from camera to camera are coordinated. It is the final point before a signal is transmitted over-the-air or sent on to a cable television operator or satellite provider for broadcast. Television master control rooms include banks of video monitors, satellite receivers, videotape machines, transmission equipment, and, more recently, computer broadcast automation equipment for recording and playback of on-air programming. The control is generally staffed with one or two operators around-the-clock, everyday to ensure continuous operation. Master control operators are responsible for monitoring the quality and accuracy of the on-air product, ensuring the transmission meets government regulations, troubleshooting equipment malfunctions, and preparing programming for future playback. Regulations include both technical ones such as those against over-modulation and dead air, as well as content ones such as indecency and station ID. On the other hand, the production control room is the place in a television studio in which the composition of the outgoing program takes place. Facilities in a PCR usually include- a video monitor wall, with monitors for program, preview, the VCRs, the cameras and most of the other video sources; vision mixer or "switcher"; audio mixing console and other audio equipment such as effects devices; character generator; digital video effects and/or still frame devices (if not integrated in the vision mixer); technical director's station, with waveform monitors, vectorscopes and the camera control units or remote control panels for the CCUs. Also VCRs may also be located in the PCR, but are also often found in the central machine room.

**Control Track.** The portion of a videotape signal consisting of timing pulses associated with video fields and frames. Used in editing and maintaining playback synchronisation.

**Control Track Editing.** Equipment that uses an electronic count of control track pulses rather than SMPTE/EBU time code numbers for its cuing and editing functions.

**Controlled Circulation.** (1) A process in which the method of circulation of a publication is controlled by some specific criterion relating to the status of the reader, and for which no separate charge is made. (2) Refers to those journals distributed free of charge to selected recipients plus those who have requested copies on publishers invitation. Most cc journals are trade and technical, and they usually have higher penetration of market than purchased journals. Consequently, publishers have adopted controlled circulation distribution in order to be able to offer advertisers larger circulation, justifying high advertisement rate. However, recent trend has been to reduce the free list and build up a subscription list. Sometimes a new magazine will start as a cc and gradually revert to one with a cover price, bookstall sales and postal subscriptions.

**Controlled Experiment.** Experimental design that uses a control group or other means, such as statistical controls or the physical control of laboratory conditions, to isolate the effects of the independent variables more accurately.

**Convergence.** Multimedia newsrooms producing news for different publishing platforms. It involves the process of coming together or becoming more alike and is usually applied to the convergence of media technologies as a result of digitalisation (computerisation). The distinctive physical characteristics of media cease to matter at least for purposes of production, processing and transmission. The contemporary increase in convergence has been used as an argument for media deregulation, since most regulatory regimes are linked to specific technologies (e.g. printing, broadcasting, cable, projection, etc.). Despite the potential, at the reception 'end' for convergence on a single apparatus, diversification seems to increase.

**Conversion Rate.** Measure of conversion of inquiries or replies to an advertisement or mailing shot into sales.

**Converter.** A device used in a cable system to change the frequencies of an electronic signal.

**Cookie.** A pattern cut out of metal or wood that is placed in front of a light source, thus projecting the pattern on the wall or backdrop of a TV studio. Formally known as cucoloris, the small three-inch pattern is usually placed in a special spotlight designed to be used with the device.

**Cool Light.** A lighting instrument that provides high light output with less heat and permits film to consistently capture more realistic colour. It provides cooler working conditions and the lights emit a steady stream of pale blue light at about 5,600x Kelvin.

**Cool Media.** Marshal McLuhan's term for participatory media such as films and TV.

**Co-operative Advertising.** Also called informal networks. (1) Joint advertising campaigns by two or more sponsors. (2) Advertising campaigns on behalf of trade or industry, paid for by levy on members. (3) Support schemes for dealers who are either supplied with standard artwork, or paid part of advertising costs. (4) Broadcast news networks created by a group of radio or TV news personnel. Also called Vertical Advertising. (slang "co-op").

**Cooperative Announcemen**t. Commercial time in network programs that is made available to stations for sale to local or national advertisers.

**Cooperative Programme**. A network broadcast that is also sold on a local basis and sponsored by both national and local advertisers; for example, "The Tonight Show". See Network cooperative programme.

**Co-production.** The sharing of costs of the production of programming between two or more stations, networks or syndicates.

**Copy.** (1) All materials to be printed, both text and illustrations. (2) From an editorial point of view, the text. (3) A single 'copy' of a publication. (4) In advertising, the text of an advertisement as produced by the copywriter.

**Copy Boy.** Obsolete term replaced in many papers with copy aide, these are men and women who keep the newsroom running by attending to various duties such as office machines, handling phones, assembling paperwork and driving around town to retrieve photos and other material.

**Copy Claim.** Benefit, or value, attributed to a product or service by an organisation in its promotional activities. Usually refers to the claim(s) made for a product in advertising literature.

**Copy Clearance.** Refers to the process whereby claims, or themes, adopted in advertising or given acceptance by specialist representatives of media concerned in order to avoid misleading or offensive statements or ideas.

**Copy Date.** Deadline when editor, advertisement department or printer requires all material for printing.

**Copy Desk.** The desk where articles are edited, headlines and captions are written, newspaper style is enforced and deadlines are either made or missed.

**Copy Fitting.** Specifying type to fit space.

**Copy Plan.** Statement of theme(s) and other materials for the development of a copy platform.

**Copy Platform.** Theme of advertising campaign, usually devised by the copywriter.

**Copy Point Recall.** Advertisement recall research which tests recall of advertisement content. This can indicate any need to modify advertisements in order to achieve better recall. Advocates of Tracking Studies consider this inadequate.

**Copy Prep.** Instructions written on copy for typesetters to follow.

**Copyright.** Legal protection for an original intellectual effort or the exclusive right to reproduce literally, dramatic, artistic or musical work, given by law for a certain period to an author etc. or his agent. This set of exclusive rights is granted by governments to regulate the use of a particular expression of an idea or information. Materials protected may include poems, theses, plays, and other literary works, movies, choreographic works (dances, ballets, etc.), musical compositions, audio recordings, paintings, drawings, sculptures, photographs, software, radio and television broadcasts of live and other performances, and, in some jurisdictions, industrial designs. It can be assigned or be bequeathed.

**Copy Rotation.** Using a systematic rota of different advertisements in order to enhance attention and impact.

**Copy Taster.** Right-hand man to the Chief Sub-Editor. He examines all copy and assesses its value in terms of space. His verdict is rarely challenged.

**Copy Test.** Text of advertising copy, either before or after publication, aiming to discover readers' comprehension, interest, brand preference, company image, etc.

**Copywriter.** Person who writes the text or copy for an advertisement, usually conceiving a theme or copy platform- consisting of display lines, text, slogan, strap line, coupon copy. He may work in an agency under a copy chief or in a creative group, in in-house advertising department, or as freelance.

**Corporate or Prestige Advertising.** Any form of advertising that has as its objective the building up of a company's reputation. Has a closer affinity to public relations activity than to advertising or sale promotional activity. Typical example in business journals such as The Economists.

**Corporate Culture.** In PR, the pattern of shared values and benefits which shapes behaviour in an organisation. Set out in mission statements.

**Corporate Discounting.** Incentives offered to advertisers with numerous brands of products; all of the corporation's advertising schedules are combined for a larger discount level.

**Corporate Identity.** Visible and physical representation of an organisation using logo, house colour, typography, clothing, livery, etc.

**Corporate Image.** Mental impression or perceived image of an organisation based on knowledge and experience. Cannot be invented but may be changed. Different people may hold different corporate images, e.g. employees, shareholders, distributors or customers according to their personal knowledge and experience. Consequently impossible to polish a poor image, but PR can build a true image by developing knowledge and understanding.

**Correction of Aberrations at Close Distance Focusing (or CRC).** In general, lenses are designed for maximum performance at infinity. Accordingly, when the lens barrel is fully extended to the shortest focusing distance, resolution is reduced. Although this is negligible for ordinary lenses, it becomes increasingly important in lens specially designed for close distance photography. Lens designers adopted a system where mechanism moves certain lens components as a unit automatically correcting for aberrations. This assures high lens performance throughout the focusing range.

**Correction Overlay.** Translucent overlay, registered on art work, on which corrections are made.

**Corrective Advertising.** Advertising that attempts to correct previous false or misleading advertising.

**Correlation.** When two things tend to vary together, for instance- that taller children tend also to be heavier. A correlation is low if there are quite a few exceptions, for instance- tall light children.

**Correlation Coefficient.** Measure of the amount of change or variation in one variable that is associated with change in another. If two variables are highly correlated, extreme values of one will commonly be associated with extreme values of the other.

**Correspondent.** A journalist who contributes material on specialised topics, e.g. agriculture, politics, shipping, automobile, education, or oil and gas. Usually a freelance, but could be editor of a specialised magazine who acts as a special correspondent on his subject to newspapers.

**Corrugated Board.** Fibreboard comprising corrugation inner fluting pasted to two flat outer paper surfaces known as inner and outer liners. Commonly constructed from Kraft paper resulting in a light, inexpensive and tough material much used in packaging, particularly for out cases.

**Cosmetic.** Refers to the appearance of a medium particularly publications: hence the use of such expression as, 'giving it a facelift'.

**Cosmopolitanism.** Literally, a citizen of the world. Also usually refer to a set of perspectives that have sought to jettison viewpoints that are solely determined by the nation, or their geographical standing within the world. A cosmopolitan viewpoint would need to carefully investigate whether or not it was reaffirming prejudice towards the West or Western nations.

**Cost per Rating Point (CPRP).** An audience research method that helps assess the effectiveness of commercials. It measures efficiency of a spot by comparing the ratings generated during the period the spot was aired with the cost of the commercial time. Often shortened to CPP. See Rating point.

**Cost-per-thousand (CPM).** Means of comparing media with different rates, circulations or readerships by dividing the rate by the number of thousands of buyers or readers.

**Cost Per Thousand Per Commercial Minute (CPM/PCM).** The cost per thousand of a minute of broadcast advertising time.

**Costing.** Allocation of expenditure where reliable costs may be determined and presented in order to provide for control of a business.

**Couch Potato.** US term for confirmed and dedicated TV viewer. It refers to a person who spends most of his/her free time sitting or lying on a couch. The stereotype often refers to overweight men who watch a lot of television, sometimes in his underwear and drinking beer.

**Counter.** Centre of a type character enclosed by strokes.

**Counter Advertising.** Advertising directed against a product or service.

**Counter Culture.** A type of sub-culture that is antagonistic or opposed to the dominant or prevailing culture of a people, tribe or community.

**Counter Programming.** A programme scheduling method where by programmes appealing to completely different audiences and demographic groups are scheduled directly opposite those appearing on competing channels. This is often used by stations or systems that have fewer viewers and is designed to attract segments of the audience that are dissatisfied with the programmes in that daypart on the competing channels.

**Coupon.** Means of obtaining response to an advertisement, either enquires or orders. Should be positioned at edge of advertisement for easy clipping, which can be encouraged by dot line and scissor symbols. Can have a Key to identify origin. It should state clearly what is being offered or sold. If there are alternatives, boxes can be printed to be ticked for choice. If payment by instalments is offered, total price must be shown. If payment may be made by credit cards, the ones accepted can be illustrated. Essential that adequate space is given for full name, address, and postcode.

**Coupon Price Reductions.** Making a price concession by providing coupons, of fixed value, sometimes printed upon the pack to encourage the initial and subsequent purchases. The coupon may, however, appear in a printed advertisement or be distributed direct to householders and may, or may not, require a previous purchase.

**Courseware.** Software used in a telecourse, including print materials like manuals, textbooks, study guides, tests and workbooks. It comprises the bulk of the telecourse.

**Cover.** Number of times advertisement is read, seen or heard. Gross cover is the total volume of cover. Net cover is the percentage of target audience who get at least one exposure. Four plus cover is the percentage receiving at least four exposures.

**Cover Date.** Publication date printed on the cover of a publication.

**Cover Page.** Either front or back page of a publication, usually available for advertising purposes at premium prices as they constitute preferred positions.

**Cover Position.** An advertisement on the cover of a publication, often at a premium cost; first cover=outside front cover; second cover=inside front cover; third cover=inside back cover; fourth cover=outside back cover.

**Cover Price.** Retail selling price of a publication printed on the cover. Some magazines have high cover prices to produce revenue when advertisement revenue is low. Few publications subsidised by advertisements and cover price, even of popular newspapers, have to contribute to revenue.

**Coverage.** (1) In advertising, the proportion (expressed in percentage terms) of a market exposed to advertising. In PR, the extent to which PR material has been used by the media. Not to be calculated on cost of advertising space or airtime. Best evaluation a mix of volume, tone i.e. how the message was conveyed, and quality i.e. where and when the message appeared. (2) In television, percentage of potential audience exposed to television advertising. Can relate to those exposed to an individual television spot, or to at least one of a campaign's television spots. Net coverage or Reach.

**Cowcatcher**. A brief commercial announcement at the beginning of a broadcast program.

**CP**. Construction Permit. Formal written permission from the FCC to build or modify a broadcast station.

**CPB**. The Corporation for Public Broadcasting. This is the agency set up to distribute federal funding for public (non-commercial) broadcasting.

**CPM**. See Cost per thousand.

**CPU (Central Processing Unit).** The electronic component that controls an electronic product's functions. Essentially, all automatic cameras have at least a CPU to control various functions of the cameras. Some top models have three to five CPU to handle individual task functions - some handle the exposure, one handle the autofocus and so on. The latest on some top models utilise 8 or 16 bits chips. Newer autofocus lenses have built-in CPUs to relay information relating to focal length, distance info, lens type to the camera body for exposure to AF processing.

**Cq.** Correct as it is; lets copy editors know that something has been checked and needs no further checking. Usually, these letters are put just after the copy they refer to.

**Cradle Head.** A sturdy camera support that sits atop a tripod or studio pedestal camera mount and supports the base of the camera, which in turn sits atop its cradle-like shape. The cradle head provides for smooth operation of the camera, particularly for tilt shot.

**Cradle-to-grave.** A programming term indicating that the audience for a show is universal. Children, teenagers, adults, parents and all demographics and psychographics are represented in the viewing audience.

**Crane.** A type of camera mount. It is a large metal device fitted with three or four wheels and has a boom arm that allows a camera to be raised smoothly from near-floor level to 10 feet in the air.

**Crawl.** A graphic effect that moves vertically or horizontally over the screen. Usually used to list the credits for a production at the end of the programme. Names of the cast and crew are superimposed or keyed over the final shots and crawl up or down.

**Creative.** Relating in advertising to the conceptual input upon which a campaign or an advertisement is based and incorporating the copy and visual content – the creative expression.

**Creative Department.** Part of an advertising agency concerned with creating ideas and expressing them in copy and design.

**Creative Group.** (1) In large advertising agencies, group of executives comprising TV producers, copywriter, visualiser, TV storyboard artist who will work as a team on major accounts. (2) Collection of individuals specialising in the development of creative ideas, particularly for the origination of advertising campaigns.

**Creative Strategy.** Statement of advertising goals, the target audience, the intended creative propositions and the means of expressing them in a particular advertisement or series of advertisements.

**Credibility.** (1) The trustworthiness or reliability of a journalist or mass media. (2) Extent to which claims made for a product or firm is believed by its markets. Exaggerated claims may often destroy a product's, or even a company's credibility.

**Credibility Factor.** Extent to which a PR message is believed.

Credit(s).

**Credit(s).** Photographer's or artist's by-line, usually in small type below or next to block. Also the list of names and titles of the people who contributed or worked on a production. Usually presented in visual crawl form or series of graphics at the end of a programme. It is sometimes accompanied by a voiceover reading the names of the cast.

**Creed.** Telegraphic printer by which communications are received from news agencies.

**Creole.** A mother tongue that originates from contact between two languages and has features of both.

**Crescendo.** An increase in the volume or intensity of a radio announcer's voice.

**Crisis PR.** Organisation of a small crisis management team which has manual of instructions, and conducts rehearsals, in readiness to deal with any crisis should one occur, especially in handling the media. A result of the spate of crisis in recent years in chemical, oil and other vulnerable industries.

**Critical News Analysis.** Generic term for a wide-ranging and complex approach to the analysis of the presentation of news in the mass media.

**Critical Path.** Technique derived from network analysis that assists planning by scheduling all necessary happenings to bring about a complex outcome at the right time and in the correct sequence.

**Critical Theory.** A general term for late Marxist versions of the part played by the mass media in maintaining a dominant ideology or hegemony. The origins are usually found in the work of the Frankfurt School, but there are several variants, especially the cultural and the political economy forms. The first of these has been associated with structuralist and semiological interpretations of texts (hermeneutics generally) and also with audience reception analysis and ethnography. The second has generally engaged with issues of structure and ownership and control of the media. Critical theory is often regarded as an alternative to empirical, behaviourist or 'scientific' approaches to the study of mass media. It is by definition normative, involving notions of an alternative and better form of society and media system.

**Cromalin.** Substitute for ordinary four-colour print.

**Crop.** To cut down in size a photograph or illustration, either to focus interest upon particular features or to make most effective use of limited space available. May also refer to the framing of the scene in the viewfinder.

**Crop Cap.** Initial capital covering more than one line, but hanging below the top line.

**Cross Fade.** To reduce volume of one form of sound whilst simultaneously increasing volume of another. That is fading in one sound source as another sound source fades out. Commonly used in radio, for instance, to introduce a scene or subject change and also in audiovisual media, like TV and cinema, where the usage of the term extends also to the gradual replacement of one scene by another.

**Cross Hatch.** Shading a drawing with crisscrossing parallel lines.

**Cross Plug.** A pitch made by a presenter or program host to promote another program on the same station. Also in alternating sponsorships, permitting each advertiser to insert one announcement into the program during the weeks when the other advertiser is the sponsor, maintaining weekly exposure for both See Alternate sponsorship.

**Crosshead.** Small heading set in centre of column, separating two paragraphs. This could be words or symbols or just white space.

**Cross-media Buy.** The purchase of advertising time and space in more than one medium. Usually implies the use of two different communications media for instance, newspaper and television while multimedia buys involve more than two media elements such as newspaper, magazines, radio and television.

**Crossover Test.** Form of split-run or A/B split testing of alternative advertisements except that alternative publications are tested. Different advertisements are placed in different journals, and then switched from one journal to the other when the next issue comes out.

**Crosstalk.** The unwanted transfer of signals transmitted on one channel or circuit to another channel or circuit. The undesired transfer creates background noise and interferes on the second channel.

**Crown.** Small poster measuring 500mm x 381mm, or 20" x 15". Basis of measurement of larger posters, e.g. 16 sheet although this does not consist of 16 separate crown size pieces of paper.

**Cryptography.** The science of analysing and deciphering codes, ciphers and cryptograms or simply an act of writing in code or cipher.

**CU.** A close-up shot.

**Cub.** A trainee reporter, also known as a rookie.

**Cue.** Audio and visual signals that trigger all aspects of a TV production to prepare a talent, sound, or video source to air. It helps coordinate the various elements in a production by preparing the talent and crew and by calling for action and execution on their part. Some are given verbally, others by hand signals. They direct presenters to speed up or slow down.

**Cue Card.** Card sent with audiotape pf radio interview to radio station, giving introductory and closing words.

**Cultivation.** An effect of heavy television viewing which distorts our perception of the world we live in making it seem more like the world portrayed by television than the world as it exists in real life. See Cultivation Analysis.

**Cultivation Analysis.** Term given to a particular type of media effect research, developed by George Gerbner. The underlying process is one of 'acculturation', meaning that people gradually come to accept the view of the world as portrayed on television (in particular) as a true representation of reality and adapt their hopes, fears and understandings accordingly. The main method of cultivation analysis is to chart the dominant 'television view of reality' in fiction and news and compare this with the views expressed by audience members, according to their degree of habitual exposure. The hypothesis is that the more people view television, the more their ideas correspond with the 'television view'.

**Cultural Imperialism/Synchronisation.** Massive flow of Western culture (especially from USA) into developing societies leading to cultural domination which could distort and displace native cultures, and lead to the adoption of foreign values, life styles and behavioural patterns often through the mass media. The process involves the domination of the media consumption in these smaller and poorer countries and in so doing impose their own cultural and other values on audiences elsewhere. However, not only content is exported, but also technology, production values, professional ideologies and ownership. The analogy is with historical imperialism where the means were military and economic power. Explicitly or implicitly, it is assumed that cultural imperialism leads to dependence, loss of autonomy and a deadline in national or local cultures. Some latitude exists as to whether the process is deliberate and about the degree to which it is involuntary at the receiving end. The concept is a fairly crude one, but it has a potent resonance.

**Cultural Memory.** That which a community recalls, re-encodes in a process of making sense of the present.

**Cultural Metaphor.** An image or series of images, seen to represent a culture.

**Cultural Relativism.** Recognition that moral and ethical standards vary across cultures. A cultural relativist recognises that behaviour considered deviant or wrong in one culture may be acceptable or even demanded in another.

**Cultural Studies.** A branch of theory and research that overlaps with the media and communication field but has a much wider reference to all forms of cultural experience and symbolic expression. It has been distinguished by a critical and humanistic orientation and also a strong focus on 'popular culture', especially of youth. It originated in Britain, but is now international in scope, very diverse and largely independent of media and communication studies.

**Culture.** In the present context it has a primary reference to the symbolic artefacts produced by media industries, but it also has a wider reference to customs, practices and meanings associated with the mass communication process (production and reception). It is sometimes used to refer to the wider framework of beliefs, ideology etc. of society (the 'superstructure') that provides the context of media operation.

**CUME.** An abbreviation of cumulative audience. See Cumulative audience.

**Cumulative Audience.** Number of different people listening to radio during a specific period of time. Cumulative broadcast rating; the net unduplicated audience of a station or network during two or more time periods; also used to describe how many different households or people are reached by an advertising schedule (also called "accumulative audience," "net audience," and "unduplicated audience"); technically, a cumulative audience include those persons who were exposed to any insertion of an advertisement in multiple editions of a single vehicle, whereas an unduplicated audience is those persons who were exposed to any insertion of an advertisement in a combination of vehicles or media, counting each person only once. It is usually expressed in actual numbers and as a percentage of the population or demographic group. (slang "cume").

**Cumulative Reach.** Number of people in a target audience reached without duplication by a given promotional schedule over a particular period of time.

**Cure.** No advertisement should employ words, phrases or illustrations which claim or imply the cure of any ailment, illness of diseases, as distinct from the relief of its symptoms.

**Current Image.** Perceived image. How an organisation is seen by outsiders.

**Cursives.** Typefaces resembling handwriting, but without joined character.

**Curvature of Field.** This optical defect causes points on an object plane perpendicular to the lens axis to focus on a curved surface rather than a plane.

**Customer Relations.** PR activity directed at customer such as external house journals, work visits, questionnaires, after sales services.

**Cut.** Deletion from a copy or type. In broadcast or stage, an instantaneous change from one picture to another. It signifies an abrupt change in action or pace. In TV production it is sometimes called 'take'. Also used in TV and film production as a command by a director to immediately stop the action on a set. The term also refers to the removal of scenes in a script or production.

**Cut-in.** The insertion of a local commercial announcement into a network or recorded program.

**Cutline.** A caption. The term comes from the day when engravings or "cuts" were used to make the impression on the page.

**Cut Off.** Horizontal rule used to separate stories in a page. Also latest time a spot is allowed to run. Cut-off in this sense is generally determined by the client. Cut-off in interpersonal communication could mean actions which block incoming visual signals when people are under stress: hands on eyes, deflected glance, gazed look, eyes shut, long blink, etc.

**Cut Screen Dots.** When screen tings and halftones are created digitally instead of by older metal plate method, the screen dots can be divided pixel by pixel. The smallest reproducible unit is therefore not the screen dot but the smallest exposable point – the pixel – of the laser image setter. Dot cutting produces improved image definition, especially of line art.

**Cutaways.** Shots that are used in TV and film productions to avoid jump cuts and to make the editing process easier and the transitions from shot to shot more graceful and smooth. A long shot is often inserted between two close-ups to cut away from the intense action for a moment or to hide an error in continuity between two close-ups. Cutaways are most often used in one-camera taped interviews where shots of the reporter nodding or asking questions are shot after the interview is over and later edited into the programme to help disguise audio edits.

**Cuttings.** (1) Clippings from newspapers or magazines of items relevant to company operations. Basically done by the public affairs department. Could also be a journalist's collection of published work. Also known as clips. (2) Surplus film pieces edited out of a commercial or programme shooting.

**Cutting Copy.** First version of a TV commercial before complete Post Production or final editing.

**Cyan.** In four-colour printing, standard shade of blue.

**Cyber-journalist.** A journalist who works on the internet, perhaps freelance.

**Cybernetics.** Study of communications systems whether of human or mechanical form. Also refers to means of controlling activities in order to keep them directed at a particular objective.

**Cyborg.** The emergence of organisms either in reality or within the imagination that call into question the boundaries between humans, animals and technology.

**Cycle of Advertising Development.** (i) Moving strategy definition – what to say and to whom; (ii) creative development – how to say it; (iii) communication assessment – have we said it; and (iv) campaign evaluation – what was the effect of what we said?

**Cyclorama.** A staging piece used in TV, stage and film production. Cyc for short, it is a continuous floor-to-ceiling background made of cloth or plasterboard that creates an illusion of infinity by eliminating a visual frame of reference. A cyc surrounds the staging area in a studio in the rear and on one or two sides without visible corners and seemingly also melts into the floor.

# D

**Dagmar.** Originally title of a book advocating evaluation of advertising effectiveness by communications goals rather than sales. Acronym for Defining Advertising Goals for Measured Advertising Response.

**Daguerre, Louis-Jacques-Mandé.** (November 18, 1787 – July 10, 1851) A French artist and chemist who is recognised for his invention of the Daguerreotype process of photography. See Camera, Daguerreotype.

**Daguerreotype.** One of the earliest types of photograph in which the image is exposed directly onto a mirror-polished surface of silver bearing a coating of silver halide particles deposited by iodine vapour. In later developments bromine and chlorine vapours were also utilised, resulting in shorter exposure times. Unlike later photographic processes that supplanted it, the daguerreotype is a direct positive image making process with no negative original. See Daguerre, Louis-Jacques-Mandé.

**Dailies.** Daily publications of newspapers. E.g. Daily Sun, Daily Champion, Daily Times, Metro, etc. Also an assemblage of footage that has been shot on any given day in film production. The dailies are projected for the director, performers and crew and are used to review the style, technique and quality of the production and the performance of the actors.

**Daily Topical.** The short bits of news items that tease the audience about the stories scheduled for presentation on an evening newscast. During station breaks, one or two announcers appear on camera, often from the newsroom, to give one-sentence summaries of news stories that will be explored in more depth later.

**Damper.** On litho printing machine, roller which moistens the printing plate before inking. This carries out the litho principle that grease and water do not mix, thus removing surplus ink from printing image.

**Dandy Roll.** On papermaking machine, the cylinder which creates watermarks.

**Darkroom.** The heart of a photo studio, an enclosed room where films are developed. It is usually light tight and used for processing films and for printing, processing paper. The room may also be used for loading and unloading film holders and some cameras. For image purist, the cycle of photograph is not complete if the darkroom process is not handled personally.

**Data.** Statistical term describing classified factual information. Singular is datum.

**Data Discman.** A small, handheld electronic device that resembles a palmtop computer with a miniature keyboard. It is essentially a paperless book. Books in form of three-and-a-half-inch in diameter optical disks, are inserted into the machine, which displays the pages on a screen about the size of a business card. One disc contain 100,000 pages of text. Pages are turned or recalled in response to commands typed on the keyboard.

**Data Disk.** A circular, rotating disk at the end of Advanced Photo System film cassettes that functions as a circular bar code, communicating the film speed, type and exposure length through a sequence of reflective bars to an optical sensor in the camera.

**Database.** In Direct Mail, a computerised Mailing List ordinarily based on information originally recorded of, for instance, customers, donors or members. Print out of labels are available for direct mail purposes.

**Data Processing.** Arrangement of data into a systematic form and its further analysis, most frequently by mechanical or automatic means.

**Dataset.** Software to send or receive keyboard data or copy from word processors to a computerised typesetter by telephone without need to re-keyboard. Saves time and errors, and makes proofing quicker.

**Dateline.** Place and date of origin of newspaper story, where the story was filed e.g. Nairobi, Kenya, at the beginning of a story that tell the reader where the story occurred. Some newspapers strictly enforce a rule that the dateline must say where the reporter was when the story was gathered. A foreign story gathered by phone at home, then, might run with no dateline.

**Date-plan.** Plan which states when and where advertisements will appear.

**Day After Recall.** Advertisement research method to measure recall of advertisements seen or heard on previous day.

**Day Glow.** Proprietary name for fluorescent inks used for printing posters.

**Day-part.** Specific segments of the broadcast day; for example, daytime, early fringe, prime time, late fringe, late night. For TV advertising, e.g. Daytime, pre-peak, peak-time, post-peak.

**Daytime.** With TV advertising, usually before 4pm on weekdays.

**dB Metre.** A device that measures sound levels in decibels.

**dB/SPL.** A unit of sound intensity based on sound pressure differences in air.

**dBm.** An electrical unit of audio level used with standard VU metres which is based on a milliwatt reference level.

**dc.** double column. Twice width of newspaper column written in lower case.

**DC.** (1) Double crown. Small poster size. Written in caps. (2) Direct current. Electrical current that maintains a steady voltage and electrical polarity. (3) Defocus Image Control- a new type of lens family introduced by Nikon, designated as DC lens. Mainly for portrait photography. The lens enables one to control background and foreground blur precisely, resulting in strikingly attractive portraits.

**Deadline.** Time by which a particular stage of a job must be completed, particularly in journalism where the story becomes dead if not completed in time. Also with advertising and broadcasting and indeed has been generally adopted as a term in planning procedure. See Closing date.

**Dealer Imprint.** The name and address of a local video store that is imprinted on a sell sheet, a national advertisement or a pamphlet.

**Dealer Magazine.** External house journal addressed to distributors.

**Dealer Relations.** PR activities directed to distributors such as dealer magazines, works visits, window dressing contests, conferences, invitations to exhibition stands, and training schemes for sales assistants.

**Dealer Tie-in**. A manufacturer's announcement that lists local dealers; not the same as "co-op."

**Decalcomania.** Transparency or transparent gelatinous film bearing advertisement that is fixed to a shop window.

**Deceptive Advertising.** A representation, mission, act or practice that is likely to mislead consumers acting reasonably under the circumstances. To be regulated, however, a deceptive claim must also be material.

**Decibel (dB).** A measure of the power of one electronic signal compared to another, unit of measurement for the loudness of sounds. It is the logarithmic unit that expresses the signal-strength ratio between the two. A bel is equal to 10 decibels; it is a more useful way of measuring signals. A decibel is as 10 times the logarithm of the ratio of the two powers. Equal to about the smallest difference of loudness normally detectable to the human ear. This was named after Alexander Graham Bell.

**Decipher.** See Decode.

**Deck.** Subsidiary section of a headline. Often incorrectly used to mean a separate line. It summarises a story. Also known as deck copy or bank.

**Deck Panels.** Outdoor advertising panels built one above of the other.

**Decode.** The act or process of converting codes into ordinary language. It involves interpreting, analysing and understanding the nature of messages- written, spoken or broadcast, etc. All communication depends on the use of codes. When the message is received, the addressee is not passive, but decoding is more than simply recognising the content of the message. Over time, each individual in the audience develops a cognitive framework of codes which will recall the denotative meaning and suggest possible connotative meanings for each signifier. But the actual meaning for each message is context-dependent: the codified relations between the signifiers in the particular context must be interpreted according to the syntactic, semantic and social codes so that the most appropriate meaning is attributed.

**Decrescendo.** A decrease in the force or loudness of an announcer's voice.

**Dedicated Channel.** One or more unused channels on a cable system reserved for later use.

**Dedicated Flash.** A fully automatic flash that works only with specific cameras. Dedicated flash units automatically set the proper flash sync speed and lens aperture, and electronic sensors within the camera automatically control exposure by regulating the amount of light from the flash. A simple glance can differentiate by identifying the multiple contacts on the hot shoe- the place where the flash is mounted.

**De-duplicate.** Deletion of repeated names from Mailing List. This depends on a name being repeated in a similar form that can be detected. Not easy to find misspelt duplicates. Accuracy will depend on original keying of names.

**Deductive.** Making a specific conclusion based on general premises. Hypothesis-testing research tests propositions based on general theories and is therefore considered deductive.

**Deep Focus.** Film making technique in which objects close to the camera and those far away are both in focus at the same time.

**Deep Throat.** Journalism parlance for anonymous sources.

**Defamation.** A legal term relating to any statement about an individual which exposes that individual to hatred, contempt or ridicule; or which causes the individual to be avoided; or which tends to injure the individual in his or her occupation. A defamatory statement could be libel or slander.

**Defamation, per se.** A legal term relating to the utterance of slanderous words, especially false and malicious words, that injure a person's reputation. As opposed to *defamation per quod,* statements which are deemed slanderous or libellous "on their face" i.e., without the need for information.

**Defamation per quod.** As opposed to *defamation per se,* statements which are deemed slanderous or libellous only when supplemental (generally, widely-known information) is considered along with the statement in question.

**Defensive Communication.** This occurs when people hear what they do not wish to hear.

**Definition.** In a photograph or its reproduction, quality of detail and sharpness.

**Degauss.** To completely erase an audio or videotape. Bulk erase.

**Degrees of Freedom (df).** Number of values of a variable that can be said to be free to vary, that is, that could take any possible value without changing important characteristics of the data set. *Df* are needed to read statistical tables appropriately.

**Delayed Action.** In photojournalism, mechanism delaying the opening of the shutter for some seconds after the release has been operated. Also known as self-timer.

**Delayed Broadcast (DB).** A programme transmitted on a broadcast station at a later time than it actually occurs or is scheduled. The programme is recorded on videotape for subsequent broadcast.

**Delayed Response.** Reaction to marketing initiative at a later time but often within the expected period of time.

**Delete.** Remove from story. Take out.

**Delivery.** The ability to reach or communicate with a certain audience or number of people by using a particular advertising schedule; the physical delivery of a publication.

**Demandingness.** The degree to which a program requires intellectual and/or emotional effort or involvement from its viewers.

**De-massification.** As originated by Alvin Toffler in his books on futurism, the fractionisation of media, especially TV as has been seen with alternatives to BBC/ITV programmes, e.g. cable, satellite, VCRs, video games.

**Demo Reel.** A collection of commercials, programmes, or segments of programmes compiled by an actor, director, producer, ad agency or an independent production company to be shown to prospective clients. Sometimes called a sample reel or a demo.

**Demo Session.** A preliminary recording session before the main demo is done.

**Demographic.** Basic, largely standard, descriptive variables used to describe audience characteristics and data on such things as age, sex, education, level, social grade, geographical distribution, religion, income and ethnic background.

**Demographic characteristics**. The population characteristics of a group or audience.

**Demographic Market Profile.** Summary of audiences according to age, sex, and so on.

**Demographic Targeting.** Directing advertising at certain sections of the public. Publications have their Demographic Profiles.

**Demographics.** Selection of people according to age, sex, income, occupation, geographical distribution and special interests and possessions.

**Demography.** Study of population and its characteristics, based on census returns.

**Demonisation.** Literally to represent something as diabolically evil. In media terms, the media takes this action against those whose view they perceive to be dangerous, destabilising, bad for business or subversive.

**Denigration.** Unfair comparison. Knocking copy or ash-canning.

**Densitometre.** Instrument for measuring tonal value of photographic or printing area.

**Density.** The blackness of an area in a negative or print that determines the amount of light that will pass through it or reflect from it. It makes the total value of a photographic or printed area. Sometimes referred to as contrast.

**Dependency Theory.** The degree to which audiences are dependent upon the mass media. One could relate this to the dependency theory taught by Marxists theorists in international relations to mean when Third World or developing countries are dependent on developed countries. This could seem useful in media parlance especially as more of the Third World media is dominated by information an entertainment from the West.

**Dependent Variable.** Statistical term describing a factor which changes as a result of some other directly linked factor-another variable-which is independent, e.g. sales, which may increase as a result of advertising. Advertising is then the independent variable and sales the dependent variable.

**Deprivation Question.** In group depth interviewing, the question which asks respondents which product they would miss most if it were no longer available.

**Depth Interview or Focused Interview.** In communication research, an interview based on open-ended questions instead of a Structured Questionnaire.

**Depth of Field.** The distance from the nearest object in a picture to the farthest object that is in sharp focus. The degree to which this area surrounding the main subject is in focus denotes the extent of the depth of field. It is determined by the distance from the camera lens to the subject, the focal length of the lens and the f-stop that is being used. The wider the aperture, the longer the focal length, and the closer the focused distance, the less the depth of field, and vice versa. In comparison to a normal lens, wide-angle lenses have inherently more depth of field at each f-number and telephoto lenses have less. Depth of field depends on the lens opening, the focal length of the lens, and the distance from the lens to the subject. In simple terms, this is the zone of sharpest focus in front of, behind, and around the subject on which the lens is focused; can be previewed in the camera and very handy for critical work.

**Depth of Focus.** The range of distance between the back of the camera lens and the focal plane within which a lens image will remain acceptably sharp. Often misused to mean depth of field. See depth of field.

**Deregulation.** Freeing broadcasters or other media from governmental restrictions concerning say, station ownership or program content. Based on a belief in market forces getting it right, or least better. It generally involves a process by which governments remove restrictions on business in order to, in theory, encourage the efficient operation of markets. The identified rationale for deregulation is often that fewer regulations will lead to a raised level of competitiveness, therefore higher productivity, more efficiency and lower prices overall. This is different from liberalisation because a liberalised market, allowing any number of players, can be regulated to protect the consumer's rights, especially to prevent de facto or even legal oligopolies. However, the terms are often used interchangeably within deregulated/liberalised industries. Most media organisations around the world have been deregulated because the media works better like other organisations when free from the shackles of government. Deregulation gained momentum in the 1970s, influenced not only by research at the University of Chicago and the theories of Ludwig von Mises, Friedrich von Hayek, and Milton Friedman, among others, but more importantly by that of Alfred E. Kahn. It was led in the US by President Jimmy Carter, with Kahn's input. Margaret Thatcher of Great Britain was Britain's most known apostle of deregulation. Olusegun Obasanjo of Nigeria has also remarkably achieved success in deregulating Nigerian media. The sale of Daily Times is a major part of this feat.

**Descenders.** Lower case letter in which the stroke drops down below the base line of the other lowercase letters in a font face, e.g. g, p, q, y. In some typefaces, the uppercase J and Q also descend below the baseline.

**Descrambler / Decoder.** Devices for transforming unintelligible, fragmented or coded pictures into cohesive images in both over-the-air and cable technology. For instance DSTV by Multichoice, etc.

**Descriptive.** Study designed to describe a particular sequence of events or social setting rather than to test theories of causation. Many descriptive studies are qualitative, but survey research is also primarily descriptive.

**Descriptive Statistic.** Statistic intended to describe a set of numbers accurately and succinctly, such as the mean value of a variable. Inferences about causation are not normally possible on the basis of descriptive statistics.

**Descriptive Video Service.** An aspect of the separate audio programme service that provides ongoing simultaneous narration of on-screen TV action for the blind. The project uses the separate audio channel to offer descriptions of the setting and action for selected dramas.

**Design.** In PR or printing, used as a generic term embracing all types of visual work, e.g. roughs, typography, graphics, finished art, for all kinds of application – advertising, exhibition, print work, house styling.

**Design Right.** (i) The designer is the first owner of any design right in a design which is not created in pursuance of a commission or in the course of employment. (ii) Where a design is created in pursuance of a commission, the person commissioning the design is the first owner of any design right in it. (iii) Where, in a case not falling within sub-section (iv) a design is created by an employee in the course of his employment, his employer is the first owner of any design right in the Copyright.

**Designated Market Area (DMA).** A term used by the A.C. Nielsen Company; an area based on those counties in which stations of the originating market account for a greater share of the viewing households than those from any other area; for example, Lake County, Illinois, belongs to the Chicago DMA because a majority of household viewing in Lake County is or can be ascribed to Chicago stations rather than to stations from Milwaukee or any other market.

**Desire.** Expression of human appetite for a given object of attention.

**Desk Research.** Study of mainly external published data and material but including other already available internal information, e.g. company records.

**Desktop Media.** Direct media sent to executives at home.

**Desktop Publishing, DTP.** The process of using computer graphics to compose electronic pages of typeface and illustrations in house journals, commercial journals and other print. This handles copy, editing, setting and layout. Typical systems used are Apple Mackintosh, PageMaker, Quark Express, Computer-aided publishing.

**Desktop Video.** The equipment and process used for the production of smaller-format non-broadcast video programming. Sometimes referred to by the initials DTV. Borrowing from desktop publishing, this video technology and technique uses the personal computer and is inexpensive, portable and versatile.

**Determinant.** Factor determining, limiting, or defining, a decision.

**Determiner Deletion.** A regular stylistic practice of journalists where the characteristics of a person and the name are linked without the use of 'the' or 'a', in the same time having the effect of labelling the named person.

**Developer.** A solution, especially used in photography to make visible an image produced by allowing light to fall on the light-sensitive material. The basic constituent is a developing agent which reduces the light-struck silver halide to metallic silver. Colour developers include chemicals which produce coloured dyes coincidentally with reduction of the silver halides.

**Developing Tank.** A light tight container used for processing film, a darkroom's essential accessory.

**Development Communication.** The use of all forms of communication, especially mass communication to achieve development. Often called devcom or communication for development, most authors call it communication in development, while others refer to it as development support communication. However, the main idea is the close relationship between development and communication. In such cases pamphlets and other means of communication could be published to aid a rural area in educating or informing the people about a development problem, say the issue on HIV/AIDS, or other subjects concerned with the people's welfare.

**Developmental News.** That which developing countries consider will help rather than harm their prospects.

**Deviant.** Person or action that is contrary to a society's rules for acceptable behaviour. Activity considered criminal, unethical, immoral, or insane in a particular culture is deviant behaviour.

**Diacriticals.** Accent marks found in foreign languages such as marks or signs above or below letters of the alphabet.

**Dialect.** A regional or social variety of a language distinguished by pronunciation, grammar, or vocabulary, especially a variety of speech differing from the standard literary language or speech pattern of the culture in which it exists. It is usually peculiar to the members of a group, especially in an occupation. This could also be the manner or style of expressing oneself in language or the arts.

**Diaphragm.** An adjustable device inside a lens which is similar to the iris in the human eye. Comprised of six or seven overlapping metal blades, it is continuously adjustable from wide open to stop down and controls the amount of light allowed to pass through the lens and expose the film when a picture is taken. It also controls the amount of depth of field the photograph will have. In lenses designed for single-lens reflex cameras, there are basically two types of diaphragms: (a) automatic: the most popular type-controlled by a single aperture ring. During viewing and focusing, the diaphragm remains wide open, allowing the maximum amount of light to go to the viewfinder for a bright and easy-to-focus image. At the instant of exposure, it stops down automatically to a particular aperture and then reopens to full aperture immediately afterward; (b) manual preset: used in some specific lenses like, PC-Nikkor lenses for Nikon for instance and controlled by two separate rings. The preset ring is first set to the desired aperture, then the aperture ring is rotated to stop down the diaphragm manually for metering or prior to taking pictures.

**Diorama.** Three-dimensional scenic illustrated point-of-sale display, or miniature set used in TV studio to simulate life-size location.

**Diary.** Method of broadcast rating measurements in which viewers or listeners keep record of programmes and stations they tune in at periodic intervals.

**Diary Method/System.** Research technique in which respondents keep a regular written record of events such as reading a publication, viewing television or purchasing certain goods. In broadcasting, a method of determining the viewership of TV programmes. Members of a family record their viewing by notations in a diary.

**Diatronic.** Superb quality digital type produced by Berthold Diatronic machines. Letterforms produced at Berthold produce faultless image. These typefaces are then laid down in negative form on high quality glass matrices. By utilising prisms and mirrors light is passed through the negative character to the photographic materials. The resultant matchless image has created the industry standard known as Diatronic quality.

**Diazo.** Copying process, e.g. blue print, using light sensitive compounds (diazonnium).

**Dichotomous Categories/Question.** Any category that is one member of a set in which there are only two choices, as used in a questionnaire when there is only a 'yes or a no' answer.

**Didone.** 'Modern' typefaces with vertical sides or thickness to letters such as 'o', as distinct from old-style faces with sloping sides.

**Die-cut.** Print or display piece cut to special shape with knife-edge die. Used in mailshots and sales literature to produce windows and Pop-Ups. May also imply the process whereby a hole is literally cut into a cover of a book or an endsheet using metal pattern.

**Dieresis.** Two dots over a vowel as in umlauts o and u.

**Die-stamping.** Intaglio printing process giving relief impression, made with male and female steel dies. Used for quality letter headings.

**Differential Perception.** The awareness of each individual or social group influenced by factors as knowledge, experience, social environment, and personality. Usually perceptions differ among different persons or groups.

**Diffuse Lighting.** Lighting that is low or moderate in contrast, such as on an overcast day.

**Diffused Light.** Soft light. Light which casts an indistinct, soft shadow.

**Diffuser.** An attachment that fits over the front of a light and softens its quality.

**Diffusing.** Softening detail in a print with a diffusion disk or other material that scatters light.

**Diffusion.** Process of spread of a given idea or practice, over time via specifiable channels, through a social structure such as a neighbourhood, a factory or tribe.

**Diffusion-Condenser Enlarger.** An enlarger that combines diffuse light with a condenser system, producing more contrast and sharper detail than a diffusion enlarger but less contrast and blemish emphasis than a condenser enlarger. See diffusion enlarger.

**Diffusion Enlarger.** An enlarger that scatters light before it strikes the negative, distributing light evenly on the negative. Detail is not as sharp as with a condenser enlarger; negative blemishes are minimised.

**Diffusion Filter.** Filter that decreases image sharpness. Used for smoothing out skin blemishes and for dreamlike effects. Filter consists of polished glass with one side smooth and the other slightly rippled which causes light passing through it to be deflected slightly to decrease image sharpness.

**Diffusion of Innovations.** The process of spreading any kind of new technical device, idea or useful information. It generally follows an S-shaped pattern, with a slow start, an acceleration of adoption and a long tail. The 'early adopters' tend to be untypical in terms of social composition and communication behaviour. The mass media have been found to play a secondary role in influencing diffusion, with personal example and known authority sources being primary. The media themselves provide typical examples of innovations that fit the S-curve pattern of diffusion.

**Diffusion of News.** A process whereby awareness of 'events' is spread through a population either by mass media or via personal, word of mouth contact with or without media involvement. Key questions concern the degree and spread of public diffusion in relation to actual or types of events and also the relative weight of media and personal sources in achieving the outcome.

**Digest Unit**. See Junior unit.

**Digital Communication.** A process that breaks down the standard analogue communications signal into a series of binary numbers (0011,0012, etc.) that are usually coded. The numbers are then transmitted digit-by-digit, decoded and interpreted.

**Digital Printing.** A printing technology which allows printed material to be produced without printing plates, image setting, film, stripping, halftone screening or scanning. The colour quality is as good as, or better than, high quality conventional litho printing. The system accepts data in PostScript form, either direct from a disk or via ISDN.

**Digital Typesetting.** Computerised typesetting whereby a character is held in a computer in a digital format. This information is sent to the laser recorder. The laser beam is then instructed to turn on and off, building up the pre-defined shapes with a series of spots light, and so exposing the photographic material. Digital technology makes it possible to produce complete made-up jobs. This process allows flexibility to be able to modify characters, reverse them out of black or tinted areas, or rotate type to varying angles, to produce a single piece of artwork for an advertisement or piece of print.

**Digital Video Compression.** A plan for reducing the amount of information necessary to reconstruct video frames at the receiving end of a transmission. The electronic signals are squeezed and thus signal capacity can be increased by factors of 8, 10 or more. The process can expand the number of channels per satellite transponder and create sufficient channel capacity to make DBS systems practical, and it will be used in high definition TV systems and hasten the advent advanced TV. Cable operations will be able to transmit hundreds of channels over a single fibre optic cable with subsequent economies.

**Digital Video Effects (DVE).** Sophisticated optical images from the surreal to the elegant, created by using video in a filmic way. Using digital communications technique, it is possible for images to be gathered, stored, broken down, clipped, dissolved, flipped, spun, squeezed, or otherwise manipulated on a frame by frame basis.

**Digital Video Recording Formats.** Professional videotape formats that use the principles of digital communications as opposed to analogue communications recording techniques. They record video in terms of 1s and 0s. The signal is measured and expressed numerically at very frequent intervals, often at 16 million samples a second.

**Digitalisation.** General word for the computerisation of all data transmission, storage and processing, employing the binary code and as such the basis for convergence of media. It is currently best known in reference to the replacement of analogue by digital transmission of television signals, leading to a large increase in potential channel capacity and scope for interactivity.

**Dimmer.** A device that controls the brightness of lighting instruments in a TV studio. The crew can adjust the lights and raise or lower their intensity by manipulating the levers or sliders that control the various lights.

**Dingbats.** Typefaces that consist of symbol characters such as decorations, arrows and bullets.

**Diode.** An electronic device that allows the transmission of electricity in only one direction. Diodes used to convert alternating current (AC) to direct current (DC) are called rectifiers.

**Direct Advertising.** Door-to-door distribution of mail drops that is under complete control of the advertiser, rather than through some established medium; for example, direct mail or free sampling.

**Direct Broadcasting Satellite (DBS).** Usually called DBS or referred to as direct-to-home signals. Broadcasting of programmes direct to homes via a dish aerial measuring between 35cm and 85cm according to power of the satellite and geographical location of the home. It covers both analogue and digital television and radio reception, and is often extended to other services provided by modern digital television systems, including video-on-demand and interactive features. Differs from low power distribution satellite which needs a larger dish. A DBS service normally refers to either a commercial service, or a group of free channels available from one orbital position targeting one country.

**Direct Input.** Paperless newsroom in which journalist keys news into computer, sub-editor subs story on VDU, and page make up on computer, final copy to mainframe computer for production of copy for plate making.

**Direct Litho.** Unlike Offset Litho, printing process which transfers an image direct from plate to paper without first printing the reversed image to a blanket and off-setting it to paper. Used especially for printing magazine covers.

**Direct Mail.** Britain's third largest advertising medium using mailing lists or databases and postal services; also used to describe advertising in other media that solicits orders directly through the mail. One of the main media of Direct Response marketing.

**Direct Mail Shot.** One single batch or mailing in a direct mail campaign. One mailing shot might therefore comprise a large number of items and a campaign might consist of several mailing shots.

**Direct Marketing.** Producer supplying direct to consumer without the use of any retail outlet rather than through intermediaries or intervening channels: includes direct mail, direct advertising, telemarketing, and so forth.

**Direct Response.** A marketing research technique that relies on advertising as the sole means of selling to the consumer.

**Directional.** An AM radio station with more than one tower to send the station's signal in a particular direction. It is possible to have FM and TV directionals but these are rare.

**Directional Hypothesis.** Hypothesis that includes a statement about the direction of a relationship as well as its existence. For example, a hypothesis that says that older children understand advertising better than younger children is directional.

**Directional Microphones.** A microphone that has a single pickup pattern, from the direction in which it is pointed. Directional mikes are often used on podiums for picking up one or two speakers. Generally narrow, it is commonly used to attenuate unwanted off-axis sound.

**Directional Stations.** Radio stations, primarily in the AM band, that utilises directional antennas to keep their signals from interfering with those of other stations.

**Director.** Responsible for directing the sound and picture of a programme.

**Directory.** Published source of reference, usually on annual basis but possibly more frequent, setting out comprehensive coverage of companies and services in a particular area of business and/or their range of products. Personalities could also be published, like Newswatch's Who is who in Nigeria.

**Directory Advertising**. Advertising that appears in a buying guide or directory; advertisements in a store directory: for example, Yellow Pages advertising.

**Direct Response.** Modern name for mail order, using Direct Mail, catalogues, mail drops, off-the-page press ads, TV, telemarketing. Also called direct marketing.

**Direct Response Marketing.** Selling by means of press advertisements which invite a direct placement of orders without further negotiation or intermediate channels of distribution.

**Direct to Plate.** Computerised plate making system, which images digital page data onto printing plates with no need for intermediate film. This technique offers savings in time, as well as labour and materials, while avoiding the environmental impact of film processing.

**Direct-wave Propagation.** Radio wave pattern in which signals travel through direct line-of-sight transmission.

**Dirty Copy, Proof.** Opposite to clean copy or proof. Original copy containing many handwriting amendments and additions, or containing many errors.

**Disaggregated Data.** From individual research returns, such as dairies from panellists, effect of advertising on purchases can be identified.

**Disempowerment.** Literally to deprive of power or influence. It involves the withdrawal of power to have control over lives of individuals, groups, communities or nations from them. It is argued in this vein that communication is a viable tool for empowerment, thus it can also be used for disempowerment.

**Disc Jockey (DJ).** More often called DJ, a person who announces and plays popular recorded music. A DJ mixes various kinds of music in an event, usually fine-tuned to suit the event or situation. The term was first used to describe radio announcers who would introduce and play popular gramophone records. These records, also called discs by those in the industry, were jockeyed by the radio announcers, hence the name disc jockey, which was soon shortened to DJs or deejays. Currently, there are a number of factors, including the selected music, the intended audience, the performance setting, the preferred medium, and the development of sound manipulation, that have led to different types of disc jockeys. However, today there are many different kinds of 'DJ's' and it does not always mean 'disc jockey' in the traditional sense, for example turntablist DJ's use actual 'discs' whilst radio DJ's may use a number of sound sources including CD's, jingles and other pre-recorded media. The term 'DJ' also applies to Personality DJ's who perform at venues and events, such as parties and product launches, where they also provide the musical entertainment.

**Discourse.** A particular way of chatting, talking, writing and thinking that can be organised into identifiable patterns of usage across time and space. Whether we are analysing a news broadcast or chat show we might be able to identify a number of different codes or ways of speaking that are more prevalent than others.

**Discourse Analysis.** This applies to all forms of language use and textual forms, but the essential idea is that communication occurs by way of forms of 'text and talk', adapted to particular social locations, topics and kinds of participant. These are sometimes known as 'interpretative communities'. 'Critical discourse analysis' investigates the dominance exerted and expressed through linguistic forms that are vehicles for carrying socially prevailing sentiments and ideologies. This idea is similar to that of rhetorical analysis, and some scholars use the terms interchangeably.

**Discourse of Power.** Term often linked with the work of French philosopher Michel Foucault (1926-1984) and Jürgen Habermas' *The Theory of Communicative Action* (1985). It clearly proposes that discourses are perceived as means of exerting influence and control over audience.

**Discretionary Income.** Extra income over the above that is required to cover basic needs. Advertising for luxuries competes for available discretionary income.

**Discriminant Analysis.** Statistical technique for identifying the characteristics that most reliably divide one group form another. For example, discriminant analysis might be used to determine what opinions predict political party preference.

**Discrimination Test.** Research test that shows how many people can differentiate between products being tested.

**Disparaging Copy.** Knocking copy.

**Dispenser.** Display device used on counters for leaflets.

**Dispersion.** (1) In communication research, the degree of scatter shown by observations in statistical analysis, usually measured against a central tendency or average, using a mean or standard deviation. (2) In photojournalism, the property of materials which have a refractive index that varies according to the wavelength of light, i.e., bend the rays of some colours more than others; a prism placed in the path of a ray of white light bends the blue and violet rays more than the orange and red, so that it spreads out or 'disperses' the colours as a continuous spectrum.

**Displacement.** An unconscious defense mechanism where the mind redirects emotion from a 'dangerous' object to a 'safe' object. For instance, some people punch cushions when angry at friends. Displacement operates unconsciously, in which emotions, ideas, or wishes are transferred from their original object to a more acceptable substitute. It is most often used to allay anxiety and is a phychological theory.

**Display.** Commonly used in retailing to refer to an exhibition of merchandise, whether in store or in window. Also describes panels – display boards. Books and published materials are often displayed in various places including book fairs and exhibitions.

**Display Advertising.** Advertising other than simple typeset lineage advertisements of the classified kind that is intended to attract attention and communicate easily through the use of space, illustrations, layout, headline, and so on, as opposed to classified advertising. Also implies an element of design, e.g. use of display typefaces as opposed to uniform body matter.

**Display Pack.** Pack which, in addition to performing a 'packaging' function, also serves as a means of displaying the product at the point of sale. Usually applies to single items as opposed to the display outer.

**Display Type/Face.** Large, bold and often decorative type used for headlines and subheadings in contrast to small text type.

**Display Outer.** Point-of-sale display piece in form of carton for small unit goods which can be converted into a dispenser with a display panel when folded out of lid. Used for counter and shelf displays.

**Displayed Advertisement.** Opposite to a run-on classified ad, in which various type faces and sizes and sometimes illustrations are used.

**Displayed Classified.** Displayed Advertisement placed in the classified columns of a publication.

**Dissolve.** A method in which a projected image fades and is simultaneously replaced by another, usually by use of two linked projectors. Also referred to as cross fade.

**Dissonance.** A perception of incompatibility between two cognitions. It is any element of knowledge, including attitude, emotion, belief, or behaviour- in lay men's terms, the uncomfortable tension that comes from holding two conflicting thoughts at the same time. The theory of cognitive dissonance states that contradicting cognitions serve as a driving force that compels the mind to acquire or invent new thoughts or beliefs, or to modify existing beliefs, so as to reduce the amount of dissonance (conflict) between cognitions. All messages, particularly those conveyed to a mass audience, are potentially a source of dissonance to someone.

**Distant Signals.** Signals that are imported by a cable system from outside the local viewing area. The transmissions are usually from broadcast stations located in other areas.

**Distortion.** An optical aberration commonly associated with an unnatural change in shape or character of an object. For an example, a rectangle may appear as a barrel or pin cushion-shaped object. There are two types of distortion: (a) barrel: straight lines are bowed in at the edges of the picture frame resembling the sides of a barrel; present in small amounts in some wideangle or wideangle-zoom lenses, but uncorrected in fisheye lenses; (b) pincushion: the opposite of barrel distortion; straight lines are bowed in toward the middle to resemble the sides of a pincushion; present in small amounts in some telephoto and telephoto-zoom lenses.

**Distribution Amplifier (DA).** A piece of electronic equipment that receives a single signal input, amplifies it and distributes it among multiple outlets. A version of the device is used in a cable system to boost the signals just prior to their reception at subscribers' homes. Sometimes called feeder amplifier or live extender amplifier.

**Distribution System.** Term used to describe the system of cables that distributes programming to subscribers.

**Dither.** A computer-aided process of adding dots to a picture in order to smooth the appearance of an image.

**Dithering.** Using a paint or image-processing program to blur the transition from one colour to another in a computer picture.

**Diversity.** Simply, it is no more than the degree or range of difference on any chosen dimension- the more difference the more diversity. When applied to mass media it can relate to structures of ownership and control, to content as produced and transmitted and to audience composition and content choices. Each of these can be emphatically assessed in terms of diversity. Diversity is associated with access, freedom, choice, change and equity. It stands as a positive value in opposition to monopoly, uniformity, conformity and consensus.

**Doctor Blade.** In photogravure and Flexography printing, a blade which removes excess ink from printing plate.

**Docudrama.** A programme format that consists of shows that are usually fictional re-creations of real events or dramatised versions of the lives of historical personalities. The first part of the term is derived from documentary and the approach is similarly serious in tone and style. They offer a sense of realism even though they take considerable liberties with history or actual events. E.g. ALI which is about the life of Mohammed Ali.

**Documentary.** Cinema or television film, or radio programme, dealing with actual facts of a situation as opposed to fiction. Often used as part of a public relations plan. Sometimes referred to as sponsored promotion i.e. where its purpose is primarily or wholly commercial. In Nigeria especially, documentaries are done to highlight dividends of democracy, with emphasis laid on the projects done by elected officials.

**Document Distribution.** Sending documents via data transmission.

**Dodging.** In photojournalism, holding back the image-forming light from a part of the image projected on an enlarger easel during part of the basic exposure time to make that area of the print lighter.

**Doggerel.** Light, often amusing and usually irregular verse sometimes used in advertisement copy.

**Dolby System.** Electronic coding process originally developed to reduce unwanted sound, such as hiss, on tape recording equipment.

**Dolly in/ Dolly out.** Camera movements which involve moving a camera toward or away from an object or subject. Although the effect is similar to zooming in or out, the perspective of the shot is less distorted when the camera physically moves toward or away from a subject. Some directors' use the terms push in, pull back, or dolly back to achieve the same effect. Ironically, the terms were derived from the dollies that support tripods.

**Dolly Shot.** A shot made with a moving dolly.

**Dominant Discourse.** Simply a discourse that is dominant over other topic or subjects, usually in the media. It takes precedence of others, may be due to importance, public interest or the frequency of the event.

**Domination.** (1) Refers to situation of market leader with significant share of total market. (2) Concentration of promotional effort in one area or medium so as to dominate that area or medium.

**Donut.** A commercial that has a blank section in the middle. While the material at the beginning and end of the commercial remains the same, new and timely information about particular products or bargains is inserted in the middle.

**Door-to-door.** Practice of selling by calls upon householders, may also be used to distribute promotional materials. See door-to-door distribution.

**Door-to-door Distribution.** Direct advertising material delivered door-to-door. There are specialist distributors, the Post Office Household Delivery Service, and distribution with free newspapers.

**Doormat Media.** Direct mail addressed to consumer at home.

**Double-barrelled Question.** A question to avoid in a research questionnaire since it poses two questions simultaneously, neither of which may be answered adequately.

**Double Billing.** An illegal and unethical method of charging a manufacturer of a product or service more than the cost listed on the rate card for commercial time or more than the established costs of print advertising.

**Double Crown.** Basic unit of size in posters, a sheet, size 20 ins wide by 30 ins deep.

**Double-decker.** Two outdoor advertising panels sited one above the other.

**Double Exposure.** Two pictures taken on one frame of film, or two images printed on one piece of photographic paper. Some cameras can have double exposure level depressed with multiple exposures one even with a motor drive.

**Double Front.** Twin poster sites arranged to utilise both sides of the front of a bus or other commercial vehicle. Usually each a 'single sheet' or smaller.

**Double Fronts, Rears.** Pairs of double crown poster on front or back of upper deck of double-decker bus.

**Double-head.** In production of a television commercial when sound and vision are still on separate tapes.

**Double Page Spread.** Two facing pages in a magazine or newspaper, used in advertising as if they were one single sheet, e.g. the design carried right across the gutter in the centre. Normally used only in tabloids. Presently some magazines use them for special ads.

**Double Pumping.** A programme scheduling technique that aims to call attention to a new series by scheduling the premiere episode of the series twice. The term is a reference to the need to pump the handle of some water pumps at least twice before the water begins to flow.

**Double Spotting**. See Piggyback.

**Double Spread Ad.** Advertisement printed across two pages either centrefold spread, or across two facing pages. See Two-page spread.

**Double Truck.** Slang term for a print advertisement that covers two full pages side-by-side, but not necessarily the two centre pages, usually for a magazine advertisement. If it prints across the gutter between the two pages, and if the pages are on the same sheet, rather than two adjacent sheets, it might be called a "true" double truck. This name comes from the days when the heavy forms for newspaper pages, largely filled with lead type, were rolled around the composing room floor on heavy carts called trucks. Two pages for one project meant a double truck. See Centre spread and Two-page spread.

**Downgrade.** A circumstance occurring when subscribers to a cable system choose to discontinue certain channels from their pay, thereby descending to a smaller number of programme choices.

**Downlink.** In cable television, main receiving station or earth station dish which accepts signals from television and also from television and radio frequencies.

**Download.** Copying a file from a web site to own computer or simply opening a file. Could also involve copying music, films or other materials to PDAs, ipods, or other electronic device.

**Downstream Keyer.** A device that allows titles to be keyed over a lineout signal.

**Downtime.** A period when a broadcast studio is inoperable and the facility and its equipment are idle. This circumstance is sometimes forced upon an operation because of equipments malfunction, but every studio schedules downtime occasionally to allow for equipment maintenance and housekeeping.

**dpi.** An abbreviation for *dots per inch*. Refers to the resolution at which a device, such as a monitor or printer, can display text and

Drag.

graphics. Monitors are usually 100 dpi or less, and laser printers are 300 dpi or higher. An image printed on a laser printer looks sharper than the same image on a monitor.

**Drag.** Amount of friction in the camera head restricting panning and tilting movements.

**Dramedies.** A term that loosely describes dramatic programmes that have some comedic elements. The shows are usually continuing series and often an hour in length. Eg. Ripples, Behind the Clouds, etc.

**Drawn-on Cover.** Method of binding sometimes used for magazines, where the cover is glued to spine of pages.

**Drip.** A regular advertising campaign as distinct from a short-term burst.

**Drip Mat.** A coaster, but usually stouter than a paper coaster and made of absorbent board, bearing advertisement, on which customers place drinks in, for example, a pub.

**Drive and Housewife Time.** Radio advertising term for segments of time when drivers are commuting or, in between, when housewives are at home.

**Drive Time.** In radio broadcasting, the time during which many listeners are driving to or from work. Then stations receive their highest audience ratings- Usually 6-10:00 a.m. and 3-7:00 p.m. This varies in different countries or towns. In Nigeria, programmes like *Oga Driver* run during these times, especially in the morning because they reach a lot of audience.

**Drop.** That section of a cable that brings the signal from the trunk or sub-trunk directly into a subscriber's home receiver.

**Drop Capital/Letter.** First character of a word at the beginning of a paragraph, set larger than the body copy. A style often used in editorials, the first letter occupying a depth of two, three or more lines of copy.

**Drop-in**. A local commercial inserted in a nationally sponsored network radio or television program.

**Drop-in-Loading (DIL).** Film cassette loading feature in all Advanced Photo System cameras that virtually eliminates film-loading problems by automatically accepting the leaderless cassette and thrusting the film forward to the first unexposed frame without any user intervention.

**Dropouts.** A phenomenon of videotape recording and playback that occurs when the spinning recording or playback heads pass over the tape and black or white lines or spots appear momentarily in the picture. The glitches occur at places where the magnetic particles have flaked off or where dirt or dust covers that portion of the tape, interfering with signal pickup. Picture signal is lost during this tape playback. It is counted as any loss of playback signal that is 20 decibels or more below the nominal playback level (16 decibels for extra high-grade and 8mm tapes) and lasting for 15 microseconds or longer (about one quarter of one horizontal scan on the TV screen).

**Dropout Compensators:** An electronic device which can, on a limited basis, restore momentary loses of video information due to videotape *dropouts*.

**Dry-brush Drawing.** A drawing made with a brush and very dry thick ink or paint.

**Dry-run.** Pre-transmission television rehearsal where action, lines, cues, etc. are perfected.

**Dry Transfer Lettering.** Sheets of characters such as Letraset from which individual letters can be transferred to paper by rubbing. Can replace display typesetting or hand lettering when producing display lines for advertisement or print.

**DTV, Digital Television.** Any one of several recently adopted systems of high definition television, including HDTV. It is a telecommunication system for broadcasting and receiving moving pictures and sound by means of digital signals, in contrast to analogue signals in analogue (traditional) TV. It uses digital modulation data, which is digitally compressed and requires decoding by a specially designed television set or a standard receiver with a set-top box. It has several advantages over traditional TV, the most significant being use of a smaller channel bandwidth. This frees up space for more digital channels, other non-television services such as pay-multimedia services and the

Dub.

generation of revenue from the sales of frequency spectrum taken by analogue TV. There are also special services such as multicasting (more than one program on the same channel), electronic program guides and interactivity. DTV often has a superior image, audio quality and better reception than analogue. However, it should be noted that DTV picture technology is still in its early stages and there are many advances yet to be made in eliminating picture defects not present on analogue television or motion picture cinema. This is due to present-day limitations of bandwidth and the compression algorithms commonly used, such as MPEG2, the effects of which are not immediately apparent unless compared side by side with the original program source, such as a 16/35mm motion picture film print.

**Dub.** (1) A G-spool. Copy of a video commercial sent to TV stations. (2) To record and add commentary, music, sound, and computer graphics to a film or video. Post production.

**Dubbing.** A slang term in audio and video production. It refers to superimposing sound upon an already complete film, as opposed to simultaneous recording.

**Dubbing in.** Adding one film or video to another, such as adding a commercial to a sponsored show where sponsored TV permitted.

**Dumping.** A global practice, led by US, where foreign markets are saturated with broadcast materials, extremely cheap to hire in comparison with the cost of home companies making their own original programmes.

**Dummy.** Booklet of blank pages used when planning a publication or pasting up proofs. Also, a specimen copy of a proposed edition of a newspaper or magazine, used when selling space.

**Dummy Layout** A rough draft of a publication page layout showing the amount of space to be occupied by copy, photos, graphics, etc. It is used for roughing layouts so corrections and changes can be made. It is also used to organise ideas for publication pages.

**Duograph.** Printing plate made from black-and-white picture to give two-tone effect, the second printing plate is flat to provide tint. Cheaper than Duotone.

**Duopoly.** A situation in which two companies own all or nearly all of the market for a given type of product or service. In this form of oligopoly, only two producers exist in a market. In reality, this definition is generally used whereby two firms must only have dominant control over a market. In the field of industrial organisation, it is the most commonly studied form of oligopoly due to its simplicity.

**Duotone.** Pair of halftone printing plates made from a one-colour picture to produce a two-colour effect.

**Duotone Pictures.** Two colour pictures, using real colours or process colours. A background colour given a screen angle of 18.4 degree, and black being printed with a screen angle of 45 degree. Highlight, mid tone and shadow tones of the two colours can be changed to achieve variations. This can be done digitally.

**Duplicated Readership.** Various journals may be read by the same people, which may produce wasteful advertising if the same ad appears in all of them. It is best, therefore, to plan a media schedule with the least amount of duplication, and the greatest reach of different readers.

**Dust Jackets.** The removable outer cover that protects a book from being spoilt. They contain useful information about the book and often, also, about the author.

**DX.** Digital Index. Coding on the film cartridges used to transmit information in relation to film speed, the length of film and the exposure latitude to the camera. Most films - except some technical films are DX coded - means you need not to worry about wrong setting of the ISO setting of film speed anymore, reducing chances of mistakes.

**DX Data Exchange.** Electrical coding system employed in 35 mm format film that communicates film speed, type and exposure length to the camera.

**Dyad.** A communication group consisting of two persons interacting. It is the elemental unit of interpersonal communication.

**Dyadic.** Paired comparison test involving informants reporting on two products or advertisements, one against the other.

**Dynamic Microphone.** A pressure sensitive device with a diaphragm connected to a wire coil that moves dynamically in a magnetic field in response to sound waves. It can tolerate very high sound pressure levels without creating distortion. It can have an omni-directional, cardioid or unidirectional pickup pattern and is often a lavaliere or shotgun microphone.

**Dynamic Range.** The range between the weakest and loudest sounds which particular piece of equipment can effectively reproduce.

# E

**e.** Frequently used to designate an electronic version or something, for example e-Commerce, for electronic buying or transactions, e-News, for an electronic newsletter, or e-Governance, to describe electronic governance.

**E6.** Kodak's standard chemical process for developing Ektachrome or compatible slide films from other films makers apart from Kodak.

**Ear, Ear Space or Title Corner.** Front-page advertisement space on one or both sides of the title of some newspapers. Some newspapers put weather or lottery information in them. (An expression sometimes heard in newsrooms, "Go stick it in your ear," has nothing to do with this.)

**Early Fringe.** TV or radio segment or daytime preceding prime time viewing. In the Central Time Zone, it extends from 3:30 to 6:30 p.m.

**Earned Rate.** The advertising rate that is actually paid by the advertiser after discounts and other calculations.

**Ears of Newspaper.** Boxes or announcements at the top of the front page, alongside the name of the paper, in the upper right- and left-hand corners. Sold for advertising space by some newspapers.

**Earth Station.** An overall generic term describing the terrestrial transmitter, antenna and associated equipment used to transmit or receive signals from a communications satellite. It is often broadened to include all of the ground electronic equipment associated with satellite transmission and reception, including the buildings that house the gear.

**Easel.** A device to hold photographic paper flat during exposure, usually equipped with an adjustable metal mask for framing.

**Eastmancolor.** Colour filmstock now used universally in film making.

**Eclectic Method.** Way of fixing advertising appropriation.

**Eco-advertising.** Often form of corporate advertising which seeks to gain credit for company's anti-pollution, wild life protection or other environmental activities.

**Eco-horror.** Term usually used to describe a film or television programme whose plot is based on the central characters for survival, usually in the wild in the face of a range of threats from forces of nature.

**Economic Life.** Period during which a machine or device works efficiently or profitably.

**ECU.** Extra close up in TV filming.

**ED**. Extra Low dispersion - usually refer to glass type. Glass with ED properties indicating special rare earth glass or special formulated glass that limits or corrects light rays passing through the lens elements to achieve all spectrum of colours to fall on the same plane of focus - especially the Red and Blue spectrum. It usually applies more to longer focal length lenses where the problem is more serious. First popularised by Nikon's Nikkor lens line - with a gold lining in the front part of the lens. Pentax, Olympus use the same name as Nikon. Canon's version is called "LD" - with red lining and usually their lenses are white in colour. While Minolta uses APO. Independent lens makers, like Tamron, uses LD, Sigma uses APO, Tokina's version is SD APO; all these trade names are basically performing the same functions.

**Edit.** To modify an original manuscript, text or film in such a way as to make the meaning clearer, improve the grammar, reduce the size, or in some other way prepare it for multiple reproduction and distribution.

**Edit Suites.** Studios used for video post-production such as editing, titling and computer graphics with equipment for adding special effects.

**Editing.** (1) In communication research, checking that questionnaires are ready for coding and analysis, or that diaries from panellists are free of inconsistencies. There are also computer edit runs to check data against criteria. (2) In film and video making, editing raw film or tape to delete, add or change sequence Editing can tighten up action and bring finished film or tape to desired length.

**Edition.** Particular issue of a publication.

**Edition Binding.** In book production, method of binding signatures of 16 or 32 pages, sewing them together and then gluing them to the book back before binding them into covers.

**Editor.** A journalist who works closely with reporters, giving out assignments and deadlines and helping them craft and build their stories. He/she has the overall responsibility for the editorial content of the publication. All other editors report to the editor; the editor reports to the publisher. Academic Journals and other publications usually have an editor or group of editors.

**Editorial.** Leading article in a publication or broadcast usually an explicit statement of the editor's views about a particular subject of interest. Sometime used to distinguish news or feature items from advertising content. The statement or article expresses an opinion rather than attempting to simply report news, as it should ideally be done without bias. In the United Kingdom such articles are often referred to as leaders. Most Nigerian publications use the traditional title of 'editorial'. Editorials are often not written by the regular reporters of the news organisation, but are instead collectively authored by a group of individuals called the editorial board without by-lines. If written by the board, they represent the newspaper's official positions on issues. Often however, there exist also one or more regular opinion columnists who present their own view. Editorials are almost always printed on their own page of the newspaper, and are always labelled as editorials to avoid confusion with news coverage. They are often about current events or public controversies. Generally, editorials fall into four broad types: news, policy, social, and special.

**Editorial Advertisement.** Advertisement design in the form of a piece of editorial matter. Such advertisements must, however, be clearly labelled 'advertisements'.

**Editorial Columns.** That part of a publication devoted to non-advertising matter, i.e. containing editorial matter.

**Editorial Matter.** News or entertainment section of publication or broadcasting, i.e. excluding any advertising matter it may carry.

**Editorial Mention.** Reference to an individual, or a company, favourable or otherwise, in the editorial column.

**Editorial Page.** A page set aside to act as the mouthpiece of the editor(s) or publisher(s) as a forum for public opinion. This page usually contain other things as letters to the editor or information about the company- publisher, and the list of its staff.

**Editorial Publicity.** Space in a journal or newspaper in which a product, service, or company is discussed or publicised at the discretion of the editor.

**Editorial Write-up.** News story or feature about an individual, product, service or company.

**Editorialise.** The act of writing in a prejudiced or opinionated way.

**Educational Advertising.** (1) Advertisements referring to educational matters. (2) Advertising devoted to improving consumers' knowledge about a product or service in order to render them more favourably disposed towards it, particularly if it involves some change in beliefs or attitudes.

**Educational Television (ETV).** A broad term that describes the use of TV to inform, enlighten and instruct. Often used in connection with programming of a non-commercial nature that illuminates ideas and brings new concepts and experiences to the viewing audience.

**Effective Aperture.** The diameter of the bundle of light rays striking the first lens element that actually pass through the lens at any given diaphragm setting.

**Effective Frequency**. Level or range of audience exposure that provides what an advertiser considers to be the minimal effective level, and no more than this optimal level or range; also called "effective reach."

**Effective Radiated Power (ERP).** The power of a station's visual signal. Often expressed in kilowatts, stations are limited in the amount of power that can be emitted from their transmitters and antennas in order to avoid interfering with other electronic communications. ERP is typically higher than actual transmitter output power in the FM and TV bands due to antenna gain. For example, a 100,000-watt FM station typically has only 20,000 watts of power leaving the transmitter. The multiple antenna bays (a bay is an actual antenna) act to increase the effective power of the station. AM radio stations would need towers more than a mile high in order to benefit from antenna gain.

**Effective Reach**. See Effective frequency.

**Effectiveness**. Ability to achieve a purpose or target by media men.

**Effects of Media**. The consequences or outcomes of the working of, or exposure to, mass media, whether or not intended. They can be sought at different levels of social analysis. There are many types of effect, but it is usual to distinguish at least between effects that are behavioural, attitudinal (or affective) and cognitive. Effects are distinct from 'effectiveness', which relates to the efficiency of achieving a given communicative objective.

**Ego**. Term borrowed from psychology, indicating an individual's conception of himself, often having an effluence over his behaviour patterns.

**Egocentric Arrogance**. Advertising which carries no brand name or logo yet succeeds in being identified, e.g. Silk Cut cigarette poster showing a piece of silk with a cut in it, MTN yellow page with no message on it.

**Egyptian**. Slab or square serif typeface like Rockwell, Cairo, Karnak which have Serifs and strokes of the same thickness.

**Eighty-twenty Rule**. A rule of thumb that states for the typical product category, eighty percent of the products will be consumed by twenty percent of the audience.

**EIBIS International**. Long established international press service which distributes translated feature articles and news releases to foreign press.

**EIS**. Electronic Image Stabiliser. A feature that minimises effect of camera shake. Originally designed for video cameras. Canon has transferred the technology over to its EF lenses; more Canon's EF lenses may adopt this feature with time.

**Elaboration Likelihood Model**. Research model for explaining consumer involvement in response to advertising. If elaboration likelihood is high, more informative advertising is justified but if it is low, more simple, repetitive advertising is necessary.

**Elasticity Method.** Method of fixing advertising appropriation on basis of supply and demand curves. The average cost of an extra unit of expenditure on advertising is compared with average return on higher profit. This shows the point beyond which further advertising is uneconomic.

**Electra.** A broadcast teletext operation consisting of a one-way information service. It contains pages of digital information from a central computer database.

**Electric Spectaculars.** Outdoor advertisement consisting of words or designs made up with electric lights.

**Electromagnetic Spectrum.** An atmospheric yardstick used to measure varying levels of electromagnetic energy, called frequency.

**Electromagnetic Waves.** Electrical impulses travelling through space at the speed of light. Used to transmit radio and television signals.

**Electronic Data Interchange (EDI).** A buzzword in retailing and the home video industry relating to a process that relies on computers for electronic messaging. EDI technique can eliminate hours of paperwork and errors in ordering, processing and invoicing products as well as in keeping track of retail sales.

**Electronic Flash.** Light source based on electrical discharge across two electrodes in a gas-filled tube. Usually designed to provide light approximating to daylight. It is often regarded as artificial light source in the dark. Electronic flash requires a high voltage, usually obtained from batteries through a voltage-multiplying circuit. It discharges a brief, intense burst of light, usually used where the lighting on the scene is insufficient for picture-taking. It is generally considered to have the same photographic effect as daylight. Most flash will correct the colour temperature back to 5000 Kelvin - the daylight colour. Modern flash has multiple TTL flash exposure control functions and even extend to autofocus control. Some specialised flash are high speed repeating flash which can be used for stroboscopic effect, UV-flash for ultra violet light photography etc.

**Electronic Mail.** Delivery of messages via personal computers and hard copy printers. For short: e-mail.

**Electronic Media.** (1) Refers to all media with electromagnetic impulses like TV, radio, computer etc. (2) Advertisements making use of neon signs or lights, and capable of movement by electric impulses.

**Electronic News Gathering, ENG.** The process of gathering sound and vision news reports electronically, usually transmitted via telephone links or from transmitter van. The portable video cameras and VTRs used for quick coverage of news event. With the ENG, television stations are able to reduce film and processing costs, reduce turn-around time from the field camera work to the newsroom editing, and lay off the obsolete film staff.

**Electronic Newspaper.** All a nation's newspapers available at the push of a button, usually accessed on the internet.

**Electronic Page.** Teletext page or pages held on Prestel or Oracle computer and available to viewers with teletext receivers. Prestel is available via telephone system, with charges for calling up pages; Oracle is on air direct to the TV set with no charges.

**Electronic Publishing.** The replacement of the traditional modes of printing, storage and dissemination of paper by electronic means.

**Electronic Retouching.** Unlike conventional hand retouching, halftone retouching by digital techniques allows direct manipulation of all grey values with exceptional level of quality and precision. Tone values can be generated in a more or less steeples range, and parts of pictures can be transplanted so that changes can be made to complex course tone areas. This is useful when retouching skin tones, or for cut-out and montage functions. Can avoid hard edges to contours of cut-out pictures on white backgrounds.

**Electronic Scanner.** Means of scanning full-colour copy wrapped round drums by reading colour densities and producing colour separations. Also transmits control readings on printing press or paper making machine.

**Electrophone.** Any musical instrument that produces sound primarily by electrical means.

**Electrotype.** Duplicate of an original printing block produced by electrochemical deposition onto a matrix. Commonly known as 'electro'.

**Element.** Single lens used in association with others to form a compound construction.

**Elite.** A group or class of persons enjoying superior intellectual or social or economic status.

**Elitist Media.** In developing countries, media which appeal to better educated or wealthier minority, as distinct from radio and folk media.

**Ellipsis.** Three dots are printed when words are omitted. In copywriting this is a means of reducing the number of words and speeding up the reading.

**Em.** Square of a given size of type, usually 12 points, used as a unit of measurement for lines, columns or type areas. This unit type of measurement is based on the "M" character.

**Embargo.** Request to editor not to print a story before a stated date and time. Frivolous use invites rejection. Should be a privilege to editor to have material in advance e.g. advance copy of a speech or report. Acceptable when international time differences need to be observed. Embargo is also the time when something can be released. News may be released early so that news outlets can be ready to publish or air it, but there may be a restriction on when it can be released to the public. Breaking an embargo- reporting information early- may cause sources to be less willing to release news.

**Embossing.** Printing a name, design or logo so that it has a raised surface.

**Emcee.** Often written as MC, short for master of ceremonies. See master of ceremonies.

**Emotional Appeal.** Product advertising appealing emotional desires rather than logic, economic or utility.

**Emotions.** Arguably defined as bodily changes, together with mental change, influencing one's decisions sometimes out of the normal pattern for the individuals used particularly in reference to buying behaviour (Persuasion).

**Empathy.** The ability of understanding and entering into another's feelings or position. The essence of this is to understand one's behaviour and perspective without filtering them through one's own value system.

**Empathy Gap.** A cognitive bias in which a person does not empathise or predict correctly how he/she will feel in the future, i.e. what kind of emotional state he/she will be in.

**Emphasis, Law of.** Dependence of emphasis on contrast such as bold headline and lighter weight text type, or use of white space.

**Emphatic Full Point.** Use of full point or full stop to give emphasis, such as by punctuating headline of an advertisement.

**Empirical.** Based on data obtained from direct, systematic observation rather than speculation or secondary information. Both qualitative and quantitative research can be empirical.

**Employee Newspaper.** Internal house journal, often tabloid format, but may be A4 magazine.

**Empowerment.** Giving more power to, or enhancing the power of, a group. Research that is designed to empower those being studied is sometimes called participatory research. This forms an apogee of many a system of self-realisation or of identity (re-)formation. Realising the solipsistic impracticality of everyone anarchistically attempting to exercise power over everyone else, empowerment advocates have adopted the word "empowerment" to offer the attractions of such power, but they generally constrain its individual exercise to potentiality and to feel-good uses within the individual psyche. It often addresses members of groups that social discrimination processes have excluded from decision-making processes through - for example - discrimination based on race, ethnicity, religion, gender. The media is an agent of empowerment. It plays this role in advocating, assisting, blocking or subverting authorisation. See disempowerment.

**Emulsion.** Micro-thin layers of gelatine on film in which light-sensitive ingredients are suspended; triggered by light to create a chemical reaction resulting in a photographic image. Basically, suspension of light-sensitive silver salts in gelatine.

**Emulsion Side.** The side of a film coated with emulsion. In contact printing and enlarging, the emulsion side of the film-dull side-should face the emulsion side of the photo paper-shiny side.

**En.** Unit of measurement, half of the EM space in width but the same in depth.

**ENAB.** Evening Newspaper Advertising Bureau. Sales organisation designed to promote the use of local evening newspapers by national advertisers.

**Encipher.** See Encode.

**Enclosure.** Object inserted into an envelope or package, usually in addition to the main or principal content.

**Encode.** The process by which a source or object performs a conversion of information into data, which is then sent to a receiver or observer, such as a data processing system.

**Encrypt.** The process of obscuring information to make it unreadable without special knowledge. While encryption has been used to protect communications for centuries, only organisations and individuals with an extraordinary need for secrecy had made use of it. In the mid-1970s, strong encryption emerged from the sole preserve of secretive government agencies into the public domain, and is now employed in protecting widely-used systems, such as Internet e-commerce, mobile telephone networks and bank automatic teller machines. It is same process with the scrambling of signals on satellite television as Sky.

**End Leaves.** Blank pages seen at the beginning or end of a book. They are usually not attached to the cover of the book. Very thick white papers are often used for end leaves. The function of the end leaves is to protect the hard cover from exerting its weight on the entire book. End leaves do not carry any information.

**End-product Advertising.** Advertising which promotes raw materials, ingredients, components or accessories to the makers of finished product.

**End Rate.** The final rate paid by an advertiser or advertising agency for commercial time on a cable or TV operation.

**End-sheet.** Heavy sheet of paper that attaches the book to the cover. There is an end-sheet in both the front and back of the book. Same as end leaves.

**End-user.** The individual or company who is the final purchaser of a product or service.

**Endorser Potential.** Qualities of a celebrity as an endorser of products in advertising. Can vanish if the celebrity is involved in scandal. For instance Glo mobile uses celebrities like Nobel Laureate Wole Soyinka, KSA, Charlie Boy, RMD, Daddy Showkey and other stars to endorse their product and services because of their potential. In the UK also David Beckam, Madonna and Kate Moss have great endorser potential. United States' Paris Hilton, Ben Affleck and Naomi Campbell are potential endorsers too.

**Enhanced Back-Printing.** An Advanced Photo System feature available in some system cameras that enables users to encode detailed information at the time of picture-taking, such as the date and time of exposure, camera settings, roll title or other custom information for subsequent printing onto the back of their photographs.

**Enlargement.** Production in size larger than the original, particularly with reference to a photographic print. See blow-up.

**Enlarger.** A device consisting of a light source, a negative holder, and a lens, and means of adjusting these to project an enlarged image from a negative onto a sheet of photographic paper.

**Enquiry.** In business terms, 'inquiry is preferred to enquiry' to distinguish between a general request for information (enquiry) and a film request for details prior to placing an order (inquiry).

**Entertainment.** A function of the media geared primarily towards providing some diversion and amusement, relaxation and respite. It further describes a major branch of media production and consumption, covering a range of formats that generally share the qualities of attracting and 'taking people out of themselves' along with the earlier stated characteristics. It also refers to the process of diversion itself, and in this sense it can also relate to the genres that are not usually regarded as entertaining, such as news, advertising or education. It is often perceived as problematic when addiction to entertainment excludes informational uses of media or when the 'entertainment' mode invades the sphere of reality content- especially news, information and politics, as it seems increasingly to do. The term 'infotainment' has been coined to describe the result.

**Ephemera.** This refers to written and printed matter published with a short intended lifetime. In the world of collectors common types of ephemera include letters, advertising trade cards, cigarette cards, airsickness bags, posters, postcards, baseball cards, tickets, greeting cards, stock certificates, photographs and zines. Decks of the Most-wanted Iraqi playing cards are recent example of ephemera because they will probably lose their original purpose and interest in a relatively short time. The word derives from the Greek meaning *of things lasting no more than a day.*

**EPS.** Abbreviation of *Encapsulated PostScript.* This is a file format for saving graphics to be printed on a PostScript printer.

**Equal Impacts.** Setting of rating points for each TV region to get balanced overall coverage in a networked campaign.

**Equity.** Actors' trade union which negotiates rates for actors appearing in television and radio commercials.

**Escalator Cards.** Advertisements placed alongside underground escalators.

**Escalator Panel.** Advertisement panel on the wall of escalator shaft, as in London Underground.

**Establishing Shot.** Opening shot or sequence showing the location of a film scene or juxtaposition of characters in action to follow.

**Ethical Advertising.** Advertising of ethical pharmaceutical products addressed to the medical profession. Also applied generally to describe honest, information advertising, as distinct from unscrupulous and misleading practice.

**Ethnic.** A term used to denote a human population whose members identify with each other, usually on the basis of a presumed common genealogy or ancestry. Ethnic groups are also usually united by common cultural, behavioural, linguistic, or religious practices. In this sense, an ethnic group is also a cultural community.

**Ethnocentricity.** Characteristic of looking at things from one's own cultural perspective. Some social science research and some news accounts are ethnocentric in that they do not take into account cultural variation in values or beliefs.

**Ethnography.** Rich, holistic description of all aspects of a culture; originally, this usually meant an anthropologist's description of a preliterate culture.

**Ethnomethodology.** Study of the ways in which the members of a particular culture make sense of their social environment. Ethnomethodology is a field rather than a method of study; ethnomethodologists commonly use qualitative techniques.

**Ethos.** A Greek word originally meaning 'the place of living' that can be translated into English in different ways. From the same Greek root originates the word *ethikos*, meaning 'theory of living', and from there, the modern English word 'ethics' is derived. In communication terms, the ethos of a communicator determines the image one has of him or her at any given time.

**ETV.** Television programming designed for educational purposes.

**Euphemism.** A mild, indirect, vague or inoffensive expression that is substituted for one that is considered harsh, blunt or offensive. For instance 'to die' may be replaced with 'to pass away'.

**Euro-branding.** Choosing Brand names for products sold throughout Europe (and especially in the Single European Market). Names must be acceptable whatever the language and not suffer from double or unfortunate meanings in other languages. Very important when advertising by cross-frontier Satellite TV.

**European Process Colour Scale.** Din 16539. Consists of cyan, magenta, yellow and black.

**EV.** Exposure value. Method of quantifying scene brightness. Most of these value apply to metering cells, how high or low e.g. a metering that can handle from EV1-EV21 means a metering system and can measure brightness level from just above the light level of a candle light to a brightly sunlight scene on a beach. Camera metering can handle more weakly on a spot metre than, say, a centre weighted average metering system. EV is commonly used in black and White photographic process. At ISO 100, the combination of a one-second shutter speed and an aperture of F1.4 is defined as EV1. The camera may be used only within the EV range of the exposure metre. For example, the exposure metering range is from EV0 to EV20 and can be used on a camera, means the camera's metre can handle broader range of exposure latitude.

**Evaluation of Results.** Assessment of achievement of a PR programme. Tangible PR based on measuring or observing whether targets were met or objectives achieved. If a PR programme sets out to achieve specific results the degree of success or otherwise can be evaluated at the end of the campaign period by means of experience, observation or scientific method.

**Even Small Caps.** Small capital letters without full-size initial caps.

**Eventing.** The systematic organisation and implementation of a programme of PR events in order to influence, educate and inform targeted publics. Includes press conferences, facility visits, dealer seminars and participation in exhibitions.

**Evergreen.** A pre-recorded videocassette that is strong and has a constant seller year after year at the video retail store. Movies like *Osofia in London* and *Living in Bondage* are instances of evergreen titles in Nigeria. The range of *Harry Porter*'s movies could be great examples also.

**Exclusive.** In press relations, relates to a story and/or illustrative photograph or other material which is supplied to one publication alone. Unwise to grant exclusive on news stories or pictures, but signed feature articles are exclusives. Syndicated articles are not.

**Exclusivity.** The singular right to use a particular product that excludes others from its use. In broadcasting, exclusivity is most often sought and granted in the area of programming. Syndicators who pick up programmes produced by an independent production company will seek exclusive distribution rights before they begin to market the product.

**Executive Gifts.** Public relations and advertising gifts, such as diaries, pens, wines and spirits, presented to clients, especially of Christmas, but also at visits and events. May be made especially as company souvenirs such as models, paperweights, etc. But of higher quality than promotional give-aways.

**Ex Gratia.** As a matter of favour. Usually refers to payments that are made where no legal obligation exists to make them.

**Exhibition.** Putting on display a company's products or services for promotional purposes. Particularly the gathering of a number of such displays which are either on view to the public in general or merely to invited guests. May be commercially or privately sponsored.

**Exhibition Train.** One which can be toured to a number of towns where it will remain at the station for a few days and be visited by invited guests.

**Existing Light.** Available light. As a matter of fact, existing light covers all natural lighting from moonlight to sunshine. For photographic purposes, existing light is the light that is already on the scene or project and includes room lamps, fluorescent lamps, spotlights, neon signs, candles, daylight through windows, outdoor scenes at twilight or in moonlight, and scenes artificially illuminated after dark.

**Exotica.** Interest in, and commodification of, ethnic differences; most strikingly demonstrated in fashion.

**Expanded.** Broad, extended version of a typeface.

**Expanded Type.** Typeface in printing which has wider dimensions than is usual. Its use is intended to exert a greater dominance or legibility.

**Experiment.** Research project in which at least one variable is artificially manipulated or changed to test its effect on other variables.

**Explanatory.** Study designed to identify or to test theories about causation. Explanatory studies can be either qualitative or quantitative, however, experimental approaches involving precise measurements are most commonly said to be explanatory.

**Exploded Drawing.** One which reveals interior of a subject which would not be visible from a photograph. Usually open line drawing.

**Exploded Views.** Special type of drawing in which a complex object is shown 'opened up' or with internal components illustrated separately and outside the main drawing.

**Exploratory Research.** Research designed to understand a new problem rather than to rigorously test hypotheses or produce a definitive description of a social setting. Exploratory research is inductive.

**Exposition.** Sometimes used as synonym of 'exhibition', but usually to imply a larger or more serious event, often accomplished by a conference or seminar.

**Exposure.** (1) Total number of shots taken or left in a camera film. Also the quantity of light allowed to act on a photographic material; a product of the intensity controlled by the lens opening and the duration controlled by the shutter speed or enlarging time of light striking the film or paper. The act of allowing light to reach the light-sensitive emulsion of the photographic material. May also refer to the amount (duration and intensity) of light which reaches the film. (2) Total number of viewers, listeners, readers or visitors to which an advertisement may be exposed according to the medium whether or not they paid any attention to it.

**Exposure Bracketing.** Shooting the same subject at a range of different exposures. Some cameras provide Auto Exposure Bracketing/Flash Exposure Bracketing.

**Exposure Compensation.** Exposure compensation for available light is activated by changing the shutter speed and/or lens aperture. This is done by using Auto Exposure Lock (AEL) and Autofocus Lock (AFL) button or exposure compensation button, or by Auto Exposure Bracketing. In flash photography with a dedicated TTL speedlight exposure compensation, it can also be performed by varying the amount of flash output. Camera-originated exposure compensation affects both the foreground subject and the background; variations in flash output amount affect only the foreground.

**Exposure Factor.** A figure by which the exposure indicated for an average subject and/or processing should be multiplied to allow for non-average conditions. Usually applied to filters and occasionally to lighting, Processing, etc. Not normally used with through-the-lens exposure metres.

**Exposure Latitude.** The range of camera exposures from underexposure to overexposure that will produce acceptable pictures from a specific film.

**Exposure Metre.** See light metre.

**Ext.** Extended type characters.

**Extension Bellows.** Device used to provide the additional separation between a lens and film required for close-up photography. It consists of extendible bellows and mounting plates at front and rear to fit the lens and camera body respectively.

**Extension Tubes.** Metal tubes used to obtain the additional separation between lens and film for close-up photography. They are fitted with screw thread or bayonet mounts to suit various lens mounts.

**External House Journals.** Those addressed to external readerships such as distributors, shareholders and customers.

**Extra.** Actor who plays minor role in TV commercial or drama and does not earn repeat fees.

**Extra High Grade.** A truly high grade tape that demonstrates its differences mostly in the quality of the image recorded. Extra high grade tape coatings are generally superior in noise immunity and lower in dropouts. This means that one gets a better recording and a better second and third generation copy. Several manufacturers have indicated on their packaging that they have done things to also provide greater longevity, but this is a claim that would be difficult to prove or disprove. For especially valuable recordings, use a high grade tape; but there is no standardisation and requirements that prevent anyone from naming a product 'extra high grade.'

**Extra Origination Charges.** Those made by publishers for four colour artwork requiring more than one transparency.

**Extrapersonal Communication.** A communication process that takes place without human involvement- machine to machine communication.

**Eye-blink Test.** Using a hidden camera, the eye-blink rate of respondents is recorded to measure extent of emotional tension provoked by the TV commercial being tested.

**Eye Contact.** The most subtle and significant feature of non-verbal communication. It involves meeting of the eyes between two people that expresses meaningful nonverbal communication.

**Eye Movement Camera.** Used in advertising research, this equipment tracks the movement of the eye over press advertisements, showing the path which the eye takes and indicating the sequence of interest that the features arouse.

**Eye Observation Camera.** Equipment used in advertising research to measure pupil dilation, so giving indications arousal of informant.

**Eye-path.** In layout or picture, a composition that directs the eye to the starting point of the design.

**Eyewash.** Exaggerated claims.

# F

**F-number.** The numbers on the lens aperture ring and the camera's LCD (where applies) that indicate the relative size of the lens aperture opening. The f-number series is a geometric progression based on changes in the size of the lens aperture, as it is opened and closed. As the scale rises, each number is multiplied by a factor of 1.4. The standard numbers for calibration are 1.0, 1.4, 2, 2.8, 4, 5.6, 8, 11, 16, 22, 32, etc., and each change results in doubling the amount of light transmitted by the lens to the film plane. Basically, calculated from the focal length of the lens divided by the diameter of the bundle of light rays entering the lens and passing through the aperture in the iris diaphragm. See F-stop.

**F-stop.** A measure of the amount of light entering the lens of a still, film or TV camera. The f stands for fixed. Numbers are etched on the iris ring on the front of the lens, denoting the extent to which the iris is closed or open. The lower the number, the larger the iris opening with more light allowed into the camera, and the faster the lens. F-stop numbers are the product of a mathematical formula where f is equal to the focal length of the lens divided by the diameter of the lens.

**Face Sheet Data.** In a research questionnaire, the respondent's personal details.

**Facial Expression.** A major aspect of non-verbal communication. It basically lies in the expression of emotions such as happiness, surprise, sadness, fear, anger, disgust, contempt, and interest. Though there are difficulties in judging facial emotions because people usually conceal negative feelings and the face more often speaks what the individual feels inside him. This however is a distinct form of communication. See Non verbal communication.

**Facing.** A billboard location with the panels facing the same direction and visible to the same lines of traffic.

**Fact-to-face Interviewing.** In communication research, street, doorstep or in-home interviewing as distinct from postal or telephone enquiries.

Facilities.

**Facilities.** The physical aspects of a TV station or production company. The term is applied more specifically to technical and production gear, including distribution amplifier (DA), camcorders, character generators, videotape formats and all other production and engineering equipment, and is often expanded to include the stations transmitter and earth station installations. The equivalent of facilities in the cable TV industry is plant.

**Facilities House.** Video producer who supplies packaged TV elements such as programme titles, station identifications and promotional fillers.

**Facing, Next Matter.** Press advertisement space next to editorial material.

**Facing Matter.** Positioning of an advertisement so that it appears opposite an editorial page.

**Facsimile.** Strictly an exact copy of writing or an illustration.

**Facsimile Pages.** In newspaper production. Pages completed on screen in editorial offices and transmitted by fax to the press at another location or to a regional contract printer.

**Factor Analysis.** Study of the component parts of an attitude research programme interview with the aim of discovering more meaningful conclusions than are apparent from the data taken as a whole.

**Facts Book.** (1) File of contact reports made by agency account executive. (2) Details about a product held by a Brand or Product Manager.

**Fade-in/Fade-out.** A production technique that creates a major change in the content of a TV or film programme. Fades are accomplished by using the leavers or faders on a switcher to gradually increase the video signal from black to a visible picture (fade-in) or by reversing the process by fading gradually to black (fade-out). A fade in begins a programme, scene or act and a fade-out has the effect of a descending curtain in the theatre, signalling the end or conclusion. Fade-ins and fade-outs are also frequently used in the audio portion of a programme, when the volume of the sound of dialogue or music gradually increases from inaudible to full volume or vice versa.

**Fair Copy.** Copy free of printing errors.

**Fairness Doctrine.** A former policy of the United States' Federal Communications Commission. It required broadcast licensees to present controversial issues of public importance, and to present such issues in an honest, equal and balanced manner.

**Familiarity.** Term refers to the perception of individuals who have had actual experience with a product or service.

**Family.** Variations of a typeface by weight, widths or design such as light, medium, bold, extra bold, condensed, expanded, roman, italic, shadow.

**Farm Magazine.** Category of magazines targeted to readers interested in farming. Subcategories include state and vocational magazines.

**Fat Face.** Typeface with extra thick contrasting strokes.

**FCC.** See Federal Communications Commission.

**Feature.** In press relations, A carefully researched article or story which is written in some depth and at some length that explains, interprets and/or provides background or tells of interesting, unusual occurrences that interest the reader; usually exclusive, Feature stories sometimes have emotional, personal, and/or humorous slants. (2) Physical description of the attributes of a product or service; these are different from Benefits.

**Federal Communications Commission.** It is an independent United States government agency, created, directed, and empowered by Congressional statute to license and regulate radio, television and other forms of electronic communication. The FCC was established by the Communications Act of 1934 as the successor to the Federal Radio Commission and is charged with regulating all non-Federal Government use of the radio spectrum (including radio and television broadcasting), and all interstate telecommunications (wire, satellite and cable) as well as all international communications that originate or terminate in the United States. It is an important factor in US telecommunication policy. The FCC took over wire communication regulation from the Interstate Commerce Commission. It's jurisdiction covers the 50 states, the District of Columbia, and U.S. possessions.

**Federal Radio Commission, FRC.** A government body that regulated radio use in the United States from its creation in 1927 until its replacement by the Federal Communications Commission in 1934. The Commission was created to regulate radio use "as the public convenience, interest, or necessity requires." The Radio Act of 1927 superseded the Radio Act of 1912, which had given regulatory powers over radio communication to the Secretary of Commerce and Labour. The Radio Act of 1912 did not mention broadcasting and it limited all private radio communications to what is now the AM band. See Federal Communications Commission.

**Feed.** (1) To supply information to another, particularly on sales lead. (2) Relaying transmission of a broadcast from one station to another.

**Feedback.** Response or reaction to a message, indicating to its communicator how the message is being interpreted.

**Feeder Cables.** An element of a tree network cable operation that connect the cable trunk lines to the cable drop lines. The intermediate potion of the distribution system carries the electronic signals from large trunk cable lines to a specific area or neighbourhood of homes. Often called feeder lines, they are stalled underground or strung between telephone poles.

**Fees, Agency.** A number of advertising agencies have replaced the anomalous commission system by charging clients net cost of media plus a fee based on time and expertise. This is more professional and the agency can earn income according to the volume and quality of work.

**Feminist.** From a woman's perspective. Research and scholarship, as well as political activity, can be feminist in this sense; when used in this way the term implies a theoretical rather than a political position.

**Fibreboard.** Two or more sheets of paperboard pasted together to form a stronger, thicker material. Usually a combination of kraft and chipboard. Solid fibreboard is a straightforward laminate often used, for example, as a book cover. Corrugated fibreboard comprises two outer 'liners' in between which is sandwiched with a corrugated 'fluting'. Both types of fibreboard are used extensive in the construction of 'cases', sometimes referred to as containers or cartons.

**Fibre Optics.** Optical fibre or fibre, it is a thin and transparent and is usually made of glass or plastic, used for transmitting light. Fibre optics is the branch of applied science and engineering concerned with such optical fibres. Optical fibres are commonly used in telecommunication systems, as well as in illumination, sensors, and imaging optics.

**Field.** A partial image informed by an electron gun in a cathode ray TV receiving tube. The gun sweeps the tube with an electronic beam from side to side and from top to bottom. This scanning process takes one-sixtieth of a second but scans only every other line, thus creating only one-half of the picture. The second scanning process of the alternate lines also takes one-sixtieth of a second. Together the two interlaced fields create a complete picture called a frame.

**Field Experiment.** Carrying out an experiment under natural (or 'field') conditions. For example, observing the introduction of a new type of technology in a media organisation would be a kind of field experiment.

**Field Force.** In communication research. Team of interviewers used for gathering information direct respondents in or around the respondents' usual habitat.

**Field Organisation.** Structure governing the operation of a field force, which may be for purposes of communication research or act as a promotional device.

**Field Research.** Communication or marketing research conducted by interviewers in the street, on doorstep or in the home.

**Field Strength.** The intensity of an electronic or magnetic field at a given point. In broadcasting, the strength of the transmission is measured in microvolts per metre at various points some distance away from the transmitting antenna, to determine the extent of the station's coverage area. In cable TV, a signal level metre measures the energy level of the cable signal at various points in the coaxial cable of the system.

**Fieldwork.** That part of a market research survey that involves face-to-face interviews with respondents by research investigators, as compared with other means of obtaining data, such as postal or telephone enquiries and the searching of relevant published material. See Desk research.

**Fill-flash.** A method of flash photography that combines flash illumination and ambient light, but does not attempt to balance these two types of illumination. See balance fill flash.

**Fill Lighting.** A TV and film lighting technique that directs broad light onto a performer, object or area from large lights positioned at the front and sides of the scene. Sometimes referred to as base lighting, this soft light is designed to complete the illumination of a scene by eliminating shadows and dark spots. Also see balance fill flash.

**Fill Rate.** The portion or percentage of an order that is fulfilled for pre-recorded videocassettes or videodiscs by manufacturing or duplicating firms.

**Filler Programming.** Additional programming used to flesh out a time period.

**Fillers.** Short paragraphs at the bottom of some columns. Anything used to fill the gap left in a page after make-up.

**Fill-in.** In Direct Mail, personal items that have to be added to a letter such as salutation, signature, or personalisation.

**Filler Spots.** On ITV, commercial supplied by advertisers which may be shown as airtime permits, and are charged at special low rates.

**Film.** A photographic emulsion coated on a flexible, transparent base that records images or scenes. More often, also used to refer to productions like drama, comedy, thrillers or other movie genre put on tape. Other programmes especially documentaries may fall in this line.

**Film Base.** Flexible support on which light sensitive emulsion is coated.

**Film Chain.** A unit that converts motion picture film or still slides into a video signal. It allows the film to be projected into the lens of a video camera and thus be recorded on videotape or transmitted to the audience. Several projectors are positioned to project into a set of mirrors in the centre of the unit, which can be changed to direct the image from any of the projectors into the lens of a video camera. It is often called a telecine.

**Film Clip.** A bit of film footage, familiarly known as a clip, that is often used as an insert in a TV production. The brief film can be introduced into a live studio programme to take the viewer outside the studio.

**Film Loop.** A short section of tape or film that is run repeatedly to produce a repetitive scene. A short (eight-foot or so) length of 16mm film is spliced into a loop and run continuously in a never-ending circle, through the projector of a film chain. Videotape machines can also be adapted to accommodate a tape loop.

**Film Make-up.** In printing, positioning Filmsettings or other film ready for plate making.

**Film Master.** Complete film positive of an advertisement from which a plate can be made.

**Film Mechanical.** Camera-Ready Copy in film form instead of paste-up artwork.

**Film Noir.** A cinematic term used primarily to describe Hollywood crime dramas that set their protagonists in a world perceived as inherently corrupt and unsympathetic. Hollywood's classic film noir period is largely regarded as stretching from the early 1940s to the late 1950s. Film noir of this era is associated with a low-key black-and-white visual style that has roots in German Expressionist cinematography, while many of the prototypical stories and much of the attitude of classic noir derive from the Hardboiled School of crime fiction that emerged in the United States during the Depression.

**Film Package.** An assemblage of several motion pictures marketed in syndication as a single unit under an umbrella label. These collections created by syndicators, sometimes contain films of a particular genre such as westerns, but often the individual motion picture titles are disparate and are grouped together under broad titles.

**Film Presence Indicator Flag.** Feature on Advanced Photo System cameras that indicates the film cassette has been loaded properly.

**Film Rush.** First print of cine film sequence; produced immediately after shooting in order to see whether a retake is necessary.

**Film Safe.** Describes the fact that film is sealed in the cassette; avoids the danger of exposure to light before shooting and mishandling of negatives after shooting.

**Filmsetting.** Typesetting on film instead of on paper.

**Film Speed**. Indicated by a number such as ISO 100 or ISO 400 etc. The sensitivity of a given film to light. The higher the number, the more sensitive or faster (and more grainer) the film. ISO is short for International Standards Organisation.

**Film Status Indicators.** The four icons on Advanced Photo System film cassettes that show the film status - unexposed, partially exposed, fully exposed or processed.

**Film Strip.** Joined sequence of positive transparencies either black and white but more usually in colour. Each strip consists of a limited number of exposures, which together tell a story or put across a message. Often produced in conjunction with a sound script which can either be spoken during showing or coupled electronically for automatic reproduction.

**Filter.** (1) Means of eliminating unnecessary information. (2) Receptionist or secretary protecting executive(s) from unexpected callers. (3) Question in research questionnaire intended to redirect interview. (4) In photojournalism, a coloured piece of glass or other transparent material used over the lens to emphasise, eliminate, or change the colour or density (ND) of the entire scene or certain areas within a scene. Technically, it is a piece of material which restricts the transmission of radiation, generally coloured to absorb light of certain colours. It can be used over light sources or over the camera lens. Camera lens filters are usually glass either dyed or sandwiching a piece of gelatine in a screw-in filter holder. See colour temperature, UV.

**Filter Question.** In a communication research questionnaire, a question which identifies the respondent's relevance to the survey. If the respondent is not relevant, the interview is discontinued.

**Final.** (1) Proof or pull of the corrected, locked-up printing form or of a block, showing the printed corrected work as it will eventually appear. It is thus distinguished from initial proofing which is for checking and correcting purposes only. (2) Also the end result of the film production process. All elements, including sound and optical effects such as titles, superimpositions and dissolves have been added to the print and the film, programme or commercial is completed. The print has been corrected for colour, checked for quality and is ready for transmission.

**Financial Advertising.** Advertising activity undertaken by companies, firms, or organisations involved in financial markets, such as Unit Trusts Assurance, Building Societies, or Banks.

**Finder.** Also known as viewfinder and projected frame. A viewing device on a camera to show the subject area that will be recorded on the film.

**Fine Grain.** Descriptive of a photographic emulsion or the developer used to process it; results in a negative which can be enlarged to a high degree without showing excessive graining.

**Fine Screen.** In printing, a halftone screen containing 100 or more lines to the inch.

**Finish.** Quality of paper surface. A paper is finished by polishing rollers, not coated.

**Finished Art.** Final drawing ready for reproduction.

**Finished Rough.** A superior advertisement visual, worked up by studio with colour separations, mechanical artwork and type overlay, for submission to agency client.

**Firmware.** Programmes built into a computer. The software is embedded in a hardware device and is often provided on flash ROMs or as a binary image file that can be uploaded onto existing hardware by a user.

**First Amendment.** The first amendment to the Constitution of the United States was enacted in 1791 and it outlawed Congressional (i.e. federal government) interference in or regulation of freedom of speech, religion and the press, etc. It has become a shorthand term to cover all matters of freedom of expression and opinion in the United States, often involving the mass media. Many other countries have equivalent constitutional provisions, although they are equally expressed in terms of the rights of the citizens. The way the First Amendment is formulated has tended to identify government as the arch enemy of freedom, strongly associating free media with the free market. See freedom of the press.

**First Colour Down.** In printing, the first colour to be printed when there is more than one colour.

**First Proof.** Early proof which is read for literals and printer's errors before submission to client.

**First Reference.** The first time someone is mentioned in an article, and generally should have their full name.

**Fisheye Lens.** Ultra-wide angle lens giving 180 angle of view. Basically produces a circular image on 35 mm, 5-9 mm lenses showing whole image, 15-17 mm lenses giving a rectangular image fitting just inside the circle, thus representing 180 across the diagonal.

**Fishing.** Targeting a Direct Response campaign by first seeking prospects by offering free sample to those who return coupon asking about use of a rival product.

**Fisk.** Detailed word-by-word analysis and critique of an article. Refers to Robert Fisk, an internationally recognised journalist for the Independent of London.

**Fix-a-Form Labels.** Packaging labels with concertina folded leaf-lets which are released by breaking perforation.

**Fixed-Focus.** Describes a non-adjustable camera lens, set for a fixed subject distance.

**Fixed-Focus Lens.** A lens that has been focused in a fixed position by the manufacturer. The user does not have to adjust the focus of this lens, applies on most entry or disposable cameras.

**Fixed Position.** A specific time for the broadcast of a commercial on a TV station. Also same on print, the rate for a fixed position is higher than that charged for a commercial purchased at run-of-schedule rates or at a pre-emptive rate. Companies like Globacom, MTN and big banks have fixed positions in some dailies and broadcast stations. In UK, companies like DELL computers, T-mobile and Capital One usually have fixed positions on dailies.

**Fixed Rate.** An advertising rate for advertising time that cannot be taken away or "pre-empted" by another advertiser; usually the highest advertising rate; commonly used in broadcast advertising.

**Fixing Bath.** A material used in the darkroom. This solution removes any light-sensitive silver-halide crystals not acted upon by light or developer, leaving a black-and-white negative or print unalterable by further action of light. Also called hypo.

**Fixer.** Solution, usually based on sodium thiosulphate, in which films or prints are immersed after development to convert the unexposed silver halides in the emulsion to soluble products that can be washed out. This prevents subsequent deterioration of the image.

**FL, Florite.** A low dispersion mineral used as a substitute for glass in some highly corrected long focal length lenses. Canon uses most of these properties on its EF-L series long teles. See ED.

**Flag.** (1) In an outdoor poster, torn paper which hangs loose. (2) Outdoor medium, useful where there are no poster sites, or there is an open area such as a petrol station forecourt. (3) The newspaper's name on page one. Also called the nameplate.

**Flags.** Lighting accessories used to shadow or block unwanted light from certain areas. They are mounted on a stand or on the grid above the studio. Sometimes called gobos or cutters, they are rectangular metal frames with black fabric stretched over them.

**Flare.** An overall decrease in contrast caused by light being reflected off, instead of transmitted through, a lens surface; controllable through the use of multilayer coating of individual lens elements in a lens. It is aggravated by unclean lens surfaces on front and rear lens elements or filters.

**Flash.** (1) Five-second TV slides with voice-over by a station announcer. Could be a report of a recent event, a news flash. (2) Also the artificial light source in the dark. Electronic flash requires a high voltage, usually obtained from batteries through a voltage-multiplying circuit. It has a brief, intense burst of light, usually used where the lighting on the scene is inadequate for picture-taking. Generally considered to have the same photographic effect as daylight, most flash will correct the colour temperature back to 5000 Kelvin - the daylight colour.

**Flashback.** A dramatic technique in which the logical progression of events that has been occurring sequentially in a story is interrupted by a character recalling a happening from a previous time. This is often used when an artist or character is telling a story or thinking of the past. It is used more often in crime dramas like Murder, She Wrote; Columbo; Crime Scene Investigation; Criminal Minds and others.

**Flash Bracket.** Often called handle mount flash. It comprised of one arm of the L-shaped bracket that extends under the camera body and uses the camera's tripod socket to mount the camera on the bracket. The vertical arm of the bracket serves as a handle and mounts a flash unit in an accessory shoe often on top of the handle portion, but there are other methods. Flash mounted in a bracket usually requires a separate electrical cord to make the electrical connection between camera body and flash unit.

**Flashbulb.** Light source based on ignition of combustible metal wire in a gas filled transparent envelope. Popular sizes are usually blue-coated to give light approximating to daylight. Flash bulbs come in various sizes and types. All work by burning metal foil in an oxygen atmosphere within the glass bulb. However, as the light is caused by combustion inside the glass envelope, light intensity increases from zero as combustion begins. It reaches a peak value and then falls off as combustion ends. The flash unit is fired or triggered by the shutter mechanism in the camera. For some flashbulb types in some cameras, the shutter mechanism fires the flash and then waits for a specified time delay before it actually opens the shutter. This delay is to allow the flash bulb to get up to full brightness. See FP (focal plane bulb).

**Flashcube.** Self-contained unit comprising four small flashbulbs with own reflectors. It is designed to rotate in special camera socket as film is wound on and can be used in a special adapter on cameras without the socket. Though this will not rotate automatically.

**Flash Exposure Bracketing.** Enables a photographer to automatically bracket exposures at varied flash output levels, in TTL auto flash shooting, without changing the shutter speed and/or aperture; this is one of the top flash features that can only be found on some high rank cameras.

**Flash Synchronisation.** Timing of the flash which coincides with the release of the camera's shutter. There are two types of synchronisation: Front-Curtain Sync, which fires the flash at the start of the exposure, and Rear-Curtain Sync, which fires the flash at the end of the exposure. See Rear-Curtain Sync, Front-Curtain Sync, and X setting.

**Flash Sync Speed.** Exposure time with a focal-plane shutter that is measured from the instant the first curtain is released, to begin its travel across the frame, until the instant the second curtain is released, to begin its travel across the frame. When the first curtain reaches the end of its travel, the film frame is uncovered, so it closes the electrical contacts for X sync and fires the flash instantly. Technically this is the shutter speed at which the entire film frame is exposed when the flash is fired in flash shooting. Most modern camera with vertical travel shutter curtain have faster flash sync speed like 1/250 sec. or slower, some top camera model like Nikon F5, changeable to 1/300 sec. with the custom setting.

**Flash output level compensation.** A control used to adjust a TTL auto flash operation, enabling an increase or decrease of flash output to lighten or darken the flash effect.

**Flash shooting distance range.** The distance range over which a flash can effectively provide light. Flash shooting distance range is controlled by the amount of flash output available. Each automatic speedlight's flash output varies from maximum duration to minimum duration. Close-up subjects will require lower (to minimum) output while more distant subjects will require more light up to the maximum output. The flash shooting distance range varies with the aperture, film speed, etc. See guide number.

**Flash Memory Card.** A storage medium used by most digital cameras. It resembles film in conventional photography and creates more than enough space for saving images onto the camera.

**Flat.** (1) One side of a signature in book publishing; the eight pages which are printed on one side of a signature. (2) Too low in contrast. The range in density in a negative or print is too short or in some cases, reflecting the low resolution produced by a low quality lens.

**Flat Colour.** Second colour produced by template or tint.

**Flat Lighting.** Lighting that produces very little contrast or modelling on the subject as well as a minimum of shadows.

**Flat Panel Television.** A new TV technology consisting of lightweight display screens that are barely thicker than a heavy pane of glass.

**Flat Rate.** (1) Standard charge for advertisement space or airtime, irrespective of volume or frequency. (2) Uniform rate for advertising space or time, i.e. without allowing for discount.

**Flatbed.** Printing press with printing image flat on bed of machine, instead of having curved plates as with rotary machines.

**Fleet Street.** Until the 1980s, the home of most of Britain's major national newspapers. Named after River Fleet, it is a famous street in London. Even though the last major news office, Reuters, left in 2005, the street's name continues to be used as a synonym for the British national press. It is now more associated with the Law and its courts and chambers, most of which are located in little side streets off Fleet Street. Many of the newspapers that formerly resided in Fleet Street have moved to Wapping and Canary Wharf.

**Flexible Budget.** Variable amount of funds for a given purpose subject only to accountability for achievement.

**Flexible Program.** Flexible Program function temporarily shifts an automatically selected shutter speed/aperture combination while maintaining correct exposure. Specifically, a desired shutter speed or aperture can be selected in programmed auto exposure mode.

**Flexography.** Rotary web Letterpress printing process. Uses flexible rubber plates and fast drying solvent or water-based inks. Used for printing packaging materials, especially delicate ones like foil wrappings. With improved photopolymer plates, inks, rivals offset litho for newspaper printing, and adopted by the Daily Mail in 1988. Flexo inks are brighter than offset inks. Good for picture reproduction.

**Flexography.** Method of printing using rubber plates; cheaper but resulting in lower quality reproduction.

**Flight(ing).** A schedule of related commercials in the media. In a winter flight the advertisements are broadcast over a long time period. A series of several spots may be called a 12-spot flight. The term is used in advertising agencies as a shorthand way of describing multiple plays of commercials.

**Float.** White space around an advertisement. Can occur when same advertisement is supplied for publications with different page sizes instead of producing adaptations to suit different pages.

**Floating Accents.** Accents in a type font which can be placed above any letter. In digital typesetting, all kinds of accents which are available to make every character combination possible, as when setting foreign names and words, or setting in a foreign language.

**Floating Time.** See Run of schedule.

**Flong.** Sheet of softened paperboard used in printing to make a mould from a full page of type and/or pictures. The metal stereotype place for rotary presses is made from the flong.

**Floor Plan.** A diagram of the floor of a TV studio as seen from above. It shows the position of set pieces, objects, talent, cameras and other production gear.

**Flow Chart.** (1) Graphical presentation of performance. (2) Stages in critical path procedure.

**Fluff.** A mistake in speech, e.g. on television or radio, made in such a way as to be obvious to an audience.

**Fluid Head.** A cheap device that is used to support some TV cameras, as well as many 16mm film cameras. It consists of a circular metal container beneath a flat piece of metal that supports the camera. Its inside components, which allow the head to pan or tilt, are encased in oil, thus allowing smoother movements than those permitted by the more limited friction head mounts.

**Flush.** To set type even with the column rule or margin on either left or right. A 'flush left' head has all the lines ranging evenly on the left.

**Flush Left.** Text which is aligned on the left margin is said to be set flush left. If the same text is not aligned on the right margin, it is said to be set flush left, ragged right. The term ragged right is sometimes used alone to mean the same thing.

**Flush Right.** Text which is aligned on the right margin is said to be set flush right. If the same text is not aligned on the left margin, it is said to be set flush right, ragged left. The term ragged left is sometimes used alone to mean the same thing.

**Flutter Sign.** Outdoor poster site made up of spangles which flutter in the breeze and appear to be consistently moving.

**Florescent Ink.** As used for shop posters, ink which reacts to ultra-violet light and gives glowing effect.

**Flyaway.** A very small satellite newsgathering earth station. The extremely portable unit can enable a live satellite feed from previously inaccessible places within hours.

**Fly Poster.** Poster pasted on site, such as on walls and windows of empty shops without permission, as with pop group/singer poster.

**Fly Posting.** Illegal fixing of posters on another's property. This is why some properties have the phrase "Post no Bill" written on them.

**FM.** See Frequency Modulation.

**Focal Length.** The distance between the optical centre of the lens and the face of the picture tube when the lens is focused on infinity. It is measured in millimetres and determines how wide an angle can be seen by the lens. The smaller the focal length the more area that can be viewed at any given distance. The larger the focal length the smaller the field that can be viewed by the lens at that distance.

**Focal-Plane Shutter.** An opaque curtain containing a slit that moves directly across in front of the film in a camera and allows image-forming light to strike the film.

**Focal Point Interviewing.** In communication research, focusing an interview on a particular theme so that the respondent is encouraged to concentrate on this when responding to questions.

**Focoltone.** Colour matching system with combination of four process printing colours so that colours can be accurately reproduced as specified by the designer.

**Focus.** In photojournalism, adjustment of the distance setting on a lens to define the subject sharply. Generally, the act of adjusting a lens to produce a sharp image. In a camera, this is effected by moving the lens bodily towards or away from the film or by moving the front part of the lens towards or away from the rear part, thus altering its focal length.

**Focus Group.** Form of qualitative research. When a small group of 6 to 12 people with common interest is taken. The group leader directs questions and records consensus of answers. Combination of brainstorming and discussion group techniques. Focus groups can be used to assess people's reactions to products, messages, or ideas.

**Focus out/Focus in.** A transitional camera or time technique that is used to dramatise a shift in reality or a flashback. A character may faint and the camera defocuses. There is a dissolve to another shot, which gradually comes into focus on a dreamlike scene. When that scene concludes, the defocus/focus technique is used again to make the transition back to the original scene.

**Focus Range.** The range within which a camera is able to focus on the selected picture subject - 4 feet to infinity - for example.

**Focus-Priority for Autofocus.** Shutter cannot be released until the subject is in focus. Used in situations when an in-focus subject is important. With the F5 camera body, focus-priority is given to single servo AF mode while release-priority is given to continuous servo AF. Using custom setting, however, one can change the priority to release-priority single servo AF or focus-priority continuous servo AF.

**Focus Tracking.** Enables the camera to analyse the speed of a moving subject according to the focus data detected, and to obtain correct focus by anticipating the subject's position and driving the lens to that position and aim the shot at the exact moment of exposure. This is basically a Nikon and Canon feature. Currently, Nikon lead the pack in this technology with the F5, the fastest among all.

**Fogging.** Darkening or discolouring of a negative or print or lightening or discolouring of a slide caused by exposure to non image-forming light to which the photographic material is sensitive, too much handling in air during development, over-development, outdated film or paper, or storage of film or paper in a hot, humid place.

**FOIA.** Used as a noun or a verb (when it is done to balky government officials), it is the Freedom of Information Act.

**Foil Papers.** Papers with metallic surfaces, ideal for Flexography printing, and used for decorative wrappings.

**Foil Stamping.** Means of showing off coins, trademarks, logos by embossing, using heat application of gold or silver inks.

**Fold-out.** Folded sheet which opens out to a larger size, or many times its folded-down size, like a map.

**Folder Technique.** Often used in advertisement pre-testing, a number of advertisements being placed in the plastic sleeves of a folder which respondents study in turn before being questioned about what they remember.

**Foliation.** Numbering of pages or folios.

**Folio.** A tag line at the bottom of the page which numbers and names the spreads. Simply a page or page number.

**Folk Culture.** This refers to the localised lifestyle of a subsistence or otherwise inward looking culture. It is usually handed down through oral tradition and a strong sense of community, and values the "old ways" over novelty. Folk culture is quite often imbued with a sense of place. If its elements are copied by, or removed to, a foreign locale, they will still carry strong connotations of their original place of creation. Folk tales are most gotten from these folk cultures.

**Folk Devils.** A person or group of people portrayed in folklore or the media as outsiders and deviant, and who are blamed for crimes or other sorts of social problems. The pursuit of folk devils frequently intensifies into a mass movement that is called a moral panic. When a moral panic is in full swing, the folk devils are the subject of loosely organised but pervasive campaigns of hostility through gossip and the spreading of urban legends. The mass media sometimes gets in on the act, or attempts to create new folk devils to create controversies. Sometimes the campaign against the folk devil influences a nation's politics and legislation.

**Follow-up Programming.** A type of programming produced and aired following an initial show that addresses the same topic or issue.

**Following Reading Matter.** Preferred position in advertising media for advertisers; an advertisement is placed immediately after a feature article or editorial and so attracts the attention of readers, whose eyes are said to migrate to the advertisement.

**Follow Up.** Further information about an event that has already been reported. Follow-up news reports; follow-up interviews. In advertising, sales contact, telephone calls or letter sometimes but not always as a result of an expression of interest by a prospect and usually after his/her receipt of an initial promotional piece, e.g. a direct mail shot.

**Follow Style.** In printing, instruction to typesetter to follow the style of a sample print.

**Font.** The entire set of characters in a typeface.

**Foot-candle (fc).** A measure of the luminance or brightness of a light. A certain level of light is required before a camera can record an image, and different cameras and lenses have different light requirements. Light metres are used to measure brightness of a scene.

**Footage.** Indicates the length of a piece of film. Each foot contains 16 frames; 35mm films runs at 1½ feet or 24 frames per second.

**Footer.** A section of text/graphics that appears at the bottom of every page in a document.

**Footprint.** Land area covered by satellite transmission.

**Force Card.** In Die-Stamping the male die.

**Forced-choice Question.** Question with a limited number of answers form which respondents must choose. A 'yes or no' question is a forced-choice question that requires someone to choose their ethnicity from a list of alternatives provided.

**Forced Combination**. A policy to require newspaper advertisers to buy advertising space in both morning and evening newspapers owned by the same interests within a market.

**Forced Development.** See push-processing.

**Forcing Distribution**. Using advertising to increase consumer demand, thereby inducing dealers to stock a product; seldom not used.

**Forecasting.** Predicting future events on the basis of historical data, opinions, trends and known future variables.

**Fore-edge.** Outside edge, opposite the binding edge, of a book.

**Foreground.** In photojournalism, the area between the camera and the principal subject.

**Form.** Number of pages printed from one sheet of paper, e.g. in 16s or 32s.

**Form-mailer.** Direct Mail shot comprising a continuous form so designed that the same piece of paper becomes an envelope containing different inserts (reply card, advertisement, etc.) all of which creates a complete message.

**Format.** (1) In print, the size and shape of a page viz- broad sheet/blanket or tabloid. (2) In photojournalism, the actual size of a photograph, either slide or negative, produced by a camera; in 35mm photography, the picture measures 24mm x 36mm and has a diagonal of 43mm; while in the new APS (Advance Photo System), several new formats were included, including panorama. Though it can also be explained as shape and size of image provided by camera or presented in final print or transparency. Governed in the camera by the opening at the rear of the body over which the film passes or is placed. The standard 35 mm format is 36 x 24 mm; half-frame, 18 x 24 mm; 126 size, 28 x 28 mm; 110, 17 x 13 mm; standard roll film (120 size), 2x 2 in. (3) In broadcasting, the form, makeup, content, style and organisation of a programme, but not its subject matter. In TV, the format can be of a game, talk, panel, comedy, dramatic, variety or musical nature. It consists of the shape, size and placement of physical and thematic elements and their arrangement within the parameters of the framework of a programme. In radio this term is used differently, where it describes the type of programme schedule on a particular station such as Call-in Talk, or MTN music chart.

**Forme.** Frame with type matter and blocks assembled in it for letterpress printing.

**Forty-eight Sheet.** Very large poster.

**Forms Close.** Copy date when material for printing must be received by publisher.

**Fount.** Complete set of characters to print a particular typeface in one size. The word has two sources of origin: (i) from old French font, to melt or cast, (ii) from early days of monastic printing in England when alphabets of printing type were stored in spare founts in the chapel.

**Fountain.** Source of ink supply in printing press.

**Four-colour Process.** Full-colour printing using yellow, magenta, cyan and black, whereby filters separate the colours of the original artwork.

**Four-colour Set.** Set of printing blocks or plates, one for each of the four major printing colours (red, yellow, blue, black) used to produce a full colour reproduction. Term sometimes refers to a set of colour proofs.

**Four Plus Cover.** Percentage of readership or audience who are exposed to an advertisement at least four times.

**Four P's.** Shorthand way of indicating the principal factors to be included in the marketing mix, i.e. product, price, place and promotion.

**Four Sheet.** Poster size of growing popularity, equal to four double crown posters.

**Fourteen-Day Rule.** This rule was an informal norm adopted during the Second World War whereby the BBC would not broadcast discussion of issues on radio and television for two weeks that had come before either the House of Commons or the House of Lords. The British public was given two weeks to make up its own mind before hearing from broadcast pundits. The norm was abandoned in 1955.

**Fourth Estate.** A term usually attributed by the historian Thomas Carlyle to the 18th century polemicist Edmund Burke and applicable to the press gallery of the English House of Commons. Burke asserted that the power of the press was at least equal to that of the other three 'estates of the Realm'- Lords, Commons and Clergy. It became a conventional term for journalists in their role as reporters of and watchdogs on government.

**FP/FC.** Full page, full colour.

**FP (Focal Plane) Flash Bulb.** A special flashbulb that can be used at certain shutter speeds, called "FP" where the initials stand for Focal Plane. It is designed for use with focal-plane shutters and it makes a nearly uniform amount of light for a relatively long time. Generally, FP flashbulbs can be used with any shutter speed and any firing delay except "X sync". The FP bulb will extinguish during exposure intervals longer than 1/60 second but enough light will have reached the film to make the exposure.

**fps.** Frames per second. Used to describe how many frames the motor can drive or winder can handle automatically on winding per second consequently. Also apply to areas like video, animations, movie cameras.

**Fracia.** In exhibitions, the headboard above a stand. Sometimes used for advertising purposes, e.g. featuring a brand name, but usually carries the identity of the exhibitor.

**Fractional Page.** Print advertising space of less than a full page.

**Fractional Showing.** An outdoor advertising showing of less than 25. See Showing.

**Fragmentation.** The increasing number of listening or viewing subdivisions in the mass audience.

**Fragrance Application.** For Direct Mail and Sales Promotion purposes, application to print of specially-formulated solution containing micro-encapsulated particles of perfume. When the area is rubbed the fragrance is released. Can prompt consumer response.

**Frame.** In cine-film, a single picture. Frames are repeated to create a movie. In Prestel Viewdata, content of TV screen. Also a complete TV picture on a cathode ray tube consisting of 525 scanning lines. It is composed of two combined fields. A frame is created by an electron gun scanning first the odd-numbered field of 262-1/2 lines and then the even numbered field of 262-1/2 lines, each one in one-sixtieth of a second.

**Frameful.** TV screen filled with Prestel information.

**Framing.** A term with three main meanings. (1) The process of composing a camera shot in TV and film. This composition is achieved by changing the camera angle, panning, tilting or dollying in or out. (2) The way in which news content is typically shaped and contextualised by journalists within some familiar frame of reference and according to some latent structure of meaning. (3) This also concerns the effect of framing on the public. The audience is thought to adopt the frames of reference offered by journalists and see the world in a similar way. This process is related to agenda-setting.

**Franchise.** A statutory right or privilege granted to a person or group by a government especially the rights of citizenship and the right to vote. As a media concept, it involves licensing broadcast stations, etc.

**Frankfurt School.** The name applied to the group of scholars who originally worked in the Frankfurt Institute of Social Research and emigrated to the USA after the Nazis came to power. The central project of the group was the critical analysis of modern culture and society in the Marxist tradition. The main figures included Theodor Adorno, Max Horkheimer, Herbert Marcuse and Leo Lowenthal. They were all very influential in the development of critical theory in North America and Europe after World War II and especially in media and cultural studies. The pessimistic view of 'mass culture' was, paradoxically, one stimulus to a later re-validation of popular cultural forms.

**Franking.** Printing or cancellation of postage upon envelopes or labels which can be used to carry an advertising slogan.

**FRCN.** Federal Radio Corporation of Nigeria. Nigeria's government owned radio corporation with big stations all over the country. Its history- radio broadcasting was introduced  to  Nigeria by the

Free.

British in 1932 when BBC signals were relayed to receivers through the re-diffusion system. In 1951, the Nigerian Broadcasting Service (NBS) was inaugurated mainly to relay the BBC programmes. In an attempt to further localise radio broadcasting in the country, the Nigerian Broadcasting Corporation was established by an Act of Parliament No 39 of 1956 and began operations as a statutory corporation on 1st April, 1957. The NBC was in operation until 1978 when the Federal Radio Corporation of Nigeria came into being by virtue of Decree No 8 1979, with retrospective effective from 1st April, 1978. By this Decree, the Federal Government dissolved the NBC and handed over twenty of its stations to state governments. The only NBC stations retained were those in Lagos, Ibadan and Enugu which were then merged with the former Broadcasting Company of Northern Nigeria (BCNN) in Kaduna also dissolved by the Decree to constitute the FRCN at inception.

**Free.** Said to be most effective word in copywriting. Can be extended to Freephone and Freepost.

**Free Circulation**. A publication sent without charge; often with controlled circulation.

**Free working distance**. In close-up photography, the distance between the front of the lens and the subject; increases as the focal length increases. It is an important consideration when photographing shy or dangerous subjects or when using supplementary illumination.

**Freebies.** Ranging from excursions to foreign countries to tickets to a church supper, these complimentary offerings are designed to entice journalists to cover a story.

**Freedom of Information (or Communication).** This has a broad meaning that covers all aspects of public expression and transmission of, and access to, all manner of content. It has been advanced as a human right that should be guaranteed internationally and not just within a society. In a narrow sense it usually refers to public rights of access to information of public interest or relevance held by various kinds of authority or official agency.

**Freedom of Information Law.** A law permitting access to government documents and meetings by the press and the public. Over sixty one countries around the world have implemented some form of freedom of information legislation, which sets rules on governmental secrecy. Many more countries are working towards introducing such laws, and many regions of countries with national legislation have local laws - for example, all states of the US have access laws as well as the national legislation. In general, such laws define a legal process by which government information is available to the public; in some countries, they may only apply to journalists, or to people with a legal need for the information. In many countries there are vague constitutional guarantees for the right of access to information, but usually these are unused unless specific legislation exists to support them. These laws may also be described as open records or (especially in the United States) sunshine laws (alluding to "letting light shine" on the process). A related concept is open meetings legislation, which allows the public access to government meetings, not just to the records of them. In many countries, privacy or data protection laws may be part of the freedom of information legislation; the concepts are often closely tied together in political discourse. In Nigeria the Freedom of Information Bill was before the National Assembly in June 2005, and was then considered likely to pass, but remains pending. A basic principle behind most freedom of information legislation is that the burden of proof falls on the body asked for information, not the person asking for it. The requester does not usually have to give an explanation for their request, but if the information is not disclosed a valid reason has to be given.

**Freedom of the Press.** A fundamental principle of individual, political and human rights that guarantees in law the right to all citizens to publish without advance censorship or permission by authority, or fear of reprisal or intimidation. This censorship is usually by autocratic governments. It allows a free flow of information and the right to individuals to impart and receive information without any fear of detention or molestation. It has to be exercised within the limits of law and to respect the rights of others. In practice, freedom of the press is often limited by (economic) barriers of access to the means of publication. The right is usually regarded as fundamental to political democracy. It is related to, but distinct from, freedom of expression, opinion or belief and also freedom of information and First Amendment.

**Free-fall Insert.** Insert tipped into journal.

**Free Interview.** Interview based on open-ended questions posed by an interviewer.

**Freelance.** Journalist not on the staff of one newspaper, but usually contributing to several. Also refers to artists, writers and other self-employed suppliers of specialist services.

**Free Newspapers.** Local newspapers with door-to-door saturation coverage of urban areas. Sometimes four to five competing titles in a large town.

**Freesheets.** Local newspapers or magazines that are distributed without charge, depending for their revenue entirely on advertising support. Most of the space in these publications is sold for advertising, leaving little room for editorial content.

**Freestanding Insert.** Loose insert in a newspaper or magazine.

**Freephone.** Facility provided in press advertisements to ring the advertiser free-of-charge. The advertiser pays for all in this case.

**Freepost.** Means of attracting response by offering post free enquiry or order service. If respondents address an envelope including the word 'Freepost' in the advertiser's address they qualify for second class post. Another possibility is to supply respondents with first or second class reply envelopes using Freepost in address.

**Freeview.** A free digital television service offering over 30 TV channels and 20 radio stations for just a one-off payment and no contract. It is received through a normal rooftop aerial and is available directly on some televisions without the box.

**Frenchfold.** A sheet of print folded into four pages, but exposing only one side which is printed, leaving a joint at the edges as with some Christmas cards.

**Frequency.** (1) Broadcast rating term to indicate how often a viewer has tuned to a given station. (2) Position on the electromagnetic spectrum. (3) The number of times that an average audience member sees or hears an advertisement; the number of times that an individual or household is exposed to an advertisement or campaign (frequency of exposure); the number of times that an advertisement is run (frequency of insertion).

**Frequency Curve.** Graphical expression of a continuous frequency distribution.

**Frequency Discount.** A reduced advertising rate that is offered by media to advertisers who run a certain number of advertisements within a given time.

**Frequency Distribution.** Simple count of the number of times that each item in a set of categories appears- for instance the number of people who saw a given number of presentations of an advertisement, especially, TV commercials.

**Frequency Modulation.** A radio transmission system that encodes audio into the signal by variations in the station's centre frequency. This form of modulation also represents information as variations in the instantaneous frequency of a carrier wave. There is a direct contrast between the frequency modulation and the amplitude modulation, in which the amplitude of the carrier is varied while its frequency remains constant. In analogue applications, the carrier frequency is varied in direct proportion to changes in the amplitude of an input signal. Digital data can be represented by shifting the carrier frequency among a set of discrete values, a technique known as frequency-shift keying. FM is commonly used at VHF radio frequencies for high-fidelity broadcasts of music and speech. Analogue (normal) TV sound is also broadcast using FM. A narrowband form is used for voice communications in commercial and amateur radio settings. The type of FM used in broadcast is generally called wide-FM, or W-FM. In two-way radio, narrowband narrow-fm (N-FM) is used to conserve bandwidth. In addition, it is used to send signals into space. FM is also used at intermediate frequencies by most analogue VCR systems, including VHS, to record the luminance (black and white) portion of the video signal. FM is the only feasible method of recording video to and retrieving video from magnetic tape without extreme distortion, as video signals have a very large range of frequency components- from a few hertz to several megahertz, too wide for equalisers to work with due to electronic noise below -60 dB. FM also keeps the tape at saturation level, and therefore acts as a form of noise reduction, and a simple limiter can mask variations in the playback output, and the FM capture effect removes print-through and pre-echo. A continuous pilot-tone, if added to the signal- as was done on V2000 and many Hi-band formats- can keep mechanical jitter under control and assist time-base correction. It is also used at audio frequencies to synthesise sound. This technique, known as FM synthesis, was popularised by early digital synthesisers and became a standard feature for several generations of personal computer sound cards.

**Frequency Response.** The reaction of an electronic device to signals at various frequencies. Most often used in measuring the quality of audio gear, the term describes the relationship between the gain or loss and the frequency in a microphone, amplifier or speakers and therefore the fidelity of the signal.

**Fresnel.** Pattern of a special form of condenser lens consisting of series of concentric stepped rings, each ring a section of a convex surface which would, if continued, form a much thicker lens. Used on focusing screens to distribute image brightness evenly over the screen.

**Friction Head.** A low-cost device that supports small TV and film cameras. It features various locks that can be tightened or loosened to curtail or allow camera movement. Friction helps accomplish smoother pans and tilts, but the device does not counterbalance the camera, making such movements somewhat unstable.

**Fringe Time.** On TV the hours before (early fringe time) and after (late fringe time) prime time, this may differ between London and regions due to different home coming from work. In Nigeria, early fringe time may end by 8am and late fringe time may begin by 4pm.

**Front Cover.** First page of magazine or journal, sometimes available for advertising.

**Front-Curtain Sync.** A process where the flash fires an instant after the front curtain of a focal plane shutter has completed its travel across the film plane. This is the way a camera operates with the flash sync mode at Normal Sync. See Rear-Curtain Sync.

**Frontlighting.** Light shining on the side of the subject facing the camera.

**Frontloading.** The practice of placing the bulk of commercials and/or print advertisements at the beginning of an advertising campaign.

**FTE.** Full Time Equivalent; an accounting term that refers to staffing. A full-time employee is one FTE; a two-day-a-week employee is four FTEs. A newsroom may have a budget number of total FTEs that will be comprised of full- and part-time workers.

**Fudge.** (1) Mistake. (2) Part of newspaper printing machine carrying second colour for late news, or announcement on ears of front page. Used editorially to mean the stop press column.

**Fugitive Inks.** Those which fade quickly and are best avoided in poster printing, e.g. light blue, mauve, pale green.

**Fulfilment House.** Firm which receives the response to Mailings, Sales Promotion offers, Direct Response marketing advertisements and dispatches what is offered. Handling house.

**Full Aperture Metering.** TTL metering systems in which the camera simulates the effect of stopping down the lens when the aperture ring is turned, while leaving the diaphragm at full aperture to give full focusing screen brilliance. The metre must be programmed with the actual full aperture, and the diaphragm ring setting.

**Full-barter Syndication.** The practice of exchanging free programming and commercials for commercial time on TV operations. The operators receive programme free but are not allowed to sell any spots within the programme.

**Full-dot Screen.** Halftone screen consisting of whole dots. With digital production, dots may be round or elliptical.

**Full out.** Not indented. The first paragraph at the beginning of a text or following a sub-heading is usually not indented. Subsequent paragraphs are indented, book style. Most legible style for Text matter.

**Full Plate.** Photographic print, approximate size 8 in by 6 in; sometimes known as Whole plate.

**Full-point.** Full stop punctuation mark.

**Full Position.** In newspaper, next matter position or special preferred advertisement.

**Full Run.** One transit advertising car card in every transit bus or car.

**Full Service Agency.** Advertising agency offering clients a wide range of activities and expertise over and above the normal creative and/or media facilities. Such services will include marketing research and planning, merchandising and below-the-line sales promotion, press and or public relations, packaging, etc.

**Full Showing.** The number of outdoor posters that are needed to reach all of the mobile population in a market at least once within a 30-day period (see Gross rating points); also called a 100 showing (see Showing).

**Function.** Basic organisation term referring to grouped activities of an enterprise, e.g. editorial, circulation, production, marketing, finance, etc.

**Functional Analysis.** In relation to mass communication, this mode of early 20th century sociological theory treats the working of mass media as in some sense necessary to the 'normal' operation of any social system (society). The main 'function' attributed to the media is to contribute to social cohesion and integration. In this light, the effects of media can be treated as either functional (positive) or dysfunctional (negative) for individuals, groups or society. The theory has largely been discarded as offering no analytic purchase and being unable to deal adequately with social conflict and change, when 'normality' is itself problematic. Even so, it still provides a general orientation to some larger questions of social process, such as integration and interdependence.

**Functionalist.** Social scientist who focuses on the way in which various social institutions contribute to the stability and harmony of the social system as opposed to examining sources of conflict.

**Funnel Technique.** In communication research, way of interviewing which directs open-ended question more deliberately than in normal Depth Interview.

**FYI.** For your information.

# G

**G.A.** Short for general assignment. A G.A. is a reporter who does not have a beat, but who might be called on to write about anything.

**G-spool.** Duplicate copy of a video commercial sent to TV stations.

**Gable-end.** In outdoor advertising, poster site or hoarding on the end wall of a building. This is mostly done for political posters or initial public offers of banks and other companies.

**Gaffer.** The chief electrician on a motion picture set. It is used in TV only in the production of long-form dramatic programmes such as miniseries. The term may have originated from carnivals in Europe where an individual was in charge of herding or gaffing people into the tent.

**Gaffers' Tape.** A unique and ubiquitous tape used in TV and film production. It is two inches wide and made of vinyl-coated cotton cloth with an adhesive backing of synthetic rubber-based resin. It is available in 12 colours and has a tensile strength of 50 pounds per inch. It is used for everything in a TV studio because of its stubborn strength and versatility.

**Gain.** Amplifying an audio or video signal.

**Galley.** First proofs of typesetting taken prior to the make up of pages.

**Galley Proof.** First proof before typesetting is imposed or pasted down, usually set solid. Originally from the galley tray in which metal type was placed before being spaced and display lines added.

**Galvanometric Response.** Change in skin conductivity due to change in moisture content (perspiration); measured by current flow as indicated on a galvanometer. Such change may have a colleration with psychological stimuli (e.g. fear or other emotion) and arguably may provide a measure of a respondent's reaction to an advertisement.

**Gang Printing.** Running more than one printing job on the same sheet.

**Gatefold.** Page in journal which folds out to make extra page or pages. Can also be applied to sales literature and mailshots.

**Gatekeeper.** Any individual directly involved in the relay or transfer of information from one individual to another through the use of a mass medium. They determine what will be printed, broadcast, produced, or consumed in the mass media.

**Gatekeeper Chain.** Chain of gatekeepers where little interaction can take place and ample opportunities for distortion exist.

**Gatekeeper Group.** A group of gatekeepers among whom there is the opportunity for interaction to take place.

**Gatekeeping.** This is a general term for the role of a gatekeeper, where initial selection and later editorial processing of event reports in news organisations. News media have to decide what 'events' to admit through the 'gates' of the media (manned by gatekeepers) on grounds of their 'newsworthiness' and other criteria. Key questions concern the criteria applied and the systematic bias that has been discerned in the exercise of the role.

**Gathering.** (1) In printing, collecting and collating pages for binding. (2) In journalism, bringing news items together or sourcing for news.

**Gaze Motion.** The effect of eyes in illustrations, and how they direct reader's attention. If eyes look in the wrong direction they can distract the reader.

**Gazetta.** The Italian coin used as an admission price to hear a reader announce the day's news event.

**Gel.** Short form of gelatin, a translucent filter material used with lighting instruments to change the colour, quality or amount of light on a scene in the theatre or in TV or film production. Sometimes called a media, this fade-resistant, cellophane-like material comes in various colours and is mounted in a frame that is attached to the front of the lighting instrument.

**Gender.** Traditionally, this is used primarily to refer to the grammatical categories of "masculine," "feminine," and "neuter," but in recent years the word has become well established in its use to refer to sex-based categories, as in phrases such as gender gap and the politics of gender. This usage is supported by the practice of many anthropologists, who reserve sex for reference to biological categories, while using gender to refer to social or cultural categories.

**Gendered Viewing.** This describes the various perception and ways of seeing between genders in relation to cultural, social and historical backgrounds.

**Gender Signals.** These are signals that represents both males and females in interpersonal conduct and appearance. It labels or places prominence upon the sex of the signaller.

**General Magazine.** A consumer magazine that is not aimed at a special interest audience.

**Generation.** A term alluding to the number of times a videotape has been duplicated from the master tape in the dubbing process. a first generation dub is the copy that was duplicated from the original tape and a second generation tape is one that has been transferred from a first generation copy.

**Generic Brand/Term.** In marketing, applied to brand name which have come to be adopted as the general descriptive term for a product, often as the result of extensive promotion.

**Genlock.** A device that links a computer to a video input/output. It synchronises the video and computer to prevent any picture break-up.

**Genre.** Essentially just a word for any main type or category of media content. It can also apply to certain subcategories of theme or plot in fiction, film, drama, etc. Soap operas and documentaries are examples of programme genres, as well as are children's programming and religious programming. Other programme genres are science fiction, travel, action, adventure, sports, horror, mystery and educational shows. It is useful for analysis because many genres embody certain 'rules of encoding' that can be manipulated by their producers and also certain 'rules of decoding' that allow audiences to develop appropriate expectations and 'read' texts as intended.

**Geodemographic Targeting.** Reaching required target audiences by means of geographic and demographic classification of residential neighbourhoods.

**Geometric Mean.** Term used in advertising schedule building where three elements (cost effectiveness, market penetration, and advertising unit cost) are treated as being entitled to an equal share of the advertising appropriation. By using the technique, selected media are given shares of the appropriate according to the extent to which they provide combinations of the three elements.

**Geostationary.** An orbiting satellite that travels at the same speed in proportion to the earth's rotation and thus appears to remain stationary over one point of the earth. Sometimes called synchronous.

**Geosynchronous Orbit.** An imaginary circle in space that is precisely 22,300 miles above the equator. A satellite in such an orbit revolves around the earth at the same angular velocity as that of the earth's rotation around its axis. Although the satellite is moving nearly 7,000 miles per hour, its centrifugal force nullifies the gravitational force from the earth and thus the satellite appears to be stationary. The satellite is then said to be in geosynchronous or geostationary orbit.

**Gestation Period.** (1) In publishing, the period or time it takes a publication to be printed. (2) In marketing, the length of time which elapses between an initial inquiry for a product and the placing of an order. More often applied to capital goods where it can amount to several years.

**Gesture.** A form of non-verbal communication made with a part of the body, used instead of or in combination with verbal communication. The language of gesture is rich in ways for individuals to express a variety of feelings and thoughts, from contempt and hostility to approval and affection. Most people use gestures and body language in addition to words when they speak; some ethnic groups and languages use them more than others do, and the amount of such gesturing that is considered culturally acceptable varies from one location to the next.

**Get.** A very good, or exclusive interview.

**Get-up.** Packaging which distinguishes and identifies a product by its shape, colour, design, typography and logo.

**GHI.** Guaranteed Home Impressions. A guaranteed number of television or radio advertisement impacts for a given sum of money.

**Ghost.** Secondary images on a TV screen just to the right or left of the main image. Simply shadow on television film.

**Ghost Images.** Bright spots of light, often taking the shape of the aperture, which appear in the camera viewfinder or in the final photograph when a lens is pointed at a bright light like the sun; controllable through the use of multilayer coating of the lens elements.

**Ghost Writer.** One who performs literally work for someone else to take the credit.

**Ghosted View.** Picture providing x-ray view of subject. See ghost images.

**Ghosting.** Providing an inner view of a package or product by cutting away part of the exterior.

**GHz.** Gigahertz. One billion hertz or one billion cycles per second.

**GIF.** Graphics Interchange Format, an image file format usually used for graphics and logos.

**Gift Coupon.** Sales Promotion method of encouraging regular purchases/habit buying by giving coupons with products which can be redeemed for gifts in a catalogue. Used by cigarette companies especially.

**Gimmick.** Idea or object that is novel or highly unusual within the context in which it is used. Lends news value to promotional activity; also helps to establish identity for a product image. Also used in PR.

**Give-away.** A free offer; a broadcast program that offers free gifts as prized. Also inexpensive promotional piece, sometimes merely a leaflet, designed for wide distribution from offices or shops or direct to prospective customers. Mainly used by companies to introduce a new product or to make known their services.

**Give-away Magazines.** Magazines depending entirely on advertising for their revenues and distributed to readers free of charge.

**Glass Painting.** Creation of illusionary background (rather like a back project shot in films) for TV commercials. The view is painted on a glass sheet and the action is shot through the glass.

**Global Advertising.** Possible when a product is universally accepted, e.g. Coca Cola, Kodak film, Procter & Gamble, but impractical when products have to be adapted or re-named to suit foreign markets. Advertisers have to be careful not to assume that a product that is popular in the home market will be accepted similarly overseas. Guinness, for example, have different brews, labels, slogans to suit foreign markets.

**Global Village.** A term which signifies the effect that all the new media have had on the world. The term was coined by P. Wyndham Lewis in his book *America and Cosmic Man* (1948). However, Herbert Marshall McLuhan also wrote about this term in his book *The Gutenberg Galaxy: The Making of Typographic Man* (1962). His book describes how electronic mass media collapse space and time barriers in human communication, enabling people to interact and live on a global scale. In this sense, the globe has been turned into a village by the electronic mass media. Modern technology and instantaneous communications have in effect made national boundaries outmoded and reduced the world to a smaller community where common experiences, ideas and events are shared by everyone irrespective of the location. Today, the global village is mostly used as a metaphor to describe the Internet and World Wide Web. The Internet globalises communication by allowing users from around the world to connect with each other. Similarly, web-connected computers enable people to link their web sites together. This new reality has implications for forming new sociological structures within the context of culture. An example of this phenomenon is The Global Sports Village. Albeit McLuhan refers to it by a toponym, the Global Village is actually a historical period, not a place. It was immediately preceded by what McLuhan calls the "Gutenberg Galaxy", another geographical designation for a chronological period. Though its roots can be traced back to the invention of the "phonetic alphabet" (McLuhan's term for phonemic orthography), the Gutenberg Galaxy, like the Global Village that followed it, was ushered in by a technological innovation, the Gutenberg press. However, the Gutenberg Galaxy phase of

Western Civilisation is being replaced- McLuhan is writing in the early 1960s- by what he calls "electronic interdependence," an era when electronic media replaced the visual culture of the Gutenberg era, producing cognitive shifts and new social organisations based on aural/oral media technologies. One sticking point in McLuhan's argument is his emphasis on the oral/aural nature of electronic media. His thinking is clearly influenced by the technology and culture of the United States in the 1950s: he often makes references and draws analogies to jazz, the radio, the telephone. Critics in the 1960s were quick to point out that the most important new electronic technologies (film, television, computers) were, in fact, predominantly oriented towards the visual. Generally his discourse stress on the importance of awareness of a medium's cognitive affects: If we are not conscious of how technology impacts cognition and society, the global village has the *potential* to become a place where totalitarianism and terror rule. On the other hand, it could create a problem-solving world-wide forum, enabling a new sense of world community.

**Globalisation.** Simply an attempt at one world community that pursues common goals, has common objectives and fights common problems. In mass communication context, it is the overall process whereby the location of production, transmission and reception of media content ceases to be geographically fixed, partly as a result of technology, but also through international media structure and organisation. Many cultural consequences are predicted to follow, especially the delocalising of content and undermining of local cultures. These may be regarded as positive when local cultures are enriched by new impulses and creative hybridisation occurs. More often they are viewed as negative because of threats to cultural identity, autonomy and integrity. The new media are widely thought to be accelerating the process of globalisation.

**Glossary.** A page that defines the technical terms that are contained in a book.

**Glossy.** Misleading term sometimes applied to magazines but true only of minority of up-market titles. In Offset litho printing, glossy inks.

**Glueing.** Direct mail shots can be given novel effect by applying different kinds of glue (remoistenable, self-adhesive, thermoreactive) to various parts of the same sheet of paper.

**Glyphic.** Chiselled style of typeface.

**GM.** An abbreviation for General Manager.

**Goal.** Synonym for objective or aim to be achieved, may be a publication date or otherwise.

**Gobbet.** Brief item of advertisement copy, isolated by white space.

**Gossip.** An unreliant mode of communication travel, though important at times. It is an idle talk, often slanderous, about someone's private or personal matters or even otherwise. While gossip forms one of the oldest and still the most common means of spreading and sharing information, it also has a reputation for the introduction of errors and other variations into the information thus transmitted. The term also carries implications that the news so transmitted usually has a personal or trivial nature.

**Gothic.** Black-letter typeface similar to handwriting, resembling Medieval script.

**GPD.** Gallium Photo Diode. Metering cells for measuring exposure, using gallium arsenide-phosphide, just like SPD or Cds cells.

**Grab.** The freezing and storing of a video image using a computer.

**Graduated Tints.** Treatment resembling airbrush effect which with digital typesetting, can be applied to either individual characters, or to a background.

**Graf.** Paragraph.

**Graffiti.** A type of deliberate application of a media made by humans on any surface, both private and public. It usually takes the form of publicly painted art, drawings or words. When done without a property owner's consent it constitutes vandalism, although in many countries the owner must press charges before it would be considered a crime.

**Grain.** In printing, folded print should flow with grain in direction of fibres in machine-made paper so that the paper is tougher across the grain and easier to fold.  In photojournalism, minute metallic silver deposit, forming in quantity the photographic image. The individual grain is never visible, even in an enlargement, but the random nature of their distribution in the emulsion causes over-lapping, or clumping, which can lead to graininess in the final image. See graininess.

**Graininess.** The sand-like or granular appearance of a negative, print, or slide. Graininess becomes more pronounced with faster film and the degree of enlargement.

**Gramophone.** An antique record player; the sound of the vibrating needle is amplified acoustically.

**Grant Projector.** Studio device for enlarging or reducing layout and artwork by viewing through screen.

**Grapevine.** Information based on rumour. Can be provoked by lack of information, or exploited as a means of leaking information.

**Graph.** A paragraph. Could also mean a statistical presentation. See chart.

**Graphic Characters.** Line, shape and other visual effects produced by computer.

**Graphic Paintbox.** Quantel's method of producing visual effects. Manipulates photographic images, produces four colour film via scanner and provides high-resolution transparencies in any format for scanning or for hard copy proofs.

**Graphics.** Pictures as distinct from lettering or typography.

**Gray Scale.** A chart of 10 steps from pure white to velvet bars of different shades of gray. It is used by engineering, staging and graphics personnel to test and balance the brightness and contrast in the TV image and to ensure that one object will stand out from another.

**Grazing.** The process of changing TV or radio channels rapidly in search of new or different entertainment or information.

**Greeked Text.** Nonsense text used for page layout before placing the real text.

**Greenwashing.** Advertising which exploits environmental issues.

**Grey Card (18% Grey Card).** Tone used as representative of mid-tone of average subject. The standard grey card reflects 18 per cent of the light falling on it.

**Grey Literature.** Published material which is not classed as 'published serials' and not usually held in libraries or catalogued. It usually has no international standard serial number (ISSN), international standard book number (ISBN) or American Coden number.

**Grid Card.** Spot broadcast advertising rates that are set in a matrix format to allow a station to set rates based on current audience ratings and advertiser buying demand; for example:

|   | 60-sec. | 30/20 sec. | 10 sec. |
|---|---------|------------|---------|
| A | £450 | £375 | £255 |
| B | £445 | £372 | £253 |
| C | £440 | £370 | £251 |
| D | £430 | £365 | £250 |

The higher the time, the more expensive. However, it is often wise to go for more time because it usually implies more value for the money paid.

**Grip.** A stagehand on a motion picture set. The term is usually used in TV only in the production of a mini-series. A grip handles most of the non-technical gear (except lighting devices) and sets up and dismantles scenery, operates a crane or dolly, and sets up stands and supports for lighting equipment.

**Gross Audience.** The total number of households or people who are "delivered" or reached by an advertising schedule, without regard to any possible duplication that may occur; also called "total audience." See gross opportunities to see.

**Gross Billing**. The cost of advertising at the highest advertising rate; the total value of an advertising agency's space and time dealings. See billing.

**Gross Impressions**. The total number of persons or the total number of audience impressions delivered by an advertising schedule. See gross audience.

**Gross Opportunities to See.** Number of advertisements or commercials appearing in a series multiplied by cumulative readership or audience.

**Gross Rate.** The highest possible rate for advertising time or space.

**Gross Rating Points (GRPs).** The sum of all rating points for a series of programmes or commercials that are earned in a particular period of time usually in a one-week period. The ratings reflect the total number of households or people tuned into the programmes or spots. They may be counted more than once during the particular time period. Thus, GRPs measure duplicated audiences, in contrast to numbers represented in a cume; in outdoor, a standard audience level upon which some markets' advertising rates are based.

**Gross Reach.** Total number of opportunities for people to see the advertisements contained in a schedule; the sum total of the readership of each publication multiplied by the total number of insertions.

**Gross Revenue.** Income from advertising if all commercials transmitted were cost at maximum rate with less special discounts.

**Grounded Theory.** A theory derived systematically and inductively from qualitative data; more specifically, theory based on a method for deriving categories from a qualitative data set rather than using pre-existing assumptions. See Constant comparative method.

**Groundprint.** Satellite Footprint.

**Group Broadcaster.** An individual company that owns a number of broadcast stations. The common ownership offers economies in purchasing programmes or equipment, sharing staff and other expenses. The BBC, Fox Television Stations Group, NBC Universal Television Group, Warner Group, and the Disney- ABC Television Group, are examples of this group broadcaster. Often other types of broadcast group exist as Sinclair Broadcast Group, Inc. one of the largest and most diversified television broadcasting companies in the USA. It owns and operates programmes or provides sales services to 58 television stations in 36 markets. Among its TV group includes 19 Fox, 18 WB, 10 ABC, 6 UPN, 2 CBS, 1 NBC affiliates and 2 independent stations and it reaches approximately 22% of all U.S television household.

**Group Buy.** The process by which a collection of public television stations temporarily band together to purchase the license to air a specific programme or series of programmes.

**Group Discussion.** Research technique in which a group of people is encouraged to express freely views and opinions on a selected subject. This might relate to the message contained in an advertisement, or any other component of a campaign upon which a viewpoint is sought. Group discussions are frequently used as a means of determining both overt and subconscious attitudes and motivation and discussions may range widely around the topic, a controlling psychologist ensuring that the topic is fully explored. The recorded proceedings are then subjected to further analysis.

**Group Interview.** Structured interview used for testing commercials or aimed at getting representative family views about a product.

**Grub Street.** This refers to the description of any form of literally or journalistic drudgery.

**GSM.** (1) General Sales Manager. A station employee responsible for directing all the sales activity, both national and local. (2) May also mean Global System for Mobile Communications, the most popular standard for mobile phones in the world. GSM service is used by over 2 billion people across more than 210 countries and territories. The ubiquity of the GSM standard makes international roaming very common between mobile phone operators, enabling subscribers to use their phones in many parts of the world. GSM differs significantly from its predecessors in that both signaling and speech channels are Digital call quality, which means that it is considered a second generation (2G) mobile phone system. This fact has also meant that data communication was built into the system from very early on. GSM is an open standard which is currently developed by the 3rd Generation Partnership Project (3GPP).

**Guaranteed Home Impacts, Impressions, Home Ratings.** Basis of selling TV airtime depending on number of homes in which the commercial is likely to be seen.

**Guard-dog Metaphor.** See Watchdog.

**Guide Number (GN).** Used to express the power output of the flash nit. It indicates the power of a flash in relation to ISO film speed. Guide numbers are quoted in either metres or feet. Guide numbers are used to calculate the f/stop for correct exposure as follows: number calculated by multiplying proper flash exposure aperture by the subject distance.

Flash-to-subject distance = $\dfrac{\text{guide number}}{\text{f/stop}}$

f/stop = $\dfrac{\text{guide number}}{\text{flash-to-subject distance}}$

**Guides.** Lines that help you arrange or align elements on a DTP or graphics program. These are invisible to the printer.

**Guiding Question.** In focused and group interviews or discussion groups, a question that enables the interviewer to keep control.

**Guilloche.** Fanciful veined design as used on security documents but which can be applied to make coupons and vouchers look realistic.

**Gum Print.** A mode of photograph printing which was used in the 19th century. It made pictures resemble oil painting.

**Gutter.** Space or margin between pairs of pages, where they may be folded, or white space between columns of type where there is no vertical dividing rule. Also the space between columns of text.

**Gutter Crossing.** Headline that run across centre margins of facing pages as in a double-page spread (not necessarily centre spread).

**Guttman Scale.** Scale that classifies subjects consistently into ranked categories along certain dimension based on their answers to a single, relatively simple series of questions.

# H

**"H" Format.** One of the three selectable Advanced Photo System print formats; identical to the 9:16 aspect ratio used in high-definition television (HDTV); suitable for wider shots than usual, such as groups; produces prints of 3.5 x 6 inches or 4 x 7 inches.

**Hackneyed.** Words or expressions that are banal or overused: like the use of 'nook and cranny' or 'new' in journalism. See Clichés.

**Hairline.** (1) Delicate stroke in a typeface. (2) A 5-point rule.

**Halation.** In photojournalism, the production of 'halos' round bright spots in an image, by light reflecting from the back of the film-base. General film bases are given a light absorbing coat the anti-halation back to prevent this.

**Half Run.** Transit advertising car cards in half the buses or transit cars of a system.

**Half Showing**. A 50 outdoor showing (see Showing).

**Half Title Page.** A page that contains information about a book or material. Usually seen before the title page. It may contain part of the book's title or its full title. Also known as half page, though not seen in every book.

**Half Track.** An audio tape recorder, or recording, that uses one-half the width of the tape for recording an audio signal. The tape can then be reversed and the other half on the tape used during a reverse pass.

**Halftone.** Applicable in all printing processes except photogravure. A continuous tonal effect in an illustration such as a photography or wash drawing, reproduced by imposing a dot screen. It causes an optical illusion of a shade somewhere between the tone of solid ink and the contrasting tone of the background paper. The effect has its limits, and when the dots (or negative spaces) get too small or spaced too far apart, the illusion becomes less pronounced and the brain may start perceiving individual dots again. A halftone, then, is typically an ink reproduction of a continuous-tone picture. The reproduction simulates the illusion of continuous tones by reproducing its many dots at a size not readily noticed by observers. These dots are usually printed at a size just below the visual acuity of an observer looking at the reproduction at a common viewing distance. This optical illusion is important because it compensates for the inability of printing presses and ink to otherwise create a scale of tones in-between the tone of solid ink (typically black) and the tone of un-inked paper (typically white). The process also involves artwork photographed through lined glass, or a screen laid on pictures according to printing process. The latter method is used for litho printing which generally uses finer screens than for letterpress printing. The advantage of this can be seen in modern newspapers in which picture reproduction has greatly improved.

**Halftone Screen Rulings.** Metric in brackets. 50 (20), 55 (22), 60 (24), 65 (26), 75 (30), 80 (32), 85 (34), 100 (40), 120 (48), 133 (54), 150 (60), 175 (70), 200 (80).

**Halo Effect.** (1) In marketing research, bias caused by popularity or prior knowledge of the subject or product surveyed. (2) In advertising, reflected glory which one product gains from another made by the same manufacturer, or by the Corporate Image. (3) In printing, ink build-up at edges of characters and halftone dots.

**Hammock.** A programming scheduling technique by which a weak show is scheduled between two strong ones on a local TV station, network or cable operation. The strategy is utilised to create an audience for a new programme or to build an audience for a show that is faltering in the ratings. The technique relies on an audience flow from the previous programme and usually requires a very strong lead in programme in order to be successful.

**Handbill.** Form of printed advertising delivered personally into the hands of likely prospects.

**Hand Held.** Film shot made without the use of a tripod.

**Hand Signals.** Production information communicated silently by the hands to on-camera talent by a floor director.

**Handle Mount Flash.** Also often referred as bracket flash. It comprises of one arm of the L-shaped bracket that extends under the camera body and uses the camera's tripod socket to mount the camera on the bracket. The vertical arm of the bracket serves as a handle and mounts a flash unit in an accessory shoe often on top of the handle portion. Though there are other methods, flash mounted in a bracket usually requires a separate electrical cord to make the electrical connection between camera body and flash unit.

**Handout.** Inexpensive leaflet for free distribution at exhibitions or for promotional purposes, especially at point-of-sale.

**Hangers.** Lighting accessories formally known as antigravity hangers. They are used to hang lights on a pipe grid above a television studio. The devices are accordion-like mechanisms that are counterbalanced with springs and thus allow the easy raising and lowering of a light to any height. They are most often used to support scoop lights.

**Hanging Indent.** Opening paragraph of text which is set to a wider measure than the following text, perhaps to the width of two columns as in some newspaper reports. With this the first line of each paragraph is set full out and the rest indented.

**Hard-bound.** Case-bound or hardback as distinct from paperback, as in book binding.

**Hard Copy.** Print out of a Prestel frame. Any written, typed or printed out copy (e.g. computer print-out).

**Hard Cover.** The thick and durable cover of a book as against the paper back cover which is flexible and not durable. This is always more expensive than the paperback type.

**Hard Light.** A sharp, focused light which casts harsh shadows.

**Hard News.** Current topical news and general news about people and events, as distinct from business or product news which may be legitimately used by feature writers. Mainly factual, news agencies deal mostly in hard news and it usually appears first in a publication.

**Hard Sell.** Very persuasive advertising. Opposite of quieter soft sell.

**Hardware.** The physical equipment used in computer or data processing.

**Harmonics.** Generally acoustical or electrical frequencies that are multiples of the basic frequency or musical tone. In acoustics and telecommunication, the harmonic of a wave is a component frequency of the signal that is an integer multiple of the fundamental frequency. For a sine wave, it is an integer multiple of the frequency of the wave. For example, if the frequency is f, the harmonics have frequency 2f, 3f, 4f, etc. In musical terms, harmonics are component pitches of a harmonic tone which sound at whole number multiples above, or "within", the named note being played on a musical instrument. Non-integer multiples are called partials or inharmonic overtones. It is the amplitude and placement of harmonics and partials which give different instruments different timbre (despite not usually being detected separately by the untrained human ear), and the separate trajectories of the overtones of two instruments playing in unison is what allows one to perceive them as separate. Bells have more clearly perceptible partials than most instruments.

**Harmony.** Essence of an advertisement or commercial teaching the desired theme or objective.

**Harmony, Law of.** In design, harmonious arrangement of elements of a layout to make a pleasing whole.

**Harry Animation/Edition System.** Full animation system which can be added to the Paintbox computerised graphic system.

**Harsh Mark.** A mark that sometimes appear across from a programme or station in rating books. It indicates that audience numbers were too low to report. The use of the mark does not mean that there was no audience, but instead indicates that it was not large enough to meet minimum reporting standards as defined by the particular research company. The mark used is – or <<.

**Haze Filter.** A filter that removes ultraviolet light and diminishes haze in a scene.

**HDTV; HD (high definition television).** Any one of several systems of television that use more than 1,000 scanning lines and an aspect ratio of 16:9. HDTV broadcast television signals with a higher resolution than traditional formats (NTSC, SECAM, PAL) allow.

Except for early analogue formats in Europe and Japan, HDTV is broadcast digitally, and therefore its introduction sometimes coincides with the introduction of digital television (DTV): this technology was first introduced in the USA during the 1990s, by the Digital HDTV Grand Alliance (grouping together AT&T, General Instrument, MIT, Philips, Sarnoff, Thomson, and Zenith). It is defined as 1080 active lines, 16 : 9 aspect ratio in ITU-R BT.709. However, in the ATSC broadcast standard used in the United States and other countries, any ATSC resolution with 720 or more active lines is considered HDTV.

**Head-end.** The human and hardware combination responsible for originating, controlling and processing signals over the cable system.

**Header.** A section of text/graphics that appears at the top of every page in a document. The header on this page is Head-end.

**Headhunter.** Recruitment agency which specialises in pinpointing very precisely just those few people known to be suitable for a certain vacancy, and then making personal contact to encourage their interest. A procedure which contrasts with the more commonplace method of placing recruitment advertisements which will probably attract more responses but may be missed by the most suitable people for the job.

**Heading.** Title of a report or published matter.

**Headline.** Dominant line of type in printing or abbreviated statement in broadcasting; intended to particularise the essence of a longer, more complex message, to which attention is thus drawn. Abbreviated as head.

**Head Margin.** White space at the top of a page.

**Head Nods.** A very good element of non-verbal communication used to communicate a wide range of messages.

**Head of Household**. The person within a family or household who is responsible for the major purchase decisions; sometimes, a male head and female head of household are considered separately.

**Headliner.** Phototypesetting machine which produces lines of large display type.

**Headphones.** Earphones. Listening device that fits over the head and covers the ears used to listen to audio sources.

**Head-on Position.** An outdoor advertising stand that directly faces the direction of traffic on a highway.

**Hearsay.** See Rumour, Gossip.

**Heat-set.** On some four-colour off-set-litho machines, means of drying each colour by passing print through heat box before printing next colour.

**Heavy-up Advertising.** The practice of scheduling a number of spot announcements during a specific short period of time on a TV or radio. The commercials are run in a concentrated manner during a period when the products being promoted are likely to be used the most, such as umbrella commercials in the rainy season.

**Heavy Viewer.** Television viewer consistently watching for many hours each week.

**Hegemony.** A term introduced by the early 20th century Italian Marxist theorist, Antonio Gramsci, to describe a certain kind of power that arises from all embracing ideological tendencies of mass media to support the established power system and exclude opposition and competing values. In brief it is a kind of dominant consensus that works in a concealed way without direct coercion.

**Heli-blimp.** Advertising balloon, completely customised with painted design, or fitted with interchangeable banners. The Balloon Stable, Bristol.

**Helical-scan Videotape Recording.** A method where the tape wraps itself around a stationary drum containing the rotating recording heads in a helix or spiral manner. The diagonal movement of the tape across the horizontally moving heads creates a slanted track on the tape; thus, the term slant-track, which is often used to describe helical-scan machines. This recording angle enables more information to be recorded on narrow tape. In contrast to segmented recording, one complete video field or frame is recorded with each pass of a video head.

**Hermeneutics.** The theory and methodology of interpretation, especially of scriptural text. It is derived from Ἑρμηνεύς, the Greek word for interpreter. This, in turn, is related to the name of the Greek god Hermes in his role as the interpreter of the messages of the gods. The Greek word thus has the basic meaning of one who makes the meaning clear.

**Herringbone Effect.** A pattern of interference in TV picture. It consists of a stationary row(s) of saw-tooth images that appear in a diagonal or horizontal manner across the screen. The effect is often caused by lack of synchronisation in the signal and in its extreme can all but obliterate the picture.

**Hertz (Hz).** Frequency measurement for broadcasting. Last name of Heinrich Rudolph Hertz, commonly used as abbreviation for 'cycles per second' in referring to electromagnetic waves. One hertz is defined as the reciprocal second ($1 \text{ Hz} = 1 \text{ s}^{-1}$).

**Heuristic.** An adjective used to describe an explanatory method of tackling a problem, in which the solution is discovered by evaluations of the progress made towards the final result, e.g. guided trial and error.

**Hi 8.** Video recording format. See High Band 8mm format.

**Hiatus**. A period during a campaign when an advertiser's schedule is suspended for a time, after which it resumes.

**Hickey.** Defect on printed sheet caused by a speck of dust or other imperfection.

**Hidden Agenda.** A situation where the causal or basic objective of an act of communication is different from that which is stated.

**Hidden Camera.** The placing of a camera in a concealed spot, which often captures the spontaneous and genuine reactions of ordinary people. The unrehearsed bits are often used in commercials and other programmes. They are used intentionally to record blunders as well as to observe everyday occurrences.

**Hidden Decision.** Any decisions taken automatically and without question; for example, killing a news story without any explanation or reason.

**Hidden Offers.** Without calling attention to the offer, something useful or interesting is offered free at the end of an ad that is wholly or largely copy. Response to the offer reveals how much attention to the ad is drawn.

**Hidden Persuaders.** Much misunderstood term sometimes mistakenly applied to PR. Actually refers to motivational research for advertising as described in Vance Packard's 1950's book Hidden Persuaders.

**Highbrow.** An individual of intellectual or erudite tastes. See Elite.

**High Contrast.** A wide range of density in a print or negative.

**High Culture.** Cultural products, such as entertainment, designed to be appreciated only by those of high socioeconomic class and educational level.

**High-density Plastic.** As used for envelops for mailing magazines and catalogues. Thin, strong, lightweight plastic film.

**High Key.** Pale grey tonal values in a photograph, wash drawing, or other picture with continuous tones. In lighting, it is characterised by minimal shadows and a low key-to-fill ratio.

**High-Z.** High impedance.

**Highlights.** Small and very bright part of an image or object. Highlights should generally be pure white, although the term is sometimes used to describe the lightest tonal value in the halftone of a photograph or other continuous tone picture, though, in this case, it may need to contain some detail.

**Hire Purchase Terms.** Under the Advertisements (Hire Purchase) Act, an advertisement for goods offered on hire purchase or credit sale must state: full cash price; total amount of instalments to be paid; length of time covered by each payment; number of instalments required before delivery of goods. Act also has regulations regarding deposit, no deposit and interest rates.

**Hiss.** Audio noise.

**Historical Method.** Way of deciding advertising appropriation by repeating a previous sum with adjustments to meet higher costs.

Hits.

**Hits.** The frequency or number of times a website is keyed into by internet visitors.

**Hitchhiker**. A broadcast advertising announcement at the end of a program that promotes another product from the same advertiser.

**HMI Light.** A type of light and lighting instrument used in both film and TV production when a great deal of illumination is needed. The initials stand for halogen metal iodide, the material that constitutes the light bulb used in the appliance. It uses low power and generates little heat, but creates a great deal of light.

**Hoarding.** (1) Withholding money or publications from circulation for later advantage. (2) Site for poster advertising.

**Hoarding Site.** Parcel of land or a building used for posters.

**Holdover Audience.** Audience inherited from a previous TV/radio show and which provides a ready-made audience for next programme. In Nigeria most producers prefer their programmes to come up before or after the daily network news because of this audience.

**Holism.** Study of cultures or societies as integrated wholes; the belief that studying particular characteristics of social groups as isolated fragments can be misleading.

**Holistic Evaluation.** Evaluation of advertising or marketing campaign as a whole, quite separately from consideration of its constituent parts.

**Hollywood.** A district of Los Angeles long associated with the American film industry. Today much of the movie industry has dispersed into surrounding areas such as Burbank and the Westside, but significant ancillary industries such as editing, effects, props, post-production, and lighting companies have remained in Hollywood.

**Hologram.** Three-dimensional picture as seen on some charge cards. Model made of image which is bathed in laser light to record master from which to produce copies.

**Holography.** Photography process in which laser is used to make a three-dimensional picture by splitting the laser's beam into two.

One beam then illuminates a photographic plate (reference beam), and the second beam is reflected off the subject back on to the place (subject beam). Produces realistic 3D effect.

**Home Page.** The main page of a website.

**Home Terminal.** Receiving set for cable TV transmissions that can be either one-way or two-way.

**Homophily.** This is the tendency of individuals to associate and bond with similar others- to share certain attributes as beliefs, values, educational background, social status, etc.

**Honorific.** Title used to precede a person's name such as Mr, Mrs, Miss, or Ms.

**Hood.** A three-sided box over a headline or sometimes a photograph.

**Hook.** (1) A repetitive musical phrase that helps listeners to identify a song. (2) A surprise ending or opening designed to capture the audience's attention.

**Horizontal Advertising.** Group or co-operative advertising, usually by trade association, to promote the industry or product, e.g. insurance or bricks. No specific firm or brand is advertised.

**Horizontal Cume.** The total number of different people tuned to a broadcast station or network at the same time on different days of the week.

**Horizontal Journal.** Journal aimed at a wide, unspecialised readership with common interests, e.g. a news magazine, compared with vertical journals which appeal to readers with special interests.

**Horizontal Publication.** A business or trade publication directed at a certain managerial level but cutting across several different industries.

**Horizontal Trade Journals.** Journals read by people of similar status, e.g. company accountants, hotel managers or factory managers.

**Horse-race Story.** An approach to news coverage of elections anchored in the metaphor of horse racing, where a political party ahead in the opinion polls is 'winning at a canter' or losing ground to the opposition which is coming up fast on the outside.

**Hosting.** Somewhat dubious system whereby sponsor pays for publication of PR articles. Usually applies to small circulation journals with limited income, which may imply that journal has little influence and sponsor is merely subsidising publisher. PR material should be published on its merits.

**Hot**. (1) Equipment that is on and operating. Hot is usually used in reference to cameras and microphones. (2) A level that is too high.

**Hot-air Balloons.** Aerial medium for advertising and PR purposes. Large and colourful, they attract attention as they travel overhead or feature at events, bearing large brand names and logos.

**Hotline.** A point-to-point communications link in which a call is automatically directed to the pre-selected destination without any additional action by the user when the end instrument goes off-hook.

**Hot Media.** Non-participatory media such as print and radio according to Canadian academic, Marshall McLuhan.

**Hot Metal, Type.** From the days when type was set with molten lead, metal type as produced by Monotype and Linotype machines for Letterpress printing. Mostly replaced by computerised Phototypesetting.

**Hot Shoe.** Usually rests around the pentaprism of the camera while some are designed around the film rewind knob. It has an electrical contact which mates with a contact in the mounting foot of the flash unit. This allows the camera to fire the flash at the proper time without any other electrical connections between flash and camera. This could be the fitting on a camera that holds a small portable flash. It has an electrical contact that aligns with the contact on the flash unit's foot and fires the flash when one hits the shutter release. This direct flash-to-camera contact eliminates the need for a PC cord. Some call it an accessory shoe. Modern flash demand more than just the main electrical contact and often has more dedicated functions such as TTL control, viewfinder ready light etc. and thus, one will find more secondary contacts other than the main.

**Hot Shop.** Creative studio which puts high value on novelty and topicality in the preparation of its advertising copy and designs.

**Hot Spot.** Undesirable concentrations of light on a set or subject matter.

**Hot Switch.** A programme scheduling technique in which there are no station breaks between programmes. Sometimes called a seamless transmission, the strategy is used to try to keep viewers from gazing and to increase audience flow. It results in more commercials within the programmes.

**House Agency.** An advertising agency wholly owned and operated by a large business organisation to which it provides services which are, however, not necessarily exclusive to that organisation. Similarly such that the organisation may additionally or alternatively use the services of independent agencies.

**House Correction.** Proof corrections marked on first proof by the printer before submitting proofs to client.

**Household.** Designation of the single family unit for research survey purposes.

**Households Using Radio (HUR).** See sets in use.

**Households Using Television (HUT).** A term used in broadcast ratings to describe every household using television. Also see sets in use.

**House Lights.** Normal, existing overhead work lights in the studio or theatre.

**House Magazine/Journal.** Periodical published by a company or other organisation for public relations and/or sale promotional purposes. Usually in one of two main forms either purely external for influencing custom, or internal for employee motivation, although the former may be circulated internally or the latter known by those outside the firm's employ. Also known as House organ. Examples are the publication of Nigerian National Petroleum Corporation- *NNPC news*, and that of its subsidiary, PPMC- *Pipeliners*, etc. University of Birmingham's BUZZ, and Society of Authors' THE AUTHOR are also good examples of house magazines/journals. See House Organ.

**House Organ.** A direct mail piece in the form of a newsletter or company magazine that is sent to all members of a certain organisation.

**House Style.** Characteristic and standardised form which is applied throughout a company to such items as letter headings, publications, advertisements, vehicles and packaging. Usually includes a distinctive logotype desire for instant recognition.

**House-to-house Distribution.** Door-to-door Distribution of sale and sales promotion material. Direct advertising.

**How-tos.** Films, programmes and videos of an instructional nature. It is usually in series, but more often are single programmes.

**HTK.** Head(line) to come. It means that the story has been edited and the headline will come later.

**HTML.** Hyper Text Mark-up Language. Basic programming code and mark-up language used for the design and display of web pages with hypertext and other information to be displayed in a web browser. It is used to structure information- denoting certain text as headings, paragraphs, lists and so on- and can be used to describe, to some degree, the appearance and semantics of a document.

**Hub System.** A cable system in which several subheadings are used throughout the distribution network to reach subscribers. Such a system is necessary in large cable operations because of the gradual degradation of the signal carried through the coaxial cables of a cable system. More than one head-end is necessary to serve a larger franchise area. Each of the subordinate centres serves as the hub for some five miles around that head-end.

**Hue Colour.** Name of a colour; for example, red.

**Hum.** An intrusive steady sound or tone caused by electrical problems. Often 60- or 120-cycle hum is heard in audio from AC power.

**Hum Bar.** Visible bar in video caused by introduction of 60-Hz electrical interference.

**Human Interest.** In contrast to *hard news*, a type of news story or format that focuses on personal actions and consequences, employs dramatic, humorous or narrative styles and usually deals with matters close to everyday emotions and experience. In such stories, news value is secondary to an appeal to feelings, emotions or sensations. It is associated with commercialisation and also with tabliodisation.

**Human Rights Watch.** The largest human rights organisation based in the United States, in New York precisely. Helsinki Watch started it in 1978 and their researchers conduct fact-finding investigations into human rights abuses in all regions of the world. HRW then publishes these findings in dozens of books and reports every year, generating extensive coverage in local and international media. This publicity helps to embarrass abusive governments in the eyes of their citizens and the world. HRW also meets with government officials to urge changes in policy and practice - at the United Nations, the European Union, in Washington and in capitals around the world. In extreme circumstances, HRW presses for the withdrawal of military and economic support from governments that egregiously violate the rights of their people. In moments of crisis, HRW provides up-to-the-minute information about conflicts while they are underway. Refugee accounts, which were collected, synthesised and cross-corroborated by their researchers, helped shape the response of the international community to recent wars in Kosovo and Chechnya. Their offices are scattered over the world in Brussels, London, Moscow, Hong Kong, Los Angeles, San Francisco, Tashkent, Toronto, and Washington.

**Hybridisation.** The process whereby new cultural forms are forged out of disparate elements, especially a combination of alien or imported forms and local or traditional cultures. Associated with globalisation- the increasing movement of peoples and culture especially.

**Hyperband.** CATV channels above the basic channels.

**Hypercardioid.** A highly directional mic pickup pattern.

**Hyperfocal Distance.** In photojournalism, distance of the nearest object in a scene that is acceptably sharp when the lens is focused on infinity.

**Hypermedia.** A theoretical, futuristic, electronic system that will manage the storage and retrieval of all human knowledge and make it available to every person on the planet in a massive relational data base. This was coined in the late 1980s by Ted Nelson.

**Hyperreal.** Connecting to the increasing number of 'real' life stories, confessional forms and 'real' time cultural forms that are currently available on mainstream television. The hyperreal aims to demonstrate that what passes for 'reality' actually depends upon certain cultural conventions. This process tends to become exaggerated in a media culture whereby programme makers and advertisers have to compete with increasing levels of competition, and where a great deal of faith is still invested in ideas of the authentic.

**Hyphenation.** Programming of computerised typesetting to break words correctly at line ends using a hyphen (-). This is useful for fitting more words on a page.

**Hyphenless Justification.** Justification of lines of type without breaking words, which can produce gaps between words. This can look bad in narrow measures, columns, or ugly condensed settings.

**Hyping.** A short-term practice of scheduling high quality or unusual programmes during a sweeps period to influence the ratings. Hyping is designed to temporarily inflate the number of viewers of the programmes or stations during the sweeps. Sometimes spelled and pronounced hypoing.

**Hypodermic Needle Theory.** Same as bullet theory. Can also be called mechanistic-stimulus-response theory. the model holds that an intended message is directly received and wholly accepted by the receiver. See Bullet theory.

**Hypothesis.** Statement logically derived from a theory. Experiments are designed to test carefully constructed hypothesis; if done correctly, their findings support, refine, or reject the theory. The term is derived from the ancient Greek, *hypotithenai* meaning "to put under" or "to suppose." A scientific hypothesis must be testable and generally will be based upon previous observations or extensions of scientific theories.

**Hypothesis Testing.** In communication research. Determining the correctness of assuming parameters, usually by sampling techniques.

# I

**IC.** (integrated circuit) A miniaturised electronic circuit consisting of scores of transistors, resistors, capacitors and diodes all in one sealed covering manufactured in the surface of a thin substrate of semiconductor material. Also known as microchip, silicon chip, computer chip or chip.

**ICA.** International Communication Association. The association was formed in 1950 bringing together academicians and other professionals whose interest focused on human communication. It maintains an active membership of more than 3,100 individuals of which some two-thirds are teaching and conducting research in colleges, universities and schools around the world. Other members are in government, the media, communication technology, business law, medicine and other professions. It is a meeting ground for sharing research and useful dialogue about communicational interests. Through its Divisions and Interest Groups, publications, annual conferences and its relations with other associations around the world, ICA promotes the systematic study of communication theories, processes and skills.

**Iceberg Principle.** Psychological concept suggesting human personality is similar in appearance to that of an iceberg, with innage desires hidden deep down under the surface. Advertisers recognise that influencing people to move in any given direction frequently demands an appeal to their less apparent desires.

**Iconic Medium.** A medium such as film, video or television in which images have realism.

**Iconoscope Tube.** An early TV pickup tube invented by Vladimir K. Zworykin. Some 13 inches long with a large electron gun at the rear, it required an enormous amount of light to create an image. He named the tube after the Greek words eikon meaning image and skopein meaning to view.

**Independent Variable.** A variable the value of which is altered, or manipulated, systematically in an experiment to observe whether changes in a dependent variable result.

**Identification (ID).** A spot television commercial eight to ten seconds in length, during a station break; the last two seconds of the visual time may be reserved for showing the station call letters ("station identification"); a ten-second broadcast commercial announcement, sometimes referred to as a "ten." Also establishing common relationship between factors.

**Identity.** Specific characterisation of person, place, etc. by self or others, according to biographical, social, cultural or other features. Communication is a necessary condition for forming and maintaining identity. By the same token, it can weaken or undermine it. Mass communication is only one amongst several contributory factors.

**Ideology.** Generally refers to some organised belief system or set of values that is disseminated or reinforced by communication. While mass media do not typically set out deliberately to propagate ideology, in practice most media content (of all kinds) does so implicitly by selectively emphasising certain values and norms. This is referred to as a 'preferred reading' in the theory of encoding and decoding. Often these reflect the national culture that provides the context of the media system, but also the class position and the outlook of those who own, control and make media.

**Idiolect.** This is the language or speech of one individual at a particular period in life. It is unique to an individual and is manifested by patterns of word selection and grammar, or words, phrases, idioms, or pronunciations distinctive to the individual. Every individual has an idiolect; the grouping of words and phrases is inimitable, rather than an individual using specific words that nobody else uses. An idiolect can easily evolve into an ecolect- a dialect variant specific to a household. See Dialect.

**IDU.** Indoor unit which decodes satellite signals for TV reception.

**Illuminated Poster.** Rear illuminated posters or light boxes displayed in public places such as stores, shopping precincts, hotel lounges, Post Offices, airports, seaports, multi-storey car parks, buses.

**Illustration.** Any pictorial representation, especially when reproduction is in print.

**Image.** (1) In PR, perceived impression of an organisation, its policy, people, products and services, based on knowledge and experience. (2) In printing, printing areas of litho plate. (3) In photography, the two-dimensional reproduction of a subject formed by a lens. When formed on a surface, that is a ground-glass screen, it is a real image; if in space, that is when the screen is removed, it is an aerial image. The image seen through a telescope optical viewfinder, etc. cannot be focused on a surface without the aid of another optical system and is a virtual image.

**Image Advertising/Commercials.** Advertising dealing with issues confronting a particular company or industry. Usually designed to place the sponsor in a favourable light. Commonly used for differentiating brands of parity products.

**Image Master.** Photographic original, or film master, for photosetting fonts of type.

**Image Study.** Form of marketing research useful in PR to determine perceived image of organisation, policy, people, products or services, usually by comparing respondent's view of similar subjects over a range of topics. Semantic differential method of assessment can be used, and results can be demonstrated with sets of graphs which show varying responses, all organisations being compared with one another, the sponsor being one of them.

**Imitation Art.** Printing paper commonly used for printing magazines. It has china clay added to wood pulp. Calendared through hot and cold steel rollers to provide polished surface.

**Immediacy.** The characteristics of quickness of action or occurrence. It is a prime news value in newspaper, radio and television news gathering and presentation. It must be considered when reporting or writing news stories for the media.

**Impact.** The effect advertising has on readers, viewers or listeners. Awareness of advertisement, TV campaign can aim to achieve certain number of impacts per viewer.

**Impact Testing.** Advertisement research to measure impact as in Recall Surveys.

**Impactive.** An advertisement is said to be impactive when it achieves desired response.

**Impact.** Gross impressions, or the total number of exposures to a schedule of radio advertisements. Not a measure of the number of different people exposed to a commercial but the degree to which an advertisement or campaign affects its audience; the amount of space (full-page, half-page, etc.) or of time (60-second, 30-second, etc.) that is purchased, as opposed to reach any frequency measures; also, the use of colour, large type, powerful messages, or other devices that may induce audience reaction (see Unit).

**Impedance.** A unit of electrical resistance. Generally expressed as high impedance (hi-Z) or low impedance (low-Z). The impedance of various pieces of interconnected video and audio equipment must match or else various types of distortion and inefficiency will result.

**Imperialism.** The policy of extending the rule or authority of a nation or empire by territorial acquisition or by the establishment of economic and political hegemony over other nations, thus, acquiring and holding colonies and dependencies. When used in mass communication, imperialism says more of a situation where media materials- news, information or entertainment- from a more powerful or privileged society is imposed on a foreign society, which may not be as advantageous as the sender in gathering these materials. It presents dependency on foreign media by developing societies especially those in the Third world. This is why there exists cultural imperialism. See Cultural imperialism, Dependency theory.

**Implosion.** The eradication of barriers that define separate social spheres. This usually occurs through the impact of media technology. For instance, the idea that in the modern world politics has become entertainment and entertainment has become politics. Thus, it will be difficult to argue that soap operas are not a political phenomenon, as advice is offered on the raising of children, masculinity is problematiced, personal ethics and relations are discussed, and of course they may be watched to avoid more troubling subjects. Further, that politics in the age of spin-doctors, image manipulation and media proliferation will all attempt to construct a certain image, as do products sold in supermarkets. To say they have imploded is to say they are becoming more alike.

**Imposition.** In printing, arrangement of sequence of pages so that 8, 12 or 16 pages may be printed together in order to cut and fold correctly for assembly or binding.

**Imposition Table.** Table on which artwork and filmed typesettings are laid out or imposed for photographing in order to make plates for litho printing or sleeves for photogravure printing.

**Impression.** As in impression cylinder which presses inked plate against paper to produce an impression, that is a piece of print. In offset litho plate cylinder prints on to blanket and impression cylinder holds paper against blanket cylinder to get offset impression. Also, complete run of a piece of print called an impression, hence first impression (or edition) of a book.

**Impression Cover.** Number of insertions it takes to cover the required percentage of population actually seeing the advertisement or commercial.

**Impressions.** The number of time a person is reached by an advertisement.

**Imprint.** Identity of publisher and/or printer stated on piece of print, useful so that printer can prove a legal claim or proof in case of dispute. Usually found at foot of last page. Also known as colophon.

**In Cue.** The recorded words that open a segment of an interview that will be dubbed and used as part of a report.

**In The Can.** Completely finished and ready to be aired.

**In The Mud.** A level that is too low.

**Incident Light.** Light falling on a surface as opposed to the light reflected by it.

**Incorporated Advertising Management Association.** Professional society representing those responsible for advertising, publicity, sales promotion, marketing and public relations of commercial, public and other organisations.

**Increasing product usage within existing markets.** Marketing objective whereby additional sales may be realised by enticing current customers to consume more of a product or service.

**Incredible Concepts.** Unusual ideas used in TV commercials, using strange figures, talking products, animation or computer graphics.

**Indent.** To begin a paragraph with a space, as in book style used in books and newspapers. The first paragraph is usually set full out or not indented. Indention makes print more readable than block paragraph used in business letters. It encourages the eye to read on.

**Independent Production Companies.** Privately owned companies that conceive, develop and produce TV programmes for transmission by cable systems and broadcast networks and for syndication.

**Independent Stations.** TV stations that are not affiliated with or owned by a network.

**Independent Variable.** In communication research. Variable subject to chance or choice factors which has an observed casual effect upon the behaviour of other variables.

**Index.** A systematically arranged information for each item in a book to be traced for easy comparison and how to trace them. In communication research, a numerical scale used, for convenience, to represent a variable that has not been measured directly. For example, grade point average might be used as an index of academic ability, but it is not a direct measure.

**Indexing.** Statistical term describing a method of standardising the base for comparative data in a time series, usually equating the initial measure to 100 and then expressing all other data in exact relation to that base; e.g. the index of wholesale prices in any year by comparison with a base year of 100 might stand at 92 or 108 to indicate a fall or rise of 8% respectively.

**Indicators.** In interpersonal communication the means by which one communicator conveys his/her attitude and response to another-feelings of attraction or rejection, of evaluation or esteem of the other person.

**Indirect Printing.** Process such as Offset-litho in which printing plate does not touch paper.

**Individual Location.** An outdoor location that has room only for one billboard.

**Induction Material.** Material for new recruits to an organisation, such as videocassettes, slide presentations and company literature. Most organisations put information about their operations on CD ROMs.

**Inductive.** Reasoning from the specific to the general; the development of theory based on observations rather than through testing hypotheses. Many descriptive studies are inductive.

**Industrial Advertising.** Advertising conducted by suppliers to industry or trades and not to the consumer public. Uses track and technical press, direct mail, trade exhibitions.

**Industrial Film.** Documentary film or video.

**Industrial Magazines.** Subcategory of business magazines.

**Inference.** The act or process of deriving logical conclusions from premises known or assumed to be true. This reasoning involves drawing conclusions or making logical judgments on the basis of circumstantial evidence and prior conclusions rather than on the basis of direct observation. Clearly in communication we need to be careful to distinguish between statements of fact and statements of inference.

**Inferential Statistics.** Statistical techniques designed to allow the researcher to draw conclusions, to test hypotheses or to estimate population values, based on limited information.

**Infinity.** In photojournalism, this means infinite distance. In practice, a distance so great that any object at that distance will be reproduced sharply if the lens is set at its infinity position, specifically, one focal length from the film.

**Inflection.** The patterns of alteration or modulation in the pitch of a person's voice.

**In-flight Magazines.** Magazines published by airlines and distributed to passengers by means of a pocket on the back of the seat. Copies are also supplied by post. Albarka Air is a good example in Nigeria. KLM and British Airways are examples of international airlines with in-flight magazines.

**In-flight Movie Commercials.** Shown to airline passengers with in-flight movies.

**Infomercials.** A relatively long commercial in the format of a television program. Often masked as adult talk shows or news specials, they are actually 30-minute or one-hour commercials for a particular product or service. The manufacturer buys time from station and provides the programme, which comes complete with a host, studio, audience and endless hyperbole.

**Info-rich, Info-poor.** Signifies levels of information gap. Countries with more information technologies and sophisticated processes, usually the developed nations are info-rich. Info-poor countries are countries with poor information technologies, little or none. They usually lack good information flow and are usually developing countries or countries in the Third World. See Information gaps, Imperialism.

**Informal Leaders.** Leaders of special interests groups, or village leaders in developing countries. May act as innovator.

**Informant.** Person answering or supplying answers to research questions or during a reporter's investigation. The person could be participating in an ethnographic study by providing data in response to the reporter/researchers questions.

**Informant, Interviewee, Respondent.** Person asked questions or to test a product during a survey.

**Information.** In a broad sense the content (messages) of all meaningful communication is information. More narrowly (but still loosely), information usually refers to verifiable and thus reliable factual data about the 'real world'. This includes opinions as well as reports about the facts of the world. Even more narrowly and precisely, information may be equated with communicated 'data' that do (or can) enable discriminations to be made in some domain of reality and thus 'reduce uncertainty' for the receiver.

**Information Gaps.** A phrase used to describe the wide gap or inequality that exist in the distribution of information among different groups in societies. See NWICO.

**Information Society.** A term widely used to describe contemporary society in terms of what is thought to be its most central driving force or source of productive power, namely information of all kinds. The justification for this assumption derives from the seeming dependence of much of modern life, materially as well as culturally, on the production, handling and application of information and on the operation of complex networks of communication. The information and communication technology sector appears to have become the chief source of wealth in more economically advanced societies.

**Information Technology.** The development, installation, and implementation of computer systems and applications. It deals with the use of computers and telecommunications to retrieve, store and/or transmit information. Often called infotech or shortened as IT, it generally combines all processes involved in communication, especially electronic and has been a major feat in the development of mass communications.

**Infotainment.** A television program with a mixture of news and entertainment features, such as interviews, commentaries, and reviews. Also called docutainment, it is generally used to draw audiences in order to increase the programmes popularity with them, the audience.

**Infrared.** Energy near visible light (beyond visible red) used by some types of film and by some autofocus camera devices.

**Inheritance Factor.** The factor whereby a television programme inherits audiences of another programme which preceded it.

**In-home Placement.** In product pre-testing, inviting people to test a product in daily use and making them complete a questionnaire on it.

**In-house.** Work handled within an organisation.

**In-line Amplifier.** Amplifier inserted between two wires that increases the amplitude of a signal.

**Ink-jet Printer.** Computer-controlled printing process in which there is no direct contact between printing head and material being printed. Small droplets of electronically charged ink, as instructed by magnetic tape, are directed from printing head to surface. Used on fast reel-fed printing machines, cheaper than Laser Printing, ideal for addressing. Often used for Direct Mail.

**Inoculation Effect.** In communication theory, the inoculation effect refers to a strategy of prejudicing one's audience against an opposing argument they may hear in the future. For instance, a Catholic priest may warn his audience that 'the devil' will tell them that the use of condoms is acceptable, with the expectation that his audience will be so advised by a government speaker. If a government representative later raises the issue with a member of the priest's audience, the representative is likely to find that audience member has pre-judged the speaker's argument, as the audience member associates such an argument with diabolic influences.

**Innovation.** Introduction of new thoughts, policies, products, markets, distribution, merchandising or other deliberate change. Given that, all things being equal, all products have a life cycle which dictates that, at some point, their usefulness will decline, innovation is an essential ingredient to long-term development of media enterprise and its absence must lead to the decline of the enterprise itself.

**Innovator Theory.** Or dispersion theory. An innovator tries and recommends. Early adopters take up idea, followed by late majority who copy. Finally there are the more reluctant, conservative-minded laggards who eventually become adopters. Useful in PR where a new idea or product depends on this process, and widely applicable in both developed and developing countries.

**In-Pack.** Item, such as free gift, inserted in pack while the product is being packed. A Waddington inserter can place coupons, gifts and other items in packs on packing line.

**In-pack Premium.** Gift offer contained within a pack, as opposed to appearing on the outside of the container, in the media or within the sales outlet.

**In-pro.** In proportion. Instruction for enlarging or reducing photographs for reproduction.

**Input Selector Switch.** A multi-position switch found on many audio control boards that connects any one of several sources to a specific audio channel.

**Inquiry.** The initial request from a prospective buyer or user of information, often following some form of advertising or sales promotion, usually with a particular purchase in mind or consideration.

**Inquiry Test.** Method of testing advertisements or media by comparing the number of inquiries received.

**Insert, Inset.** (1) Information to be inserted into the body of a story. (2) Placing of loose advertisements in publications. Great increase in use of inserts, and publishers with modern plants have machines for placing inserts. Saves postage if material otherwise direct mailed, but inserts are liable to be tipped out and discarded by readers. More successful if insert is of similar size to the page of the publication. Sometimes encountered as 'insert' but this usage is not recommended since 'insert' more usually refers to the insertion of a separate photograph or chart within an overall illustration.

**Insert Envelopes.** Envelopes inserted inside Direct Mail shots, perhaps acting as teasers, containing a special offer, a prize offer, or a gimmick. May be plain or printed. May convert a static advertisement into some thing more active, or may provoke overkill.

**Insert Editing.** As opposed to assembly editing, an editing process that inserts video and audio information over an existing control track.

**Insert Mode.** A video editing approach that uses a tape containing only a control track onto which segments from one or more other tapes are recorded. By not transferring a control track with each edit (as in the case of assembly editing) a more stable picture results.

**Insert Shot.** A close-up shot of something within the basic scene which is used to show features or details. See Shot.

**Insertion Loss.** Loss of signal strength due to connection to a device.

**Insertion Order.** A statement from an advertising agency to a media vehicle that accompanies the advertisement copy and indicates specifications for the advertisement.

**Insertion Weights.** Used for weighing advertising expenditure; means of varying expenditure according to the impression value of alternative publications. It reflects the likelihood of an advertisement being seen.

**Inside.** Not on the front page, as in, "we'll run this story inside."

**Institutional Advertising.** Corporate image or prestige advertising, done by an organisation speaking of its work, views, and problems as a whole, to gain public goodwill and support, rather than to sell a specific product. usually found in business press.

**Institutional Magazines.** A type of business publication directed toward a specific institution.

**Interspersed Aspect Ratio.** A basic requirement of certified photofinishers and certified photofinishing equipment; specifies the three system print formats - C, H and P - that users select during picture-taking and must be available at photofinishing.

**Interchangeable Lens.** Lens designed to be readily attached to and detached from a camera.

**Intrapersonal Communication.** Language use or thought internal to the communicator. It is the active internal involvement of the individual in symbolic processing of messages. The individual becomes his or her own sender and receiver, providing feedback to him or herself in an ongoing internal process. It can be useful to envision intrapersonal communication occurring in the mind of the individual in a model which contains a sender, receiver, and feedback loop. Although successful communication is generally defined as being between two or more individuals, issues concerning the useful nature of communicating with oneself and problems concerning communication with non-sentient entities such as computers have made some argue that this definition is too narrow. Intrapersonal communication however can encompass: day-dreaming; nocturnal dreaming, including and especially lucid dreaming; speaking aloud ("talking to oneself"), reading aloud, repeating what one hears; the additional activities of speaking and hearing (in the third case of hearing again) what one thinks, reads or hears may increase concentration and retention; writing (by hand, or with a wordprocessor, etc.) one's thoughts or observations: the additional activities, on top of thinking, of writing and reading back may again increase self-understanding ("How do I know what I mean until I see what I say?") and concentration. It aids ordering one's thoughts; in addition it produces a record that can be used later again. Copying text to aid memorising also falls in this category; making gestures while thinking: the additional activity, on top of thinking, of body motions, may again increase concentration, assist in problem solving, and assist memory; sense-making e.g. interpreting maps, texts, signs, and symbols; interpreting non-verbal communication e.g. gestures, eye contact; communication between body parts; e.g. 'My tummy is telling me it's time for lunch.' See interpersonal communication.

**Instructional Design.** A process used in schools and colleges as well as in business, health care and government to improve the efficiency and effectiveness of instruction, often with audiovisual communications devices. It is often a collaboration involving a team of teachers and experts in the field who originate or rework training lessons, individual lectures, units, modules and entire courses.

**Instructional Television (ITV).** The TV systems and programmes that are used in a systematic manner in a formal educational environment. The term ITV implies a more specific use of the medium for teaching purposes than the broader and nearly obsolete phrase educational television.

**Instrument.** Tool used for measurement. In social science, this term most commonly refers to a paper-and-pencil tool, such as a questionnaire.

**Insult Signals.** Signals that are generally always insulting, no matter what the context in which it has been made. This however vary substantially between different nationality. Such signals may communicate mockery, disinterest, boredom, superiority, impatience, rejection or contempt.

**Intaglio.** Printing process in which an image is recessed below surface of plate with photogravure and copper engraving.

**Integrated Commercial.** A broadcast advertising message that is delivered as part of the entertainment portion of a program.

**Integration.** (1) Concept of unifying the media, especially the addition of Direct Mail to existing advertising and Sales Promotion campaigns. Critics consider such a single strategic plan and budget as impractical, and that Direct Response Marketing should be regarded as a separate new marketing force. (2) Also this term is used to signify a degree to which communication interconnects members of a social system by interpersonal communication channels.

**Intellectual Property Rights.** Ownership of information. In research, questions about who has the right to examine or analyse data are intellectual property rights issues.

**INTELSAT.** International Telecommunications Satellite (Consortium). Now Intelsat Limited., it is the world's largest commercial satellite communications services provider. On July 18, 2001, it became a private company, 37 years after being formed as International Telecommunications Satellite Organisation (INTELSAT), an intergovernmental consortium owning and managing a constellation of communications satellites (Intelsats) to provide international broadcast services. Ownership and investment in INTELSAT (measured in shares) was distributed among INTELSAT members according to their respective use of services. Investment shares determined each member's percentage of the total contribution needed to finance capital expenditures. The organisation's primary source of revenue came from satellite usage fees which, after deduction of operating costs, was redistributed to INTELSAT members in proportion to their shares as repayment of capital and compensation for use of capital. Satellite services were available to any organisation (both INTELSAT members and non-members), and all users paid the same rates.

**Intensity.** Exceptionally great concentration, power, or force in the media by some news stories that tend to dominate or stifle competing stories. General elections provide useful illustrations of the intensity of media coverage.

**Intensive Interview.** Technique used in communication research to endeavour to formulate a true pattern of human behaviour by a process of continued patient probing into beliefs and desires.

**Interaction.** A mutual, interchanging or reciprocal action and communication, verbal or non verbal, between two or more individuals, or two or more social groups.

**Interaction Effect.** Effect on a dependent variable resulting from the interaction of two or more independent variables.

**Interactive Multimedia.** A sophisticated electronic system through which an individual can retrieve data from various media. Based on a multimedia concept but controlled by the user at a computer workstation, it is also often referred to as interactive video.

**Interactive Television.** A type of TV where the viewers, by use of computer or communications technology, actively participate in the programme.

**Interactive Video.** A video that involves the active participation of individuals in the communication process. it can be as simple as coding frames on a pre-recorded videocassette so the user can fast-forward to any segment. A more sophisticated form is laser videodisc technology that enables random and instantaneous recall of any segment or frame on the disc.

**Interactivity.** The capacity for reciprocal, two-way communication attributable to a communication medium or relationship. Interactivity allows for mutual adjustment, co-orientation, finer control and greater efficiency in most communication relationships and processes. The single most defining feature of 'new media' is their degree of interactivity, made increasingly possible by digitalisation.

**Intercoder Reliability.** Measure of the extent to which two or more coders agree on the classification of material into categories for research purposes. In media research, these measures are most commonly used in content analysis.

**Interconnects.** Regional organisations that sell commercial time for a number of systems in a geographic area.

**Intercultural Communication.** Communication between cultures or subcultures; the study of the problems that arise in communication among different people of different cultural or ethnic backgrounds.

**Interfacing.** Getting one computer to talk to another as when a text generated on one computer cannot automatically be read by another. The author or client's floppy disk will not drive the printer's laser typesetting computer until it has been interfaced through the printer's multi-disk reader. This is because different disks have different directions, may slow down or speed up as they spin, or be single-sided, double-sided, hard-sectored or soft-sectored, and they may store data in their own peculiar ways. Also, the author may use a particular software package, many of which have non-standard control codes.

**Interlaced.** The scanning process which combines the odd and even fields to produce a full video frame.

**Interleaves.** Sheets of paper, often flimsy, inserted between printed sheets to prevent set-off from wet ink. Also, placing of paper of a different kind between text pages, especially to print pictures on a better class of paper as is done in biographies and autobiographies.

**Intermedia Comparisons.** Comparing one medium against another or others according to cost, characteristics of the audience, and the atmosphere of the audience.

**Internalisation.** The cognitive process of acquiring skill or knowledge, thus Learning values or attitudes, etc. that is incorporated within oneself.

**International Broadcasting Trust.** Established twenty years ago as an independent television production company, it specialises in making programmes on development, the environment and human rights. Since its establishment, it had made over 200 programmes for all the major UK broadcasters, including mainstream documentaries and drama, and others specifically targeted at schools and young people. IBT is also an educational charity, set up by a consortium of seventy aid and development agencies, educational bodies, churches and trades unions, as a unique partnership between non-governmental organisations and broadcasters, educationalists and film makers. It has produced a range of support materials to accompany their programmes to highlight the issues they raise. Many of its mainstream programmes have been adapted for subsequent educational use. Materials to accompany programmes include action packs, study guides and websites. In 2001, IBT ceased making programmes in house and began to collaborate in programme development and production with other independent production companies and broadcasters. Its main areas of interests is- dialogue with all the main public service broadcasters; development of a slate of innovative and wide ranging programme ideas on international issues; conducting television monitoring research covering both news and non news factual international programming; and lobbying government, regulators and broadcasters to provide high quality and imaginative international programming.

**International Communication.** The exchange of meanings across national frontiers and between two or more countries; the study of the problems that arise in communication of this type and of the variations in media systems and philosophies that exist among contemporary human societies.

**International Federation of Journalists, IFJ.** This is the world's largest organisation of journalists. First established in 1926, it was re-launched in 1946 and again, in its present form, in 1952. Today the Federation represents around 500,000 members in more than 100 countries. It promotes international action to defend press freedom and social justice through strong, free and independent trade unions of journalists and does not subscribe to any given political viewpoint, but promotes human rights, democracy and pluralism. It is opposed to discrimination of all kinds and condemns the use of media as propaganda or to promote intolerance and conflict. IFJ believes in freedom of political and cultural expression and defends trade union and other basic human rights. It speaks for journalists within the United Nations system and within the international trade union movement and supports journalists and their unions whenever they are fighting for their industrial and professional rights. It has established an International Safety Fund to provide humanitarian aid for journalists in need. Its policy is however decided by the Congress which meets every three years and work is carried out by the Secretariat based in Brussels under the direction of an elected Executive Committee.

**International Programme for the Development of Communication, IPDC.** The only multilateral forum in the UN system designed to mobilise the international community to discuss and promote media development in developing countries. The Programme not only provides support for media projects but also seeks an accord to secure a healthy environment for the growth of free and pluralistic media in developing countries. The efforts of the IPDC have had an important impact on a broad range of fields covering, among others, the promotion of media independence and pluralism, development of community media, radio and television organisations, modernisation of national and regional news agencies, and training of media professionals. It has mobilised some US$ 90 million for over 1000 projects in 139 developing countries and countries in transition.

**Internet.** Referred to the worldwide system of interconnected networks, using the telecommunications infrastructure that now supports a large number of types of computer-based communication exchanges, including consultation of databases, websites and home pages, conversational interactions, email, many kinds of electronic commerce and financial transactions. The Internet is gradually taking over many functions of 'traditional' mass media (e.g. advertising, news and information). Access to the Internet is still restricted by costs to the user, plus barriers of language, culture and computer literacy, this is noticed especially in developing or Third World countries.

**Interpersonal Communication.** Communication between two or more persons. This kind of communication is subdivided into dyadic communication, public communication, and small-group communication.

**Interpolation.** In communication research, mathematical term referring to the technique of judging a value of values between known value points. More generally, it may be used to describe the process of drawing conclusions from known data.

**Interpretive.** Research, usually qualitative, in which the reactions and interpretations of the researcher are seen as an integral part of the methodological approach rather than as a source of distortion.

**Intertextuality.** This refers to the tendency for different media texts to refer to each other at different levels and across genres and also the process by which 'readers' make meaningful connections across formal boundaries of texts and genres. The connections extend from media texts to material objects of consumption by the way of branding and merchandising. Advertising makes much deliberate use of intertextual connections. Conversational texts of media audiences extend the influence of the original texts into everyday life and language.

**Intertype.** A type composing machine which sets solid lines of type according to the measure fixed by the operator.

**Intervening Variable.** Variable believed to mediate, change, or control the influence of an independent variable (IV) on a dependent one (DV). For example, perhaps income of parents (IV) influences educational achievement, which in term influences income (DV).

**Intervention.** Mainly describes the policy and practice of governments to intervene in a situation so as to alter or hinder an action, development or control the nature of information flow.

**Interview.** (1) Contact between parties, either face-to-face or through a communications medium, e.g. telephonic or postal means. (2) Communication research interviewer obtaining information. (3) Salesmen giving information and obtaining data as basis for a sales transaction. This usually involves a situation where a person is asked about views, activities; as by a reporter on a radio or a published account.

**Interview Schedule.** List of questions for use in a semi-structured depth interview. Unlike survey questions that are to be asked in the same order in the same way of each respondent, an interview schedule (or interview guide) is flexible.

**Interviewer.** Person who conducts an interview. Should be capable of restraining bias. Part-time interviewers trained for the task, conduct much fieldwork. They should carry a card identifying the organisation responsible for the quest. A researcher in this sense may as well carry an introductory letter to identify himself/herself and maybe, the purpose of his interview.

**In-theatre Research.** Used to pre-test TV commercials and also posters. The audience is assembled in a theatre or hall and shown the advertisements. They may be asked which product they would prefer as a gift, or would buy, both before and after being shown a TV commercial.

**In-the-can Films.** Movies that have already been seen in movie theatres but whose income is assured through releases and release to television.

**Intimisation.** Manner of dealing with information, especially news, and focusing on human interest; presented in a manner which is intimate and personal.

**Intramedia Comparisons.** Comparing publications or channels one against another or others within the same medium.

**Intranet.** A private computer network inside an organisation or institution for internal use only. Most universities in UK have intranets for staff and students.

**Intransient.** Applies to message transmitted and capable of retention, such as those within newspaper or magazines. Television and/or radio messages are transient, i.e. transitory, and, although the meaning or content of the communication may be retained, it will be a matter of memory or notation rather than sight of the original message. This distinction may possibly become absolute with the spread of techniques of audio/video recording.

**Intrapersonal Communication.** Communication within a person, usually known to him alone.

**Invasion of Privacy.** The law of privacy which limits the mass media to operate in their efforts to gather information without infringing upon the privacy rights of others.

**Inventory.** (1) In advertising, the total amount of commercial time spots that are available for sale by a media. They keep running account of their inventory, in order to accommodate advertisers or advertising agencies that seek availability for the time periods. (2) In broadcasting, the amount of programming that has been prepared or licensed but not yet broadcast. Stations buy film packages and syndicated programmes for transmission over a period of time, and the motion pictures or programme titles that have not yet been broadcast are said to be the inventory. (3) In home video and consumer electronics, the total number of pre-recorded videocassettes machines that are in stock in a retail store at any given time. The retailer must keep a reasonable amount of inventory to be able to serve customers.

**Inverted Pyramid.** The structure of a news story which places the important facts at the beginning and less important facts and details at the end, enabling the editor to cut bottom portion of the story if space is required.

**Inverted Telephoto Lens.** Lens constructed so that the back focus (distance from rear of lens to film) is greater than the focal length of the lens. This construction allows room for mirror movement when short focus lenses are fitted to SLR cameras.

**Investigative Reporting.** Reporting that requires a careful search to uncover facts and determine the truth.

**Invisibility.** That is, invisible to the public as represented by the media. In this sense certain things are dodged and not looked at when writing or reporting an event. Such thing may be the colour of an individual or even the physical ability.

**Ionosphere.** Upper level of the atmosphere that reflects radio waves (normally below 30 mHz-ie, the AM band but not the FM band) back to earth.

**IPS.** (inches per second) Generally refers to tape speed or tape writing speed.

**Iris.** Strictly, iris diaphragm. An adjustable circular opening that controls the amount of light entering a TV, film or still camera lens. the device consist of thin overlapping metal leaves pivoting outwards to form a circular opening of variable size to control this light transmission through the lens. Made of metal or plastic, the iris is adjusted by a ring located on the barrel of the lens. When the ring is rotated, interlaced flaps are closed or opened in varying degrees, permitting different amounts of light to enter the camera through the lens. The size of the iris opening is measured in F-stops.

**ISBN.** International Standard Book Number. A unique number given to a book for identification like that on this book. The ISBN system was created in the United Kingdom in 1966 by the booksellers and stationers W H Smith and originally called Standard Book Numbering or SBN (still used in 1974). It was adopted as international standard ISO 2108 in 1970. From 1 January 2007, ISBNs will be 13 digits long. The number is either 10 or 13 digits long, and consists of four or five parts: if 13-digit ISBN, a GS1 Prefix, either 978 or 979, the country of origin or language code, the publisher, the item number, and a checksum character. See ISSN.

**ISDN.** Integrated Systems Digital Network. A digital telephone exchange line which enables the user to send and receive large volumes of information in a variety of forms. These include voice, data, images and video.

**ISSN.** International Standard Serial Number. A unique eight-digit number given to a publication that is published periodically, like newspapers and magazine, for identification purposes. It was adopted as international standard ISO 3297 in 1975 and the format of the ISSN is an eight digit number, divided by a hyphen into two four digit numbers. The last digit, which may be 0-9 or an X, is a check digit. See ISBN.

**Island Position.** Advertisement surrounded entirely by editorial or margin. A print advertisement that is not adjacent to any other advertising; a broadcast commercial that is scheduled away from any other commercial, with program content before and after; often at premium advertising rates. Also known as solus position.

**Island Sites.** Press advertisement surrounded on at least three sides by editorial. Exhibition site with aisles on all sides.

**ISO Speed.** The international standard for representing film sensitivity. The emulsion speed (sensitivity) of the film as determined by the standards of the International Standards Organisation. In these standards, both arithmetic (ASA) and logarithmic (DIN) speed values are expressed in a single ISO term. For example, a film with a speed of ISO 100/21° would have a speed of ASA 100 or 21 DIN. The higher the number, the greater the sensitivity, and vice versa. A film speed of ISO 200 is twice as sensitive as ISO 100, and half that of ISO 400 film.

**Isolated 30**. A 30-second broadcast commercial that runs by itself and not in combination with any other announcement; usually found only on network television.

**Isolated Camera.** A camera that is separate from the others covering an event, which concentrates on a single individual or specific action within the event. Called an iso, the segregated camera is often attached to its own videotape machine. The technique has become standard for most sports coverage and has also been used in documentaries and occasionally on news programmes.

**ISP.** Internet Service Provider. See Access provider.

**Issues.** Situation or event that is thought about. It may be social, cultural, political or economical concerns, or ideas, which are at any given time considered important and which are the source of debate, conflict or controversy. The Clinton/Lewinsky issue and the September 11 terrorist attack in the US were big issues.

**Issue Advertising.** Or advocacy advertising which presents an organisation's point of view on current issues such as the environment or government policy.

**Issue Life.** Period between publication dates. A publication's life is said to have terminated once a subsequent issue of the same name has been released. Refers specifically to newspaper and magazine advertising of course, their text matter may be retained or subsequently consulted.

**Issue Readership (Average).** Number of readers, on average, who read a publication.

**Italic.** Typeface which slopes to the right. Invented by Italian printer, Aldus Manutius, 15th century.

**ITU.** International Telecommunication Union. An international organisation established to standardise and regulate international radio and telecommunications. It was founded as the *International Telegraph Union* in Paris in May 17, 1865, and is today the world's oldest international organisation. Its main tasks include standardisation, allocation of the radio spectrum, and organising interconnection arrangements between different countries to allow international phone calls—in which regard it performs for telecommunications a similar function to what the Universal Postal Union (UPU) performs for postal services. It is one of the specialised agencies of the United Nations, and has its headquarters in Geneva, Switzerland, next to the main United Nations campus.

**ITV.** Instructional television, programming, specifically designed for direct or supplemental teaching.

**Iwe Irohin.** Believed to be the first newspaper in Nigeria published in Abeokuta and founded by an Anglican missionary, Reverend Henry Townsend.

**IX Information Exchange.** The ability of Advanced Photo System film to communicate with devices, and devices to communicate with film. This can be accomplished optically or magnetically using a thin magnetic layer on the film that records digital data.

# J

**J-Curve.** Economicllay this shows the shape of the trend of a country's trade balance following a devaluation. However, in media terms it represents the relationship between the overall extent of awareness people have of such an event and the proportion of those learning of it through interpersonal sources.

**Jack.** A female electrical connection typically a phone-plug receptacle. Or a brace for scenery.

**Jargon.** The specialised or technical language- speech or writing of a trade, profession, or similar group. It is usually an unusual or pretentious vocabulary, with convoluted phrasing, and vague meaning. Some word when used are only known or understood by a certain group or profession, say journalists.

**Jiffy-bags.** Lightweight protecting envelopes, padded or with bubbled – cushioning.

**Jingle.** Short catchy tune to which the advertising message of a television, radio, or cinema commercial is sung. Not necessarily an original tune since often different words are sung to an already familiar tune.

**Jingoism.** Extreme nationalism characterised especially by a belligerent foreign policy; chauvinistic patriotism.

**Jitter.** A technical aberration in a jerky unstable jumping of the image. The rapid unsteady effect is often caused by improper synchronisation in the playback of a videotape recording.

**Job Press.** Platen printing press used for small jobs such as business cards.

**Job Sheet.** Sheet bearing job number, client code and job title on which PR consultants records orders and expenditures in order to bill client for work done. Similar to that used by printer to record all details and progress of a print job. This is basically a means of controlling work and charging out.

**Jog.** The slow, frame-by-frame viewing of a videotape, generally to make edit decisions.

**Journalese.** The style of writing often held to be characteristic of newspapers and magazines, distinguished by clichés, sensationalism, and triteness of thought.

**Journalist.** Someone who works in the news gathering business, such as in a mass media. This person is involved in the gathering and dissemination of information about current events, trends, issues and people. Reporters are one type of journalist. They create reports as a profession for broadcast or publication in mass media such as newspapers, television, radio, magazines, documentary film, and the Internet. Reporters find the sources for their work, their reports can be either spoken or written, and they are generally expected to report in the most objective and unbiased way to serve the public good. Depending on the context, the term also includes various types of editors and visual journalists, such as photographers, graphic artists, and page designers. See journalism.

**Journalism.** Literally, this refers to the product or the work of professional 'news-people'. The discipline involves collecting, analysing, verifying, and presenting information regarding current events, trends, issues and people. As a product it typically means informational reports of recent or current events of interest to the public. In this sense, journalism is another word for 'news', with its many typical and familiar features, especially the aim of being up to date, relevant, credible and interesting to a chosen audience. As a work process, journalism has mixed connotations, reflecting uncertainty about the status of the profession. There are several styles and schools of journalism differentiated by purpose and audience and also by national media cultures. See journalist.

**Journals.** Publications, usually scholarly, published at certain intervals, bi-weekly, monthly, quarterly or yearly. Very prominent journals include *Journal of Black Studies*, *European Journal of International Law*, *International Journal of Human Rights*, *Journal of Mass Communication Research*, *Global Media Journal*, *Journalism and Mass Communication Quarterly*, *Journal of Advertising Research* and many others. Journals could also be a record of events, thoughts or personal experiences, or even a day to day record of business transactions.

**Journo.** Short for journalist or journalism.

**Joystick.** A hand-operated control which can be moved in any of four directions (sometimes even vertically) to control various computer operations.

**JPEG.** Joint Photographic Expert Group. An image file format often used for photographic images.

**Judgment Sample.** Group selected without use of statistical methods in order to obtain its views and ideas. Usually comprise the more important figures in a particular sector. This is a major constituent of the Delph method of forecasting.

**Jumbo Pack.** Sales Promotion device, a number of associated brands such as individual packs of breakfast cereals or ban of chocolate are packed together. Often used at Christmas. Also, very large economy packs, jars and bottles for detergents or drinks.

**Jumbotron.** A giant presentation TV unit that measures 23-1/2 feet by 32 feet and is used for outdoor display.

**Jump.** The part of a story that continues on another page. Also called a break. The readers get directions from jump lines.

**Jump Cut.** An undesirable cut in TV or film production that occurs when a director or editor makes an abrupt transition from one camera angle or scene to a similar one for no apparent reason. A jump cut is also created by an extreme change between shots. In both cases the effect is to make it look like the picture has jumped from one shot to another.

**Jump Line.** Line of type at the bottom of a column which directs the reader to somewhere else in the paper where the story is completed, allowing more space for stories to begin on the front page.

**Junior Unit.** In press advertising, a standard page size advertisement that can be enlarged or reduced to fit different journals, or can be reproduced at the same size with or without next matter. If based on smallest size, the advertisement will not suffer from reduction

Junkets.

> making small type difficult to read. similarly, using a Reader's Digest-size advertising page in a larger magazine is usually called a "Digest unit."

**Junkets.** Excursions for journalists, compliments of someone seeking news coverage of an event.

**Junk Mail.** Unsolicited but especially badly targeted, duplicated, wrongly addressed and generally careless Direct Mail. Whether or not it is junk mail will depend on the response of the recipient. But sometimes applied to all direct mail as 'advertising which masquerades as personal post'.

**Justification.** Spacing out type matter to fill lines of equal length. More legible than if there is a free right hand edge.

**Justify.** To adjust the position of words on a printed pass so that the left or the right hand margin is regular.

**Juxtaposition.** Unfortunate placing of rival advertisements next to one another. Also generally, the act of putting together things close together or side by side.

# K

**K 14.** Kodak's chemical process for developing Kodachrome slides.

**K & N Absorbency.** Way of testing ink absorbency of various papers.

**Kaolin.** Fine clay used in making papers such as Imitation Art.

**Keen Price.** Low price.

**Keeper Gift.** Gift made to encourage a request for information about an advertised product or service, or for a trial or sample. The enquirer is allowed to keep the gift, whether or not sale results.

**Kelvin (K).** A unit of measurement used in photography and broadcast to calibrate the colour temperature of a light source. It is sometimes referred to as degrees Kelvin or °K or simply K. in Kelvin temperature scale, 0° K is equal to – 273.15° C.

**Kenaf.** Tropical plant which offers cheap alternative to word for making paper.

**Kern.** In a typographical character, extension beyond body such as tail of a 'Y'. This could mean moving characters closer to give a tighter appearance.

**Kern Pairs.** Pairs of letters (such as 'Wa') that need to be kerned to prevent unsightly gaps between the two letters.

**Kerning.** The adjustment of horizontal space between individual characters in a line of text. Adjustments in kerning are especially important in large display and headline text lines. Without kerning adjustments, many letter combinations can look awkward. The objective of kerning is to create visually equal spaces between all letters so that the eye can move smoothly along the text. Kerning may be applied automatically by the desktop publishing program based on tables of values. Some programs also allow manual kerning to make fine adjustments.

**Kettle Stitches.** Stitches that sew together signatures of a book.

**Key.** Device which enables advertiser to identify source of enquiry as when a coupon has an unobtrusive key printed in the corner. Keys can be included in the address. A different person's name can be used in each journal, or there can be a variation in the address such as 11a, 11b, 11c. By means of keys it is possible to calculate the cost per reply by dividing the cost of the space by the number of enquires. Similarly, cost per conversion to sales can be calculated.

**Key Factors.** Essential elements of a given PR or other situation, i.e. those factors which are crucial to achieving a specified goal.

**Key Forme.** In colour printing, the plate which is used first.

**Key Lighting.** A TV and film lighting technique that directs light onto a performer, object or scene from the top and side. Key lights are highly directional and are the primary and most concentrated lights used to highlight the subject in a dramatic way by creating shadows, often with the aid of barn doors. Along with fill lighting, background lighting and backlighting, key lighting is one of the four basic illumination techniques in film and TV production. It establishes the form, dimension and overall appearance of a subject.

**Key Size.** Unit of type measurement in phototypesetting.

**Key Source.** A video source keyed into background video.

**Keyed Advertisement.** Advertisement designed to cause an enquirer to indicate the source of his information, for instance by including a code number or a particular 'department' within the return address.

**Keyline, Key Drawing.** Outline used for positioning artwork in a piece of print.

**Keystone.** An undesirable visual effect created when a camera is not positioned precisely perpendicular to the plane of a television graphic. It is the result of a camera shot that is just off-centre or at an angle from the artwork, with the result that the near side of the graphic appears somewhat larger than the far side. Keystoning is most noticeable with lettering. When the camera is not at the correct angle in relationship to the letter card, the lettering appears distorted. The term is derived from the trapezoidal or keystone geometric shape.

**Keystroke.** Depression of a keyboard key as with direct input in a computerised newsroom, or with computerised phototypesetting.

**KHz.** Kilohertz. 1000 hertz or 1000 cycles per second. See Hertz.

**Kicker.** The lead of a story, a short line set in smaller type than the headline and larger than the body text of the story. Was invented by Arthur Christiansen of London's Daily Express for the type of story which may not be the day's most important but which will make the biggest talking point. Similar to panels but longer and more leisurely or more sensational. Also a light typically placed between the backlight and the fill lights. Sometimes used to simulate the light from a window behind a subject.

**Kid Fringe.** A daypart in a broadcast station that is generally considered the period between 3.00pm and 5.00pm Monday through Friday. Although this period varies from station to station, the time slot is most often filled with children's shows and cartoons on independent stations. It immediately precedes the early fringe period.

**Kill.** Deleted unwanted typesettings or story.

**Kill Fee.** A bargain fee paid to a journalist for an unused story.

**Kilobyte.** (K or kB) A unit of information or computer storage equal to either 1024 or 1000 bytes. It is commonly abbreviated KB, kB, Kbyte, kbyte, or, very informally, K or k. The term was first used to refer to a value of 1024 bytes ($2^{10}$), because the binary nature of digital computers lends itself to quantities that are powers of two, and $2^{10}$ is roughly one thousand. As computers became more widely used, this misuse (according to the BIPM) of the SI prefix spread from the slang of computer professionals into the mainstream lexicon, creating much confusion.

**Kineme.** A segment or fraction of a whole communicative gesture; a kinetic parallel to a phoneme.

**Kinescope Recording.** The first method of preserving a TV programme on film. Introduced in 1947, the technique used a 16mm film camera to record images and sound from a cathode ray picture tube. The camera was synchronised with the television image and focused on an especially bright monitor. A programme was usually recorded from beginning to end and the negative was developed as a regular film processing. The resulting product was called kine. It was often grainy, of poor contrast and inferior to regular film quality.

**Kinescope Tube.** Invented by Vladimir K. Zworykin in 1925, this tube made electronic television possible. This is a cathode ray vacuum tube that operates by shooting a beam of electrons onto the interior of the face of the tube, which is coated with phosphorescence. When the electrons hit the face of the tube, the phosphorescence glows. The kinescope tube converts the video signal from the pickup tube to an identical pattern on its face.

**Kinesics.** The study of non-linguistic bodily movements, such as gestures and facial expressions, as a systematic mode of communication.

**Kinetoscope.** Forerunner of the motion picture developed by Thomas Edison, it was a crude device with a peephole through which a viewer could see pictures move.

**Kiss Impression.** Very light printing impression.

**Klischograph Hard-dot Gravure.** Advance on traditional recessed Photogravure where the plate has surface areas of various sizes to give depths of tone instead of cells of various depths.

**Knocking Copy.** Advertisement copy which deliberately exposes competitive products to adverse comparison(s).

**Knowledge Gaps.** A term coined to refer to the structured differences in information levels between groups in society. The original promise of mass communication was that it would help to close the gaps between the 'information-rich' and 'information-poor'. The concept has stimulated research to investigate how far this has happened and what types of media use and other conditions are associated with such an 'effect' (or its reversal). The dominant outcome has been that newspapers have been better at closing gaps than television. Current expectations are that new media are more likely to widen than to close gaps because of their differential availability to the already better informed.

**Kodak Still-picture Process.** A hybrid technique of traditional and electronic photography from Kodak Company. It uses the traditional photographic method but also permits pictures to be manipulated and viewed electronically.

**Kodatrace.** Clean film overlay placed on artwork, with extra instructions to printer.

**KpH.** Body height of a typeface.

**Kraft Board.** Paperboard noted for its strength and water resistant characteristics, manufactured from bleached or unbleached sulphite wood pulp. Main use is in packaging.

**Kraft Paper.** Paper, usually brown, and noted for its strength. Much used in packaging.

**Kroy Lettering Centre.** Desktop microcomputer with 'qwerty' keyboard, capable of producing thousands of different character sizes and style variations.

**Ku-band Satellites.** Communication satellites that contain transponders on frequencies in the KU-band from 11.7 to 12.2 gigahertz. Signals of these high frequencies can be received by relatively small television receive only dishes, thus making Direct Broadcast Satellite services possible. Its transmission is sensitive to atmospheric changes.

**Kuleshov Effect.** A cinematic montage effect demonstrated by Russian filmmaker Lev Kuleshov in about 1918. He edited a short film in which shots of the face of Ivan Mozzhukhin were alternated with various other shots (a plate of soup, a girl, a child's coffin). The film was shown to an audience who believed that the expression on Mozzhukhin's face was different each time he appeared, depending on whether he was `looking at' the plate of soup, the girl, or the child's coffin, showing an expression of hunger, desire or grief respectively. As a matter of fact the footage of Mozzhukhin was identical, and rather expressionless, every time it appeared. Kuleshov used the experiment to indicate the usefulness and effectiveness of film editing. The implication is that viewers brought their own emotional reactions to this sequence of images, and then moreover attributed those reactions to the actor, investing his impassive face with their own feelings. See Kuleshov, Lev Vladimirovich.

Kuleshov, Lev Vladimirovich.

**Kuleshov, Lev Vladimirovich.** (1899-1970) A Russian filmmaker known for his work on film editing and the impact it has on the viewers. The Kuleshov Experiment showed the ability of viewers to associate emotions with images. This and other techniques were explored by Kuleshov in his work in Marxist film theory. See Kuleshov effect.

# L

**L-side.** Bus side advertisement space with horizontal bus side position on double Decker plus vertical space at rear.

**Label.** Card, tag, patch or other attachment to a product or package in order to give it a particular identity.

**Labelling Theory.** Theory that says that how people and their behaviour are labelled, or categorised, creates social expectations that influence future actions. For example, those labelled deviant will begin to act according to others' expectations.

**LAD, Language Acquisition Device.** A postulated 'organ' of the brain that is supposed to function as a congenital device for learning symbolic language ie. language acquisition. First proposed by Noam Chomsky, the LAD concept is a component of the nativist theory of language which dominates contemporary formal linguistics, which asserts that humans are born with the instinct or 'innate facility' for acquiring language.

**Ladder.** The overall map which shows the placement of every layout in a yearbook.

**Ladies of the House (LOH).** A term used by A.C. Nielsen Company in some of its reports, referring to female heads of households.

**Lading.** Portions of copy not necessary for narrative, to pad out is to make a story or headline longer than the message or sense strictly demands.

**Laid Paper.** Paper with parallel watermark lines.

**Lamb, Charles.** Author and poet who was one of the first copywriters, writing Government lottery advertisements in 1800.

**Laminate.** To give print a glossy, protective finish by sticking transparent plastic film to the surface. Used for covers of brochure/books, record sleeves, picture postcards or wall charts. Similarly, artwork and proofs may be so protected.

**LAN, Local Area Network.** A system that links together electronic office equipment, such as computers and word processors, and forms a network within an office or building.

**Landscape.** Horizontal orientation of page, picture or print, wider than it is deep.

**Language.** A systematic means of communicating thoughts and feelings by the use of sounds, conventional symbols or arbitrary signals, such as voice sounds, gestures, or written symbols. It could be the special vocabulary and usages of a scientific, professional, or other group

**Language Inflation.** Repeated use of words such as new, good, free, now, and special, which may seem banal and yet can be effective clichés of copywriting.

**Language Noise.** Expressions which cause misunderstanding because they are capable of having double meanings. It may even be an offensive meaning in another language or culture. Nigger brown was once a common colour, but because of racial implications it is rarely used today.

**Language Pollution.** Language pollution according to Gail and Michele Meyers is said to occur when a language is used by people to say what they do not believe, when words are used, sometimes unknowingly or deliberately, to conceal rather than to explain reality.

**Language Production.** What people say, sign, and write, as well as the processes they go through to produce these messages.

**Lapdog.** See Watchdog.

**Laser.** Acronym meaning light amplification by stimulated emission of radiation. A narrow beam of light used to create images, as in Linotronic computerised typesetting machine.

**Laser Printing.** Much used in Direct Mail printing for typographical and colour effects and Personalisation within sales letters. Operates by means of a photoconductive material which holds the image of individually produced characters by low power laser-beam scanning material. The image is coated with toner which is then transferred to the printing surface by a heated roller. Computer software is applied and each character is individually produced at up to 10,000 per hour.

**Laser Videodisc (LV).** Electronic optical machine that contains low-power lasers that reflect off the surface of the videodisc and create electronic signals that can be seen on the screen when the device is attached to a TV set.

**Lasswell, Harold Dwight.** (1902-1978) A leading American political scientist and communications theorist. He was a member of the Chicago school of sociology. Along with other influential liberals of the period as Walter Lippmann, he argued that democracies needed propaganda to keep the uninformed citizenry in agreement with what the specialised class had determined was in their best interests. As he wrote in his entry on propaganda for the *Encyclopaedia of the Social Sciences*, we must put aside "democratic dogmatisms about men being the best judges of their own interests" since "men are often poor judges of their own interests, flitting from one alternative to the next without solid reason". See Lasswell's model of communication.

**Lasswell's Model of Communication.** In this model of communication developed by Harold Dwight Lasswell, he argues that in studying communication we should consider the elements- Who (says) What (to) Whom (in) What Channel (with) What Effect. This model of communications is significantly unique since it includes different types of media. For example, newspapers, magazines, journals and books are all text media, but are assumed to have different distribution and readership, and hence different effects. Lasswell was primarily concerned with mass communication and propaganda, so his model is intended to direct us to the kinds of research we need to conduct to answer his questions- 'control analysis', 'effects research' and so on. In fact, though, it is quite a useful model, whatever category of communication we are studying. The model consists of five major components, though this is by no means obligatory. See Lasswell, Harold Dwight.

**Late Fringe.** A daypart that is generally considered to be the time slot between 11.30pm and 1.00am on affiliated stations, although the period varies from station to station.

Late Night.

**Late Night.** In broadcasting the time slot beginning from 1.00am Sunday through Saturday until morning on local TV stations, networks and cable systems. During this daypart syndicated programmes and infomercials are generally scheduled.

**Latent Image.** The invisible image left by the action of light on photographic film or paper. The light changes the photosensitive salts to varying degrees depending on the amount of light striking them. When processed, this latent image will become a visible image either in reversed tones (as in a negative) or in positive tones (as in a colour slide).

**Latitude of Acceptance.** As identified by Donald Granberg, this consists of the alternatives regarded by the receiver as basically acceptable. In this vein there will be one position that represents a receiver's actual position on the subject, this position is the most acceptable and comes the closest to that person's actual point of view. See Latitude of rejection, Latitude of non-commitment.

**Latitude of Non-commitment.** This can be described as indifferent. In other words, the option the receiver has been given falls neither in the latitude of acceptance, nor the latitude of rejection. In clear terms, the latitude of non-commitment states that the receiver is undecided about the option or idea with which he or she has been presented. See Latitude of acceptance, Latitude of rejection.

**Latitude of Rejection.** This consists of opinions, or options that a person finds totally unacceptable. Donald Granberg describes the latitude of rejection as being an option that is regarded as totally unacceptable or undesirable. See Latitude of acceptance, Latitude of non-commitment.

**Lavaliere Microphone.** A small omni-directional (personal) microphone usually referred to as lav. Used for talk shows and interviews and is worn on a cord around the neck or clipped to a lapel. They are named after Madame de La Valliére, a onetime mistress of Louis XIV, who always wore a jewel suspended on a chain above her bosom.

**Law of Minimal Effect.** A point of view that the media have little or no effect in forming or modifying the attitude of the audiences.

**Lay Down.** Impose a print job.

**Layout.** Plan or design of an advertisement or piece of print, exactly set out as distinct from a visual with measured areas for type and illustrations and display lines drawn, together with typographical instructions, for the printer to follow. May be finished up to show client what the job will look like, or to serve as guide to making up camera-ready artwork. Also the way the newspaper is designed and laid out on the page.

**Layout Editor.** The person who begins the layout plan, considering things like placement and amount of space allotted to news and advertising copy, graphics, photos, and symbols.

**LCD panel (Liquid Crystal Display).** An electronically generated text, numeric and symbols. Before the popularity of the LCD, LED is the most common method. LCD consume only one fifth (1/5) of the power of the LED and thus have a wider application in photographic line. The only problem is, it turns dark at very high temperature and will resume to normal when temperature is cool; it gradually fades in extended time. Used most commonly on cameras that show such information as remaining exposures, flash status and aspect ratio selected. Most televisions now come in LCD, they are usually lighter in weight, though more expensive, but handy especially when below 20 inch.

**Lead.** (Pronounced lede) Strips of metal less than type high used to space out headings and text. Also the first sentence or first few sentences of a story. Pronounced lede, and sometimes spelled that way, too.

**Lead Generation.** Advertising which produces sales leads, especially by means of coupons. Also methods by which prospects are identified.

**Lead-in Programme.** A show on TV station or network that begins a daypart or a particular sequence of programming. the programme strategy is to schedule a strong initial programme with great appeal in order to create good audience flow for the remainder of the time period.

**Lead Story.** Story supporting the main display headlines on a page. It is the principal story.

**Leader.** A short piece of film or videotape that is placed on the front of a videotape recording or film used in television. It consist of 30 seconds of film that contains 15 or 20 seconds of black blank film for threading the projector and 10 seconds of timing numerals.

**Leader, Editorial.** The editorial comment of a newspaper, sometimes called editorial or leader. Hence, leader writer.

**Leaders.** (pronounced: ledding). Dots and lines that direct the reader's eye in lists, e.g. completing the line between words and prices. It is the amount of space added between lines of text to make the document legible. The term originally referred to the thin lead spacers that printers used to physically increase space between lines of metal type. Most applications automatically apply standard leading based on the point size of the font. Closer leading fits more text on the page, but decreases legibility. Looser leading spreads text out to fill a page and makes the document easier to read. Leading can also be negative, in which case the lines of text are so close that they overlap or touch.

**Leadership.** Individuals within groups or institutions who have influence, provide focus, coordinate and direct activities of the group are leaders. The major role of a leader in mass communication thought is that of managing group interaction.

**Leading.** In printing, putting space into text or type matter usually between lines. This is achieved by locking lead blocks into the printing forme.

**Leading/Lagging Chrominance Effect.** A technical aberration in a TV picture. This occurs when the chrominance or colour portion of the video signal leads or lags behind the luminance signal. The result is an undesired effect in which the colours appear to the left (leading) or to the right (lagging) of the image.

**Leading Question.** (1) Particularly pointed question suggesting further concealed particulars. (2) Question in market research suggesting a particular answer is sought – otherwise known as loading a question.

**Leaf.** A single sheet comprising two pages, back and front.

**Leaflet.** Printed piece of paper, single or folded-over to make four pages. It can be stitched with additional sheets to make into more pages. Term is, however, usually applied to a publication with no more than twelve pages, i.e. there folded sheets.

**Leaks.** A conventional way in which governments disseminate information, often through the president's or prime minister's close sources, with the aim of manipulating the media.

**LED.** Light Emitting Diode. Light producing transistors used to display dots, numeric and text in the viewfinder. Slowly the LCD is replacing this technology.

**Lede.** The start of a story, same as Lead. It is spelled this way to prevent confusion with lead, a metal that was used extensively in hot-type days, and a term that refers to the spacing of lines in a story.

**Leg.** A column of type. A two-column headline will likely have two legs of type under it.

**Legend.** Title or description of an illustration.

**Legged Efforts.** Bonus sales which occur when advertising continues to produce results after a campaign has ended and in excess of the target. Some couponed advertisements in magazines may go on producing replies for months afterwards.

**Lens.** One or more pieces of optical glass or similar material designed to collect and focus rays of light to form a sharp image on the film, paper, or projection screen.

**Lens Aberration.** Optical flaws which are present in small amounts in all photographic lenses; made up of chromatic aberration, spherical aberration, curvature of field, distortion, etc.; a perfect lens would show the image of a point as a point and a straight line as a straight line. However, in practice, lenses are never perfect. It could reproduce a point as a patch and a straight line as a more or less curved band; most of the trouble is caused by aberrations, inherent in the lens construction. Moreover, it is the job of the lens designer to control most of the aberrations as much as possible by combining a number of single lenses in such a way that the aberrations of one lens tend to be cancelled out by opposing aberrations in the others. See aberration.

**Lens Flare.** A bright spot in an image caused by a bright light hitting the elements of a lens.

**Lens Opening.** A perforated plate or adjustable opening mounted behind or between the elements of a lens used to control the amount of light that reaches the film. Openings are usually calibrated in f-numbers. The more blades used will have a more natural and rounded spots.

**Lens Shade.** A collar or hood at the front of a lens that keeps unwanted light from striking the lens and causing image flare. May be attached or detachable, and should be sized to the particular lens to avoid vignetting.

**Lens-Shutter Camera.** A camera with the shutter built into the lens; the viewfinder and picture-taking lens are separate.

**Lens Speed.** The smallest f-stop number which transmits the maximum amount of light for a specific lens. This is the largest lens opening (smallest f-number) at which a lens can be set. A fast lens transmits more light and has a larger opening than a slow lens. Determined by the maximum aperture of the lens in relation to its focal length. The speed of a lens is relative: a 400 mm lens with a maximum aperture of f/3.5 is considered extremely fast, while a 28mm f/3.5 lens is thought to be relatively slow.

**Letrachrome.** Letraset colour imaging system.

**Letrajet.** Letraset device that converts a Pantone marker into an airbrush.

**Letraset.** Make of Dry Transfer Lettering consisting of sheets of ready-printed characters which can be transferred to paper by rubbing.

**Letterbox(ing).** Term used for one method of adapting a 16X9 aspect ratio to 4X3 which results in a black or patterned bar at the top and bottom of the 4X3 image. Since this technique does not involve altering original images or scenes in any way, it is considered the "most honest" form of conversion. It shows widescreen pictures in their original dimensions on TV and, with increasing frequency, on home video.

**Letterhead.** Formal printed stationary in which the name of a company is printed at the top of the paper, often in a characteristic 'house style'. Such stationary will also include address, telephone and telex numbers, and often names of directors, logotypes, symbols, slogans and other matter.

**Letterpress.** Relief printing process. All printing areas are raised to take ink and transfer this to paper. Similar to a date stamp. There are three kinds of machines; platen, flat-bed and rotary. Largely supersede by offset-litho as in newspaper industry.

**Letter-spacing.** Increasing emphasis by spacing out characters, as in display lines.

**Level.** The strength or amplitude of an audio or video signal.

**Level of Measurement.** Usually divided into nominal, ordinal, interval, and ratio, this term refers to the degree to which a particular measurement has certain properties that some types of statistical tests require.

**Levelling Off.** Balancing the columns of a paper. One double column story should not be run immediately under another.

**Lexis.** Used to describe the total set of words in a language as distinct from morphology; vocabulary

**Libel.** Publishing or broadcasting false information that identifies and defames an individual. Constituted when a defamatory statement is written, or is in any other permanent form like pictures, effigies, etc.

**Liberalism.** A political philosophy that emphasises the capacity of individuals to make autonomous and informed decisions. In terms of mass media, it was thought that a free media enabling individuals to maximise autonomy would be best delivered by the market rather than by state control.

**Libertarian.** Describes a press privately owned and providing a check on government in addition to meeting other needs of society.

**Library.** A very important morgue of the mass media which stores reference books, old newspapers, video and audio tapes, biographies, history of countries, documentations of institutions, micro films of printed matters and other valuable that could be referred to in future. Most media organisations have their libraries in-house. It can also refer to an individual's private collection, but more often it is a large collection that is funded and maintained by a city or institution. This collection is often used by people who choose not to-or cannot afford to-purchase an extensive collection themselves. However, with the collection or invention of media other than books for storing information, many libraries are now also repositories and access points for maps, prints or other artwork, microfilm, microfiche, audio tapes, CDs, LPs, video tapes and DVDs, and provide public facilities to access CD-ROM and subscription databases and the Internet. Thus, modern libraries are increasingly being redefined as places to get unrestricted access to information in many formats and from many sources.

**Library Music.** Recorded music on disc or tape held by music libraries which may be hired for a fee to use as background music in TV commercials, films or videos.

**Library Shot.** Either specially taken film (e.g. of famous locations, airlines taking off, in flight and landing), or scenes from existing films, which can be inserted in new productions such as TV commercials. Supplied by film libraries and archivists. Companies (such as airlines, tourist organisations) may shoot pictures for such processes by other users.

**License Renewal.** The process of extending a broadcast station's authorisation to continue operations.

**Licensing.** A license is government authorisation to operate a broadcast station. For radio and TV stations, legal arrangement transferring the rights to operate on a certain frequency. Such an arrangement, also known as franchising, is usually formalised by contract in which there is a consideration, perhaps, in the form of a regular fee, or of a commission or royalty. The body that license and control stations in Nigeria is the National Broadcasting Commission.

**Life**. The length of time during which an advertisement is used; the length of time during which an advertisement is judged still to be effective; the length of time that a publication is retained by its audience.

**Life-style.** The idea has a long history in commercial market research and has affinities with theories of taste and family background developed by Pierre Bourdieu. It refers to patterns of personal consumption and tastes of all kinds that are generally self-chosen but also shared with some others. They can be relatively independent of social class and material circumstances although they are likely to be shaped by a number of external factors, amongst which income is certainly one, along with age, education, social milieu and outlook. A life-style may be a way of expressing an individual identity, but for the media it can also be a way of constructing and managing consumer markets. See also life-style profiles and taste culture.

**Life-style Profiles.** Classifying media audiences on the basis of career, recreation, and/or leisure patterns or motives.

**Lift.** In print, pick up matter already set in type and included in a news story. In broadcast, the process of increasing the number of subscribers of a cable television system. Also refers to the acquisition of first time subscribers.

**Ligature.** Letters joined together on one type body.

**Light Metre.** An electronic instrument with a light-sensitive cell that measures the level of light utilised in a TV or film production or in photography, the light reflected from or falling on a subject. The hand-held device contains a photoelectric cell that measures light reflected off a subject, ambient light and direct light. The measurement is expressed in foot-candles (FC) or lux. The same as exposure metre.

**Light Reader.** Revealed in a TV Times 'How People Read' survey, conducted by BMP Solutions in Media, that more than one-third of adults spend less than 4.5 hours a week on leisure reading. 25.4% classified as light readers. Those who read for less than two hours amounted to 11.7%. Spread over all social grades. Not necessarily Light Viewers, more likely, Heavy Viewers.

**Light Viewer.** Those of higher-social grades or whose activities reduce their possible viewing time, who watch less television than majority of viewers. About 30% of viewers watch only 9% of TV transition.

**Lighting.** Used in a studio or stage to brighten or reflect a situation especially when a camera is on stand by. This is usually used for conveying the mood of a picture.

**Lighting Cameraman.** A member of a film crew, responsible for the pictorial composition of the film image as well as the arrangements for lighting.

**Lighting Plot.** A diagram showing the position of all light instruments in a production. The layout is sketched as seen from above and shows the placement of key, fill and backlights. It is prepared in advance of the show and acts as a blueprint for the positioning of scoop light and spots, which are often represented by symbols. It sometimes also indicates the dimmer circuit numbers for each instrument.

**Lighting Ratio.** The relationship between light and dark in a TV picture. The film camera can distinguish something that is 100 times brighter than another part of the picture, but the TV camera is less sensitive. It can only handle a difference of approximately 30 times brighter (a 30:1 ratio) than something else in the same scene without creating a blooming or washed-out effect. One way of measuring the lighting ratio in a TV set is to determine the brightness level of the fill lighting compared to the brightness level of the key lighting as measured in foot-candles by a light metre. The ratio is derived by dividing the lower number of the fill light into the higher number of the key light.

**Likert Scale.** Series of questions answered on a numerical, usually 5- or 7-point, 'agree- disagree' scale. Likert scale items must be chosen according to a specified procedure; however, the term is often misused to refer to all questions in this form.

**Limited-play Videocassettes.** A type of videocassette that can be rented and watched for limited number of times before automatically erasing itself. It is built on a counter that knows how many times it has been viewed and an internal magnet that erases the tape after 25 screenings.

**Limiter.** Audio circuit that automatically keeps audio levels from exceeding a certain level.

**Limiting Aperture.** The actual size of the aperture formed by the iris diaphragm at any setting. Determines, but usually differs from, the effective aperture.

**Linage.** In print, the number of agate lines to be used for an advertisement or for a series of advertisements, now made somewhat obsolete by the declining use of agate-line measurements. See Agate line.

**Line-level.** In contrast to a mic-level input, a high-level audio input associated with pre-amplified sources of audio.

**Line Block.** Printing block for reproducing line illustrations. Face of metal is solid, without any halftone screen.

**Line Chart.** Two-dimensional diagram showing relationship between two different sets of data.

**Line Drawing.** Pictorial illustration in solid lines only without any tones.

**Line Feed.** In digital typesetting, equivalent of set solid, e.g. without leading or white space between lines of type. Baseline to baseline distance in mm.

**Line Feed Factor.** In digital typesetting, a value (e.g. 1.6) used to multiply capital height of a typeface, which is then divided by 18 to produce one unit for spacing purposes.

**Line Gauge.** Type rule with different point sizes, used for Copyfitting and measuring type.

**Line Manager.** Functional head, with powers of command and carrying executive responsibility as compared with staff appointments with merely advisory powers.

**Line Mechanical.** Paste-up of line copy ready to photograph for making litho plate.

**Lineage.** Method of charging for classified advertising or sponsors of PR stories by the line.

**Linear.** Relationship between two variables that can be described by a straight line when the vertical axis of the graph represents one of the variables and the horizontal axis represents the other.

**Linear Editing.** As opposed to random access editing, an editing approach that requires edits to be entered and done in the sequence required for the final edited version. Each segment has to be found, cued and then recorded in sequence, which necessitates the stopping of both tapes as each segment is located and cued.

**Linear Fader.** As opposed to a rotary fader, a volume control device which is moved along a straight line.

**Linear Programming.** Any procedure for locating the maximum or minimum of a linear function of variables which are subject to linear constraints and inequalities.

**Line-by-line.** Selection of outdoor advertising positions site-by-site from a poster contractor's list. Or cinema advertising by precise geographical targeting. Campaigns can be targeted at certain towns or for one or any number of weeks.

**Linefeed.** In phototypesetting, means of inserting space between lines of type.

**Line Monitor.** The master or programme monitor which shows the picture being recorded or broadcast.

**Line Notes.** Notes prepared by a radio station executive from which a disc jockey will promote a contest, an up coming feature or another D.J's show.

**Line Rate.** The print advertising rate that is established by the number of agate lines of space used; somewhat obsolete because of the declining use of agate-line space measurements.

**Linespacing.** Spacing between lines of photoset type.

**Lineale.** Sans-serif typeface.

**Linear Graduated Screens.** Use of vertical and horizontal graduated halftone screens, for both black and white and colour printing, to give a shaded or almost airbrush effect, by means of digital typesetting.

**Linguistic Determinism.** The proposition that the language of a culture determines the way in which the world is perceived and thought about.

**Linguistics.** The scientific study of the nature, structure, and variation of language, including phonetics, phonology, morphology, syntax, semantics, sociolinguistics, and pragmatics.

**Linotype.** A typesetting machine similar to the intertype. So called because it sets type in lines.

**Lip Synchronisation.** A technique used in TV and film production, that matches the voices of performers speaking or singing with their lip movements. It is called 'lip sync' for short.

**List Broker/Manager.** Employee, agent or the owner of a Mailing List who maintains it, is responsible for its use, and may market it.

**List Sample.** Selection of names taken from a mailing list for a test mailing to measure responsiveness of the list.

**List Selection.** Characteristics used to select certain groups of names and address, as with a Database when filters can be included in the software so that particular names can be called up and printed.

**Listening.** In commercial radio research, listening is recorded in terms of 15 min. segments and is defined as 'any listening' within a particular segment. Between midnight and 0600 hours listening is recorded in 30 minute segments.

**Listings.** Term for radio and television programme details. In Britain, publication of programmes is restricted to the day of broadcast in newspapers, with highlighted information in other journals. Radio Times and TV Times monopolise listings the week ahead. With the sale of TV Times and other changes under new broadcasting legislation, the listings monopoly is unlikely to survive.

**Literacy.** Ability to read and write is common form of literacy, but in developing countries there is also oral literacy or ability to remember and recite messages, and visual literacy consisting of mental pictures.

**Literal.** Printer's typesetting error, which printer is responsible for making correction without charge. Not an author's correction.

**Lithography.** Planographic printing process based on principle that water and grease will not mix. Invented by John Aloysius Senefelder in Munich, 1796. With the original system, image was drawn in reverse on porous stone. For posters artists had to draw design in reverse for each colour to be printed. With introduction of photography, metal plates replaced stone.

**Litter-bin Advertising.** Supply of street litter bins by a contractor, on which advertising space is cold, or advertiser sponsors a litter bin bearing his name.

**Live Programme.** Performance and broadcast transmitted simultaneously.

**Livery.** Form of Corporate Identity, vehicles, ships, aircraft, railway wagons, distinguished by company's House Style, name display, Logotype or other designs. Historical origins: emblems on soldiers' shields or sails of ships, colours of stage coaches, leading up to ship's funnels and currently airlines.

**Living Newspaper.** A style of theatre created during the Federal Theatre Project. Plays were presented as documentaries on social issues of the day including labour, race relations, and health care. The theatres sought to both help people recognise the social problems around them and ring a clarion to action, so that they might be solved.

**Lloyd's List.** One of the world's oldest continuously-running journals, having printed shipping news in London as early as 1734. It was begun by the proprietors of Lloyd's Coffee House in the City of London as a reliable but terse source of information for the merchants and underwriters who met there regularly. Initially it only listed movements of merchant and naval vessels, but expanded over the centuries to provide news, including casualty reports, and, occasionally, opinion. In 2002, a long tradition came to an end when the journal ceased to refer to ships as "she", adopting the neutral word "it" instead. The publication is edited in Fenchurch Street.

**Loaded Question.** To be avoided in a communication research questionnaire because it implies an expected answer and is biased.

**Lobby Correspondent.** Journalist accredited to mix Ministers and party officials to write about political events and to report off the record statements from non-attributable sources which are usually politicians not wishing to be named. Privileged to receive White papers 24 hours before publication. Not to be confused with Press Gallery reporters who make verbatim reports on speeches made in the House.

**Lobbying.** A process of trying to influence the thinking of legislators or other public officials, specifically those in power, for or against a specific cause.

**Lobbyists.** Not to be confused with lobby correspondents who are journalists, lobbyists represent pressure groups and will endeavour to inform government officials and civil servants of their causes. Various groups such as farmers, teachers, nurses, doctors, old age pensioners and so on have their lobbies or representations to politicians. There are specialist PR consultancies which undertake lobbying on behalf of clients.

**Lobster Shift.** Working in the hours after a publication has gone to print. Also known as dog watch.

**Local Advertising.** Placed and paid for by the local merchant or dealer.

**Local Origination Channels.** Specific cable channels designated for locally originated programming. Some of the programming is as simple as slides or billboards for a weather forecast. Many are usually swap channels listing items for rent or sale or community calendar channels promoting local events.

**Local Press.** Local newspapers, usually covering a borough or rural district. Published once or twice a week.

**Local Marketing Agreement (LMA).** In this practice, two or more stations enter into an agreement in which they share facilities, staff and equipment at times frequency.

**Local Rate.** An advertising rate offered by the media to local advertisers that is lower than the rate offered to national advertisers.

**Location.** Real-life setting for still or motice photography or for television filming, or opposed to an artificial setting.

**Lockbox.** A device that allows a cable subscriber to block out reception of a particular channel at any given time. It is installed at the back of a TV set and contains a trap that can be activated by a key.

**Log.** A broadcast station's record of its programming.

**Logistics.** Term borrowed from the military describing the science and practice of estimating the likely flows and timings of company resources for any particular project or campaign and providing the means to achieve them. Primarily used in physical circulation management of newspapers, journals, magazines and other published matter.

**Logotype.** Often abbreviated to logo. Usually in simple design, part of corporate identity scheme, a visual presentation of a company name. Often in a special shape like a badge, or using handwriting as with Ford, Cadbury, Coca-Cola logos, or special lettering. Can be registered as trade mark but may be additional to trade mark.

**Lombard.** Acronym for Psychographic type.

**Long-focus.** Lens of relatively long focal length designed to provide a narrower angle of view than the normal or standard lens, which generally has an angle of view, expressed on the diagonal of the film format, of about 45 degrees. The long focus lens thus takes in less of the view in front of it but on an enlarged scale.

**Long Lens.** A telephoto or long focal length lens.

**Long-range Plan.** Quantitative plan of development for the future, usually at least five years.

**Long Shot (LS).** A shot from a great distance. This is a type of shot from a TV or film camera that encompasses the entire scene and involves a wide view of the area. Sometimes referred to as a 'wide' or 'full' shot as a cutaway when it hides errors created by jump cuts. When a long shot is used in the opening of a sequence it is often called an 'establishing' shot, in that it orients the audience to the surroundings or the circumstances of what they are going to see. Also known as a 'cover' shot.

**Longitudinal Videotape Recording (LVR).** A pioneer reel-to-reel videotape format that is operated on the principle of recording electrical impulses on narrow magnetic tape, which moved rapidly over stationary recording heads. The tape had to move 100 inches per second over the heads, however, and the resulting black-and-white image had poor resolution and produced jitter. Additionally, fewer than 16 minutes could be recorded on a reel.

**Lookism.** Discrimination or prejudice against people based on their appearance. It is also a theory that suggests- the better looking one is the more successful one will be in life. The theory is offered by American psychologist Nancy Etcoff.

**Loose Inserts.** Advertisements distributed separately with a publication, and usually inserted loosely within its pages.

**Loss Leader.** An item that is advertised and sold at a price that represents a loss of profit for the retailer. The pricing technique is used to draw or lead customers into the store with the hope that they will buy other items.

**Lossy.** Picture compression method that discards some data and to some degree degrades picture quality.

**Loudness.** The perceived strength or intensity of a sound. It is a perceptual dimension of sound influenced by the amplitude of a sound wave; sound waves with large amplitudes are generally experienced as loud and those with small amplitudes as soft.

**Loudness Metre.** A volume units meter which responds to the loudness of sounds as humanly perceived, as opposed to only the milliwatt DB reference used by most VU metres.

**Lowbrow.** Used to indicate a low level of intellectual capacity of cultural appreciation judged against the standards of highbrow elite. See Highbrow.

**Low Culture.** Cultural products, such as entertainment, for which the intended audience is primarily those of limited educational level and lower socioeconomic status.

**Low-Frequency Roll-off.** An audio circuit associated with microphones and amplifiers which attenuates undesirable low frequencies.

**Low-key Lighting.** Lighting characterised by a high key-to-fill ratio which results in predominant shadow areas. Typically used for night scenes in dramatic productions.

**Low Pass Filter.** An electrical filter that passes frequencies below a specified frequency and attenuates those above. Required in digital audio to prevent sampling of signals above one-half the sampling frequency.

**Low-Power TV / LPTV.** A classification of TV station designed to serve a small community through the use of a transmitter with very limited power. It broadcasts at very low power and low cost. These stations tend to serve small towns, or communities within large cities. There are close to 3,000 LPTV stations in U.S. The terms "low-power broadcasting" and "micropower broadcasting" (more commonly "microbroadcasting") should not be used interchangeably, because the markets are not the same. LPTV is regulated by the FCC and operates in a commercial manner, whereas LPFM is a not for profit industry. The former term is more often used to describe stations who have applied for and received official licences. The relationship between broadcasting power and signal range is a function of many things, such as the frequency band it uses e.g, SW or FM, the topography of the country in which it operates (lots of mountains or flat), atmospheric conditions, and finally the amount of radio frequency energy it transmits. As a general rule, the more energy it transmits, the further the signal goes.

**Low Profile.** Attempt to avoid publicity. Rather negative and silly PR tactic by companies which are afraid of criticism.

**Lower Case.** Small characters in typesetting. Printing convention designating small letters, as against capital letters, which are referred to as upper case. Originates from hand setting when small letters kept in lower case or drawer of type-cabinet containing individual type characters.

**Lower Power Television (LPTV) Stations.** Broadcast stations that transmit a signal to a limited geographic area. Their proponents sometimes call them 'community broadcasting stations'. They utilise the same frequencies as their full power UHF and VHF brothers but transmit at a lower wattage.

**Lowest Unit Charges (LUC).** Mandated minimum costs related to political broadcasts.

**Loyalty Factor.** Supposition that the more a periodical is read the more likely it is that its readers will pay attention to its content.

**LS.** In scripts an abbreviation for long shot.

**Lumen.** Measurement of light quantity. Lumens per square foot equals foot-candles.

**Luminance.** The black-and-white aspect of a television signal. Also called the Y-signal. When part of a composite colour signal, the luminance signal consists of 0.30 red, 0.59 green and 0.11 blue.

**Lux.** The lux (symbol: lx) is the SI unit of illuminance. It is the unit used in photometry as a measure of the intensity of light, with wavelengths weighted according to the luminosity function, a standardised model of human brightness perception. In English, "lux" is used in both singular and plural. It is a derived unit based on lumen, and lumen is a derived unit based on candela. One lux is equal to one lumen per square metre, where $4\pi$ lumens is the total luminous flux of a light source of one candela of luminous intensity. One Lux in video means light level of a candle light (moonlight).

# M

**M.** 1,000.

**MacBride Commission.** Also known as The International Commission for the Study of Communication Problems, it is popularly named after the President of the Commission, Sean MacBride who was an international human rights activists and Nobel Peace Prize winner. The Commission had other fifteen members drawn from all parts of the world. It was convened by United Nations Educational Scientific and Cultural Organisation (UNESCO) to review the problems of a New World Information and Communication Order (NWICO). It published a popular report, *Many Voices, One World*; it is the most comprehensive text on the issue of media imbalance and related issues. *See NWICO.*

**Machine Coated.** Paper which is coated or given a special surface on the papermaking machine.

**Machine Proof.** Proof which is checked at the printers, as often as necessary with colour printing to avoid holding up the machine.

**Macro Lens.** A lens that provides continuous focusing from infinity to extreme close-ups, often to a reproduction ratio of 1:2 (half life-size) or 1:1 (life-size). See micro lens.

**Macro Marketing.** Overview of society's needs in the interplay of marketing actions within a country's economy.

**Macro-media.** Mass circulation or mass audience media such as press, radio, TV, cinema.

**Macro Photography.** The process of taking photographs of small objects with regular photographic lenses at reproduction ratios of 1X or greater; also referred to as photomicrography.

**Magalogue.** Free magazine, usually distributed to AB readers, and containing expensive items mostly bought by charge-card holders.

**Magazine.** (1) A lighttight metal container (cartridge) that holds 135 film (cylindrical magazine) or when apply to medium format, magazine back refer to the inter changeable container that holds the films for mounting on the back of the camera for exposures. (2) A periodical publication containing a variety of articles, generally financed by advertising and/or purchase by readers. They are typically published weekly, biweekly, monthly, bimonthly or quarterly, with a date on the cover that is in advance of the date it is actually published. They are often printed in colour on coated paper, and are bound with a soft cover. In practice, magazines are a subset of periodicals, distinct from those periodicals produced by scientific, artistic, academic or special interest publishers which are subscription-only, more expensive, narrowly limited in circulation, and often have little or no advertising. It may cater for news, gossips, pictures, special interest groups, etc. Magazines fall into two broad categories: consumer magazines and business magazines. Consumer magazines are aimed at the public and are usually available through retail outlets. They range from general-interest titles such as *Time*, *Newswatch* and *Ovation*, which appeal to a broad spectrum of readers, to highly specialist titles covering particular hobbies, leisure pursuits or other interests. Among the hundreds or thousands of topics covered by specialist magazines are, for example, computer games, fishing, particular marques of automobile, particular kinds of music, and particular political interests. They are sometimes called general interest or popular magazines because they are written for a more wider audience. They can focus on one subject or cover many different subjects. Each magazine is usually tailored to a specific audience. They are easy to read and provide information the average person would like to know about. Articles and stories are written by staff or freelancers. There are usually many pictures and photographs. The main idea of these types of magazine is to entertain, sell products and promote viewpoints. On the other hand business magazines are available only, or predominantly, on subscription. In some cases these subscriptions are available to any person prepared to pay; in others, free subscriptions are available to readers who meet a set of criteria established by the publisher. This practice, known as controlled circulation, is intended to guarantee to advertisers that the readership is relevant to their needs. Very often the two models, of paid-for subscriptions and controlled circulation, are mixed. Advertising is also an important source of revenue for business magazines. Magazines may also be classified further- Pictorial: publishing more pictures than words, like the *Encomium*; Literally: publishing literature or materials that appeal to a literal audience, may be poets, playwrights or novelists, like *The ANA Review*; Teen: Publishing materials that basically appeal to younger audiences at times it may not necessarily be tied to only those between the ages of 13-19, it may appeal to other youths; Arts. Other classes of magazines may include scholarly and sensational magazines. Scholarly magazines are academic focused. They provide in depth information on various subjects. The information in a scholarly magazine is presented in a serious, textbook-like manner. There are charts and graphs, but rarely pictures or photos. The articles are professionally written by experts. The main purpose of these magazines is to teach and provide help in research. Then again, sensational magazines often have a newspaper-like look to them. They are larger and thinner than other magazines. They thrive on creating a stir. They use flashy headlines and focus on amazing-type stories or stories about celebrities. Articles are written by staffers or freelancers. These magazines include many pictures, most often more pictures than stories. These are generally known as tabloids.

**Magazine-card.** Promotional vehicle consisting of a card formed by a perforation on a magazine cover, the card being protected and reinforced by a resistant PVC film. Can be used for claiming a benefit such as a discount on a purchase.

**Magazine Concept.** Buying a certain number of broadcast announcements from a station with a certain guaranteed audience level, without selecting the specific times or programs.

**Magenta.** Standard red colour used in four-colour printing.

**Magic Hour.** A time of the day, particularly dawn or dusk, that is the ideal period to photograph a scene on television remote or on a film location. There is little need to adjust the lighting or camera f-stops at that time because the colour temperature is nearly perfect for the conditions of the shoot.

**Magicube.** Special form of flashtube which is fired by mechanical (not electrical) means. Can be used only on cameras fitted with the appropriate socket.

**Magnetic Film.** Generic, term for film coated with substance capable of retaining magnetic variations transferred to it by a magnetic head on a recorder. Used for the sound or audio input for a film, for example.

**Magnetic Sound Track.** Sound track recorded on magnetic tape, in much the same way as on a domestic tape recorder.

**Magnetic Tape.** Usually plastic strip coated with magnetic recording medium.

**Magnification Ratio.** Ratio that express greatest possible on film magnifying power of a lens. Used commonly on the macro setting of the zoom lenses, macro lens or with bellows.

**Mail Drop.** Advertisement delivered door-to-door.

**Mail-in.** form of Sales Promotion in which the applicant sends in a coupon from a press advertisement or token from a pack for a free offer. There may be a small charge for postage and payment, but it is not a premium offer requiring payment for a special price offer. Alternatively, a cash refund or cash voucher may be offered.

**Mail Order.** Trading by post. Now mostly called Direct Response marketing. Not to be confused with Direct Mail which is an advertising medium. Mail order is conducted by direct mail, catalogues, Off-the-page press advertisements, TV, etc. The big growth area has been financial services.

**Mail Order Publisher.** Publisher who sells books, magazines, gramophone records, cassettes, compact discs, videos and other publications by post, such as book and record clubs or a subscription publisher.

**Mailing List.** List of prospects used in Direct Response marketing. It is important that this list is up-to-date, and frequently purged of dead addresses or de-duplicated, especially when several lists which can include repeat addresses are being used.

**Mailing Piece.** Letter, leaflet or other article sent through the post on a widespread basis.

**Mailing Response Analysis.** Use of regression techniques to measure neighbourhood characteristics which seem to deliver the best mailing response. Then possible to score postcodes in a prospect-scoring model which seeks to maximise response from a later mailing.

**Mainbar.** Formed in a backward sort of way, a main bar is simply the main story, but stated this way to distinguish it from secondary sidebar stories. It's a little like calling the city's main library the main branch to distinguish it from the true, secondary branches.

**Make-good.** Re-run of press advertisement or TV/radio commercial following a dispute or failure to insert or transmit as Scheduled. Mainly to compensate for an error, omission, or technical difficulty with the publication, broadcast, or transmission of the original.

**Make-up.** (1) In pre- production, to prepare the artists or presenter in terms of appearance. (2) Arrangement of type and plates in page form for advertising. (3) Layout and design of pages of a publication.

**Malredemption.** Malpractice of abusing coupon offers by theft from printers or stores, or other criminal misuse of premium offers. Term loosely used for misredemption.

**Mammum Aperture.** The widest aperture which the diaphragm is capable of opening up to. It is engraved on the lens in this manner; 1: 1.4.

**Managed News.** Managed and sometimes leaked news by politicians. Attempt to control political news.

**Management.** (1) The owners, or directors, of a media or any organisation. (2) The generic term employed to designate those executive tasks in a business which ensure that diverse resources are utilised in such a way that pre-planned economic performances are achieved. Commonly regarded as comprising the interlocking activities of planning, organising, staffing, directing, controlling and co-ordination, using all liaison and communications resources available for these ends.

**Managing Editor.** The person who co-ordinates all news departments at a newspaper by collecting all copy and ensuring that all instructions for printer or typist are clear and consistent. Or the person who meets and consults with the staff to make a plan.

**Manual.** (1) Printed document of any number of pages usually containing specific instructions, e.g. sales manual, operating or service manual, relative both to products and services as well as company policies, regulations and practices. (2) Also in photojournalism, where user selects both shutter speed and aperture, following or ignoring the metre's recommendations to achieve the desired exposure.

**Manual Flash.** Flash output is controlled manually in manual flash mode unlike in auto flash mode, where flash output power varies automatically according to the selected aperture. Some speedlights like the Nikon SB 27, SB 26, SB-25. SB-24 and SB 20, provide selectable manual outputs (full, 1/2, 1/4, 1/8, 1/16 etc.), while others provide full manual output only.

**Manual Iris.** Diaphragm controlled directly by a calibrated ring on the lens barrel.

**Manuscript.** Derived from the Latin *manu scriptus*, literally "written by hand," it is the final draft of a written document as submitted to a publisher for typesetting and subsequent reproduction. It may be any written document that is put down by hand, in contrast to being printed or reproduced some other way. Information may be hand-recorded in other ways than in manuscripts, as inscriptions that are chiselled upon a hard material or scratched as with a knife point in plaster or with a stylus on a waxed tablet, (the way Romans made notes), or are in cuneiform writing, impressed with a pointed stylus in a flat tablet of unbaked clay. Thus, they may not only be defined by their contents, which may combine writing with mathematical calculations, maps, explanatory figures or illustrations. It may be in the form of scrolls or in book form, or codex format. Illuminated manuscripts are enriched with vignettes, border decoration, elaborately engrossed initial letters and full-page illustrations. Abbreviation MS.

**Mapping.** Graphic geodemographic reports to show customer density and penetration, target markets and areas of business density.

**Margin(s).** Normally the make-up given to the cost price of a product by a distributor to cover his costs and include some level of profit. Is sometimes referred to as the difference between the arbitrary cost of a product and the actual selling price. (2) In printing, back, head, for-edge and tail, four to a page and best proportioned 1, 1 ½, 2 and 2 ½ respectively.

**Margin of Error.** Range of likely population values. If 60% of people sampled agree with a statement and the margin of error is 2%, the population value is believed to be between 58% and 62% agreement.

**Marginalisation.** Putting off to the margins,; making less important, less powerful, or less visible. Minority ethnic groups and women are marginalised in many countries.

**Markas.** Acronym for psychographic type middle-age renester, kids away.

**Marked Proof.** One on which printer has made corrections before it is submitted to the client.

**Market.** (1) Group of person and/or organisations identified through a common need and with resources to satisfy that need. (2) Place where buyers and sellers gather to do business. (3) To market; to indulge in trade, i.e. buying and selling for pecuniary advantage. See Target market and Target group.

**Market Coverage.** Measurement of extent to which advertising media reach target audiences. The same calculations may be applied to estimate: (1) the extent to which sales forces cater for all prospective customers; and (2) sales outlets are supplying for all available custom.

**Market Leader.** Brand or product securing the greatest proportion of total sales within its field. May sometimes refer to the company marketing the brand or product concerned. The market leader of computer software is Microsoft.

**Market Penetration.** The extent to which a product captures the potential sales in a market- expressed as market share.

**Market Place.** Figurative; applies to any or all places where trading takes place.

**Market Potential.** The reasonable maximum market share or sales level that a product or service can be expected to achieve.

**Market Profile.** A demographic and psychographic description of the people or the households of a product's market. It may also include economic and retailing information about a territory. See Target Market and Target profile.

**Market Reach.** Total number of prospects which is possible to reach through a given campaign.

**Market Research.** Research, usually conducted by advertising agencies, into the potential market for products. It involves the systematic gathering, recording, analysing and use of data relating to the transfer and sale of goods and services for producer to consumer.

**Market Segment.** A section or sub-group of the total market as with special blends of coffee, or different sizes of cars. Advertisements need to be written, designed and placed according to the market segment they aim to reach. May be special interest groups or particular social grades.

**Market Segmentation.** The theory and practice of dividing a market into definable groups, usually to improve marketing performance. Frequently different segments of a market have individual behaviour patterns and require a different approach for success to be achieved.

**Market Share.** A company's or brand's portion of the sales of a product or service category.

**Market Threshold.** The critical point at which a media artefact justifies, financially, its existence; and the greater the competition within the market, the more essential the threshold becomes.

**Marketing.** (1) News, features on marketing, sales promotion. (2) There are numerous definitions of marketing, most notably among them are:

A.    Marketing is an organisational function and a set of processes for creating, communicating, and delivering value to customers and for managing customer relationships in ways that benefit the organisation and its stakeholders. It is also the process of planning and executing the conception, pricing, promotion, and distribution of ideas, goods, and services to create exchanges that satisfy individual and organisational goals. (American Marketing Association)

B.    Marketing is the management process responsible for identifying, anticipating and satisfying customer requirements profitably. (Chartered Institute of Marketing, UK).

The copious definitions of marketing reflects multi-diversity and its importance. But it is important to know, the whole intention of marketing is to promote a product or service to attract customers for the mutually advantageous exchange or transfer of products and services.

**Marketing Communications.** Every element of the Marketing Mix or strategy which involves communications with sales force, distributor and users/consumers. Not limited to promotional communications such as selling, advertising and sales promotion. Also includes public relations at all levels, and forms of communication such as branding, labelling, packaging, pricing and marketing research.

**Marketing Concept.** Business philosophy starting with the needs of the costumer.

**Marketing Function.** (1) An all embracing term covering every contributory factor in the marketing process. (2) Considered to be the responsibility of marketing management.

**Marketing Information.** Data and news relevant to a marketing operation.

**Marketing Mix.** All the elements contained in the marketing strategy as originated by Neil Borden, but taking in many more elements than the original set, and preferably considered in chronological order of application rather than in the narrow four Ps concept of product, price, place and promotion. Public relations is not a separate part of marketing mix, as advertising is, because there is a public relations aspect to most elements of the mix.

**Marketing Research.** All kinds of scientific study applied to marketing, including pre-testing of advertisements, post-advertising research such as tracking studies, and media research. This is broader than market research which is limited to studies of the market.

**Marque.** Name or brand which distinguishes a product in a range of products such as different coffee blends or cars. This can also lead to a marque personality or image which attaches to a product.

**Married Print.** Film print or videotape combining picture and sound.

**Marxism.** Theory of society based on the work of Karl Marx, according to whom human progress takes place on the basis of conflict between succeeding 'classes', whose dominant power depends on ownership of the current main factor of production (e.g. land, raw material, capital or labour). The dominant class exploits other classes in order to maximise profit and output. The relevance for mass communication lies in the proposition that the media are an ideological asset that can be used to defend, or attack, a dominant class position. In Marx's own time and later, the mass media were owned and operated in the interests of the dominant class. This remains an issue to be determined.

**Masculinist.** Done or said from a male perspective; promoting male values; sexist. This term is usually used to indicate the opposite of feminist or the absence of feminism.

**Mask.** Frame, usually rectangular, used to cover those parts of an illustration which are not required to be reproduced, e.g. cropping of a photograph for this purpose.

**Masking.** (1) Placing a protective layer over area(s) of a picture while retouching or airbrushing other parts (2) Blocking out part of a picture to prevent it being reproduced, or to permit correction (3) Way of adjusting colour values and tone in photomechanical reproduction.

**Maslow, Abraham.** (1908 –1970) An American psychologist. He is mostly noted today for his proposal of a hierarchy of human needs. See Maslow's hierachy of needs.

**Maslow's Hierarchy of Needs.** Abraham Maslow developed the Hierarchy of Needs model in 1940-50's USA, and the Hierarchy of Needs theory remains valid today for understanding human motivation, management, and personal development. Maslow proposed this theory in his 1943 paper A Theory of Human Motivation, which he subsequently extended. It contends that as humans meet 'basic needs', they seek to satisfy successively 'higher needs' that occupy a set hierarchy. Maslow studied exemplary people such as Albert Einstein, Jane Addams, Eleanor

Mass.

Roosevelt, and Frederick Douglass rather than mentally ill or neurotic people, writing that "the study of crippled, stunted, immature, and unhealthy specimens can yield only a cripple psychology and a cripple philosophy." The hierarchy of needs is often depicted as a pyramid consisting of five levels: the four lower levels grouped together as deficiency needs are associated with physiological needs, while the top level termed growth needs, is associated with psychological needs. It argues that while our deficiency needs must be met, our being needs continually shape our behaviour. The basic concept is that the higher needs in this hierarchy only come into focus once all the needs that are lower down in the pyramid are mainly or entirely satisfied. Growth forces create upward movement in the hierarchy, whereas regressive forces push prepotent needs further down the hierarchy. The five needs-

• *Physiological needs* are to do with the maintenance of the human body. If we are unwell, then little else matters until we recover.

• *Safety needs* are about putting a roof over our heads and keeping us from harm. If we are rich, strong and powerful, or have good friends, we can make ourselves safe.

• *Belonging needs* introduce our tribal nature. If we are helpful and kind to others they will want us as friends.

• *Esteem needs* are for a higher position within a group. If people respect us, we have greater power.

• *Self-actualisation needs* are to 'become what we are capable of becoming', which would be our greatest achievement.

These are the needs that are most commonly discussed and used. Maslow later added three more needs by splitting two of the above five needs. Between esteem and self-actualisation needs was added: Need to know and understand, which explains the cognitive need of the academic and the need for aesthetic beauty, which is the emotional need of the artist. Self-actualisation was divided into: Self-actualisation, which is realising one's own potential, as above; transcendence, which is helping others to achieve their potential.

**Mass.** This term describes a very large but amorphous set of individuals that engage in similar behaviour, under external influence, and are viewed by their would-be manipulators as having little or no separate identity, forms of organisation or power, autonomy, integrity or self-determination. It represents one view of the media audience and is used with the same negative connotations in a number of related expressions, including mass behaviour, mass opinion, mass consumption, mass culture, mass society, etc. and of course 'mass communication' itself.

**Mass Advertising.** Using the mass media to reach markets.

**Mass Communication.** Process by which messages are communicated to a target audience and larger number of people utilising mass media such as national press and television. As a field of academic study, it is used to describe the various means by which individuals and entities relay information to large segments of the population all at once through mass media. See mass media.

**Mass Culture.** When current (approximately 1930-70), this term described the 'culture of the masses', generally meaning 'lower' forms of entertainment and fiction appealing to the uneducated and 'uncultured' majority, as opposed to the 'high culture' of the majority. Cultural change and new perceptions of popular culture have changed the meaning of the term and made it largely reluctant or undesirable. When current it was more ideological (upholding elite cultural values) than empirically valid, since all but a small minority tended to participate in at least some aspects of 'mass culture'.

**Mass Media.** This term is used to denote, as a class, that section of the media specifically conceived and designed to reach a very large audience (e.g. popular press, radio, TV, outdoor, cinema), typically, at least as large as the whole population of a nation state. It was coined in the 1920s with the advent of nationwide radio networks and of mass-circulation newspapers and magazines. The mass-media audience has been viewed by some commentators as forming a mass society with special characteristics, notably atomisation or lack of social connections, which render it especially susceptible to the influence of modern mass-media techniques such as advertising and propaganda. It is also gaining popularity in the blogosphere when referring to the mainstream media.

**Mass Society.** A form of society theoretically identified as dominated by a small number of interconnected elites who control the conditions of life of the many, often by means of persuasion and manipulation. The term was first applied both to the post-war United States by radical critics (especially C. Wright Mills) and also by political theorists to the European societies that fell under the spell of fascism and communism. Large-scale and centralised forms of social organisations are typical, accompanied by feelings of anomie and powerlessness. The mass media are necessary instruments for achieving and maintaining mass society.

**Massification.** A process where a population is regarded and treated as a lumpen mass with similar if not identical tastes and attitudes.

**Mast.** A long pole of wood or metal, upright and set for carrying radio serials, satellite and other transmission gadgets for wide broadcast. Can be seen in many broadcast stations.

**Master.** The original or primary recording.

**Master Control.** An audio and video control centre which is the final switching point before signals are sent to the television transmitter. See control room.

**Master Control Console/Switcher.** Heart of television control room operation through which both the audio and video images are fed, joined together, and improved, perhaps through special effects for the 'on-air' image. Most such switchers control video and audio simultaneously.

**Master of Ceremonies (MC).** Sometimes spelled *emcee* or called a compere, an MC is the host of a staged event or other performance. The individual usually presents performers, speaks to the audience, and generally keeps the show moving. An example in fiction is the Joel Grey role of the MC in the theatre and film musical *Cabaret*, and an example from reality is Ikenna Nndaguba, Nigeria's most influential MC, at the annual national awards given by the president. The term originates from the Roman Catholic Church. At a large Catholic church or cathedral, the MC organises and rehearses the proceedings and ritual of each mass. He may also have responsibility for the physical security of the place of worship during the liturgy. At major festivals such as Christmas and Easter, when the liturgies are long and complex, the MC plays a vital role in ensuring that everything runs smoothly. In the 1970s and 1980s, the term MC became associated with hip hop music, and is the traditional title for a person who today is commonly called a rapper. Traditionally, an MC uses rhyming verses, whether pre-written or free-styled, to introduce and praise the DJ he works with, and hype up the crowd. Within hip-hop, "MC" is also an acronym for "Microphone Controller", "Mic Checka", or "Music Commentator".

**Master Proof.** Galley or Page Proof, bearing printer's corrections, and submitted to author or client for corrections. New copy changes (author's corrections) liable to charge.

**Master Session.** The final recording session in which a song is put on tape. Costing many thousands of money, this uses full orchestration, a major control console, and a recording engineer.

**Masthead.** This term is used to mean three things and can get confusing. It is used to mean the distinctive title design of a newspaper or magazine. In readership surveys, cards bearing mastheads are used for recall purposes. Also the page of a publication that gives its staff and editorial information- names of top editors, and for the box of names, phone numbers and addresses. It usually appears inside the publication usually close to editorial comments. At times it appears across the front page and identifies the newspaper and the date of publication. (Slang "banner").

**Mat Service.** A service to newspapers that supplies pictures and drawings for use in advertisements; entire prepared advertisements may be offered ("mat" is slang for "matrix").

**Match Code.** An abbreviation of data taken from names and addresses on a mailing list so that editing or identification of the records is simplified.

**Matching Transformer.** An impedance-changing device used to make different pieces of equipment electronically compatible. Often used to alter the output of high-impedance mics so they can be used with low-impedance equipment inputs.

**Matrix.** (1) Paper or plastic mould from which duplicate printing blocks are produced. (2) Horizontal and vertical lines or columns used for established relationships between sets of data.

**Matrix Metering System.** An exposure metering system using a multi-segment sensor and computer. Available in some Nikon SLRs. With

Matt.

the classic techniques of evaluating for 18% reflectance, factors such as brightness and contrast are primarily used to determine exposure. As well, it is essential to evaluate each scene's esthetic factors such as colour to get the best exposure.

**Matt.** Dull, unpolished paper surface for finish.

**Matt Calendar.** On papermaking machine, the cylinder which creates a smooth dull finish and bulk for blade coated offset litho papers. Improves ink gloss.

**Matter.** Type or copy in print or gathered together for printing purposes.

**Maximail Rate.** The cost of an agate line of advertising space at the highest milline rate; somewhat obsolete as the usage of agate lines has declined.

**McDonaldisation.** Term used by sociologist George Ritzer in his book *The McDonaldisation of Society*. He describes it as the process by which a society takes on the characteristics of a fast-food restaurant. It is a reconceptualisation of rationalisation, or moving from traditional to rational modes of thought, and scientific management. Where Max Weber used the model of the bureaucracy to represent the direction of this changing society, Ritzer sees the fast-food restaurant as having become a more representative paradigm contemporarily.

**McLuhan, Herbert Marshall.** (July 21, 1911– December 31, 1980) A Canadian educator, philosopher, and scholar, professor of English literature, literary critic, and communications theorist, who is one of the founders of the study of media ecology and is today an honorary guru among technophiles. He was perhaps the first communication theorist to achieve the status of cultural icon. In the mid-1960s, his books drew attention to the complex interactions among media and societies. His ideas, which related much to media and such issues as gender, technology, politics, economics and culture, were widely influential, and his eclectic approach and twisted writing style still makes for interesting reading. Most of his writings are major references for mass communciation studies. Among this distinguised publications include- *Report on Project in Understanding New Media-* National Association of Educational Broadcasters (1960); *Explorations in Communication* (1960); *The Gutenberg Galaxy: The Making of Typographic Man* (1962); *Understanding Media:*

*The Extensions of Man* (1964); *The Medium is the Massage* (1967); *War and Peace in the Global Village* (1968); *Culture is Our Business* (1970) *City As Classroom: Understanding Language and Media*, With Eric McLuhan(1977); *Laws of Media: The New Science* With Eric McLuhan (1988); *The Global Village*, with Bruce R. Power (1989); and *Understanding Me* (edited by Stephanie McLuhan and David Staines) published in 2004.

**MCU.** Script designation for medium close-up.

**Mean.** Arithmetic average where a total of distinct values are related to the number and distribution of each value to arrive at a figure intended to be representative of all the values. The mean is the most common measure of central tendency.

**Meaning.** A dynamic interaction between reader/viewer/listener etc. and the message; an interpreted goal, intent, or end.

**Meanline.** The X-height of a typeface, that is of small letters without extension, e.g. a, e, o. With some typefaces the x-height can be low, making type less legible in small point sizes. Such type is best used in large sizes for display purposes.

**Measure.** In printing, length of line to which type is set.

**Measure(s) of Central Tendency.** Term used in statistical method to describe the various forms of average, based on the tendency of quantitative data to cluster around some middle value or values in sets of variable values. The mean, median, midpoint, and mode are all measures of central tendency.

**Measure of Dispersion.** Standard approximation of the extent to which scores in a distribution deviate or vary from the typical, common, central values. Variance and standard deviation are well-known measures of dispersion.

**Mechanical Binding.** Binding which opens flat. Useful for ring binders or spiral bound publications. Requires wide margin for punching to take binding.

**Mechanical Data.** As specified in media-owner's rate card or in Brad data setting out production details such as column lengths and widths, printing process, halftone screens and colour facilities.

**Mechanical Pulp.** Produced by grinding instead of through chemicals and used to make Newsprint.

**Media.** Means of communication such as press, radio, TV, film, video, exhibition, sales literature, direct mail, catalogues, telephone, posters, signs, newscasters, etc. Plural of medium.

**Media Accountability.** A composite term for the idea, and the associated processes for realising it, the media can and should be held to account for the quality, means and consequences of their publishing activities to society in general and/or to other interests that may be affected. This brings accountability into potential conflict with freedom. The idea of media accountability is sometimes, though not necessarily, associated with ideas of social responsibility. It does presuppose some mutual relationship between media senders and receivers. It is also closely linked to the idea of there being a public interest in the media.

**Media Advertising.** The traditional above-the-line-media, press, radio, TV, outdoor, cinema, and those on which advertising agencies relied for commission income, although many these days charge service fees.

**Media Analysis Staff.** Advertising agency worker (usually) employed to maintain and collate media statistics.

**Media Broker.** Independent agency, usually dealing exclusively with buying space or time in the media on behalf of a client. May or may not include media planning or other support services.

**Media Budget.** Amount of advertising appropriation allocated to media advertising, classified by medium, vehicle and time periods.

**Media Buyer.** Executive in advertising agency (or large in-house advertising department) who negotiates purchase of space and airtime. Originally called space buyer. Large agencies have separate buyers of space and airtime, and also Media Planners.

**Media Buying.** The purchase of space and airtime on the mass media usually for adverts or sponsored programmes.

**Media Commission.** Commission allowed by publishers and television contractors to 'recognised' advertising agencies in consideration of the space or time they book on behalf of their clients.

**Media Communication.** The mode of communication between direct, face-to-face address and mass communication.

**Media Concentration.** The coming together of media organisations to form larger units either by vertical or horizontal integration of firms. The former refers to joining of various sequences in the media process (e.g. paper production, printing, publishing and selling of books), the latter to conglomeration of firms at the same stage in the sequence. Both lead to greater monopoly and less diversity. Concentration can also take place within the same national market or transnationally. The usual main reference is to concentration of ownership, although it is possible for there to be varying levels of concentration of different work processes in a media conglomerate.

**Media Co-ordination.** Way of buying media more competitively. One agency co-ordinates the media buying for different product accounts of one company which are handled creatively by other agencies.

**Media Control.** Concerns ownership of the mass media, which could be owned privately or by government. It is also often used to denote the level of laws used to get rid of freedom of information or expression of the media. Also some writers have used this to mean the effect the mass media have on individuals. But the main categories of media control generally recognised are authoritarian, paternal, commercial and democratic. See Media influence.

**Media Credibility.** The believability of a medium in which a message appears. For example, one particular newspaper might be considered more believable than another newspaper.

**Media Data Form.** Established format for presenting data regarding a publication so as to facilitate comparison, particularly of circulation and rates. Also available for exhibitions.

**Media Ethics.** Principles of good conduct for media practitioners, bearing in mind the public role of the media in a given society, as well as the claims of individuals. The relevant conduct relates especially to the ways in which information is obtained and to decisions about what and how to publish, especially bearing in mind the consequences that might follow for all concerned. In non-informational content areas, there are also numerous ethical issues, although these are less likely to have been codified or play a part in decision making. The claim of journalism to be a profession depends in some degree on the voluntary development and acceptance of ethical standards. See media accountability.

**Media Evaluation.** Consideration of alternative media prior to selection, to determine the significance of both qualitative and quantitative factors relevant to advertising objectives.

**Media Explosion.** Rapid development of new press, radio, TV, teletext and other media, aided by new publishing and broadcasting techniques which have occurred in recent years, including international media using satellite facilities.

**Media Exposure Analysis.** Measuring and interpreting exposure of respondents to various media. Also allowance necessary for those who may not read, see or hear certain media.

**Media Images.** Conventional stereotypes which the media operate in the definition and redefinition of consensus and by which they define and sometimes police, the normative contours of society.

**Media Imperialism.** A process whereby ownership, structure, distribution, or content of media in any one country singly or together is subjected to the external pressure from the media interests of any other country or countries without a proportional reciprocation in influence by the country so affected.

**Media Independent.** Advertising agency which plans and buys media but does no creative work.

**Media Influence.** This refers to the way in which the mass media in all forms- television, film, advertising and similar forms- affect the way an audience behave and act in everyday live. See Hypodermic Needle Theory.

**Media Manipulation.** This is the way in which individuals or groups use various tricks in dealing with the media in order to create an image of their side of an argument that is most favourable to the receiver.

**Media Mix.** Explanation of amount of advertising appropriation allocated to each medium within the media budget.

**Media Owners.** Publishers and contractors supplying media, including press, cinema, TV and radio broadcasting, and posters available for carrying advertising. More broadly, those offering any channel of communication used for mass communication.

**Media Planner.** Agency executive who plans media schedules for approval by client, using rate card details, circulation, readership and audience figures, to select the most economical and effective media to reach target market.

**Media Register, The.** Run by Advertising Research Services. Monitors advertising expenditure in competition with Meal. Provides slides or prints of any roadside poster displayed, and supplies poster expenditure data.

**Media Research.** Investigation and analysis of media, comprising: (1) Media characteristics; (2) Qualitative factors; (3) Quantitative factors: (4) Cost factors; (5) Mechanical data. In practice, is largely concerned with readership, audience and circulation data.

**Media Schedule.** Chart drawn up by an advertiser, usually with the aid of an advertising agency, setting out the media to be used in a campaign indicating the weight, timing and cost of each time. Also plan of media bookings showing titles (or stations), dates, times, positions, costs.

**Media Selection.** Deciding which are the appropriate media to achieve programme or advertising objectives in line with media strategy and evaluation. Will normally be based on most cost-effective communication to pre-determined target audiences.

**Media Species.** Classification of the public in terms of attitudes to advertising.

**Media Strategy.** Amount of advertising appropriation defined by its purposes and allocated to the factors of impact, coverage, frequency and duration.

**Media Technology.** See Information technology.

**Media Tiredness.** Failure of media to retain their pulling power due to excessive use. Necessary to determine the lowest number of insertions, spots or mail shots before law of decreasing returns applies.

**Median.** Midpoint of a series of numerical data. Often referred to as a kind of average. If there is an even number of scores, the midpoint is halfway between the two scores in the middle. Observed by inspection, e.g. 4, 7, 13, 16, 20; median is 13. Where the number of items in a series is even, interpolation may be used.

**Mediaspeak.** Literary corruption or pollution such as 'at this point in time' instead of 'now'.

**Mediasphere.** Term coined in relationship to public sphere to represent the collective ecology of the world media, including newspapers, journals, television, radio, books, novels, advertising, press releases, publicity and the blogosphere, and to include any and all media both broadcast and published.

**Media-weight.** Used for weighing advertising expenditure; means of varying expenditure or actual decision criteria according to the value of particular media characteristics, especially the qualitative factors. It reflects the effectiveness with which an advertisement will work in a particular medium or publication.

**Mediate, Mediation.** Changing the meaning of any real event through the application of media technology.

**Medium.** Channel of communication, e.g. press organ, television station, exhibition or direct mail. Plural form is media, often used to refer specifically to periodical publications.

**Medium is the message.** A classical statement by Marshall McLuhan, which means that the form of a message- print, visual, musical, etc.- determines the ways in which that message will be perceived. McLuhan argued that modern electronic communications- including radio, television, films, and computers- would have far-reaching sociological, aesthetic, and philosophical consequences, to the point of actually altering the ways in which we experience the world.

**Mediums of Communication.** The possibility that different mediums (radio, television, or the internet) have a direct and differentiated impact on shaping human behaviour. This also refers to the various media in a communication process.

**Megahertz / MHz.** One million cycles per second.

**Melodrama.** Often used in very approximate ways to mean 'exaggerated', 'hysterical' or 'extreme' originally a kind of drama which, coming out of censored theatre in the seventeenth century, developed an elaborate language of gesture and used in highly polarised scenarios often pitting 'vice' against 'virtue'. It could be a play, film, or television program, characterised by exaggerated emotions, stereotypical characters, and interpersonal conflicts.

**Memory Factor.** Problem when conducting research surveys that respondents cannot always remember correctly. Even claim, for instance, to have seen an advertisement that has not appeared. Can be overcome by aided recall methods such as Mastheads of publication in Readership Surveys or, better still, with diaries in which consumers record TV programmes watched.

**Merchandising.** The promotion of an advertiser's products, services, and the like to the sales force, wholesalers, and dealers, promotion other than advertising to consumers through the use of in-store displays, guarantees, services, point-of-purchase materials, and so forth; display and promotion of retail goods; display of a mass media advertisement close to the point of sale.

**Merge.** Combining of Mailing Lists as occurs when names and addresses are obtained from different sources.

**Merge-purge.** Weeding out of duplicate names when two or more mailing lists are merged.

**Merger.** Amalgamation of two or more organisation with the object of growth, possibly to improve spending efficiency or to improve market performance but also to absorb competition.

**Metro Rating.** The broadcast rating figure from within a metropolitan area.

**Metropolitan Area.** A geographic area consisting of a central city of 50,000 population or more, plus the economically and socially integrated surrounding area, as established by the federal government; usually limited by county boundaries (slang "metro area").

**Metropolitan Bias.** The argument that too much of the UK media is based in London and takes little interest in affairs outside the capital.

**Message.** Communication transmitted by words, signals, or other means from one person, station, or group to another. It provides information and can be this information itself. Therefore its meaning is dependent on the context, the term may apply to both the information and its form. More precisely, in mass communications, a message is information which is sent from a source to a receiver. It could be a thought or idea expressed briefly in a plain or secret language, prepared in a form suitable for transmission by any means of communication. This is a very vital part of a communication process and one can strongly say it is the essence of mass communication.

**Message Distribution**. Measurement of media audience by the successive frequency of exposure, for example, saw once; saw twice, and so on.

**Metallic Inks.** Those which have metallic powders for printing in gold or silver.

**Metamessage.** The underlying message in a communication act or process.

**Metaphor.** A figure of speech in which a word or phrase that ordinarily designates one thing is used to designate another, thus making an implicit comparison, as in *"a sea of troubles"* or *"All the world's a stage"* (Shakespeare).

**Metasignals.** The propagation of signalling information among the nodes of a system. Simply put, a signal that comments on another signal or set of signals.

**Metre Advertisements.** Advertisements placed on parking metres. They have a repetitive effect on passers-by.

**Metre Method.** A broadcast rating measurement in which a monitoring device installed on TV sets is connected to a central computer which then records channel selection at different times of the day.

**Methodology.** Principles underlying the choice of particular research techniques. It strictly relates to the basis of a research design application and analysis. Commonly used as a synonym for 'method', but more properly should apply to a set of methods.

**Metonymy.** Figure of speech in which one word or phrase is substituted for another with which it is closely associated, as in the use of *Washington* for *the United States government* or of *the sword* for *military power.*

**Metric Type Sizes.** Although the original Point System continues to be used (unlike the replacement of halftone screens by metric versions), metric type sizes are widely used on the continent and with computerised photo typesetting or digital typesetting 1.00mm CH (4pt), 1.50mm CH (6pt), 2.60mm CH (8pt) up to 18mm CH (72pt). CH stands for capital height.

**mf.** More follows, as used in bottom right-hand corner of a news release when there is a continuation.

**MF.** Machines or mill finished paper, calendared on papermaking machine to produce smooth finish.

**MG.** Machine or mill glazed paper with glossing finish on one side. Used for posters.

**MHz.** Megahertz. One million hertz or one million cycles per second. One hertz simply means "one per second" (1 / s); 100 Hz means "one hundred per second", and so on. The unit may be applied to any periodic event – for example, a clock might be said to tick at 1 Hz, or a human heart might be said to beat at 1.2 Hz. Frequency of aperiodic events, such as radioactive decays, is expressed in becquerels. To avoid mix-up, periodically varying angles are typically *not* expressed in hertz, but rather in an appropriate angular unit such as radians per second. A disc rotating at 1 revolution per minute (RPM) can thus be said to be rotating at 0.105 rad/s or 0.017 Hz, where the latter reflects the number of complete revolutions per second.

**Mic Fright.** A fear to perform in front of a microphone.

**Micro Lens.** A lens for close-up photography, designed to focus continuously from infinity down to a reproduction ratio of 1: 2, or with a matched extension ring or teleconverter down to 1: 1. it is available in normal or telephoto focal lengths to provide a variety of free working distances. With the exception of Nikon, this type of lens is called a "Micro Nikkor" lens. See above Macro or Makro (usually for German origin lenses).

**Microfiche.** Method of storing publications and other records photographically on sheets of film, which can be viewed on optical viewing equipment.

**Micro-marketing.** Emphasis on advertising and Sales Promotion to sell goods rather than going beyond advertising to rely on price, performance or reputation, wider use of variable being macro-marketing.

**Microphone, Mic.** A communication device that picks up sound and amplifies it. It is sometimes referred to as a mike or mic (pronounced "mike"), it increases the sound of ones voice and is an acoustic to electric transducer that converts sound into an electrical signal. Microphones are used in many applications such as telephones, tape recorders, hearing aids, motion picture production, live and recorded audio engineering, in radio and television broadcasting and in computers for recording voice, VoIP and numerous other computer applications. A microphone's directionality or polar pattern indicates how sensitive it is to sounds arriving at different angles about its central axis. The polar pattern represents the locus of points that produce the same signal level output in the microphone if a given sound pressure level is generated from that point. Its types include;

(1)     Dynamic: This produces excellent frequency response and is good for outside broadcast because of its resistance to wind blasts. The diaphragm is attached to a coil of wire located near a magnet. When sound waves strike the diaphragm, they are passed on to the coil and the movement of the coil generates a small electric current. As the sound becomes louder, the movement of the diaphragm increases as does the amount of the electrical energy produced. Also called pressure.

(2)     Ribbon: This has a thin metallic ribbon supported at the ends between the poles of a permanent magnet.  A small current is generated when sound waves hit the coil and is then relayed to the audio console. Though not as rugged as dynamic, the sound production is always rich especially in closed areas. Also called velocity.

(3)  Condenser: Almost similar to pressure microphones because it has a diaphragm instead of a coil. It uses condenser which is also called capacitor. It has a powerful audio response. Its diaphragm acts as one plate of a capacitor, and the vibrations produce changes in the distance between the plates. Since the plates are biased with a fixed charge (Q), the voltage maintained across the capacitor plates changes with the vibrations in the air, according to the capacitance equation: $Q = C.V.$ where $Q =$ charge in coulombs, $C =$ capacitance in farads and $V =$ potential difference in volts. The capacitance of the plates is inversely proportional to the distance between them for a parallel-plate capacitor.

**Microphone Boom.** A device for suspending, directing and moving a mic over a production area.

**Microprism.** Minute glass or plastic structure of multiple prisms set in a viewfinder screen to act as a focusing aid. Breaks up an out-of-focus subject into a shimmer but images a focused subject clearly. Will not work satisfactorily at lens apertures smaller than f5.6.

**Microwave.** A very short-wave frequency located above the area on the electromagnetic spectrum where standard broadcast transmission takes place.

**Mid-Market.** In classifications of media texts (especially newspapers), the middle position between tabloid and quality.

**Mid-roll Change.** Feature available on the some APS camera that enables users to remove a partially exposed film cassette, insert it again later, and start shooting exactly where they left off.

**Middle Tones.** Mainly in black and white pictures, the grey tones. The finer the half tone screen, the better the range of tonal values.

**Midpoint.** Point halfway between the highest score and the lowest score in a frequency distribution; the mean of the highest and lowest scores.

**Migration.** (1) Switching from one television channel to another; may occur as a reaction to television commercials or choice of programme. (2) Switching attention from a feature or news item in the press to an advertisement.

Mike.

**Mike.** *Microphone mic.*

**Mileage.** Measure of reaction gained from a media communication.

**Milieu.** The social environment or setting of an individual, group, culture or nation.

**Milk Bottle Advertising.** Silk-screened advertisements on milk bottles.

**Milline (Rate).** An advertising measure; one agate line appearing in one million copies of a publication. A unit for comparing newspaper advertising rates in relation to circulation. This comparison is done with uneven circulations by calculating the line-rate-per-million circulation; determined by multiplying the line rate by 1,000,000 and dividing by the circulation; now somewhat obsolete because of the declining use of agate-line measurements and advertising-line rates. See minimil rate.

**MiniDisc.** Format designed by Sony to provide both a smaller CD for customer playback and a recording medium for the audio industry. Only the latter use has been taken up widely.

**Mini Doc.** A short documentary usually produced as a series for a radio or news program.

**Mini-Lab.** Also 1 hour colour lab. Photofinishing operation that operates on a retail level, serving consumers directly and processing film on-site.

**Minimil Rate**. The cost of an agate line of advertising at the lowest possible milline rate; somewhat obsolete as the usage of agate lines has declined. See milline rate.

**Minicuts.** Collection of pages of camera-ready stock artwork, printed on one side, ready for paste-up. Hundreds of pictures in 100 A4 pages.

**Mini-page.** Portrait page advertisement at premium rate filling about three-quarters depth and which of page, with editorial surround.

**Mining.** Seeking new prospects in Direct Response campaign by using large public database.

**Mirror Lens (Reflex Lens).** Lens in which some (usually two) of the elements are curved mirrors. This construction produces comparatively lightweight short fat long focus lenses. They cannot be fitted with a normal diaphragm.

**Mirror Image.** How an organisation sees itself which could be contrary to that held by outsiders, usually used in public relations.

**MIS.** Marketing Information Service.

**Mise en scene.** Literally 'putting together the scene'; 'putting into the scene' or staging the events of the script for the camera. Usually refers to visual processes at pre-edit stage, though some critics include sound in this term.

**Mix.** (1) In films and video, to fade out one image and introduce another. (2) To combine two or more sources of audio or video. (3) The range of products – the product mix-sold by one manufacturer. See dissolve.

**Mix-down.** The process by which numerous audio tracks are appropriately combined into the final one or two audio tracks needed for program distribution.

**Mix-effects Bank.** A double row of buttons on a switcher which can be used in the creation of video effects.

**Mix-effects Monitors.** Video monitor dedicated to setting up and viewing video effects from one or more *mix-effects banks.*

**Mixed Media.** Using more than one medium in any advertising campaign. Most often used where more than one advertising objective has been set for the campaign.

**Mixed-sources.** Two or more light sources with significantly different colour temperatures. Commonly, sunlight and incandescent light.

**Mixer.** A device that blends two or more audio or video sources.

**MLS.** Script designation for medium long shot.

**Mnemonic.** Set of initials which make it easier to say or remember series of words, and whereby the initials form a new word.

**Mobile.** (1) Point-of-sale display device suspended from ceiling of shop so that it moves with air currents. (2) In some countries, especially Third World, touring film, video or demonstration show. (3) Loudspeaker van or car. (4) Exhibition or hospitality vehicle. (5) Travelling advertising medium such as car, taxi, trailer, van or bus.

**Mobile Advertising.** Advertising on vehicles such as vans, buses, cars, taxis or trains. Can display posters where static sites are scarce; has dramatic appeal of movement and can reach succession of audiences. Flexible medium which can be used for short-term promotions such as opening of new store, or to launch new cars.

**Mock-up.** Rough presentation of an idea for print, package, display piece or exhibition stand which may be a drawing or model.

**Mod.** Modification of which may include type characters, halftone and line art.

**Mode.** Most commonly recurring value(s) in any recorded numerical data. Such clusters are often referred to as averages and may sometimes be more representative of the data than the arithmetic mean. For example, the modal age among college freshmen is probably 18, although the mean age is probably much higher.

**Mode of Address.** The way a text speaks to its audience, the tone and pitch.

**Model.** (1) Mathematical representation of real life situation. (2) Person used to illustrate an advertisement. (3) Reproduction on a small scale. Mostly used in communication research, this is an abstract and simplified representation of a complex system or process. Where multiple variables are known to interact, statistical techniques can be used to model the most important relationships.

**Modelling.** Representation by lighting of the three-dimensional nature of an original in a two-dimensional reproduction.

**Modem.** Electronic coupler connecting a computer and telephone, permitting access to other computers and databases.

**Modern Face.** Typeface with upright thickness to sides of letters such as 'O'. used mainly in the late 18th century.

**Modernism.** Innovative, often self-reflexive artistic movements which ran roughly from the 1920s to the 1970s.

**Modernity.** (1) An alternative to post-modernity as a way of describing the contemporary, emphasising attempts to rethink enlightenment values such as belief in progress, rationality etc.; (2) In post-modern theory such pre-contemporary processes as Fordism.

**Modulation.** The superimposition of audio and video signals on a radio frequency carrier wave so that the signals may be broadcast.

**Modulation Transfer Function (MTF).** The method used to measure a lens's ability to hold diminishing details of a subject. It is used because everything is done electronically and eliminating any errors in human judgement or vision and results can be repeatable to counter check earlier tests. Secondly, a precise comprehensive rating is made possible by incorporating huge amount of data into a single reading; lastly it is very fast and permit its use on just out from production lenses.

**Monaural.** Single-channel audio as opposed to stereo audio.

**Monica.** A marketing research database tool which predicts the likely age group of consumers on the basis of their first names.

**Monitor.** A TV set, normally without an RF tuner or audio circuitry, used for the checking of colour, composition, etc., during a production. To check performance at regular intervals in relation to pre-established norms. Also to record radio and TV programming.

**Monitor Pre-flash(es).** In photojournalism, when performing automatic balanced fill-flash with TTL multi sensor, the speedlight fires a series of scarcely visible pre-flashes to enable the camera's computer to pre-analyse the scene. The TTL multi sensor in the camera body reads the amount of reflected light, then the camera's microcomputer determines the area of the TTL sensor to be used for flash output control and adjusts the flash output level. The Monitor Pre-flashes are visible but not recognisable. First adopted by Contax RTS III, now Nikon is using this for its top flagship model, the F5.

**Mono Press.** Publication printed in black and white only.

**Monochrome.** Although it means one colour, it generally denotes a black and white television picture.

**Monofunctional.** The term ascribing to a literary work, radio, film, or television as a single function.

**Monoline.** Typefaces, such as Sans Serif faces, whose strokes are of equal thickness.

**Monopod.** A one-legged camera support.

**Monopoly.** Any market situation where one seller controls prices and the supply of product. In the UK usually a 25 per cent share will attract the interest of regulators.

**Monopoly Advertisers.** Advertisers who take all the available advertising space in or on a medium, e.g. bus, or whole issue of publication.

**Monotone.** One colour printing of pictures, usually black.

**Montage.** (1) Showing of rapid succession of scenes in television filming. (2) Bringing together into one illustration a number of different artistic materials edited in sequence in which a juxtaposition of seemingly unrelated shots is designed to create a mood or basic theme.

**Montage Editing.** Although the term as used in early film work had a different meaning, today montage editing refers to a rapid, impressionistic sequence of disconnected scenes linked by a variety of transition devices that are designed to communicate feelings or experiences. A montage does not tell a story by developing an idea in a logical sequence.

**Mood.** (1) Advertisement copy which creates an atmosphere, as with many charity advertisements. (2) The mood of reader, viewer or listener at different times of day, or on different occasions, which can affect response to advertising.

**Mood Advertising.** Advertising which is deliberately aimed at putting potential customers into a frame of mind conducive to acceptance of the product.

**Mood Music.** Background music, as in TV and radio commercials, which can enhance appeal of the advertising by being dramatic, modern, romantic and so on.

**Mood Programming.** Maintaining a single approach or characteristic in broadcast programming.

**MOR.** Middle of the road. A radio format that describes a station that plays a wide spectrum of popular music. MOR stations play everything from Glen Miller to current "soft" rock.

**Moral Panic.** The term was first applied by the criminologist Jock Young to apply sudden expressions of often irrational mass anxiety and alarm directed at supposed 'crime waves' or other supposed evidence of disorder and social breakdown (including promiscuity and immigration). The media are implicated through their tendency to amplify such 'panics'. They are also sometimes objects of moral panics, when alarm at their harmful effects suddenly gains currency (e.g. in the form of crime waves, suicides, or rioting). New media, such as computer games and the internet, tend to generate some degree of panic at alleged harm to their (young) users.

**More/mf.** Written at the foot of a copy to show that more is to follow.

**Morgue.** In newspaper offices, ready written obituaries of VIPs. Also outdated term for newsroom library where past copies of news materials are stored.

**Morphing.** Special computer graphics effect often used in TV commercials. It creates bending and stretching effects. This effect makes a person or object progressively transform into another person or object. Achieved by computer software, e.g. the shape-changing Terminator in *Terminator 2* (US 1991).

**Motivation.** A psychological feature that arouses an organism to action toward a desired goal; the reason for the action; that which gives purpose and direction to behaviour. It could cause initiation, direction, intensity and persistence of behaviour. It could be a temporal or dynamic state and should not be confused with personality or emotion which is the temporal state that do not immediately link to behaviour as anger, grief or happiness. A motivated person can be reaching for a long-term goal such as becoming a professional footballer or a more short-term goal like learning how to spell a particular word.

**Motivation Research.** A kind of research used to investigate the psychological reasons why individuals behave in a certain way, say buy specific types of merchandise, or why they respond to specific advertising appeals, to determine the base of brand choices and product preferences.

**Motivation Theory.** A theory that identifies the social factors that push people to engage in a certain behaviour. Motivation is derived from the Latin word *movere,* meaning "to move." It can broadly entail forces that act on or within a person that cause the arousal, direction, and persistence of goal-directed, voluntary effort. Motivation theory is thus concerned with the processes that explain why and how human behaviour is activated.

**Motor Drive.** A mechanism for advancing the film to the next frame and recocking the shutter, activated by an electric motor usually powered by batteries. Popular for action-sequence photography and for recording images by remote control.

**Mouse.** A hand-held, button-activated input device that when rolled along a flat surface directs an indicator to move correspondingly about a computer screen, allowing the operator to move the indicator freely, as to select operations or manipulate text or graphics. The device has now become very sophisticated to include wireless and laser features.

**Moving-coil Mic (Dynamic microphone).** Microphone which depends upon a diaphragm connected to a moving coil suspended in a magnetic field. See Microphone.

**MP3 (MPEG- 1 Audio Level 3).** The standard format for compressing video data for editing and playback.

**MPEG.** Moving Pictures Experts Group. A file format used for digital video. MPEG- 2 is a standard for compressing video data for editing and playback.

**MPPA, Motion Picture Association of America.** America's trade association formed by the major Hollywood studios to protect their interests. The Motion Pictures Association (MPA) is the international arm of the organisation which has successfully defended the studios' rights to free trade and exploitation of international markets.

**MS (medium shot).** Object seen from a medium distance. Normally covers framing between long shot and close-up.

**Mug.** A mug shot or a small photo of someone. If someone says, "get me a mug," don't come back with coffee.

**Multifunctional.** Involving numerous independent variables or treatments (factors). Multifunctional experimental designs can be extremely complex.

**Multi-image Presentation.** Combined audio tape/35mm slide presentation.

**Multilayer Coating.** The depositing of multiple coats of anti-reflective materials on a lens surface to reduce ghost images and flare produced by internal reflections and insure faithful colour rendition; in the Nikon Integrated Coating system, the number of layers is determined by the type of optical glass and the position of the element in the lens design.

**Multimedia.** Used to describe a range of different delivery formats such as text, images, video and audio, often accessible concurrently on the internet.

**Multiple-choice Question.** One which presents respondent with list and questions such as 'which of the following makes of phone do you use?' Best to rear range order of lists for different respondents when danger of first and last items becoming favourites.

**Multiple Camera.** A video tape production where several cameras are used.

**Multiple Exposure.** (1) Single picture made by superimposing images on others. (2) Extent to which readers see a page in a journal more than once.

**Multiple Image.** Problem that different representatives of the same organisation give individual images. Hence, attempts at creating uniformity such as staff clothing, for example in banks, building societies and retail stores.

**Multiple-screen Slide Presentation.** Theatrical show with large screen made up of multiples of 35mm slides back-projected by batteries of computerised projectors. Screen can be split into two, four, eight or more smaller pictures simultaneously.

**Multiple Readership.** More than one reader per issue, usually involving secondary and tertiary readers. In trade and technical press, can amount to double figures for each copy.

**Multiple Regression.** Technique for developing an equation that best represents the relationship between continuous independent and dependent variables.

**Multiplex.** (1) Combining several signals into one. For example, most FM stations transmit a main signal and sub-signals that create the stereo sound heard on that station. (2) Also multi-screen cinemas which have resuscitated cinema exhibition.

**Multiplexer.** A mirror device which is part of a film island that selectively directs the light from multiple projectors into a single television camera.

**Multiplier Effect.** An economics terminology used to decribe an occurance of a change in spending which causes a disproportionate change in aggregate demand. It is particularly associated with Keynesian economics; though some other schools of economic thought reject or downplay the importance of multiplier effects particularly in the long run. But in media term, It is used to describe a situation where culture as a commodity, usually in forms of films and television programmes exported to other countries, open up markets for other goods.

**Multi-stage Sample.** Sample assembled by combining proportionate numbers of respondents of different characteristics represented in a universe. Selection is random within each category. Satisfactorily combines the benefits of both quota and random sampling. For example, a sample collected in the United Kingdom and then collecting other samples from other countries would be multiple.

**Multivariate Analysis.** Any statistical technique, such as multiple regression or multivariate analysis of variance, designed to study relationships among variables simultaneously.

**Municipal Advertising.** Advertising that stresses the favourable attributes of a municipality. Used many times to try to attract businesses to an area.

**Music Production Libraries.** Collections of music covering a wide variety of moods and needs, which have been especially designed for productions.

**Must.** An instruction on a copy. Editorial item which is considered essential and should appear.

**Muybridge, Eadweard.** (April 9, 1830 – May 8, 1904) A British-born photographer, known primarily for his early use of multiple cameras to capture motion, and his zoopraxiscope, a device for projecting motion pictures that pre-dated celluloid film strip still used today. See Zoopraxography.

**MVDS.** Microwave digital sound.

**Myths.** Traditional stories through which societies reinforce and explore their beliefs about themselves; in Media Studies, associated with the work of the anthropologist Levi-Strauss, and then Roland Barthes, who uses it to mean almost the same as ideology.

**Myth of Marginality.** Term applied to the practice by news media of covering events that are not usually given important ranking order in agenda setting, thus giving it low or marginal status when news values are applied.

# N

**NAB.** National Association of Broadcasters. This is a full-service trade association that promotes and protects the interests of radio and television broadcasters in Washington and around the world, assisting them in technical, legal, financial, and other matters. NAB is the broadcaster's voice before Congress, federal agencies and the Courts. They also serve a growing number of associate and international broadcaster members. NAB work to keep their members out front on policy issues, technology and management trends. Their staff provides ongoing and "late breaking" broadcast news, industry research and legal expertise.

**NAB Code.** A code of ethics for broadcasters developed by the National Association of Broadcasters.

**NABJ.** The National Association of Black Journalists. An organisation of journalists, students and media-related professionals that provide quality programs and services to and advocates on behalf of black journalists worldwide. Founded by 44 men and women on December 12, 1975, in Washington, D.C., NABJ is the largest organisation of journalists of colour in the U.S. It is committed to-strengthening ties among black journalists; sensitising all media to the importance of fairness in the workplace for black journalists; expanding job opportunities and recruiting activities for veteran, young and aspiring black journalists, while providing continued professional development and training; increasing the number of black journalists in management positions and encouraging black journalists to become entrepreneurs; fostering an exemplary group of professionals that honour excellence and outstanding achievements by black journalists, and outstanding achievement in the media industry as a whole, particularly when it comes to providing balanced coverage of the black community and society at large; working with high schools and colleges to identify and encourage black students to become journalists, and to diversify faculties and related curriculum; and providing informational and training services to the general public.

**Nameplate.** The newspaper's name on page one. Also called the flag or masthead.

**NAN.** News Agency of Nigeria. NAN was created in May 1976, by Decree No. 19 as amended by Decree No. 10 of 1978, solely as an organisation established for the purpose of news gathering, distribution of news and as a channel of information to the people and more especially to those who require the services. NAN like most world news agencies, belongs to the group of National News Agencies. It is owned and controlled by the Nigerian government. However, rather than use NAN as an instrument of propaganda, the Nigeria Government established NAN with the bid to ensure that news about Nigeria and Nigerians is not only made available to the world press but ensure that news from all around the country is made available to the media. While the primary duty of NAN is to uphold the integrity of the Federal Republic of Nigeria as well as promote harmonious relationship between the various ethnic groups of the country, NAN must always ensure that news items and comments from the agency does not jeopardise peace and harmony in the country. The news agency operates on the following functions and objectives: (1) to make available, international, regional and local news and other news materials; (2) to distribute such news, news materials and news features to subscribers against payment either in the form of fees or news exchange or on such terms as may be agreed; (3)to present impartial information on any matter of public or national interest within and outside the country; and (4) to present objective news and views, without prejudice of all sections of the country. It also offers commercial services otherwise known as the Bizcomm Services. The Business and Communication Services commenced since November 1991and it delivers and receives messages for clients throughout the country.

**Nanosecond.** One-billionth of a second.

**Narcotising Dysfunction.** A social consequence of the media upon audiences. Literally It indicates inducing stupor or narcosis; "narcotic drugs". However, it was proposed by one of the early television researchers, Paul Lazarsfeld, in 1955. He argued that one of the social effects of television viewing was 'narcotising dysfunction', in which viewing came to substitute knowing for doing, leading to an eventual diminishment of social involvement and engagement. He contributed much to the development of empirical methods in the social sciences during his work at the Columbia Bureau of Applied Social Research. The most famous of the studies he conducted was that into voting behaviour carried out in the 1940s and which also led him to develop the highly influential Two Step Flow Model of mass communication.

**Narration.** The process of telling a story, the selection and organisation of the events for a particular audience. For instance this could be the way a print reporter or broadcaster tells a story to his/her audience.

**Narrative.** Complex term referring to a sequence of events organised into a story with a particular structure.

**Narrative Paradigm.** A theory proposed by Walter Fisher that all meaningful communication is a form of storytelling or to give a report of events and so human beings experience and comprehend life as a series of ongoing narratives, each with their own conflicts, characters, beginnings, middles, and ends. It sees people as essentially storytellers, thus it defines humankind as *homo narrans*.

**Narrowband.** A communications system that utilises a narrower and lower frequency range compared to the higher wideband services. A service using frequencies below 1 megahertz is considered a narrowband service, whereas television at 6 MHz is commonly considered a wideband service.

**Narrowcasting.** A program that appeals to a select target audience, demographic, or special interest group instead of a large mass audience.

**National Advertising**. Advertising by the marketer of a trademarked product or service sold through different outlets, in contrast to local advertising.

**National Brand.** Brand which is advertised nationally by the manufacturer, as distinct from a retailer's own brand or own label.

**National Campaign.** Marketing operation covering the entire country.

**National Film and Television Archive, NFTVA.** One of the world's greatest collectors of film and television. The majority of its collection is British material but it also features internationally significant holdings from around the world. It also collect films which feature key British actors and the work of British directors. There is a wealth of material of every genre from silent newsreels to CinemaScope epics, from home movies to avant-garde experiments, from classic documentaries to vintage television, from advertisements to 3-D films, soap opera to football. The archive contains more than 50,000 fiction films, over 100,000 non-fiction titles and around 625,000 television programmes. As guardians of vast and growing national film heritage, they recognise the responsibility of ensuring continued survival of these materials. Lately, they have made significant investment in new storage facilities, epecially in the last 18 months and have also upgraded their existing stores. It is run by the British Film Institute.

**National Film and Television School.** United Kingdom's national centre of excellence for education in film and TV programme making. The National Film School (as it was first named) opened in 1971, the culmination of four years of planning to create an institution to train new talent for the British film industry. Concerned that the UK was being left behind by Europe and the USA, where formal training for filmmakers was already well-established, the Department of Education and Science had in 1967 recommended the creation of a national film school for the UK, and in 1969 an inquiry led by Lord Lloyd of Hampstead began to develop the recommendation into concrete plans. From the outset, the NFS rejected the vocational-school style, casting itself as a purveyor of in-depth film and television training. The curriculum in the early days was a loosely structured affair; sporadic seminars and workshops were secondary to production, with students spending most of their time doing exactly what they had come to the School to do - making films. But by the early 1980s, a more structured curriculum was introduced. Links with the Industry were strengthened, allowing students' idealism and creative talent to be matched with collaborative, financial and production expertise. The School changed its name to The National Film and Television School in 1982, reflecting the fact that many of its graduates went on to make their careers in TV. It today has some 160 full-time students, another two dozen part-timers on the Script Development course and around a thousand a year on its short courses. The only UK film school with its own film and television studios, and post-production facilities rivalling those of professional companies, its talented community of students makes around a hundred films a year on courses that are still over

90% practical and unlike anything offered at any other UK film school.

**National Identity.** In terms of representation, the set of ideas constructed around the concept of 'nation' and the ways in which individuals and groups relate to them.

**National Press.** Newspapers and magazines with national circulation. May be printed in or near Lagos or Abuja, but some use contract printers strategically placed throughout the country. Special feature of British press; most foreign publishers are regionalised, either because of the size of the country or because modern countries are federations of states. However, satellites have made national presses possible elsewhere. In Nigeria, This Day Newspaper publishes its newspaper simultaneously in Abuja and Lagos daily.

**Natural Break.** Requirement in broadcast media that commercial breaks occur only between normal gaps in the continuity of programmes. Almost impossible to achieve in a network involving many different programmes being broadcast simultaneously to different geographical regions, and so operates in principle rather than being applied rigidly.

**Naturalistic illusion of Television.** A concept that suppose the visual qualities of television can lead to the assumption that it is merely a window on the world.

**Naturals.** Centrefold Spread.

**NBC.** National Broadcasting Commission. Nigeria's broadcasting regulatory body. The Act of the National Assembly, Act 38 Of 1992 as amended by Act 55 of 1999, empowers the Commission, to carry out a number of duties, some of which include, licensing monitoring, regulating and conducting research in broadcasting in Nigeria. It is also the duty of the Commission, to ensure the development, in a dynamic manner, through the accreditation of the mass communication curricula in all the tertiary and other institution related to broadcasting. The National Broadcasting Commission is mandated by Section 2 subsection (1) of Act No 38 of 1992 as amended by Act No 55. of 1999 to carry out the following functions; (a) advising the Federal Government, on the implementation of the National Mass Communication Policy, with particular reference to broadcasting; (b) receiving, processing and considering applications, for establishment, ownership or operation of Radio and Television stations including; (i) Cable Television Services, Direct Satellite Broadcast and any other medium of broadcasting. (ii) radio and television stations owned, established or operated by the Federal, State and Local Government. (iii) and stations run under private ownership. (c) recommending applications, through the Minister of Information and National Orientation, to the President, Commander-In-Chief of the Armed forces, for the grant of radio and television licenses; (d) regulating and controlling the broadcast industry; (e) undertaking research and development in the broadcast industry; (f) receiving, Considering and investigating complaints from individual and corporate bodies, regarding the contents of a broadcasting station and the conduct of a broadcasting station; (g) upholding the principles of equity and fairness in broadcasting; (h) establishing and disseminating a national broadcasting code and setting standards with regards to the contents and quality of materials for broadcast; (I) promoting Nigerian indigenous cultures, moral and community life through broadcasting; (j) promoting authenticated Radio and Television audience measurement and penetration; (k) initiating and harmonising government policies on Trans-border direct transmission and reception in Nigeria; (l) regulating ethical standards and technical excellence in public, private and commercial broadcast stations in Nigeria; (m) monitoring broadcasting for harmful emission, interference and illegal broadcasting; (n) determining and applying sanctions, including revocation of licences of defaulting stations, which do not operate in accordance with the broadcast Code and in the public interest; (o) approving the transmitter power, location of stations, areas of coverage as well as regulate types of broadcast equipment to be used (p) ensuring qualitative manpower development in the broadcasting industry, by accrediting curricula and programmes for all tertiary training institutions that offer Mass Communications in relation to broadcasting; (q) intervening and arbitrating in conflicts in the broadcast industry; (r) ensuring strict adherence to the national laws, rules and regulations relating to the participation of foreign capital, in relation to local capital in broadcasting; (s) serving as national consultant on any legislative or regulatory issues on the broadcasting industry; (t) guaranteeing and ensuring the liberty and protection of the broadcasting industry with due respect to the law and; (u) carrying out such other activities as are necessary or expedient for the full discharge of all or any of the functions conferred on it under, or pursuant to this act.

**Necci Enlarger.** Japanese equipment for making full-colour printed enlargements direct from photographs on flexible textiles, vinyls, Formica laminate for interior/exterior displays/posters.

**Neckline.** White space below a headline.

**Needle Drop.** The single use of a transcribed musical piece, generally for a fee.

**Negative**. In photojournalism, the developed film that contains a reversed tone image of the original scene.

**Negative Correlation.** Relationship between two variables in which an increase in one is associated with a decrease in the other. For example, number of hours spent watching television might be associated with children's decreased school performance.

**Negative Holder.** A device designed to hold the negative in proper position in an enlarger.

**Negative Line Art.** Reversing line drawings white on black. Care has to be taken that fine lines are not so weak they will fill in. Can be done digitally.

**Negotiated.** In audience theory, the idea that a meaning is arrived at a result of a process of give and take between the reader's assumptions and the 'preferred meaning' offered by the text.

**Neologism.** The creation or use of new words or senses, or giving an old word a new meaning, such as 'viewer' from the French 'voyeur to indicate someone who views other people sometimes illicit activities. In psychology terms, the invention of new words is regarded as a symptom of certain psychotic disorders, such as schizophrenia.

**Net**. Money paid to a media vehicle by an advertising agency after deducting the agency's commission (also, slang for "network").

**Net Audience.** Total audience for a TV/radio airtime schedule, less duplication.

**Net Cover.** Percentage of the target audience receiving at least one exposure to a commercial or advertisement.

**Net Paid Circulation.** Part of total circulation paid for by readers, i.e. after deduction of free or complimentary copies and of unbought copies published.

**Net Price.** Final price after all discounts and allowances have been deducted.

**Net Rate.** Publisher's rate after deduction of agency commission.

**Net Reach.** Number of people who will have at least one opportunity to see an advertisement after allowing for duplication of readership between issues and between publication.

**Net Unduplicated Audience.** The number of different people who are reached by a single issue of two or more publications. See Cumulative audience.

**Network.** Any interconnected set of points, which could be persons, places, organisations, machines, etc. in communication, interest focuses on the flow of information through the 'lines' of a network, with particular reference to their carrying capacity and interactivity, and of course to who or what is connected more or less rightly and exclusively. The term 'network society' has been coined by theorist (e.g. Castells and Van Dyke) as an alternative way of expressing the reality of the Information Society. Also, a network may connote television or radio stations linked together for transmitting identical programmes simultaneously (not always necessary), like most of the programmes on the Nigerian Television Authority (NTA) or probably the British Broadcasting Corporation's linked services. Refers also to the facility by which other TV regions may retransmit programmes, and thus similar to syndicated press features.

**Network Advertising.** Advertising placed by the network which the station agrees to accept when it contracts to carry the network programming. The network keeps most of the money from the spot and pays the station in accordance with the size of the audience.

**Network Analysis.** Breaking down a complex project into component requirements and recording these in a diagrammatic form which incorporates a critical time scale, so that planning and control can be effected in the most expedient manner.

**Network Compensation.** The dollar amount a network pays an affiliate station for broadcasting a network feed.

**Network Cooperative Programme**. A network program with provisions for inserting local commercials. See Cooperative programme.

**Network Feed.** The sending of programming over the network distribution system to affiliates.

**Network Option Time**. Broadcast time on a station for which the network has the option of selling advertising.

**Network Radio Advertising.** Radio advertising on all ILR stations, booked in packages of days and times.

**Network TV Advertising.** Television advertising on all ITV stations.

**Neutral Density Filter; ND Filter.** A filter that reduces the light coming into a camera lens without altering its colour. In some filters, half ND filters can be very effective to lower the contrast, especially the sky to achieve more balance effect. Lens like reflex lenses, where its aperture is fixed, ND filter can be the only way to play around with exposures. Certain 617 format is provided with a central ND filter.

**New International Information Order, NIIO.** See NWICO.

**New Media.** New technological systems used for mass communication, such as fibre optic cables, computers, satellites, videoconferencing facilities, or electronic mail systems.

**News.** Gotten from the word 'new'. Information that is not already known to its recipients. It is the main form in which current information about public events is carried by media of all kinds. There is a great diversity of types and formats as well as cross-cultural differences, thus, it can be reported by such sources as newspapers, television and radio programs, wire services, and web sites. News reporting is a type of journalism, typically written or broadcast in news style. Most news is investigated and presented by journalists and can be distributed to various sites via news agencies. If the content of news is significant enough, it eventually becomes history. To be considered newsworthy, an event usually must have broad interest due to one or more news values- (a) Effect- how many people were, are or will be affected? (b) Timeliness- did the event occur very recently? (c) Revelation- is there significant new information, previously unknown? (d) Proximity- was the event nearby geographically? (e) Oddity- was the event highly unusual? (f) Entertainment- does it make for a fun story? (g) Celebrity- was anyone famous involved? News items and journalism can be divided in various ways, although there are gray areas. Distinctions include between hard news (serious and timely topics) and soft news (lighter topics); breaking news (immediate events); news analysis; and enterprise or investigative reporting, in which a topic is examined in great detail. News coverage traditionally begins with the "five W's"—who, what, where, when, why. See journalism.

**News Agency.** News gathering and information service, usually computerised such as News Agency of Nigeria, Press Association, Reuters, Associated Press, TASS. They sell them to broadcasters and newspaper publishers.

**News Cooperative.** A broadcast station association in which news stories are exchanged between members.

**News Desk.** Part of a newspaper office which receives news from various sources such as reporters, wire services, PR practitioners and so on.

**News Diffusion.** The process by which news is diffused to the receiving public.

**News Director.** The person responsible for the content, production and presentation of a newscast. Exact responsibilities depend on the news organisation.

**News Frameworks.** Shared set of assumptions by reporters and editors about what is newsworthy.

**News Hole.** Available space or time for a news story to appear or be aired based on the news value of competing stories and the space or time taken up by competing stories. Ads, promotional material, and public service materials decrease the news hole.

**News Management.** The strategy employed by those usually in power or government to shape the news to their own advantage, or to control events in such a way as to win favourable or positive publicity.

**News Producer.** Although responsibilities vary widely, producers are generally under the news director and in charge of specific newscasts. Producers often write basic transitional news copy.

**News Professionals.** The media workers who are trained to process news stories according to institutional norms.

**News Proof.** Advertisement proofed on Newsprint.

**News Release.** News story or item handed out officially to the media usually associated with news emanating from government sources, commercial companies, or other corporate bodies. Should resemble a news report as printed in the press. Subject should be in first few words. Opening paragraph should summarise whole story and should be capable of telling basic story even if nothing else is printed.

**News Selection.** See Agenda setting, News value.

**News Value.** The value or importance of an event or the potential impact of an event in relation to other events or potential news stories. This criteria is applied by journalists and editors in news organisations to determine whether or not to carry particular items of news. In commercial media, the consensus 'value' is whether or not the item concerned is likely to interest a potential audience. However, there are other sources of value, including a judgement of intrinsic significance or the pull or pressure of influential interests other than the audience.

**Newscaster.** Electronically operated, moving lighted sign, spelling out news items interspersed with advertisements, placed high on building and visible at a distance. Usually sited in city centres and railway terminals.

**Newspaper.** Traditionally this has referred to a print media form appearing regularly (usually not less than once a week), containing (at least) reliable reports of recent or ongoing events of general interest and offered for public sale (though may be free at times). Associated characteristics are usually independence or transparency of ownership and editing and a geographical range of coverage and circulation. Variant forms have emerged, including the 'free newspaper', paid for by advertising, and more recently the 'electronic newspaper' that is offered on-line and lacks the limits of time and location of the traditional newspaper.

**Newspaper Network.** Groups of newspaper linked together in a cooperative arrangement permitting an advertiser to purchase space in all of the newspapers within the group at the same time with one bill.

**Newspapers Publishers Association.** Trade association of national newspaper and London evening newspaper publishers.

**Newspaper Society.** Trade association of regional newspapers.

**Newspaper Syndicate.** A firm that sells special material such as features, photographs, comic strips, and cartoons, for publication in newspapers.

**Newsprint.** Poor quality absorbent paper made from mechanically pulp and used for printing newspapers and some magazines.

**Newsroom:** An office where journalists work, usually there are a lot of tables in the room with various writing materials. Also communication gadgets like TV, radio and computers are provided there. It is sometimes called the 'heart' of a mass media organisation.

**Newsworthiness.** Elements which make a news story interesting and noteworthy from the perspective of an audience.

**Next-day Recall.** Advertisement research to test impact and awareness of an advertisement and its content on the day following its appearance.

**Next Matter.** Press advertisement position next to editorial material.

**Next-to-reading Matter.** Advertisement position immediately adjacent to editorial; may be at premium rates.

**NFC.** Nigerian Film Corporation. Fully owned by the Federal Government of Nigeria and is under the supervision of the Ministry of

Information and National Orientation. The Federal Government being the only shareholder, the Corporation is compelled by law to provide social services to the Nigerian public and the Federal Government. The NFC is slated for full commercialisation.

**NFVCB.** National Film and Video Censors Board. Body that regulates and censor videos especially the home made in Nigeria.

**NIB.** News-in-brief. Often confused with fillers. The dividing line is thin. When there is a bounteous harvest of stories, some can be condensed into briefs without loosing the vital facts.

**Niche Marketing.** Marketing, including advertising and retailing, aimed at special Market Segment.

**Niépce, Joseph Nicéphore.** (March 7, 1765 – July 5, 1833 A French inventor, most noted as a pioneer in photography. He produced the first successful permanent photograph. He began experimenting with processes to set optical images in 1793. Some of his early experiments produced images, but they faded rapidly. He was said to have first produced long lasting images in 1824. The earliest known existing example of a Niépce photograph or any other photograph was created in June or July of 1827 or 1826, as some sources report. Niépce called his process "heliography", meaning "sun writing". The exposure time require is an issue still debated today, somewhere between 8 and 20 hours. Because of the improbably long exposure time, the process was used to photograph buildings and inanimate objects, but could not be practically used to photograph people. See Camera.

**Nielsen.** The A.C. Nielsen Company; a firm engaged in local and national television ratings and other marketing research.

**Nielsen Station Index (NSI).** A rating service for individual television stations.

**Nielsen Television Index (NTI).** A national television rating service, primarily for network programming.

**NIPR.** Nigerian Institute of Public Relations. Nigeria's PR organisation with membership drawn from the media and other institutions. Its function is similar to those of other PR institutes around the world. It holds conferences annually and usually absorbs new members during these conferences.

**No change in rate (NCR or NCIR).** Used when some other format or specification change has occurred.

**No Comment.** Negative statement which should be avoided. Journalists should not be snubbed and are entitled to even a generalised answer.

**NOA.** National Orientation Agency. Coordinates public orientation and enlightenment in Nigeria.

**Noddies.** Cutaway shots of an interviewer's visual responses (nodding, smiling, etc.). Noddies are useful as transition devices during editing.

**Noise.** Something that interferes with the communication process, it disrupts the free flow of information. Typically manifested as hiss or hum on sound tracks, and as snow or graininess in video.

**Nominal.** Data based on classifying cases into meaningful categories that cannot be ranked or ordered in a logical way from lowest to highest. Eye colour is an example of nominal data, as is ethnicity.

**Non-composite Video Signal.** Video signal containing picture and blanking information but no sync signals.

**Non-directional Microphone.** A microphone with a circular polar pattern of response, equally sensitive to sound from all directions.

**Nonlinear.** Relationship between two variables that is best represented graphically by anything other than a straight line. See Linear relationship.

**Non-linear Editing, NLE.** In contrast to linear editing, an editing approach that can assemble segments in a random order, in the same manner as a word processor. Segments can be moved, deleted, copied and altered before being output to an edited master. In film and video editing, this is wholly performed on a computer. Video and audio images are digitalised and can be compiled for playback from the computer, before a final version is 'printed' to film or tape. Analogue video and audio editing are 'linear'. Film editing has always been 'nonlinear'.

**Nonparametric.** Refers to a large group of statistical techniques that make minimal assumptions about the data to which they are applied and that can be used with nominal data, data for which the shape of the distribution is unknown, and other special cases.

**Nonverbal Behaviour.** A non verbal action that indicates or directly suggests something to another. It could be in form of nods, smiles, grunts, blink, glancing away, or even beckoning the first finger which may mean 'come here'.

**Nonverbal Communication.** Communication that takes place without words; body language. This can include facial expressions, gestures, and even posture; some nonverbal communication is probably unconscious.

**Nonverbal Vocalisations.** Sounds that are not necessarily speech but used in communication to convey an important or otherwise message.

**Normal Distribution.** Statistical term central to sampling theory. On a line chart, it shows the point at which the mean, mode, and median averages share the same value and has a characteristic bell-shaped profile. Standard deviation is calculated upon a formula derived from this distribution, enabling the confidence level (e.g. 95%) within which results are confined to be stated. In the example given, this would be accuracy defined to within ± 5%. See Bell curve.

**Normal Frequency Curve.** Pattern of distribution of values encountered frequently in statistical analysis where the mean, mode and median values are identical or very close together. The curve is symmetrical, bell-shaped, and the average value lies at the peak of the curve.

**Normal Lens.** A camera lens that gives a normal image perspective similar to that of the original scene (approximately 45°)and has a shorter focal length approximately equal to the diagonal of the focal plane. It also has a wider field of view than a telephoto lens, and a longer focal length and narrower field of view than a wide-angle lens. Normal lenses corresponds to the portion of human vision in which one can discern sharp detail. In 35mm photography, the diagonal measures 43mm, but in practice, lenses with focal lengths from 50mm to 60mm are considered normal.

**Norms.** Rules or guidelines for behaviour accepted in a given culture. Many sociologists believe that norms are a key characteristic of every society; the mass media help establish these behavioural expectations.

**Noticeability.** Impact of advertising on radio and television.

**Noting.** Term used in advertisement research. Indicates that a reader's attention was drawn to an advertisement when first looking through the newspaper or magazine in which it appeared, though not necessary that he reads it, but fully understood or acted upon this stimulus.

**Nothing Score.** Average number of readers found to have noted a specific advertisement or editorial item expressed as a percentage of total readership.

**NMMA.** Nigerian Media Merit Award. Awards given to deserving media organisations and practitioners in Nigeria. It is usually organised annually and recipients are nominated before the main ceremony where they attend to know the winners.

**NPA.** Newspaper Publishers Association. A trade association for British national newspapers and its role is to represent, protect and promote the national newspaper industry. It was founded in 1906 and its current members comprise Associated Newspapers, Express Newspapers, Financial Times, Guardian Newspapers (UK), Independent Newspapers (UK), MGN (Trinity Mirror national titles), News International and Telegraph Group. Other associations as this exist in other countries, but their names may differ, depending on their mandate.

**NPC.** Nigeria Press Council.

**NRB.** National Religious Broadcasters. An organisation that assists religious formatted broadcasters with technical, legal, financial, and other matters.

**NRIC.** Negative Returned In Cassette - required Advanced Photo System feature that returns processed film in its original, closed cassette. It liberates one from the hassle of storing and handling film negatives.

**NRS, National readership Survey.** This is the organisation that supplies information on UK readership of national newspapers and magazines.

**NTA.** Nigerian Television Authority. It was established by Decree 24 of May 1977 to take over the operation of television services in Nigeria. It also has established stations in the states as part of National Television Authority. There are over 36 functional television stations including NTA 2, channels 5, Lagos, under the umbrella of NTA, operating on very high frequency (VHF) channels. Its viewership is estimated at 50 million and it has over 53 transmitters dispersed through out the federation

**NTSC, National Television System Committee.** A professional group that sets television standards. The TV colour system laid down by the National Television Standards Committee is used in the United States and Japan. PAL's the standard in Great Britain and the commonwealth countries. SECAM is used in many countries in the European community.

**NTSC Standard.** Normally refers to the 525-line, 60-field system of broadcast television which combines chroma with luminance information into one composite signal.

**NUJ.** Nigerian Union of Journalists. Trade union for journalists in Nigeria.

**Null Hypothesis.** Exact complement or opposite of the hypothesis. Statistical tests test null hypotheses rather than hypotheses themselves; only if the data clearly force rejection of the null hypothesis are then said to support the hypothesis.

**Number.** Single issue of a newspaper or magazine. Occasionally there may be a special number on a particular topic.

**Numbers Buying.** Buying media on basis of quantities, e.g. cost per thousand impacts.

**Numeral.** Name of symbol to identify a number.

**Numerical Concentration.** Selection of the most economic or effective media based on readership figures which most closely match those of the chosen target audience, after duplication and wasted readership have been eliminated.

**Nut.** Same as the En or half EM.

**Nut Graf.** Paragraph containing the vital elements of a story. This paragraph tells readers what the story is about and why they should care. Some papers have rules about how close this should be to the top of the story.

**NWICO.** New World Information and Communication Order. Was formed by UNESCO in 1977 and the MacBride Commission was set up to study communication problems all over the world, as in response to the need for a new international information order. The root of this was the issue of communication imbalance, communication flow was not balanced in quality and quantity of global mass communication. As a result the side effects affected developing nations, Latin America, Asia and Africa. This conference gave birth to the popular report, "Many Voices, One World." See MacBride Commission, Information gaps.

# O

**180 Degree Rule.** A narrative continuity 'rule' on the placement of the camera in film-making. Also known as 'not crossing the line.'

**O & O Station.** A broadcast station that is "owned and operated" by a network.

**OAAN.** Outdoor Advertising Association of Nigeria. Founded in 1990, this is the umbrella association of outdoor advertising companies in Nigeria. The objective is to provide a forum for representation of all members. It presently comprises of about ninety-five corporate members.

**OB Van.** Outside broadcast van built to have a prototype transmitter that is used to convey signals to the control room for onward transmission to the transmitter.

**Object Language.** Meanings attributed to objects with which one surrounds himself/herself.

**Objectivity.** The state or quality of being without bias or prejudice; detached, impersonal. A journalist's job is to report the facts, not coloured or embellished by his personal opinion; except in the case of opinions or editorials. This term is theoretically contested when applied to news, although in 'common-sense' terms it sums up a number of the qualities that make for trust and reliability on the part of the news audience. These include factual accuracy, lack of bias, separation of fact from comment, transparency about sources, not taking sides. The reasons for controversy about the term stem mainly from the view that true objectivity is unattainable and it is misleading to pretend otherwise. In brief, all news is said to be ideological, and objectivity is held by critics to be another ideology. The requirements of objectivity make it possible for sources to manipulate the news and only serve to conceal 'bias', whether this is intended or unintended.

**Oblique Stroke.** A slash (/).

**Oblong.** Landscape-shaped. A booklet or catalogue bound at shorter side.

**Obscenity, Law of.** An obscene publication that has the tendency to corrupt those whose minds are open to such immoral influences and into whose hands such publication may fall.

**Observation.** Research technique; in which data is collected by researchers witnessing or recording the actual events which take place.

**Obsolescence.** Generally being in the process of passing out of use or usefulness; becoming obsolete. In communication sense, it refers to the link between social habits and media-using habits; thus, the act of dumping former institutionalised modes of conduct related to some established cultural activity.

**Oeuvre.** French for work, generally the sum of the lifework of an artist, writer, or composer, or at least a substantial part of it.

**OFCOM.** Regulator of the UK broadcasting and telecommunications industries proposed in 2000.

**Off Air.** TV programme received directly off the air as broadcast, not by intermediary means such as cable or tape recording.

**Off-card Rate.** Special negotiated price for media advertising, i.e. other than that published in the official rate card.

**Off Mic/Off Camera.** Terms used to describe any action or sound in a television production that occurs out of range of a microphone or camera. Voices or sounds made off camera give the impression of action happening there and references to movement or business out of camera range imply that such activity is taking or has taken place.

**Off Peak Time.** All airtime segments (television and radio) other than those occurring at peak time. Usually offered at significantly lower rates.

**Off-The-Film Metering.** A metre which determines exposure by reading light reflected from a film during picture-taking. The metre light reflects off the film plane during exposure. First pioneered by Olympus on its famous OM2n, which is real time metering for normal exposure and flash exposures. Most flash mode for modern cameras are available with OTF flash mode.

**Off-the-record.** Statement made to a journalist unofficially. Best avoided in general PR interviews as stricture may be overlooked, but normal when dealing with non-attributable sources like politicians when journalist will refer to say 'A usually reliable source'.

**Off-the-screen Sales.** Direct Response sales using TV commercials and often-computerised acceptance of telephoned orders with credit facilities. TV company supplies advertiser with print-out of orders received.

**Offending Images.** Images used in advertising which offend certain groups such as feminists, animal, non-smokers, teetotallers, environmentalists and ethnic groups.

**Offset-litho.** Lithographic printing using a rotary machine, plate cylinder printing on to blanket cylinder which offsets on to paper. It is merely that part of the process by which the image on a litho plate is transferred to a rubber sheet which then prints onto paper, thus avoiding a mirror or reversed reproduction.

**Old Face, Style.** Early 17th –century typeface with slanting sides to letters such as 'O'.

**Old-shoe Language.** Words that are familiar to most people. Copywriter has to avoid using words which provoke mental block because of unfamiliarity. Once reading flow is halted, reader's concentration and interest is lost.

**Oligopoly, Oligopolisation.** An industry controlled or dominated by a small number of producers.

**Ombudsman.** Personnel who accept feedback from readers on any issue, from suggestions to complaints.

**Ominopolis.** This is the view that new media has not so much opened up a diversity of new realities, but has lead to a reduction in the field of vision. The media, in this respect, has imposed upon us a culture of speed and immediacy that has blunted the human senses.

One-tailed Test.

**Omnibus Questionnaire.** Questionnaire consisting of sets of questions inserted by different fee-paying sponsors. Complete questionnaire mailed by Research Company to a recruited Consumer Panel.

**Omnidirectional.** Microphone pickup pattern equally sensitive to sounds in all directions. See microphone.

**On-air Testing.** After transmission of TV commercial(s) depth, interviews are conducted among a recruited sample of housewives. Or recall testing of an unrecruited sample of housewives.

**On-line Computing.** Direct telephone line link between journalist and newsroom, or between DTP editor and printer.

**On-pack Leaflets.** Fix-a-form labelling/leafleting system, where leaflets are attached to packs.

**On-sale Date.** Date when a publication is on sale at the news-agent. Some monthly journals are on sale during the month before the month on cover. Actual selling date could be important to timing of an advertising campaign. Radio Times. TV Times are on sale some days before programme listings become effective.

**On-screen Layout.** Direct input of layout and other copy into a computer or DTP system, and viewed on computer screen. Can often be viewed on computers or terminals throughout the newspaper or magazine editorial department, PR department or printing organisation. Done prior to film and plate-making, it makes paste-up irrelevant.

**On Spec.** Submitting a work on the speculation that the publication will accept it. Usually a technique used by freelance writers.

**On the Air.** Indication that broadcasting is taking place. May be indicated by a red light above the door or a very visible area.

**On the Run.** While printing presses are running. As when full-colour is printed in a continuous run on a web-offset-litho machine.

**One-tailed Test.** Statistical test based on the assumption that the hypothesis is directional. Where there is good justification for this assumption, it is easier to meet the criteria for rejection of the null hypothesis.

**One-time Rate.** See Open rate.

**One Time Only (OTO).** A commercial announcement that runs only once.

**One-off Payments.** Method of paying an actor a once-and-for-all fee for appearing in a TV commercial, thus avoiding repeat fees or disputes with Equity, the actors union.

**One-stage Advertising.** Direct Response, Off-the-page, press advertisement, seeking to sell right away.

**One-way ANOVA.** Analysis of the relationship between the variance in a single independent variable and that in a dependent variable.

**Onomatopoeia.** The formation or use of words such as *buzz, crackle, bang, hiss, twitter, thud, quack* or *murmur* that imitate the sounds associated with the objects or actions they refer to.

**Op-ed.** Opposite editorial. A feature page, usually by a prominent journalist, presenting an opinionated story. Usually contains columns, articles, letters for readers, and other items expressing opinions. Also a tactic of placing corporate, issue or advocacy advertisement on, say, leader page of a newspaper.

**Open-end Transcription.** A transcribed broadcast with time for the insertion of local commercial announcements.

**Open-ended Question.** In communication research questionnaire, a question which is not coded for expected answers, but which invites the respondent to speak freely. Verbatim answer summarised by interviewer.

**Open Rate.** In press advertising, highest rate on which discounts are based. Also called "basic rate" and "one-time rate."

**Opera omnia.** Latin for 'all his works", it signifies a total prohibition on an author's writings imposed by the Roman Catholic *Index Librorum Prohibitorum*, first issued in 1559.

**Operating Budget.** Amount of money set aside to achieve a particular objective or to finance a functional department's activities.

**Operationalisation.** Finding a way to measure or assess a variable; turning an abstract concept into a variable on which concrete empirical data can actually be collected.

**Opinion.** Letters or articles that express the subjective opinion of the writer.

**Opinion Leader.** A term introduced by Elihu Katz and Paul Lazarsfeld, in early research into the influence of mass media, to describe the social role of persons who influence the thinking or behaviour of others in informal social relationships. Opinion leaders influence thinking on a particular subject(s) because their opinions are respected, and they may be regarded as authorities. Their attitudes and actions are held to be likely to affect those of others. The identifying characteristics vary according to the 'topic' of influence and social setting, but the people concerned are generally better informed, make more use of mass media and other sources, are gregarious and likely to be respected by those they influence. The failure of early research to find 'direct' effects from mass media was attributed in part to the variable and often invisible contribution of opinion leaders (known as personal influence).

**Opinion Polls.** Quantitative polls, whose results are highly structured by editorial decisions about which results to emphasise, which give a snapshot of how a supposedly representative sample of people feel about an issue. E.g. numerous broadcast and print media organised opinion polls to measure and analyse the support for the US led war in Iraq in 2004.

**Opinion Research.** Gathers together, from a statistical sample of the population, views that are taken to represent those of the entire population.

**Opportunities to Hear.** Number of times a member of a target audience is exposed to a station broadcasting a commercial.

**Opportunities to See.** Originally applied to poster advertising, but has become generally applied to all visual media. With poster and transportation advertising, provides a yardstick similar to cost-per-thousand circulation or readership with the press.

**Opportunity To See (OTS).** Average number of exposures experienced by the audience covered by a particular medium.

**Opportunity to Recall.** In radio survey each individual multiplied by the number of commercials while they were listening/viewing.

**Oppositional.** Actively opposed to the dominant; in audience theory describes a reading which rejects the 'preferred meaning' offered by the text.

**Optical Letterspacing.** The way in which an impression of even spacing is created by varying space between letters according to their shape.

**Optical.** In TV, and video-making, visual effects created by laboratory processes and camera devices. Fade-ins and fadeout open and close sequences. Dissolve, or mix, is fade-in or fade-out superimposed on another. Wipe is complete change of picture with no double-image. Matte or mask effects used when pictures taken at different times to make eventual one whole, as when packs or cartoon characters are superimposed on live sequences in commercials. A super is lettering superimposed on a picture, and a pop-on is an optical device for flashing prices slogans on and off.

**Optical Transfer Functions(OTF) Test.** Evaluates lens performance in terms of resolving power, contrast rendition and aberrations. Most people believe the test is the only way to determine how good a lens is in the lab, at least the tester (especially photo magazines) does the same.

**Option.** In Hollywood, a purchased right to develop a property such as a novel for a new film.

**Opto-mechanical Typesetting.** After more than 500 years of using metal type, printers were (in the early 60s) able to use a new typesetting technique. A film strip, glass disc or plate replaced hot metal setting. From a master Fount any number of characters in desired sizes could be exposed to photophobic paper of film. The photographic master was superseded by the digital method in the 70s. By the mid-80s it became possible to output graphic elements and technical screens.

**Opus.** Latin for 'work', the plural of which is *opera*. Mostly applies to music, pieces of music by composers are given opus numbers, which generally run in order of publication or creation.

**Oracle.** Optical Reception of Announcements by Coded Line Electronics. ITV teletext alphanumeric information system available free of charge on sets fitted to receive it. Pages on sale to advertisers. Not linked to the telephone, and there is no charge for viewing pages, as with Prestel. Information generated by computer, constantly updated, and covers numerous topics such as news, motorway traffic reports, City prices, sports results, etc.

**Oral Culture.** A culture or subculture in which principally most communication is by word of mouth. Pictures may be an appendage, but reading and writing play a minor role in the communication process.

**Oramedia.** In developing countries, traditional forms of communication, an interplay between a traditional community's customs and conflicts, harmony and strife, cultural convergences and divergences, cultural specific tangibles, interpersonal relations, symbols and codes and moral traditions which may include: rumour, oratory, poetry, music, singing, the drum, linguists, ornaments, rites, rituals, charms and insignia, masks, market gossip, festivals, gong men or town criers, folk theatre, folk tales, puppet and shadow shows. It encompasses a people's factual and cosmological existence from birth to death and even beyond death. It is based on local culture and symbolism. Also called folk media. This term was coined by Frank Ugboaja.

**Ordinal.** Data involving categories that can be assigned to a logical rank order without assumptions about the distance between one category and the next. For example, answers to Likert-type scale questions are ordinal.

**Ordinary Position.** In press advertising, Run-of-paper or no special position.

**Orientalism.** The study of Near and Far Eastern societies and cultures, languages and peoples by Western scholars. It can also refer to the imitation or depiction of aspects of Eastern cultures in the West by writers, designers and artists.

**Orientation.** An element of non-verbal communication. It could mean a complex mental state involving an integrated set of beliefs and feelings, values and dispositions to act in certain ways; a course introducing a new situation or environment; or the angle to which people sit or stand in relation to one another.

**Originals.** Artwork for reproduction

**Ornamented.** Typeface with fancy flourishes.

**Orphan.** First or last lines of a story, cut off from the rest of the piece by a page break.

**Ortho (Orthochromatic).** Denotes film sensitive to blue and green light.

**OSCAR.** Outdoor Site Classification and Research. It is the UK poster audience reses arch system, launched in October 1985 by the Outdoor Advertising Association.

**OTC.** Over the Counter.

**OTH.** Opportunities to Hear, Frequency.

**OTR.** Opportunity to Recall.

**OTS.** Opportunity to See.

**Out-home Media.** All media seen outside the home such as cinema, outdoor, transportation, point-of-sale and exhibitions.

**Outdoor Advertising.** Advertising out-of-doors such as posters and signs, other than advertising on transportation vehicles and property.

**Outlet.** Setting or trading unit.

**Outline.** (1) Typeface with only an outline and no solid body. Could be a drawing also, but this typeface is usually used for desktop publishing based on a mathematical formula describing the shape, also sometimes known as 'vector graphics' (cf bitmap). Outline drawings and fonts maintain the same quality even when enlarged. (2) Term for an idea forming the basis for negotiating a production commission.

**Outside Broadcast.** OB. Television or radio programme produced and transmitted from a particular location and not from the studio.

**Outside Broadcast Van.** A mobile vehicle that houses broadcasting equipments from where programmes could be transmitted. Often shortened to OB van.

**Out-take.** A piece of film which is not actually used in the completed version.

**Overexposure.** In photojournalism, condition in which too much light reaches a film, producing a dense negative or a very bright/light print or slide.

**Over Matter.** Typesetting which exceeds available space and do not get into the paper but is generally preserved for subsequent editions (if necessary).

**Overlap.** Normally refers to those areas of the country which are covered by two or more ITV transmitters.

**Over-redemption.** Excessive response to Sales Promotion offers. Sometimes difficult to gauge likely response, and wise to place in limit such as first so many applications. Otherwise embarrassing if apologies necessary. Could be financial loss if excess demand had to be satisfied.

**Overall Painted Bus.** Bus painted to design of a single advertisement. Available with many private companies. ABC Transport is a very good example of this in Nigeria, where Glo Mobile and Nescafe design the buses with their names.

**Overhang Cover.** Book cover larger than pages, as with some bibles with leather covers.

**Overkill.** Result of excessive advertising appeals, when claims or promises defy credibility or methods used, as with some mail shots, are overdone, causing irritation or disbelief.

**Overlay.** Transparent or translucent sheet of paper laid over one piece of artwork carrying further artwork which is to be reproduced in a different colour; or for protection; or to facilitate instructions on how it should be used or modified for production.

**Overmatter.** Excess of type in printing, in relation to the space available.

**Overprint.** Superimpose one negative over another to produce one combined print.

**Overrun.** Additional copies of an advertisement beyond the number actually ordered or needed; extra copies to replace damaged out door posters or transit car cards.

**Overset.** Printing term, used when more text is set than is required to fill space available.

**Overspill Media.** Media which have circulations or audiences extending beyond the original area or country, as with many European newspapers. But particularly relevant to cable and satellite TV.

**Ozalid.** Diazo copying process used for page proofs.

# P

**P.** Page. Plural pp.

**PAC.** Pinpoint Address Code.

**Pack Recognition.** Linkage between advertising and point-of-sale. If the package is clearly shown in advertising especially where there are opportunities for colour, a customer can seek or recognize it in the store.

**Package.** (1) A series of broadcast programs that an advertiser may sponsor. (2) A completed television news story on tape, which is edited before a news show goes on air and contains reporters stand-ups, narration over images, and an out-cue for the anchor to start speaking at the end of the tape.

**Package Plan Discount.** A spot television discount plan for buying a certain number of spots, usually within a one-week period.

**Package Unit system.** The basis for Hollywood film production which replaced the studio system in the 1950s. each film is treated as a one-off and a package of director, stars and crew brought together for a specific production.

**Packager.** An individual or company that produces packaged program series; also called "syndicator."

**Packaging.** Way in which a product is packed for protection, as a container, as a means of identifying product, and as a means of advertising it. Pack Recognition is an important link between advertising and POS presentation.

**Pad.** Additional material to make a program longer.

**Page.** (1) On Prestel, one or more numbered frame of information. (2) In printing, one side of a leaf.

**PageMaker.** Computer software basically used for typesetting and page layout- desktop publishing. Now more a business and education application. See Quark Xpress for the industry standard.

**Page Make-up.** Assembly of text and pictures in a page to complete whole design. Can be done by computer on a VDU.

**Page Proof.** Proof resembling eventually printed page, that is with spacing, display lines, and complete as opposed to a run-on galley proof. At this stage corrections must not affect succeeding pages, and only mirror ones or ones confined to the page, should be made.

**Page Rate.** Price per page for advertising purposes.

**Page Traffic.** Breakdown by Social Grade, sex and other classifications of readership of different pages of a journal. In Gallup noting and reading research detailed scores are given for each page of a publication, with full-page advertisements identified.

**Page Zero**, **Page 0.** Top index page of teletext material.

**Paginate.** The act of making a page on a computer screen.

**Pagination.** Contents list of a brochure, book, catalogue, magazine or newspaper, showing printed materials to appear page by page.

**Paid Circulation**. The number of print copies that are purchased by audience members.

**Paintbox.** Quantel's design computer, a video paint system with images created with curves and natural colour mixing. Popular in video and TV production.

**PAL.** (Phase Alternation Line) The System for minimising hue errors in colour transmission and  a TV colour standard used in most of western Europe and other parts of the world, including Australia, India, China, Argentina, Brazil and most of Africa.

**Pamphlet.** Short, printed but unbound treatise promoting a product, service, organisation or idea.

**Pan and Scan.** Technique for showing widescreen films on a standard-shape television set.

**Pan/Panning.** Abbreviation from panorama; slow movement of camera from left to right, or vice versa, across a scene, with camera set-up remaining stationary. This movement is usually horizontal from the pan head and the eventual effect creates a strong sense of movement.

**Pan Format.** In photojournalism, one of the three selectable Advanced Photo System print formats, a 1:3 aspect ratio that produces prints of 3.5 x 10.5 inches or up to 4.5 x 11.5 inches and is suitable for panoramic shots and tall or wide subjects.

**Pan Handle.** The handle attached to the pan head of a camera that enables the cameraperson to pan or tilt the camera.

**Pan Head.** Device connecting the camera to the camera mount which allows the camera head to be tilted vertically and to be panned horizontally.

**Pan Media.** Media such as journals with international circulations or satellite TV which have cross-frontier readerships and audiences.

**Pan Pot.** An attenuator-based device which can "place" a sound to varying degrees in a left or right stereo channel by raising or lowering the volume of the sound.

**Panchromatic.** Also shortened as PAN, a designation of films that record all colours in tones of about the same relative brightness as the human eye sees in the original scene, sensitive to all visible wavelengths.

**PANA.** Pan African News Agency. It was founded on 20 July 1979 in Addis Ababa, with the adoption of a convention by African Ministers of Information. PANA took over the activities of the Union des agences d'informations Africaines, which had been set up in April 1963 in Tunis. It was officially inaugurated and commenced news agency activities on 25 May 1983. It is a specialised agency of the African Union (AU), formerly Organisation of African Unity (OAU) and has its headquarters in Dakar, Senegal, with regional offices in Khartoum, Sudan; Lusaka, Zambia; Kinshasa, Democratic Republic of the Congo; Lagos, Nigeria; and Tripoli, Libya.

**Panel.** (1) In papers a useful display alternative to pictures. Often amusing, surprising, piquant, attractive, and eye-catching. It is a good way of giving emphasis to a story that is big yet lacking details especially if it predicts something. (2) In outdoor advertising, a poster site. (3) Recruited respondents, often housewives or householders, who provide regular reports on continuous surveys such as consumer panels and TV surveys. Data usually recorded in daily diary.

**Pantone Matching System (PMS).** A popular system for colour printing inks. It is a system of matching colours and choosing printing inks, using numbered colour samples and shades. Pantone ink check standard trade mark for colour reproduction and colour reproduction materials such as Pantone markers. By using the official PMS name and number for a specific colour, users are assured that the desired colours will match when the file is printed using a four colour press (CMYK).

**Paparazzo.** A freelance photographer who doggedly pursues celebrities to take candid pictures for sale to magazines and newspapers.

**Paper.** Sheet material manufactured mostly from wood-pulp and used in printing and packaging in a variety of grades, e.g. Kraft, a very tough paper for bags and sacks; glassine, a specially processed paper which is grease resistant.

**Paperboard.** Commonly known as cardboard. Comprises a number of layers of wood fibres, sometimes of differing qualities, which are bonded together during their formation on a board machine.

**Paper Sizes.** ISO sizes are; A1 594' 841mm; A2 420' 594mm; A3 297' 420mm; A4 210' 297mm; A5 148' 210mm; A6 105' 148mm; A7 74' 105mm. RA sizes untrimmed. Silently larger SRA sizes which allow trimming of grip edges and Bleeds. B sizes in between A sizes for posters and big envelopes. C sizes for envelopes.

**Paradigm/Paradigmatic.** A class of objects or concepts. Defined along with syntagm: an element which follows another in a particular sequence. For example in choosing from menu, the paradigms (starters, main courses, desserts) are elements from which you choose, and the syntagm is the sequence into which they are arranged (soup/fish/ice cream). Sometimes these structures are treated as horizontal (across time) and vertical (along values) aspects of narratives. It is used specifically in social sciences to explain theoretical frameworks, pattern or model involving a set of assumptions, concepts, values, and practices that constitutes a way of viewing reality for the society that shares them, especially in an intellectual discipline.

**Paragraph Opener.** Box symbol to emphasise opening of paragraph.

**Parallax.** With a lens-shutter camera, parallax is the difference between what the viewfinder sees and what the camera records, especially at close distances. This is caused by the separation between the viewfinder and the picture-taking lens. There is no parallax with single-lens-reflex cameras because when you look through the viewfinder, you view the subject through the picture-taking lens.

**Parallel Processing.** The ability of the brain to concurrently process incoming stimuli. This becomes most important in vision, as the brain divides and conquers what it sees. It breaks up a scene into four components: colour, motion, form, and depth. These are individually analysed and then compared to stored memories, which helps the brain identify what you are viewing. The brain then combines all of these into one image that one sees and comprehends. This is a continual and seamless operation.

**Parallel Readership.** Reduction of the average claim period for readership research, where a second reading event occurs during original claim period so introducing error into estimated average readership figures leading to understatement of readership.

**Parameter.** (1) A quantity whose value specifies or partly specifies the process under consideration or the values of other quantities. (2) A quantity which changes relatively infrequently during a computation; in particular, in a routine, a quantity which may be given a different value each time the routine is used, but which remains unchanged throughout any one routine.

**Parametric.** Type of statistical test that makes specific assumptions about the variables and parameters being approximated. Use of parametric tests is normally restricted to interval and ratio data.

**Paraphrase.** To summarise or rewrite in your own words a quote. Paraphrasing should not have quote marks.

Paraproxemics.

Paraproxemics.

**Paraproxemics.** The study of the manner the media, especially film and TV, simulate the way people handle the space between themselves in real-life dialogue and hence induce a sense of belonging in the viewer/listener. In radio's case, this reproduces the apparent interpersonal distance between radio's performers and the listener. Proxemics is the study of body-to-body relationships.

**Para-social Interaction.** A term for the pseudo-interaction that can take place between individuals in audiences and fictional characters or media personalities. Some degree of loss of contact with reality is involved, and it may be the basis for influence on behaviour.

**Partial Showing.** An outdoor showing of less than 25.

**Participant Observation.** Qualitative research technique associated with ethnography. In participant observation, the researcher tries to become a member of the culture being studied, and his or her own reactions become part of the analysis.

**Participation.** A commercial announcement within a broadcast program, as compared with one scheduled between programs; also called "participating announcement."

**Participation Program.** A broadcast program with each segment sponsored by a different advertiser.

**Participatory.** Research that takes into account the objectives of the people being studied; a reaction against the tradition of researchers pursuing their own goals without asking about their effects on those who are the objects of study.

**PASE.** On-line availability and booking systems for outdoor advertising, with separate systems for contractors and agencies.

**Pass-along Readers.** Readers of a publication who acquire a copy other than by purchase or subscription. See Secondary audience.

**Pass for Press.** Final approval of a publication before printing.

**Passivity.** The condition or quality of being passive; inactivity, quiescence, or submissiveness. It is a long and widely held view of mass audiences being unreflective and essentially passive to media products- advertising, news, television programmes, etc.

376

**Pass-read-readership.** Secondary readership as when a journal is passed round the office. The Financial Times has a small circulation but a large pass-on-readership.

**Paste-up.** Dummy with proofs pasted in position.

**Paste-up-Artist.** Studio artist who sticks copy in position as camera-ready artwork, but make-up of artwork or pages can be done on computer screen.

**Pasteboard.** Cardboard made of thin sheet stuck together Ticketboard.

**Patch.** (1) Using cables or electronic circuits to interconnect video and audio equipment. (2) Pasting corrections on to film or artwork before making litho plate.

**Patch Cord.** The cord on a patch panel used to complete a connection between various audio or video sources and desired pieces of equipment. See patch panel.

**Patch Panel, Patch Bay.** Traditionally, a master controlling device in which patch cords are used to route various audio and video sources to appropriate pieces of production equipment. Today, patch panels rely on solid-state or computer-based switching.

**Path Analysis.** Technique based on correlation data that try to establish which among a set of interrelated variables are most reasonably thought of as causes and which as effects.

**Patriarchy.** A social system in which the father is the head of the family and men have authority over women and children.

**Patronage.** Of consumers, habitual use of a mass medium.

**Pay Cable.** A system in which cable subscribers pay an additional amount beyond the standard monthly rental fee in order to receive special programming.

**Payola.** Illegal payment for airing or promoting a recording on the air.

**PBS.** Public Broadcasting Service. A non-profit public broadcasting television service with 349 member TV stations in the United States. Its headquarters are in Arlington, Virginia. PBS was founded in 1969, at which time it took over many of the functions of its predecessor, National Educational Television (NET). it commenced broadcasting in October 1970. Also PBS may be used in the media to mean a service system for public broadcast.

**PC.** (1) Short for Personal Computer. (2) in photojournalism, this means Prontor/Compur - the clip on socket of the flash mode terminal. (3) May also mean perspective control. Also known as tilt or shift lenses. Lenses that allow for correction of linear distortion resulting from high or low camera angle. Most are with gear or sliding mechanism and most require manual metering.

**PC Cords.** The purpose of sync cords is to allow the camera to control the flash, so the flash fires at the correct time. Other common names for electrical cords to connect flash to camera are PC cord, sync cord and synch cord. One type of electrical connector on camera bodies is called a PC socket, whence the name, PC cord.

**PC Terminal/PC Socket.** Some older flash units may not have a hot shoe on the flash unit and would need cable connection to fire timely. This terminal/socket is a threaded collar surrounding the centre electrical part of the socket. Some flash cords have a connector that makes electrical contact with the centre part of the socket and is held securely in place by a threaded ring which screws into the outer part of the socket on the camera body. It is another alternative way to sync the electronic flash on the camera. Some of the modern autofocus cameras have omitted this feature on the body. It can also be used to activate another flash unit via sync cord in a multiple flash setup. PC sockets and common PC cords fit together by pushing the connector on the cord into the socket on the camera. It remains connected only because of friction.

**PCC.** See **Press Complaints Commission.**

**PD.** Program Director. Person responsible for selecting programs for airing, scheduling air time for programs and talent, and oversees local programming.

**PDA, Personal Digital Assistant.** A small palm-size computer, usually with an email programmer, diary and organiser tools. Could be called a palm electronic diary or palmtop.

**PDF.** Portable Document Format, an open standard file format, proprietary to Adobe Systems, for representing two dimensional documents in a device independent and resolution independent format. Each PDF file encapsulates a complete description of a 2D document (and, with the advent of Acrobat 3D, embedded 3D documents) that includes the text, fonts, images, and 2D vector graphics that compose the document. Importantly, PDF files do not encode information that is specific to the application software, hardware, or operating system used to create or view the document. This feature ensures that a valid PDF will render exactly the same regardless of its origin or destination. PDF is also an open standard in the sense that anyone may create applications that read and write PDF files without having to pay royalties to Adobe Systems; Adobe has a number of patents relating to the PDF format, but licenses them on a royalty-free basis for use in developing software that complies with the PDF specification. PDF files are most appropriately used to encode the exact look of a document in a device-independent way. While the format can describe very simple one page documents, it may also be used for many pages, complex documents that use a variety of different fonts, graphics, colors, and images.

**Peak Listening Hours.** Hours when most people listen to the radio. This can vary according to the type of listener, e.g. breakfast time, morning and afternoon (car commuters), mornings (housewives), lunch time, late night (teenagers).

**Peak Point.** In cinema advertising, point between feature films when commercials are shown, so that commercials are included in each complete programme. There are no Natural Breaks as with showing of films on TV.

**Peak Time.** Segment of television airtime, usually the middle part of the evening, where the highest rate is charged and, theoretically, the highest number of people are viewing. Has similar application in radio transmissions.

**Peak Time Band.** In television advertising, a span of time during which it can be forecast when the maximum audience will be viewing. Potentially applicable to radio commercials.

**Peak Viewing Hours.** Mid-evening when TV attracts largest audience. Usually begins earlier on weekends. In Nigeria it may begin by 8pm on weekdays.

**Pearson's r.** Common correlation coefficient used with interval or ratio data. Like those for most other correlation coefficients, values for this statistic range from positive 1 to negative 1, with zero indicating no relationship between two variables.

**Ped Down.** To lower the height of a camera through the action of the camera pedestal.

**Ped Up.** To use the camera pedestal to raise the camera vertically.

**Pedestal.** (1) An adjustable camera dolly or support with wheels. Pedding the camera up or down refers to raising or lowing the camera on the pedestal. (2) The black level of a television picture as shown on a waveform monitor.

**Pedestrian Housewife Poster.** Poster measuring 5 foot high and 3' 4" wide consisting of four double crown sheets. Mounted at street level where it will be seen by most shoppers. Often illuminated.

**Pedestrian Traffic Flow.** Number of people using certain routes. It is used as a measure of opportunities to see poster sites.

**Peer Group.** Class of people who, for one reason or another, are held in high esteem by others, i.e. they regard them as their 'peers'. Thus, rank and film trades unionists may feel inclined to follow their officials' advice because they respect their experienced judgment. Some may regard Peer groups as a category of Opinion formers and the term has obvious connections with the way they perceive the media.

**Peer Review.** System through which articles for publication in academic journals, papers intended for presentation at academic conferences, and grant applications are reviewed by specialists with appropriate expertise.

**Perforations.** Regularly and accurately spaced holes punched throughout the length of film for still cameras. Basically the perforation acts as a guide for precision registration of film and also provide mechanical movement from frame to frame.

**Penetration.** (1) The percentage of households that have a broadcast receiving set. (2) Extent to which an advertisement has been accepted by, or has registered with the total of possible users, usually expressed as a percentage.

**Penetration, Market.** Ability of advertising medium to reach the market, and extent of its reach. Controlled circulation magazines and free newspapers have great penetration because the circulation is not limited to buyers.

**People Metre.** Slang for a broadcast ratings measurement device that records individual audience members who are present during a program.

**Per Inquiry.** A method used in direct-response radio and television advertising, whereby orders as a result of a commercial are sent directly to the station or the station's agent. The advertiser pays the station on a per inquiry (or order) received basis.

**Per Issue Rate.** A special magazine advertising rate that is determined by the number of issues that are used during the contract period; similar to a frequency discount, except not based on the number of advertisements, but rather on the number of issues in which an advertising campaign appears.

**Per Single Column Centimetre (PSCC).** Basic unit for charging for advertisement space.

**Perception.** Personal interpretation of what one sees, hears, smells, i.e. the reception of sensory stimuli and conscious or unconscious application of them to form an acceptable interpretation of their meaning. This impression is most commonly held by a target market about a product, service or company; or a group of people or person about a particular program or event. Perceptions may not necessarily reflect reality.

**Perfect Binding.** Method of binding where leaves backs are trimmed and glued to cover. Badly done, can result in pages bursting free. Used for paperback books, telephone directories. Also called adhesive, cut-back or thermoplastic binding.

**Perfecting.** Printing both sides of a sheet at one pass in a perfector press.

**Performatives.** Relating to or being an utterance that performs an act or creates a state of affairs by the fact of its being uttered under appropriate or conventional circumstances, as a justice of the peace uttering *I now pronounce you husband and wife* at a wedding ceremony, thus creating a legal union, or as one uttering *I promise*, thus performing the act of promising. These words are considered action words and are very vital in news reporting since they often embody evaluative connotations. Words like insist, declare, announce or denounce are performatives.

**Peripheral Media.** Small circulation journals of little if not questionable advertising value.

**Periodical.** Publication which appears at regular intervals, e.g. daily, weekly, monthly.

**Periodicity.** In terms of action, the quality or state of being periodic; recurrence at regular intervals. It also describes the time-scale of the schedules of news organisations; thus daily newspapers have a 24-hour periodicity.

**Permissions.** Agreements to film on specific locations or by rights holders that images, sounds and text may be used in a media production.

**Persistence of Vision.** A theory that thinks the perceptual processes of the brain or the retina of the human eye retains an image for a brief moment. A visual form of memory known as iconic memory has been described as the cause of this phenomenon. Persistence of vision is said to account for the illusion of motion which results when a series of film images are displayed in quick succession, rather than the perception of the individual frames in the series.

**Perspective.** The rendition of apparent space in a flat photograph, that is how far the foreground and background appear to be separated from each other. Often associated with the renaissance and the growth of individualism since it suggests a single viewpoint on a scene. It is determined by only one factor: the camera-to-subject distance. If objects appear in their normal size relations, the perspective is considered 'normal'; if the foreground objects are much larger than the ones in the background, the perspective is considered 'exaggerated'; when there is little difference in size between foreground and background, one can say the perspective looks 'compressed'.

**Personal Column.** Newspaper column which carries small personal classifieds. If commercial advertisements are placed in personal column they are usually inserted after genuine personal ads.

**Personal Interview.** Meeting between two or more people, with a view to discussing a project or proposition or eliciting answers to questions as in market research.

**Personal Space.** That which every individual feels easy in and which, if encroached upon, causes anxiety, tension or resistance.

**Personality.** (1) Term which attempts to aggregate that combination of traits which may indicate what a person will do, or how an individual will behave when placed in given or differing situations. (2) Well-known person such as may be used to feature in an advertisement or a campaign.

**Personality Promotion.** (1) Use of well-known persons to endorse a product or service in advertising. (2) Use of readily identifiable, often gaily dressed, persons from whom a prize can be claimed if approached with the use of a promotional phrase or saying.

**Personalised Book.** A 'gift' book where the actual name of the person receiving the book is interwoven into the story through quick printing by computer. Personalised books are frequently directed towards children.

**Perspective.** Method for two-dimensional drawing in such a way that an impression of three-dimensions is given, e.g. by drawing converging lines away from the basic outline.

**Persuasion.** Personal process with the aim of changing a person's attitude or behaviour with respect to some object. In advertising, the development in a person of a desire to purchase a product or, service, or more properly, to acquire the perceived benefit.

**Persuasive Communication.** Any form of communication which is primarily intended to exercise persuasion, e.g. advertising, editorial publicity, sales presentations, speeches, films and filmstrips, etc.

**pH.** P –descenders which affect body height of a typeface. Their height from base line.

**Phantom Power Supply.** Power which comes from a mixer that is used to operate a condenser mic.

**Phase.** Timing relationship between two signals.

**Phase Alternating Line.** Standard colour television system used by most western European countries.

**Phase Cancellation.** Interference resulting in reduced audio levels caused by a sound source being picked by two microphones.

**Phase Distortion.** Changes in desired picture colour caused by shifts in chroma phase.

**Phatic.** Of, relating to, or being speech used to share feelings or to establish a mood of sociability rather than to communicate information or ideas.

**Phoneme.** The smallest phonetic unit in a language that is capable of conveying a distinction in meaning, as the *m* of *mat* and the *b* of *bat* in English.

**Phonetics.** A branch of linguistics that deals with the sounds of speech and their production, combination, description, and representation by written symbols.

**Phonogram.** A convenient, though not very much used, term for all forms of recorded and personally replayed music, which were originally (almost) only available via the 'gramophone', previously 'phonograph', later 'record-player'. The word covers records, tapes and discs of all kinds.

**Phonology.** The study of speech sounds in language or a language with reference to their distribution and patterning and to tacit rules governing pronunciation.

**Photo Agency.** Supplier of news photos to press or other users. Newspapers usually receive pictures via computers.

**Photocomposition.** Photoelectronic cold typesetting. Characters are photographed to require size using the same size master photo-matrix for all type sizes. Direct film positives are introduced at once to imposition and plate making. Copy held in computer memory, usually on floppy discs, making corrections easy when copy is called up on VDU. Also called phototypesetting, manuscripts are prepared in this sense for printing by the projection of images of type characters on photographic film, which is then used to make printing plates.

**Photo File Index Print.** A basic system feature that makes ordering reprints and enlargements easy; the small print shows a positive thumbnail-sized version of every picture on an Advanced Photo System film roll. It accompanies all prints and negatives returned in the sealed film cassette by the photofinisher; each thumbnail picture is numbered on the index print to match negative frames inside the cassette.

**Photofinisher Service Certification.** Program developed by the System Developing Companies to give special recognition to photofinishers and retailers who provide the minimum Advanced Photo System feature set. An identifying logo signals to consumers which photofinishers and retailers provide all of the mandatory benefits of the system.

**Photogenic.** Attractive in photographs.

**Photograph.** often shortened to photo, it is an image or a representation of that on e.g. paper, created by collecting an array of photons onto special photo-sensitive paper. The most common photographs are those created of reflected visible wavelengths, producing permanent records of what the human eye can see. Most photographs are made with a camera, which focuses the light onto either photographic film or a CCD or CMOS image sensor. Photographs can also be made by placing objects on photosensitive paper and exposing it to light (the result is often called a photogram) or by placing objects on the platen of a flatbed scanner. Most traditional photographs are produced with a two-step chemical process. In the two-step process the film holds a negative image (colours and lights/darks are inverted), which is then transferred onto photographic paper as a positive image. Another widely used film is the positive film used for producing transparencies, usually mounted in cardboard or plastic frames called slides. Slides are widely used by professionals mostly due to their sharpness and accuracy of colour rendition. Most photographs published in magazines are still originally taken on colour transparency film. Originally, all photographs were black-and-white if not hand-painted in colour. Although methods for developing colour photos were available as early as the late 19th century, they did not become widely available until the 1940s or 50s, and even so, until the 1960s most photographs were taken in black and white. Since then, colour photography has dominated popular photography, although the black and white format remains popular for amateur photographers and artists.

Photographer.

> Black and white film is considerably easier to develop than colour. Digital photos can be stored in various file formats, of which JPEG is one of the most popular. Many other graphic formats are used, including TIFF, GIF, TGA and RAW.

**Photographer.** A journalist who takes photos. He may be independent, employed or hired by an organisation.

**Photographic Truth.** The belief that photography can produce documentary evidence- now challenged by digital imaging.

**Photogravure.** Intaglio printing process using metal plate or cylinder (sleeve) with cells recessed to depth required by quantity of ink. Used for printing popular magazines on super-calendared paper, although competition from offset-litho. Good quality gravure used for printing postage stamps, fine art prints.

**Photojournalism.** A shot hand expression of photographic journalism. It is the communication of news, information, education, idea, etc to the target audience through pictures with the aim of influencing such audience to act in a particular manner or direction.

**Photolamp (3400K).** Photographic lamp giving more light than a normal lamp of the same wattage, at the expense of filament life. Often referred to by the trademark Photo Hood and used with type A colour films.

**Photomatics.** Method of testing TV programmes, taping photographs of storyboard sequences. More expensive than animatics.

**Photomechanical Transfer.** Paper negative used to produce positive print by chemical transfer.

**Photomicrography.** See microphotography.

**Photomontage.** The technique of making a picture by assembling pieces of photographs, often in combination with other types of graphic material.

**Photo-offset-lithography.** Planographic printing process.

**Photorealistic.** Referring to the realistic effect achieved by photography.

**Photoshop.** Computer software developed and published by Adobe Systems and used for image manipulation. It is the current market leader for commercial bitmap and image manipulation, and, in addition to Adobe Acrobat, is one of the most well-known pieces of software produced by Adobe Systems. It is considered the industry standard in most, if not all, jobs related to the use of visual elements. It is usually referred to simply as "Photoshop". Photoshop is currently available for Mac OS and Microsoft Windows; versions up to Photoshop 9.0 can also be used with other operating systems such as Linux using software such as CrossOver Office. Past versions of the program were ported to the SGI IRIX platform, but official support for this port was dropped after version 3.

**Phototypesetting.** See Photocomposition.

**PI.** See per inquiry.

**Pi characters.** Typographical characters not found in ordinary alphabet or fount. Special symbols.

**Pica.** A pica is equal to 12 points. Typographical measurement. The pica em is the standard measure of width by printers. A unit of measure that is approximately 1/6th of an inch in PostScript printers. The traditional British and American pica is 0.166 inches.

**PICT.** Abbreviation of *PICTure* – a file format for saving graphics.

**Pictogram.** Used to represent volumes of data in round figures or proportions, e.g. a pie chart. Symbols on a chart to represent quantities.

**Pictorial Presentation.** Expression of data or information in picture form in order to ease, or further, comprehension.

**Picture Angle.** The angle of coverage of a lens usually measured across the diagonal of the picture frame; varies with focal length- the longer the focal length, the narrower the picture angle; the shorter the focal length, the wider the picture angle. Telephoto ratio is derived by dividing the distance from the front vertex of a lens to the front vertex by the focal length. The smaller the telephoto ratio, the smaller the total length of the lens.

**Picture Cards.** Either inserted in or cut from packs, giveaway cards which can be collected to form a set. Sales promotion scheme which encourages having buying.

**Picture Caption.** Heading or description of photograph for publication.

**Picture Wire.** Wire services through which photo transmission takes place.

**Pidgin English.** It is a pidgin or contact language created, usually spontaneously, out of a mixture of other languages as a means of communication between speakers of different tongues. They Pidgin English have simple grammars and few synonyms, serving as an auxiliary contact language. It is a common language spoken in sub-Saharan Africa, usually in rural areas and among those who may not be very fluent in English language. They are learned as second languages rather than natively.

**Pie Chart.** Pictorial presentation, showing the parts of a total activity or performance as sectors of a circle. May also be used to contrast the behaviour of two sets of variables by comparing the angular dimensions and/or area of each piece and changes occurring over time.

**Piece.** News item or feature.

**Pied Type.** Used by printers to describe words or lines of type rendered meaningless by displaced or wrong letters, i.e. type all mixed up.

**Piercing.** Extracting rectangle of white space from picture and using space for a caption.

**Piggyback.** (1) Slang for two of a sponsor's commercial announcements that are presented back-to-back within a single commercial time segment; for example, two 30-second commercials in a 60-second time slot; also called "double spotting." (2) Piggybacking-In communication research, placing a set of questions on a mailed omnibus questionnaire containing questions from various sponsors.

**Pilots.** Sample broadcasting programmes produced either by networks or production companies for possible programming adoption.

**Pilot Study.** Small-scale study designed to generate ideas, refine techniques, and test methods prior to initiating a larger-scale project.

**Pilot Survey.** Initial small marketing research survey to test the validity of a questionnaire and feasibility of a full survey.

**PIN.** Pinpoint Identified Neighbourhoods.

**Pincushion Distortion.** The opposite of barrel distortion; straight lines are bowed in toward the middle to resemble the sides of a pincushion; present in small amounts in some telephoto and telephoto-zoom lenses.

**Pinstripe.** Bar code in form of 3in stripe holding up to 1,000 characters or can carry a signature and monochrome photograph. Indecipherable to human eye, easily machine-read by special scanner.

**Pirate Radio.** refers to illegal or otherwise unwelcome types of broadcasting, often taking the form of an unlicensed FM station on the commercial FM band. Sometimes radio stations are deemed legal where the signal is transmitted, but illegal and considered "pirate stations" where the signals are received-especially when the signals cross a country's border. In other cases, a broadcast may be considered "pirate" due to the nature of the content, even if the broadcast is not technically illegal- such as a webcast.

**Pirated Records and Tapes.** Illegally recorded music sold in violation of copyright and contractual agreements with artists.

**Pitch.** (1) Story idea sent to an editor by a reporter. (2) In advertising, colloquial term describing an ad agency presentation before a prospective client. (3) Also the highness or lowness (frequency) of a sound.

**Pixel.** In digital production of screen tints and halftones, the smallest exposable point of the image setter.

**Placard.** Small double-crown poster or bill as used to advertise newspapers outside newsagents shops or by street newsvendors.

**Placing.** Process of selecting, organising and implementing a choice between marketing alternatives.

**Plagiarism.** The act of taking ideas and writings from another and passing them off as one's own. It is a form of cheating, and within academia is seen as academic dishonesty. It is a matter of deceit. Plagiarism is a serious and punishable academic offense, when the goal is to obtain some sort of personal academic credit or personal recognition. It is not necessarily the same as copyright infringement, which occurs when one violates copyright law.

**Plane.** Level surface. Used in photography chiefly in respect to focal plane, an imaginary level surface perpendicular to the lens axis in which the lens is intended to form an image. When the camera is loaded the focal plane is occupied by the film surface.

**Planned Obsolescence.** Phrase made famous by US consumer rights and Green campaigner Ralph Nader. In addition to the drive to keep up with fashions, manufacturers of certain products (especially cars) deliberately built in avoidance of lasting for as long as they could, thus encouraging (unnecessary) repeated acts of purchase.

**Planning Director.** In advertising agency, usually the head of Account Planning.

**Plans Board.** In some advertising agencies, a committee of departmental heads, chaired by account executive, which discuss new assignments and has meetings to plan strategy before presentation is made to client. The committee reviews campaign plans for clients.

**Plate.** Printing block or litho plate.

**Plate Cylinder.** In rotary press, the cylinder which carries printing plate.

**Platform.** Copy theme of an advertisement.

**Platen.** Small letterpress printing machine, used for jobbing work, which works like an oyster, bringing paper and type-bed together under pressure.

**Play.** Editorial term indicating emphasis to be given to a story. Points in a story can be played up or down or played lightly; if the story is played up it is given a high display.

**Playing Cards.** Give-away advertising medium with advertisement on backs of cards. Artwork, printing by playing card manufacturer.

**Playlists.** Form of feedback for the recording industry in which individual radio stations list the songs popular in their listening area for a given period of time.

**Plot.** A story line. The arrangement of incidents or events to achieve certain artistic and emotional purposes. It is the skeleton of a story.

**Plug.** Free advertising, e.g. when a product is plugged in the media. Not to be confused with public relations which is concerned with factual information. Consequently, PR material should not be capable of being accused of plugging because company and brand names appear too frequently or obviously.

**Plugola.** Illegal payment for promoting a product on air without disclosing that payment was made.

**Pluralist.** Usually used to describe a political position which allows for several competing ideologies to be accepted as valid.

**PMS.** See Pantone Matching System.

**PMT.** Photo-Mechanical Transfer.

**Point.** (1) Unit of type – 0.0138 inches, 12 points to the pica, approximately 72 points to the inch. Used for measuring typographical elements. (2) Full-stop.

**Point-of-purchase.** Arguable alternative term to point-of-sale, but may differ in some respects, e.g. in mail order where the points-of-purchase differs from the point-of-sale in terms of time span, or where vending machines are in use.

**Point-of-sale (POS).** Usually referring to retail sales outlet. Place at which a sale is made; also refers to publicity material used there, e.g. posters, showcards, display units, dispensers and leaflets.

**Point of Sale/Purchase.** Display material supplied by manufacturers to advertise products in shops.

**Point Size.** Measure of the size of text characters in typesetting: 72 points is strongly one inch.

**Point System.** 72 points = inch, and 1 point = 0.0138 inch, based on Didot's typographical measurement system. Type sizes are stated in points, e.g. 6pt, 12pt, 72pt. 10 on 11 means 1pt spacing between lines.

**Polar Pattern.** Pickup pattern. The range of sensitivity surrounding a microphone as plotted in a two- or three-dimensional drawing.

**Polarised Light.** Light waves vibrating in one plane only as opposed to the multi-directional vibrations of normal rays. It is a natural effect produced by some reflecting surfaces, such as glass, water, polished wood, etc., but can also be simulated by placing a special screen in front of the light source. The transmission of polarised light is restrained by using a screen at an angle to the plane of polarisation.

**Polarising Screen (Filter).** A filter that transmits light travelling in one plane while absorbing light travelling in other planes. When placed on a camera lens or on light sources, it can eliminate undesirable reflections from a subject such as water, glass, or other objects with shiny surfaces. This filter also darkens blue sky.

**Political Advertisements.** While not permitted on broadcast media (not to be confused with allocated time for party political broadcasts) permitted in most other media such as press, outdoor and direct mail. All advertisements which contain 'political' claims should be readily recognisable as advertisements, cause no confusion as to be identity or status of the advertiser, and wherever such information is not otherwise readily accessible, state the advertiser's address or telephone number. In Nigeria it is allowed as was seen in the 2003 general elections.

**Political Economy.** The original word for theoretical economics but for some time used by critical theorists working in the neo-Marxist tradition to refer to a general view of media and society in which material (economic) factors play a determining role and in which politics is primarily about economic power. This study of social relations- particularly power relations, constitute the production, distribution and consumption of resources.

**Poll.** Survey of attitudes, awareness, opinions, originated by Mass Observation Poll.

**Polysemic.** Literally 'many-signed', a text in which there are several possible meanings depending on the ways its constituent signs are read. Often now abandoned in favour of the position that audience activity as part of meaning production means that no sign can have, securely, only one meaning.

**Pool.** A certain number of reporters or one reporter who goes out and represents everyone else. For example, a high-interest court case, a presidential appearance or a concert may not have room for all the journalists who want to cover it, so the organisers may restrict coverage to a press pool. Pool coverage is usually shared with other media outlets.

**Pool System.** Practice of governments, particularly in wartime, challenging media access to news through a regulated 'pool' of reporters; and subsequently the 'pooling' of information for publication or broadcast.

**Pop Filter.** A screen placed over a microphone that reduces the effect of speech plosives and wind.

**Pop Video.** As seen in some TV commercials, use of abstract forms in contrast to traditional narrative style.

**Pop-ups.** Die-cut effect which allows parts of a piece of print, e.g. mail shot, to physically pop up when opened. Examples are pointed fingers, noses.

**Poppagraph.** Direct Mail shot technique whereby a die-cut shaped image stands in relief when a printed item is opened. Can have a dramatic humorous effect, giving movement to static piece of print.

**Population.** In communication research, all the people relevant to an enquiry. In social science, flow of people through time. In census-taking, the total number of people.

Popular.

**Popular.** Widely used term, literally meaning of the people. Negatively, in contrast to high culture, art, etc. and as synonymous with mass.

**Popular Culture.** Cultural elements that prevail in any given society, mainly using the more popular media, in that society's vernacular language and/or an established *lingua franca*. It results from the daily interactions, needs and desires and cultural moments that make up the everyday lives of the mainstream. It can include any number of practices, including those pertaining to cooking, clothing, mass media and the many facets of entertainment such as sports and literature.

**Populism.** Political philosophy supporting the rights and power of the people in their struggle against the privileged elite. In media terms, this signifies a nature whereby the mass media is seen as agents through which leaders control and exploit the masses.

**Pornography.** Sexually explicit pictures, writing, or other material whose primary purpose is to cause sexual arousal. The presentation or production of this material has grown lately and the Internet has become the most popular channel for these presentations.

**Portrait.** Opposite to landscape, an upright page or picture, vertical sides being longest.

**Portunus.** The Roman god of communication.

**Position.** The location of an advertisement on a page; the time when a program or commercial announcement will run in a broadcast; special positions may cost premium prices.

**Positioning.** Aiming a product at an appropriate Market Segment, and addressing the advertising to this segment in the appropriate media.

**Position Media.** Advertising media with fixed site or position, such as posters. Usually used as a blanket term to cover poster and transport advertising.

**Positive.** The opposite of a negative, an image with the same tonal relationships as those in the original scenes-for instance, a finished print or a slide.

**Positive Correlation.** Relationship between two variables in which an increase in one is associated with an increase in the other. For example, number of hours spent studying might be associated with children's better school performance.

**Positive Recall Rating.** In radio survey percentage of individuals who recall, either prompted or spontaneously, commercials broadcast at times when they were listening/viewing.

**Positivist.** Proponent of stance asserting that the goal of social science is precise empirical measurement of phenomena of interest and that this goal is attainable.

**Poster Session.** Special session at an academic meeting in which researchers put up poster presentations describing their research. The use of poster sessions allows more researchers to describe their work and to interact with others.

**Post-feminism.** Position which argues that the condition of women after the successes of the 1960s and 1970s wave of feminist struggles means that they can enjoy ironic pleasures and playfulness around traditional femininity.

**Post-Fordism.** Method of commodity production which subcontracts part of the production process to a number of firms and uses new technology to make production more responsive to consumer demand.

**Postmodernism.** A widely current (cultural) theory that underwrites the view that the 'age of ideology' is over along with the 'industrial society' and its massive forms of social organisation and control and dedication to rationality. Instead we are leaving in an era of unstructured diversity, uncertainty, contradictions, open-ended creativity and individual freedom from imposed rules and social constraint. It has become fashionable to discern in the exuberant growth of mass media forms as the essence of popular post-modern culture. Neither the material conditions of contemporary society nor forms of organisation of mass media exhibit clear signs of postmodernism. Much as with earlier critical cultural theory, post-modern thinking can support divergent optimistic and pessimistic outlooks.

**Post Office.** (1) Individual or regional office used for relaying messages. (2) Public corporation providing services in telecommunications and mailing.

**Post-production.** After a video has been shot, all the additional work such as special sound, music and computer graphics effects, titling and perhaps voice-over necessary to complete video. It combines any production work done after all the main taping has been completed. The term typically refers to editing.

**Postproduction Switcher.** A video switcher which is capable of interfacing with two or more videotape machines and designed to meet the specific needs of editing.

**Post-recording.** Any audio work done after the main taping has been completed.

**Postscript.** Page description language used in print publishing which is platform-free- not dependent on the type of computer used.

**Post-test.** Generally test or other measurement administered after the treatment in an experiment. Post testing reflects the effects of the treatment, conditions that were already present, plus any changes that might have occurred incidentally during the experiment. In advertising, evaluation of a campaign or an advertisement after it has run and has had time to have an effect. Could also apply to a new product launch.

**Post-testing.** Method of testing advertising after it has appeared, e.g. Reading and Noting Tests, Next-day Recall, Tracking Studies.

**Postal Diagnosis.** An old racket, which says no advertisement should contain any offer to diagnose, advise, prescribe or treat by correspondence. One dubious advertiser used to ask people to mark where it hurt on a drawing of the human body, and a so-called treatment was supplied for a fee.

**Poster.** One of the oldest forms of advertising. Printed advertisement bill pasted on various kinds of poster site, or displayed elsewhere such as in windows and shop displays. Some, like Guinness', have become collector's pieces. They have great power-because of size, position, colour, repetition – to be remembered for a very long time.

**Poster Panel.** Fixed position for poster advertising, usually found in underground/railway trains and stations or other transportation media.

**Poster Site Classifications.** Based on type of location, category of road, and degree of visibility, for each poster site.

**Poster Sizes.** 4 sheets = 5ft' 3ft 4ins; 12 sheets = 5ft' 10ft; 16 sheets = 10ft 6ft 8ins; 48 sheets = 10ft' 20ft; 64 sheets = 27ft' 10ft; 96 sheets=40ft' 10ft. Unit sheet size is double crown (small billboard/window bill/placard size). 'Quad Crown is often used for small posters advertising entertainments, e.g. walls of Underground, British Rail stations. Posters are not printed in 'sheets' of the above sizes: the term 'sheets' is simply one of measurement.

**Posture.** An element of non-verbal communication used to denote a range of aspects of behaviour- an attitude, a pose, body carriage or even stance on a particular issue.

**Pot.** Short for potentiometer. The volume control on a console.

**Potential Audience/User.** Maximum possible audience or likely future user.

**Power Elite.** Members of a society who combine social and political privilege with power and influence.

**Power Zoom.** A lens with a servomotor that makes possible electrically controlled zooms.

**pp.** Pages.

**PPA.** Periodical Publishers Association. The organisation for magazine and business-to-business media publishers in the UK. Its role is to promote and protect the interests of the industry in general, and member companies in particular. The association's membership consists of almost 400 publishing companies, who together publish more than 2,260 consumer, business and professional magazines. They also produce a large range of directories and websites, in addition to organising conferences, exhibitions and awards. A number of the larger companies also have TV and radio brands linked to their publishing interests. PPA's mission is to: pursue relevant activities to promote and protect the interests of magazine and B2B media publishers; embrace at least 80 per cent of magazine publishing by turnover and secure more than 50 per cent of funding through the provision of services reflecting the developing needs of members and associate members; and maintain professional publishing standards, seeking to raise minimum levels where necessary to ensure a healthy, visible industry.

**PPV, Pay Per View.** A method of charging television viewers for a single viewing of a programme, rather than subscribing to a channel for a set period. Used first for sports events and concerts, now also for some film screenings.

**PR.** Abbreviation of public relations.

**Pragmatics.** A branch of semiotics that studies language as it is used in a social context, including its effect on the interlocutors. It deals with the relationship between signs, especially words and other elements of language, and their users.

**Preamp; Preamplifier.** The initial electronic device used to increase the strength of signals from microphones and other audio equipment.

**Pre-approach.** Preparation of all relevant material in relation to objective prior to an interview.

**Pre-coded.** Questions to be put and the possible answers which may be received in a survey are keyed to enable easy tabulation of results using a numerical coding system. This facilitates computer analysis making possible the rapid handling of a high volume of data.

**Pre-empt Spot.** In television, an advertisement spot bought in advance in a particular time segment at a discount but which will not be screened if another advertiser offers to take up that time at the full rate.

**Pre-empt System.** Much criticised method of selling TV airtime subject to latest bid, making it impossible to plan spots economically. Whereas an advertiser cannot cancel within six to eight weeks, contractors can cancel if they are offered better price.

**Preemptible Rate.** An advertising rate that is subject to cancellation by another advertiser paying a higher rate, usually in broadcast; the protection period varies by station. and ranges from no notice to two-weeks notice or more. See fixed rate.

**Pre-emption.** Cancellation of a broadcast program for special material or news; the right of a station or network to cancel a regular program to run a special program; a commercial announcement that may be replaced if another advertiser pays a higher or "fixed" rate.

**Preferred Reading.** This is from Hall's encoding/decoding theory of audience readings, and is the most likely reading of a text by audiences, given the operation of power structures and dominant values both in the institution producing the text and in audiences. Hall argues it always struggles with other possible meanings.

**Preliterate.** Culture that does not have a written language. Anthropologists once referred to such cultures as 'primitive'; more recently, recognition of the technological complexity of preliterate societies has made that term obsolete.

**Pre-print.** Part of print-job run off in advance, as sometimes occurs with colour pages in newspapers, especially when colour pages pre-printed by a different process. Part-printed reels fed into press for black and white printing.

**Pre-sale.** The possibility of selling the distributions rights to a product before production is completed, giving some security to the production.

**Preset Iris.** Diaphragm with two setting rings or one ring that can be moved to two positions. One is click-stopped, but does not affect the iris, the other moves freely and alters the aperture. The required aperture is preset on the first ring, and the iris closed down with the second just before exposure.

**Pre-test.** (1) Trial run of direct mail shot. (2) Pre-test of different prices for direct response offer to see which price wins best response. (3) Advertisement Pre-testing, Folder Technique, In-theatre Research, Product Pre-test to get people's reactions to new product. (4) In a general usage, test or other measurement administered before the treatment in an experiment. Pre-testing reflects the effects of conditions that existed prior to the experiment.

**Pre-test Post-test Design.** Experiment design in which the measurement of the dependent variable takes place both before and after the administration of the treatment (manipulation of the independent variable).

**Preferred Position.** A special, desired advertisement position in a publication against which a premium charge is made.

**Prelims.** First pages of a book preceding the text and containing details of title, contents, copyright and printing history.

**Premium.** An item that is offered to help promote a product or service; a higher-cost advertising rate. See Premium price.

**Premium Price.** A special advertising rate, usually higher, for special positions or other considerations.

**Preprint.** Advertising material that is printed in advance of the regular press run, perhaps on another printing press with greater capability for colour, and so forth.

**Preproduction.** The planning stage of a production.

**Preroll.** The time needed between the start of a videotape and when it stabilises.

**Presence.** Refers to a form of measurement which endeavours to indicate whether members of a target audience are actually present during the transmission of commercials as well as the programmes within which they are slotted. Crude viewing figures require modification for translation in terms of attention value. Also the subjective feeling of special "closeness" a listener has to a performer, typically as achieved through a specific balance of frequencies within a reproduced audio signal.

**Presentation.** (1) The way an advertisement is set out. Its use of layout, typography, illustration. Presentation of copy. (2) The way a proposed advertising campaign is explained and demonstrated by the agency to the client.

**Presenter.** Actor, celebrity, or an anchorperson in a broadcast programme.

**Press.** All periodicals, whether national, local, trade, or technical.

**Press Advertising.** Advertising in print media, e.g. newspapers, magazines, catalogues, programmes, directories, yearbooks.

**Press Complaints Commission.** An independent body that deals with complaints from members of the public about the editorial content of newspapers and magazines. Their service to the public is free, quick and easy and they aim to deal with most complaints in 25 working days. No cost is involved in the complaining process. The PCC received 3,654 complaints in 2005. Of the complaints that were specified under the terms of the Code of Practice approximately two in three were about accuracy in reporting and approximately one in five related to intrusion into privacy of some sort. All complaints are investigated under the editors' Code of Practice, which binds all national and regional newspapers and magazines. The Code- drawn up by editors themselves- covers the way in which news is gathered and reported. It also provides special protection to particularly vulnerable groups of people such as children, hospital patients and those at risk of discrimination.

**Press Conference.** An informal media briefing at which journalists are given a statement.

**Press Cuttings.** Excerpts on a particular subject cut from any kind of periodical. Used as a monitoring device to indicate the extent to which a subject is receiving publicity.

**Press Date.** Date on which a publication or a section of a publication is due to be passed for press.

**Press Kit or Pack.** Means of assembling press information for use at a press event. Should be convenient to carry and contain only essential material. Too many are over-elaborate printed cardboard wallets stuffed with irrelevant material, and are soon discarded by journalists who merely want a story.

**Press Officer.** Member of a team, usually a former journalist, who specialises in press relations.

**Press Reception.** Meeting to which press representatives – editors, journalists, reporters – are invited in order to be informed of an event, and to have the opportunity of questioning or commenting. A press conference.

**Press Relations.** The part of public relations activity aimed at establishing and maintaining a favourable relationship both with and through the press, thus providing them with news material and other vital information.

**Press Release.** Written statement describing an event or item which is considered to be of sufficient interest to readers for an editor to publish some reference to it. Sometimes referred to as a news release – a more appropriate term as it includes the use of broadcasting media.

**Press Office.** At an exhibition, the place where journalists are supplied with media and product information.

**Prestel.** TV set has to be modified to receive pages transmitted from a computer via the telephone line. Advertisers can buy pages. Viewers pay for pages called up. Not on air or free-of-charge to viewer.

**Press Visit.** Visit of members of the press to a place of interest, usually coupled with a special event, such as the official opening of a new establishment or launching of a new activity.

**Pre-test.** Test of product or advertisement prior to full scale testing programme.

**Pre-testing.** See product evaluation.

**Pre-testing Copy.** Exploratory research to check the efficacy of a particular piece of advertising copy prior to its being used in an actual advertisement.

**Preview.** Showing of a film, commercial or advertising campaign to a selected audience, in advance of general public viewing.

**Preview Bus.** A switcher bus, generally connected to a preview monitor, used for setting up and checking video sources before use.

**Preview Monitor.** A video monitor that can be used to check any camera or video effect before use.

**Price.** Agreed exchange value forming the essential basis for a trading agreement.

**Price Tag.** Price declared on an item or in an advertisement describing an item.

**Price Mechanism.** The movement of prices in any market that some economists argue operates the laws of supply and demand.

**Primary Audience.** Individuals in the print media audience who purchase or subscribe to the publication. See Secondary audience.

**Primary Colours.** In printing inks, yellow, magenta (red) and cyan (blue). In light, red, green and blue.

**Primary Data.** Information which is specially collected by means of a research programme carried out for a specific purpose.

**Primary Household.** A household in which a publication has been subscribed to or purchased.

**Primary Listening Area.** The geographic area in which a broadcast transmission is static-free and easily received.

**Primary Media.** In an advertising campaign, the main media which spearhead a campaign. Other media are secondary or support media. The choice depends on the type of advertiser and campaign. For a FMCG advertiser, primary media could be press or TV; for an industrial advertiser, primary media could be the trade press or a trade exhibition; for a Direct Response (mail order) advertiser primary media could be direct mail and catalogues.

**Primary Readership.** Readership figures based upon initial purchasers of a publication, e.g. paid for by any member of a household.

**Primary Research.** New, original marketing research as distinct from existing, published secondary research material such as Government statistics.

**Prime Lens.** A fixed-focal-length lens.

**Prime Time.** Most expensive TV airtime because audiences are at their largest. Peak viewing airtime; usually the evening hours, i.e. 19.30 to 22.30 p.m.

**Principal Photography.** The production phase on a film shoot.

**Print.** A positive picture, usually on paper, and usually produced from a negative.

**Print Media.** Blanket term covering printed media and it is distinguished from broadcast or position media.

**Print Run.** Total number of copies printed.

**Print-through.** The undesirable transfer of an audio or video signal from one layer of magnetic tape to another on a tape reel.

**Printing Frame.** A device used for contact printing that holds a negative against the photographic paper. The paper is exposed by light from an external light source.

**Printing-in.** See burning-in.

**Prior Restraint.** Legal term describing the rights in some states for censorship to be exercised before publication. It requires a person to seek governmental permission in the form of a license or imprimatur before publishing anything, constituting prior restraint every time permission is denied. More recently, prior restraint has often taken the form of an injunction or other governmental order prohibiting the publication of a specific document or subject. Sometimes, the government become aware of a forthcoming publication on a particular issue and seeks to prevent it. In other cases, the government attempts to halt ongoing publication and prevent its resumption. These injunctions are also usually considered to be cases of prior restraint, because future publications are stopped before they start.

**Privacy in Photographs, Films.** A person who for private and domestic purposes commissions the taking of a photograph or the making of a film has, where copyright subsists in the resulting work, the right not to have (a) copies of the work issued to the public, (b) the work exhibited or shown in public, or (c) the work broadcast or included in a cable programme service.

**Privatisation.** Process by which services or utilities in the public sector are transferred to private ownership. The sale of Nigeria's Daily Times is a good example of this transfer.

**Probability Sampling.** Basis of sampling theory; where providing sufficient history of an event is known, then the probability that it will occur again is calculable. Probability sampling presents a form of random sampling used to select participants in an experiment or survey. In probability sampling, every member of the population has an equal chance of being included in the sample.

**Probe.** Used to obtain further information when the initial inquiry does not produce a satisfactory response, or to make sure at interview that the respondent has answered the question fully.

**Process Colours.** The four colours used to produce full-colour print: yellow, magenta, cyan and black.

**Processing.** Developing, fixing, and washing exposed photographic film or paper to produce either a negative image or a positive image.

**Producer.** The creator and organiser of television shows, usually in charge of financial matters.

**Producer Choice.** BBC policy encouraging producers to consider less expensive non-BBC facilities.

**Product.** Anything that is capable of forming the subject matter of an advertisement. It is most often a tangible object of trade, but may also be, for example, a service or facility, an idea, a cause or an opportunity.

**Product Acceptance.** Measurement deciding degree of success of product launch.

**Product Allocation.** The various products that are assigned to specific times or locations in an advertiser's schedule, when more than one brand is advertised; the amount of the advertising budget that is allocated to individual products.

**Product Benefits.** Factors which go towards satisfying the requirements of a customer. Fundamentally, the purchasing decision is based upon the perceived product benefits rather than the product itself or its specification or performance.

**Product, Cash.** One on which no money is spent to advertise or promote it.

**Product Development Cycle.** Chain of events leading up to the birth of a new product, i.e. concept, mock-up, prototype, pre-production batch, full production.

**Product Life Cycle.** The stages through which your product's life passes, including: introductory, acceptance, maturity and decline.

**Product Placement.** Payment to TV companies and filmmakers to include products or advertisements such as shop signs in their productions.

**Product Protection.** A time separation between the airing of broadcast commercial announcements for competitive goods or services.

**Production.** Creation of advertising materials such as camera-ready copy for publishers.

**Production Assistant.** An assistant to a producer or director can be assigned responsibilities for a wide variety of production details, including script changes, personnel issues, talent coordination, logistical arrangements, etc.

**Production Circle.** In the Hollywood studio system, the constant film production process involving strict division of labour.

**Production Companies.** Commonly called production houses, these businesses produce broadcasting programmes for adoption either by networks or by individual stations via syndication.

**Production Department.** In an agency or in-house advertising department, the section which both maintains progress chasing, production of materials to be published such as typesettings and dispatches copy to the publisher to meet copy date. Also handles the arrival of proof and dispatch of corrections. Sometimes called traffic department, this department exist in all mass media organisations.

**Production Manager.** In an advertising agency or in-house media department, the person responsible for the production department. Often combines duties of progress chaser and print buyer. He simply manages the production department.

**Product Research.** Research, usually instigated by advertising agencies, into a company and its product.

**Profane Language.** Profane is gotten from a Latin word *pro fana*, meaning outside the temple. It is a corrupt kind of communication that takes the form of religious, excretory or sexual character. Such expressions should be avoided in writing or reporting for the media.

**Professional Magazines.** A type of business publication directed at readers in a specific profession, such as law or accounting. See magazine.

**Profile.** Used interchangeably with "audience composition", it is the breakdown of the readership of a publication by social grade, age groups, sex, occupations, interests and geographical distribution to describe the demographic characteristics of audiences.

**Programme Audio.** Final audio mix intended for recording, broadcast or distribution.

**Programme Bus.** The master bus on a video switcher which determines the output signal of the switcher.

**Programme Compatibility**. Broadcast programming or editorial content that is suitable for the product or service that is being promoted; suitability of the advertisement or campaign theme with program content.

**Programme Exposure.** An exposure mode on an automatic or autofocus camera that automatically sets both the aperture and the shutter speed for proper exposure.

**Programmed Auto.** When a camera sets both shutter speed and aperture for correct exposure.

**Programming.** A product of broadcasting. It is the act of selecting and placing programme content or items appropriate and suitable to a particular segment of predefined target audience at a particular point in the air.

**Progressive Proofs.** Proofs pulled from each colour plate, in sequence and building up to full-colour.

**Projected Audience**. The number of audience members calculated from a sample survey of audience size; the number of broadcast viewers, either in total or per receiving set, based on the sample for the rating percentages.

**Projected Frame.** See finder.

**Projection.** (1) Forecasting process (extrapolation) using trends in a time series to estimate future values. (2) An estimate of the characters of a total universe based on a sample of that universe. (3) Psychological research technique to identify true attitudes, for example, towards a product, rather than the socially acceptable reasons which may be put forward by a respondent.

**Promo.** An announcement for a station, its programming, or of its programs, or a personality at the station.

**Promotional Clothing.** Body media such as T-Shirts, sweatshirts, hats, visors, ties and other clothing bearing promoter's name or logo, given away (but sometimes sold). Often associated with sponsorship.

**Promotional Games.** Prize contests and games used as sales promotion games. Some lucky number, fruit machine, or bingo games. To comply with gaming law, purchase of the product is not essential, as with free entry in prize draws.

**Promotional Mix.** The mix or combination of Above-the-line and Below-the-line advertising which makes up an advertising campaign.

**Proof.** (1) Preliminary printing, usually by a manual process, to facilitate checking and approval prior to final mechanical printing. (2) An annual test of a broadcast station's technical equipment required by the FCC or the regulatory body of the region the station is based.

**Proof or Pull.** A trail; a galley proof pulled before the story is put into the page. A page proof is an impression of the whole page; a reader's proof contains the corrections made by the proof reader.

**Proofing.** The process of checking the text in the final version of a media product before publication for errors in placement, spelling, etc.; test printing a colour image on paper because colours on a computer screen are not reliable guides.

**Propaganda.** This is the process and product of deliberate attempts to influence collective behaviour and opinion, thus, gaining support for this opinion, cause or belief. This is done by the use of multiple means of communication in ways that are systematic and one-sided. Propaganda is carried in the interest of the source or sender, not the recipient. It is almost certain to be in some respects misleading or not fully truthful and can be entirely untrue, as with certain kinds of disinformation. It can also be psychologically aggressive and distorted in its representation of reality. Its effectiveness is variable depending on the context and dispositions of the target audience more than on 'message' characteristics. Not to be confused with advertising or Public Relations. The misleading expression 'trade propaganda' is sometimes used for advertising in the trade press.

**Property.** Any original story the rights to which have been acquired by a production company.

**Propinquity.** A significant determinant of group membership and liking through proximity, it is the property of being close together.

**Proportion, Law of.** Pleasant arrangement of layout so that elements are in proportion to one another. Also, sizes of sheets of paper, print, type areas, margins, pleasantly proportioned, rectangular rather than square, more space at the foot than on other three sides.

**Proposal.** Idea for a new media product submitted speculatively by a freelance to a major producer, including an outline and an argument that a market exists.

**Proposition.** A scheme setting out ideas and costs, as with a proposed advertising campaign presented by agency or consultant to client.

**Prosodic Signals.** Timing, pitch and stress of utterances to convey meaning.

**Prosumer.** Marketing term used to describe professional consumers.

**Protocol.** Software controlling the interface between computers in a network. Protocols cover every aspect of using the internet.

**Protolanguage.** A language that is the common ancestor of a set of related languages; that is a language family; or a system of communication during a stage in glottogony that may not yet be properly called a language.

**Provincial Press.** Newspaper, circulating daily or weekly in a restricted geographic region, e.g. a city or country. Otherwise referred to as local press or regional press.

**Proxemics.** The study of the cultural, behavioural, and sociological aspects of spatial distances between individuals.

**Proximity Effect.** The exaggeration of low-frequency response associated with most microphones when they are used at very close distances. Some microphones have built-in adjustments that can compensate for proximity effect.

**PSA.** See Public Service Announcement. Pre-Sunrise Authorisation. Permission from the FCC for a daytime radio station to transmit before local sunrise usually with reduced power.

**Psychoanalytic.** Concerned with analysing unconscious processes. Now primarily a branch of psychotherapy, the psychoanalytic approach has contributed much to our general knowledge of human psychology.

**Psychodrawing.** Psychodoodle. Research method requiring respondents to draw stick men, caption cartons, or fill in thought bubbles in drawings. Releases spontaneous responses. Form of Motivational Research.

**Psychogalvanometer.** Measuring device used in advertising research to determine the emotional effect of advertising messages by reaction to the rate of perspiration flow exhibited by the viewer.

**Psychographics.** Study of the psychological characteristics of the mass media. It is used in describing a purchase decision-making influence using psychological and social criteria.

**Psycholinguistics.** The study of the influence of psychological factors on the development, use, and interpretation of language.

**Psychology.** The word "psychology" is the combination of two terms - study (ology) and soul (psyche), or mind. The derivation of the word from Latin gives it this clear and obvious meaning: a science that deals with the mind and mental processes, especially in relation to behaviour. It is an academic and applied field involving the study of the human mind, brain, and behaviour. It also refers to the application of such knowledge to various spheres of human activity, including problems of individuals' daily lives and the treatment of mental illness. There are a number of fields of psychology. Clinical psychology is concerned with diagnosing and treating disorders of the brain, emotional disturbances, and behaviour problems. Child psychology is the study of the mental and emotional development of children and is part of developmental psychology, the study of changes in behaviour that occur through the life span. Cognitive psychology deals with how the human mind receives and interprets impressions and ideas. Social psychology looks at how the actions of others influence the behaviour of an individual. Just as it is useful to other academic disciplines, it is a core point of study in mass communication, particularly as it is helpful in communication research and understanding audience behaviour.

**Public.** As a noun it refers to the general body of free citizens of a given society or some smaller geographical space. Its connotations are strongly influenced by democratic theory, since freedom and equality (of rights) are generally only available in a democracy. The members of a genuine public in a democracy are free to associate, converse, organise and express themselves on all subjects, and government is ultimately accountable to the will of the 'public as a whole' according to agreed procedures. This large notion of what constitutes the public is one reason why public communication has a certain claim to protection and to respect in a democracy. See also public opinion; public interest; public sphere.

**Public Affairs.** Form of Public Relations more concerned with corporate, political and financial affairs of a company than with products or services. An American concept, and separation to be public affairs and public relations considered being artificial by those who prefer to unite both under single term 'public relations'.

**Public Address System.** A microphone and amplifier system which enables a speaker etc. to be heard at a distance.

**Public Broadcasting.** The operation of the various non-commercial radio and television stations.

**Public Communication.** Alternative term to mass media or mass communication.

**Public Domain.** Describes any media product for which copyright has expired, or has never been claimed, implying that no payment to a rights holder is required. This applies only to the work itself and not to a particular publication of it- i.e. the text of a Soyinka play, but not the Spectrum printed version.

**Public Interest.** Expresses the idea that expectations from, and claims against, the mass media on grounds of the wider and longer term good of society, can be legitimately expressed and may lead to constraints on the structure or activity of media. The content of what is 'in the public interest' takes various forms. Its most minimal interpretation is that media should meet the needs of their audiences, but ethical, ideological, political and legal considerations may also lead to much stronger definitions. The expression of public interest also takes place in many ways, including public opinion, politicians, critics and many interest groups affected by public communication. See also media accountability.

**Public Opinion.** The collective views of a significant part of any public. This part is sometimes taken to mean a numerical majority as measured by polling, but this far overstates the capacity of the measuring instruments and misses the essential point that opinion is always diverse, dynamic and variable in strength. Historically and in certain contexts public opinion may be taken to refer to 'informed opinion', or the general view of the more educated and aware members of the society. No statement concerning public opinion is likely to be unambiguous or beyond dispute without some clear definition. See spiral of silence.

**Public Relations.** Now a reference to all forms of influence carried out by professional paid communicators on behalf of some 'client' and designed primarily to project a favourable image and to counter negative views that might exist. Public relations practice as defined by Frank Jefkins is the planned and sustained effort to establish and maintain goodwill and mutual understanding between an organisation and its publics, such as employees, customers, shareholders, local communities, trade unions. It is the art and social science of analysing trends, predicting their consequences, counselling organisation leaders, and implementing planned programmes of action which will serve both the organisation's and the public interest. The means are various, ranging from direct communication to providing gifts and hospitality. Public relations is not to be confused with either advertising or propaganda. It is often a source of supply for news media or seeks to influence news in other ways. It implies to the total organisation, internally, externally, commercial or non-commercial. The basic purpose of PR is to create understanding. See also advertising and propaganda.

**Public Relations Research.** The means of probing the opinions, attitudes and reactions of persons affected by the acts and policies of an organisation, then evaluating their consequences.

**Public Sector.** The part of the economy comprising organisations funded by central or local governments. A public limited company (plc), however, is in the private sector, being owned by shareholders it is listed on the stock exchange with shares available for sale to the public.

**Public Service Advertising/Announcements.** Advertising supporting non-profit causes and organisations and provided free as a service to the public by the print or broadcast media where the ads appear.

**Public Service Broadcasting (PSB).** The (mainly European) system of broadcasting that is publicly funded and operated in a non-profit way in order to meet various public communication needs of all citizens. These were originally virtually all needs (i.e. inclusive of entertainment), and the justification for PSB lay in the 'natural monopoly' character of broadcasting distribution. This justification is no longer valid, and PSB survives on grounds of general public interest and because it can meet certain communication needs that tend to be neglected in commercial systems because they are not profitable. These include universal service, special needs of certain minorities, certain kinds of educational provision, and services to the democratic political system by giving some degree of open and diverse access supporting general informational aims and meeting the specific needs of politicians in the electoral and government process.

**Public Sphere.** The conceptual 'space' that exists in a society outside the immediate circle of private life and the walls of enclosed institutions and organisations pursuing their own (albeit sometimes public) goals. In this space, the possibility exists for public association and debate leading to the formation of public opinion and political movements and parties that can hold private interests accountable. The media are now probably the key institution of the public sphere, and its 'quality' will depend on the quality of media. Taken to extremes, certain structural tendencies of media, including concentration, commercialisation and globalisation, are harmful to the public sphere.

**Publication.** When published (verb). A newspaper or magazine (noun). From the Latin verb *publicare*, meaning to seize for public use. The term means the act of publishing, and it also means any writing of which copies are published, and any website. Among publications are books, and periodicals, the latter including magazines, scholarly journals, and newspapers. To publish is to make publicly known, and in refernce to text and images, it can mean distributing paper copies of the public, or putting the content on a website.

**Publication Date.** Officially stated date when a publication becomes available for purchase or distribution.

**Publicity.** Another loose term like promotion. Strictly speaking, good or bad result of making known over which there is little control. But used as synonym for advertising and wrongly for public relations, and 'publicity manager' is used as superior title for 'advertising manager'. However, in some activities a publicity manager may seek publicity rather than use advertising, e.g. in holiday resort.

**Publicity Manager.** Person responsible for managing a company's publicity.

**Public Relations Consultant.** Individual or firm employed by an organisation to advice and/or act on its behalf in the field of public relations.

**Public Relations Officer.** Executive responsible for planning and implementing the public relations policy of an organisation.

**Publics.** In public relations the groups of people that a PR programme is planned to reach. In a lipstick-manufacturing organisation, the publics likely may consist more of ladies and other stakeholders.

**Public Service Advertising.** Non-commercial advertising, sometimes provided by media at reduced rates or free of charge, and concerned with the welfare of the community in general.

**Publisher.** In publishing, the person or firm responsible for ordering, printing and distributing copies. May also be responsible for promotion and profitability.

**Publisher's Statement.** Statement by a publishing company of a circulation and other information relating to a particular publication. Not necessarily independently audited.

**Publishing.** Business of producing books, magazines, newspapers, and other periodicals, and distributing them to the public via bookshops, newsagents, mail or other outlets.

**Puff, Puffery.** Old name for advertising, still used by editors, especially when a news release is not limited to facts and resembles an advertisement. News release should not contain self praise and superlatives.

**Puff Piece.** A news story with editorialised and complimentary statements.

**Pulitzer Prize for Journalism.** An American award regarded as the highest honour in print journalism, literary achievements, and musical compositions. It is administered by Columbia University in New York City. Prizes are awarded yearly in twenty-one categories. In twenty of these, each winner receives a $10,000 cash award and a certificate. The winner in the Public Service category of the Journalism competition is awarded a gold medal, which always goes to a newspaper, although an individual may be named in the citation. The prize was established by Joseph Pulitzer, a Hungarian-American journalist and newspaper publisher, who left money to Columbia University upon his death in 1911. Part of the bequest was used to found the university's journalism school in 1912. The first Pulitzer Prizes were awarded on June 4, 1917, and they are now announced each April. Recipients are chosen by an independent board.

**Pull.** (1) Printer's proof pulled up on small proofing machine. (2) A marketing strategy that calls for end-user demand to be created in order to convince pipeline influences to carry/represent a product or service.

**Pull-out.** Section or supplement in a publication which can be pulled-out. Often used for special numbers of publications, and as means of selling extra advertisement space, e.g. gardening, travel, Christians gifts.

**Pull Quote.** A quotation from an article displayed in larger type as a figure to the body of the article.

**Pulp Magazine.** A publication, usually printed low-quality paper, with sensational editorial material; for example, a mystery, detective, or "TV/movie" magazine.

**Pulsation Method.** Heavy advertising, following by a pause, following up by further burst of intensive advertising. In short, pulsing.

**Punch-out.** Cut out in print by means of Die-cutting.

**Puppets.** Used in TV commercials instead of actors or animation, or in conjunction with them, or with products.

**Push.** A marketing strategy that calls for pipeline influences to promote a product or service to the end-user.

**Push Processing.** Increasing the development time of a film to increase its effective speed (raising the ISO number for initial exposure) for low-light situations; forced development.

# Q

**QTV.** Mounted screens that play video advertisements to queuing customers. Operated by the Post Office in main post offices, or other premises, with take-away leaflets on display. Operates nationally.

**Quad.** Sheet of paper four times standard size, e.g. quad crown poster.

**Quad Crown.** Poster size equal to two double crowns.

**Qualified Circulation.** The distribution of a publication that is restricted to individuals who meet certain requirements; for example, member physicians are qualified to receive the *Journal of the American Medical Association*, or in the instance of the *Human Rights Quarterly*, distributed to mainly lawyers or human rights workers.

**Qualified Reader.** A person who can prove readership of a publication.

**Qualifying Questions.** Questions which identify the relevance of a respondent to a survey, e.g. Did you watch television last night?

**Qualitative.** Information in the form of reasons, opinions, motives as produced by Motivation Research, Discussion Group research or intensive unstructured interview. It involves any method of doing social science research that uses general observations, depth or semi structured interviews, and verbal descriptions in place of numerical measures.

**Qualitative Research.** Marketing research which obtains information based on reasons, opinion or motives by means of clinical tests, in-depth interviews, group discussions. The findings are not represented numerically or in percentages as with Quantitative Research.

**Quality.** In film and television, subjective term used by critics and commentators to describe certain types of films and television programmes. Although there are no strict guidelines, the concept has been used in the licensing of UK television channels in the form of the 'quality threshold'- a commitment to broadcast a specified amount of 'quality programmes'. Could refer to high production values, popular appeal or unusual.

**Quality Circles.** Of Japanese origin, regular meeting of groups of employees with supervisors to brainstorm ideas.

**Quality Document.** An audit document showing how an organisation maintains the integrity of its administration systems.

**Quality Press.** Daily and Sunday newspapers considered more intellectual. Usually you brand the 'serious' newspaper- in the UK synonymous with broadsheet (but not in the rest of Europe).

**Quantification or Ideal Method.** Way of basing advertising appropriate on advertising agency proposals for the most effective campaign to achieve target. What it will cost to achieve an assignment.

**Quantitative Analysis.** Also called content analysis, based on counting the frequency of certain elements in clearly defined sample, and then analysing those frequencies. The selected quantise must be 'coded', i.e. a set of descriptive categories or labels are attached to them (e.g. 'headlines involving the word 'asylum seeker'). These should be unambiguous such that different researchers at different times using the same categories would code the images in exactly the same way. What matters is the quality of the questions asked.

**Quantitative Research.** Research findings which may be expressed numerically. It generally involves any method of doing social science research that uses numerical counts or measures and statistical analysis in place of verbal material. They may then be subjected to mathematical or statistical manipulation to produce forecasts of future events under differing environmental conditions.

**Quantity Discount**. A lower advertising rate for buying a certain amount of space or time.

**Quark Xpress.** Industry standard computer application used in page layout for Mac OS X and Windows, produced by Quark, Inc. The first version was released in 1987. XTensions technology, which allows developers to create custom software add-ons for Quark products, was introduced in 1989. QuarkXPress Passport is

QuarkXPress with the added ability to handle multiple language documents. Compare with other desktop publishing applications for home and small market as Adobe PageMaker, Microsoft Publisher and CorelDraw.

**Quarter-dot Screen.** Method used to create a semi-half tone effect when a tonal picture is to be reproduced on rough paper such as newsprint. Achieves increase in quality of fine detail reproduction, e.g. photograph of vehicle. Quarter-dot technique differs from Full-dot since a dot is made up of four quarter circles, each of which can reproduce an individual tone value.

**Quarter-Run.** One-fourth of the car cards that are required for a full run in transit; a card in every fourth transit system vehicle.

**Quarter Showing.** One-fourth of a full showing in outdoor advertising.

**Quarterly.** Publication issued four times a year. So many popular journals like *Human Rights Quarterly*, *International and Comparative Law Quarterly*, etc. fall within this category of publications. They are more often scholarly or corporate materials.

**Quartile.** Any of four parts into which, in statistics, a population is divided. In a cumulative frequency distribution, the lower values occur in the lower quartile, the higher values in the upper quartile and the remainder in mid-position around the median value.

**Quarto.** Original manuscript and letter heading size (10ins 8ins, 254mm '203mm) and magazine size (crown 4to). Quarter of a sheet of such paper.

**Quasi-experiment.** Social science research that follows the general principles of experimental research but does not take place under completely controlled conditions. An example is a field experiment.

**Questionnaire.** Best document for research studies which provides the questions and the structure for an interview and has provision for respondents' answers. Requires considerable skill in design, involving understanding of human nature and communication processes.

**Question.** A communication research questionnaire usually has various styles of questions, both to obtain particular kinds of information and to avoid monotony. Any word or sentence forwarded to a person in expectance of a reply.

**Quintile.** Any five equal groups within a measurement. One fifth, for example, can represent the magnitude of television viewing in an audience measurement system such as the heaviest or lightest viewing quintile within the sample. Usage in advertising often refers to audience members who have been divided into five equal groups (quintiles), also ranging from the heaviest to the lightest media usage levels.

**Quire.** Twentieth part of a ream, or 25 sheets of paper. Newsagents usually buy publications in quires.

**Quota.** A designated amount of production, minimum or maximum, which is specified for purposes of regulation or to protect specific producers from competition e.g. attempts to limit Hollywood's share of film markets by insisting that cinemas show home nation product.

**Quota Sample.** In communication research, a sample of respondents found by the interviewers to conform with requirements to interview quotas or numbers of people of prescribed characteristics such as social grades, age, ethnicity, sex, gender, marital status, and so on. While not as satisfactory as probability sampling, quota sampling technique is often more practical, especially for market research and it is less expensive but less reliable than random sample.

**Quotations Marks.** These should be restricted to quotes such as reported speech or from printed statements. Quotation marks should not be used to give emphasis or be given to product names.

**Quotations.** A news release may be strengthened if it contains a quotation from an important person whose remarks add useful information.

**Quotes.** Inverted commons. Many publishers use single quotes.

**QWERTY.** Of, relating to, or designating the traditional configuration of typewriter or computer keyboard keys, devised in 1873 to overcome jamming problems on the world's first production machine, a Remington.

# R

**R3000.** Chemical process for making prints from slides.

**RA4.** Process that involves producing slides from negatives.

**Racism.** The stigmatising of difference along the lines of racial characteristics in order to justify advantage or abuse of power, whether economic, political, cultural or psychological.

**Radical Press.** See Underground press.

**Radio Ballads.** An audio documentary format created by Ewan MacColl, Peggy Seeger, and Charles Parker in 1958. It combines four elements of sound: songs, instrumental music, sound effects, and, most importantly, the recorded voices of those who are the subjects of the documentary. The latter element was revolutionary, for previous radio documentaries used by professional voice actors.

**Radio Drama.** With no visual component, a drama meant to be broadcast on radio. It depends on dialogue, music and sound effects to help the listener imagine the story.

**Radio Frequency.** RF Electromagnetic radiation within a certain frequency range. Radio and television transmitters both utilise RF energy to broadcast their signals.

**Radio Ratings.** Recall as a percentage of the population group being measured, which can be all people or any demographic group.

**Rag Right, Rag Left.** Not justified. Uneven on either the right or the left. Unjustified on the right-hand edge to column or page of typesetting or otherwise. Can be effective for small items of text, such as simulating readers' letters, but is irritating and difficult to read if overdone.

**Ragged.** In which no attempt is made to line up or 'justify' lines of type setting, i.e. one edge or both edges are left 'ragged'.

**RAID.** Redundant Array of Inexpensive Drives. A system of teaming together numerous computer hard drives, generally for storage in non-linear editing systems.

**Rails.** Tracks for camera mounts laid on the ground (resembling small railroad tracks) which allow for smooth follow shots for cameras.

**RAJAR, Radio Joint Audience Research.** The industry body which collects and publishes data on radio audiences in the UK. It is the standard survey of radio listening in the U.K. It was established in 1992 to operate a single audience measurement system for the radio industry i.e. the BBC, UK licensed and commercial stations.

**Random Sample.** As used in communication research, in which every member of Universe or Population has an equal chance of being selected. Not really random but very precise. An interval or probability sample. Names and addresses (every nth name) are chosen at regular intervals from a list such as the electoral roll or a membership list. Gives a cross-section of population. By law of averages, and because it is not subject to human error, more accurate than a quota sample. Interviewer required to make at least three attempts to locate a respondent before using a replacement. This, and more scattered location of respondents, makes random sample more expensive than quota sample. Used for National Readership Survey.

**Range.** Difference between the lowest and highest scores or values obtained for a particular variable. In a distribution with a lowest score of 10 and a highest score of 80, the range is 70.

**Range Advertisements.** In a Meal report these are advertisements in which more than one brand appears in a single advertisement and the total cost of the insertion is divided pro rate to each of the brands advertised.

**Rangefinder.** Instrument for measuring distances from a given point, usually based on slightly separated views of a scene provided by mirrors or prisms. May be built into non-reflex cameras. Single-lens reflexes may have prismatic rangefinders built into their focusing screens. The Leica and the Contax G2 are still leading in this area.

**Rate.** A charge for advertising media space or time.

**Rate Book**. A printed book that is designed to provide advertising rates for several media vehicles; for example, Standard Rate and Data Service.

**Rate Card.** Document issued by publishers or advertising contractors showing the charges made for various types and sizes of advertisement and including the relevant mechanical data to govern advertisement production.

**Rate Differential.** The difference between the local and the national advertising rates in a vehicle.

**Rate Guarantee.** Media commitment that an advertising rate will not be increased during a certain calendar period.

**Rate Holder.** A small print advertisement used by an advertiser to meet contract requirements for earning a discounted advertising rate. Must appear within stated time.

**Rate Protection.** The length of time that an advertiser is guaranteed a certain advertising rate without an increase. When a new rate-card is issued, existing media bookings are honoured at originally agreed rate.

**Rating.** Applied especially to broadcasting media and meaning the relative audience or viewership achieved by a programme or station, as compared with others during a certain time period e.g. a popularity rating. Used also in research studies.

**Rating Point.** A rating of one percent: one percent of the potential audience; the sum of the ratings of multiple advertising insertions; for example, two advertisements with a rating of 10 percent each will total 20 rating points.

**Raw.** Data that have not been processed or modified. This term often refers to frequency distribution data that have not yet been summarised in any other way.

**Raw Sound.** Recorded or live sounds from the scene of news stories that add to the "reality of reports". Raw sounds include aircraft flying overhead, crickets, chirping of birds, people chanting and the sound of marching bands at a parade.

Reach.

**Reach.** The total audience that a medium actually reaches; the size of the audience with which a vehicle communicates; the total number of people in an advertising media audience; the total percentage of the target group that is actually covered by an advertising campaign.

**Reaction Shot.** A term used in motion picture production and cinematography referring to a basic unit of film grammar in which an actor or actors are shown reacting to another actor's action or words, or to an event supposedly witnessed by the reacting character(s). It usually implies the display of some sort of emotion on the face of the actor being shown, and is thus most commonly a close-up shot- although a group of actors may be shown reacting together. A reaction shot is also generally bereft of dialogue, though this is not an absolute rule. Its main purpose is to show an emotional response to the immediately preceding action or words of another character in the scene, or to an event in the immediately preceding scene which may or may not involve another actor- e.g., an explosion, monster, empty room, etc.

**Read Most.** Term used in assessing the effectiveness of an advertisement in the press. Respondents are asked to indicate whether, if they noted an advertisement, they then 'read most' of its copy. This data can then be expressed as percentage of total readership.

**Reader.** Someone who has 'read' a publication or periodical as opposed merely to having 'received' it. Hence the difference between circulation and readership. A person receiving a publication, whether free or at a price, may never read it. Thus there could be fewer readers than the circulation or print order might imply. Equally, the opposite might apply.

**Reader Advertisement.** One presented as if it were editorial. Disliked by editors. Publishers usually distinguish by adding words at top such as 'Advertisement' or 'Advertiser's Announcement' which minimizes the intended effect. Some reader advertisements are special features, often illustrated with sketches.

**Reader Interest.** An expression of interest through inquiries, coupons, and so forth; the level of interest in various products.

**Reader Panels.** Groups of readers who can be questioned about their responses to a media product.

**Reader Profiles.** Research surveys designed to ascertain both the demographic and the psychographic characteristics of specialised audiences.

**Reader Research.** Research into who reads a media producer.

**Readership.** The percent or number of persons who read a publication or advertisement.

**Readership Profile.** Classifications of readership of publications expressed in percentage form relative to total readership.

**Readership Replication.** Extension of the claim period for readership research where a second reading event occurs during or after original claim period, so introducing error into estimated readership figures, leading to overestimation of readership.

**Reader Service.** Publisher's service to both readers and advertisers, encouraging a response without the readers having to clip coupons or write to advertisers.

**Reader Service Card.** A device that gives magazine readers an opportunity to request additional literature and information about an advertiser's products by circling a corresponding number on a reply card. In case of free holiday brochures, request may be restricted to 4-6 to avoid wasteful applications.

**Readership.** Those who read a publication, including secondary readership. The readership figure is likely to be at least three times that of the circulation figure based on net sales.

**Readership Survey.** Detailed analysis of a newspaper's audience.

**Reading and Noting.** Readership research index of actual audience for advertisements appearing on particular pages or average pages in specific publications.

**Reading and Noting Test.** Sometimes stated in reverse order. Method of testing published advertisements for recall and impact. Respondents are questioned on each component of an advertisement, percentage ratings being collated for men and women readers for each component. An advertisement may be run in a regional edition of national newspaper and, as a result of test, it may be amended before it is run nationally. Can also be applied to evaluation of parts of a newspaper, on behalf of publisher.

**Reading Notice.** A print advertisement that is intended to resemble editorial matter.

**Real Colour.** A single selected colour as distinct from colours produced by process colour printing (cyan, magenta, yellow and black).

**Real Time.** Time taken for an event in an audiovisual text which exactly matches the time taken for the same event in the real world.

**Realism.** A fiercely contested term which emphasises taking seriously the relationship between media texts and the rest of the real world.

**Realism Effect.** The real-seemingless image, achieved through artifice.

**Realist Aesthetic.** An approach to presenting an image which seeks to achieve realism.

**Reality TV.** Form of factual television on British television from about 1989. The term was first applied to magazine format programmes based on crime, accident and health stories or trauma television (*Crimewatch UK Lifesavers* etc.). Now used for television which blends apparently raw authentic material with news magazine format and, even more loosely, of any unscripted programme. The Big Brother reality episodes are contemporary examples of this kind of programme.

**Ream.** Set of 500 sheets of paper, but under metrication also the 1,000-sheet ream.

**Rear-Curtain Sync.** A feature when flash fires an instant before the second (rear) curtain of the focal plane shutter begins to move. When slow shutter speeds are used, this feature can create a blur effect from the ambient light, that is a flowing- light pattern, following a moving subject with subject movement frozen at the end of the light flow. Most mid range and top flight auto camera models have this feature. See front-curtain sync.

**Rears.** Spaces available on the backs of buses for advertisement poster. Especially suitable for certain products, e.g. garages, motor tyres and spares, travel, and driving school services.

**Rebate.** Discount or refund paid to advertisers by publisher when new publication fails to achieve circulation on which original rates were based. The payment may also be returned by the media vehicle to an advertiser who has overpaid, usually because of earning a lower rate than that originally contracted.

**Rebating of Commission.** Advertising agencies receive commission on media purchases, but in order to charge fees based on time and expertise this commission may be rebated by charging a client net rates, i.e. less commission.

**Recall Survey.** Survey with no Aided Recall. Used for next day surveys, usually in the street, to test recall of press or TV advertisements.

**Recce.** Reconnaissance- part of pre-production, checking out venues for performances or locations for recording.

**Receiver.** See Sender/receiver.

**Received Pronunciation (RP).** A form of pronunciation of the English language which has been the prestige British accent. It is a form of English English, sometimes defined as the "educated spoken English of southeastern England". It is often taught to non-native speakers; used as the standard for English in most books on general phonology and phonetics; and represented in the pronunciation schemes of most British dictionaries.

**Reception Analysis.** An alternative to traditional audience research (concerned with counting and effect) that takes the perspective of the audience rather than the media sender and looks at the immediate contextual influences on media use and the interpretation and meaning of the whole experience as seen by the recipient. Ethnographic and qualitative methods are usually required.

**Reciprocity.** Most films are designed to be exposed within a certain range of exposure times-usually between 1/15 second to 1/1000 second. When exposure times fall outside of this range-becoming either significantly longer or shorter-a film's characteristics may change. Loss of effective film speed, contrast changes, and (with colour films) colour shifts are the three common results. These changes are called reciprocity effect. Generally, as a quick reference, exposure beyond one second needs to compensate for this characteristic of film.

**Recognised Agency.** An advertising agency recognised by the various publishers or broadcast stations and granted a commission for the space it sells to advertisers.

**Recognition.** (1) Method of testing effect of advertising. (2) Advertising agencies apply to controlling media organisations for recognition and are then entitled to receive commission from media owners. It is difficult for an agency to operate if denied this form of recognition, which is most frequently a credit-rating device but may also be used as a means of supplying pressure to conform.

**Recognition of Advertising Agencies.** For purpose of claiming commission from media owners, recognition is granted by bodies representing media. Two requirements: agency must have credit worthiness (in order to pay media bills promptly), and must accept the Code of Advertising Practice. Media bodies do not guarantee rate of commission, which is negotiable between agencies and media owners.

**Recognition Survey.** Form of advertisement research in which recall of press, radio, TV advertisements is measured by Reading and Noting, Text-day Recall, tracking and other tests.

**Recognition Test.** Survey to measure the recognition of advertisements with obscured or removed names.

**Record Head.** The electromagnetic device that places an audio or video signal onto a recording medium (such as videotape) for later playback.

**Recruitese.** Euphemisms used in staff recruitment advertisements which usually mean the opposite or gloss over unattractive aspects, e.g. 'flexible hours' for no payment for overtime.

**Recruitment Advertising.** Advertising designed to recruit staff of any kind. Consist mostly of classified and semi-display advertisements.

**Recto.** The right hand page in a print publication.

**Red-letter.** Exclusive, breaking news coverage of a major news event, printed in red type. Like the Indian Ocean tsunami disaster in 2004 was alerted in red-letter on CNN.

**Reductionism.** Approach to research that emphasises the study of component parts instead of the whole; usually meant critically. Quantitative techniques are reductionist in comparison to qualitative ones.

**Redundancy.** In communication terms, the number of bits used to transmit a message minus the number of bits of actual information in the message. Data compression is a way to eliminate unwanted redundancy, while checksums are a way of adding desired redundancy for purposes of error correction when communicating over a noisy channel of limited capacity.

**Reel.** (1) Web or roll of paper used on rotary printing machines. (2) Also an object around which lengths of another material (usually long and flexible) are wound for storage. Generally it has a cylindrical core and walls on the sides to retain the material wound around the core. In some cases the core is hollow, although other items may be mounted on it, and grips may exist for mechanically turning the reel.

**Reel Fed.** Printing by reel rather than with flat sheets of paper.

**Reel-to-reel.** In contrast to a cartridge or cassette tape format, a tape format that depends on two separate reels: a supply reel and a take-up reel.

**Re-establishing Shot.** A wide shot intended to re-orient an audience to the basic elements of a scene and their relative positions.

**Refer.** Pronounced reefer, but spelled this way, it refers readers to inside or related stories. At some papers, these have been called whips.

**Reference Black.** The darkest portion of the video picture, generally with a reflectance value of 3 percent.

**Reference White.** The whitest portion of the video picture, generally with a reflectance value of 60 percent or above.

**Referent.** In semiotics, the real world object to which the sign or signifier refers.

**Reflected Light Metre.** A photoelectric device that measures the amount of light reflected from a subject. In determining exposure, reflected light metres assume an average 18 percent reflectance.

**Reflector.** Any device used to reflect light onto a subject to improve balance of exposure (contrast). Another way is to use fill in flash.

**Reflector Board.** A silver or bright white surface used to reflect light onto a subject. Generally used outside to soften and fill in the light from the sun.

**Reflexivity.** The ability to be able to revise your actions in the light of new information. The argument is often that information societies are becoming reflexive societies. That is as the world becomes defined through information overload rather than information scarcity, it is argued, it also becomes increasingly reflexive. This means opening up questions on nature, gender, sexuality, etc. that were repressed in previous historical eras.

**Refractive Index.** A technical term used to describe the effect of a lens in causing light rays to bend; important aspect in lens design.

**Refutation.** The act of employing counter arguments, evidence, proof to dispute the arguments of another person.

**Regional Networks.** A system that provides broadcast programming and information to specific geographic regions of the country.

**Regional Press.** Newspapers, magazines and other publications which do not have national circulations, serving provincial areas of the country.

**Regional Production.** Obligation by the BBC to spread production around the regions and nations of the UK. This kind of production usually applies to other national television networks like Nigeria's NTA.

**Register.** Correct printing of sequence of colours so that the final effect is sharp, not blurred as when colours are out of register. Correct alignment of pages with consistent margins.

**Register Marks.** In colour printing, marks for the correct positioning of paper.

**Registration.** Adjusting the chroma channels in a tube-type TV camera so that the video from the three primary colours perfectly overlaps (registers).

**Regression Analysis.** Mathematical technique for establishing the relationships between observed and quantifiable variables, both past and present.

**Regulation.** The process of monitoring the activities of industries. Some media industries regulate themselves and others are regulated by bodies set up by legislation like the National Broadcasting Commission, Nigeria's regulatory body once headed by Tom Adaba.

**Reification.** Treating imaginary or illusory things as though they were real; usually meant critically. For instance, some opinion research might erroneously assume that attitudes exist as concrete objects rather than researches' abstractions.

**Reinforcement.** A special role of the mass media in reinforcing and underpinning certain social and political values and structures.

**Reiteration.** One of the most powerful devices in advertising. The repetition of names, slogans, selling points and the repetition of advertisements themselves, especially in regular positions.

**Rejig.** The amendments to a story already set in type inserting or adding new matter.

**Relative Aperture.** Numerical expression of effective aperture, also known as f-number. Obtained by dividing focal length by diameter of effective aperture. See f-number.

**Relay Satellite.** An artificial device capable of bouncing messages back to earth.

**Release Form.** As signed by models or others being photographed, filmed or videotaped, giving permission for a picture to be used in advertising.

**Release Patterns.** The geographical patterns of the release of media texts, especially feature films.

**Release-Priority.** For autofocus, shutter can be released anytime even when subject is not in focus. It helps one avoid missed opportunities when one is not concerned with absolute focusing precision, it applies primarily for Nikon.

**Reliability.** Whether repeating the same measurement or experiment will yield the same or similar results. For quantitative research to be meaningful, reliability must be reasonably high.

**Relic Gestures**. Physical gestures that have outlived their original situation, yet continue to be used to effect, even though their derivation is no longer palpable or explicable.

**Religious.** Category of magazines targeted to readers with an interest in religion. Denominational magazines fall into this category.

**Reminder Advertising.** An advertisement, usually brief, that is intended to keep the name of a product or service before the public; often, a supplement to other advertising. Expenditure devoted to overcoming memory lapse. Accounts for a significant proportion of advertising.

**Reminiscence.** Improvement in retention of factual data over time without further relevant communications.

**Remote.** TV production done outside the studio.

**Rep**. A media representative (slang for a national sales representative).

**Repeat Fees.** Controversial subject concerning fees to actors when commercials are repeated. Has been the subject of an agreement between IPA and Equity. High repeat fees can deter advertisers from repeating commercials in minority programmes. Present system relates fees to number of transmission. Argued that fees should relate to audience size.

**Repeater Satellite.** A series of satellites that could both receive and retransmit signals back to earth.

**Repertoire of Elements.** The fluid system of conventions and expectations associated with genre texts.

**Repetition and Difference.** The mix of familiar and new characteristics which offer pleasures and attract audiences to generic media texts.

**Repetitive Question.** In a research questionnaire, question asked in different ways to check whether the same answer is forthcoming. Clarifies possible misunderstanding and checks accuracy of response.

**Replacement.** A substitute for a broadcast commercial announcement that did not clear the original order, that is, that was not broadcast as specified on the advertiser's order.

**Replicability.** Unambiguity of research findings such that different researchers at different times would interpret the evidence in exactly the same way. See quantitative analysis.

**Reporter.** A journalist who gathers information and writes news stories. This type of journalist researches and presents information in certain types of mass media. Reporting is usually distinguished from similar work, such as writing in general, by news judgment (determining newsworthiness) and journalism values (such as trueness). Reporters gather their information in a variety of ways, including tips, press releases, and witnessing an event. They perform research through interviews, public records and other sources. The information-gathering part of the job is sometimes called "reporting" as distinct from the production part of the job, such as writing articles. They split their time between working in a newsroom and going out to witness events or interview people. Most reporters are assigned an area to focus on, called a beat. They are encouraged to cultivate sources so they won't miss news.

**Representative Sample.** Sample that contains close to the same proportions of various demographic groups as the population. This can be achieved through probability sampling, quota sampling, or some other means.

**Reprint.** Copies of an advertisement printed after appearance in a publication.

**Repro Pulls.** Good quality proofs of typesetting, usually for use in making up artwork, or in enlarging for display purposes.

**Reproduction Fee.** Fee payable to copyright owner for publication of photograph, cartoon or other artwork which may be supplied by, say, photo agency or photo library.

**Reproduction Ratio**. Term used in macro-photography to indicate the magnification of a subject; specifically the size of the image recorded on film divided by the actual size of the subject. For instance, if the image on film is the same size as the subject, the reproduction ratio is written as 1:1 or 1X.

**Requesting Circulation.** With Controlled magazines ABC certification requires evidence of requested circulation, usually based on return of request cards inserted in magazines.

**Research Method.** Basic approach to obtaining empirical data, whether quantitative or qualitative. Surveys, experiments, participant observation, and focus group work are all examples of research methods. See Method and Technique.

**Research Service.** Business that specialise in providing research on current topics for subscribers, primarily newspapers and broadcast executives.

**Researchable Problem.** Problem that can be solved or at least illuminated by the application of some social science research methods. Many media related policy issues are actually matters of judgement than researchable problems.

**Residual of Previous Year's Surplus Method.** Way of taking the following year's advertising Appropriation out of the previous year's profits, instead of more correctly relating the appropriation to the cost of achieving future sales.

**Resistive Reading.** A situation that occurs when an audience choose not to accept without question the preferred reading media messages.

**Resolution.** Efficiency of photochemical or computer system or camera in reproducing fine detail, hence expression 'high resolution' and to distinguish and reproduce fine detail. The image resolution in a final photograph depends on the resolving power of the sensitive emulsion and on that of the lensóthe. Though both are not related, the effective resolution is a function of both. For reasonably accurate photographic measurements of lens resolution, the sensitive material must therefore have a much greater resolving power than the lens.

**Resolution Chart.** A test pattern used to set up and check a camera which shows camera sharpness and the condition of the camera system.

**Resonance.** The intensification of vocal tones during speech as the result of vibrations in the nose and cheekbones.

**Respondent.** A research informant, someone who participates in a survey by answering questions; the term for a study participant most commonly used in sociology. .

**Response.** Reaction evoked by a stimulus. In behaviourist psychology, the researcher is concerned with observable behavioural responses, not internal, emotional or cognitive states.

**Response Bias.** Tendency to give the researcher what he or she wants; a bias toward the answers believed to be seen as 'correct,' socially appropriate, and so on.

**Response Function.** Set of numbers, often in percentage form defining the relative value of given numbers of advertising impressions per person or section of the target population.

**Response Handling.** Services offered by media to encourage and handle response to advertising, especially on TV, e.g. British Satellite Broadcasting offer such a service to Direct Response advertisers. BSB packages includes on-screen phone number on the ad. Respondents receive information by phone or mail.

**Response Rate.** Measure of advertising effectiveness, e.g. in direct mail, the number of replies per thousand; in other forms of advertising, the number of replies per insertion. Taken in conjunction with readership/viewership figures for example, this measure enables a comparative cost per inquiry structure to be compiled for use in media selection.

**Retail Advertising.** Advertising which promotes local merchandisers' goods and services.

**Retail Trading Zone (RTZ).** The geographic area in which most of a market's population makes the majority of their retail purchases.

**Retainer.** Term often used wrongly to mean fee but should refer to an exclusivity fee should professional services be required from time to time.

**Retention Time.** Length of time an advertising message can be retained. Some advertising, such as press and direct mail, can be kept permanently, whereas cinema, radio and TV ephemeral. Posters enjoy repetitive seeing.

**Reticulation.** Cracking or distorting of the emulsion during processing, usually caused by wide temperature or chemical-activity differences between the solutions.

**Retouch.** To modify a photograph or negative by hand, using paints, dyes or chemicals, in order to improve or change it in some way, or to introduce additional features or eliminate existing ones. It develops a photograph so that it reproduces better, e.g. by strengthening or to alter tones of highlights by use of dyes, painting out blemishes, backgrounds.

**Retraction.** Withdrawal of a previously published story or fact.

**Retrofocus Design.** In a retrofocus design, which is advantageously applied to wideangle lenses, the back focus is designed longer than the lens' focal length to allow clearance for the movement of the reflex-mirror No mirror lock up or separate viewing accessory attachment is required. It consists of front diverging apd rear converging lens groups, as opposed to the telephoto design, and is also called the inverted telephoto design.

**Retrospective Analysis.** Study of a situation after the events; colloquially referred to as 'post mortem'.

**Returns.** Measure of income arising from an investment. Could also mean the usefulness of a broadcast device during a said period.

**Reuters.** Great Britain's news agency founded in 1951. Just like other news agencies it provides reports from around the world to newspapers and broadcasters. However, news reporting accounts for less than 10% of the company's income. Its main focus is on supplying the financial markets with information and trading products. These include market data, such as share prices and currency rates, research and analytics, as well as trading systems that allow dealers to buy and sell such things as currencies and shares on a computer screen instead of by telephone or on a trading floor like that of the New York Stock Exchange.

**Reverb; Reverberation.** Subtle echo effect accompanying a sound.

**Reverberation Unit.** A mechanical or an electronic device that creates controlled sound reverberation or echo. Used for special effects and in postproduction sweetening to balance location presence between different sources of audio.

**Reverse Indents.** First few characters of paragraph not indented, but all succeeding lines of paragraph indented.

**Reverse Out.** Printing white lettering on black or other colour background. If the background is not sufficiently dark or solid, white lettering loses its legibility. The reverse lettering should be large, and there should be little of it, otherwise legibility will be poor.

**Reverse Plate.** Printing block in which the contents – illustrations and lettering– are in white upon a black or coloured background.

**Reverse Video.** Polarity reversal. Negative image. Changing from dark characters on a light background to light characters on a dark background, for example.

**Reverse-angle Shot.** Used in dialogue scenes where a shot of someone speaking is followed by a shot of a person who is listening. Normally taken from over the shoulder at an angle of about 140 degrees.

**Review.** The act or art of analysing and judging the quality of a literary or artistic work.

**Review Board.** In a media organisation, a group which reviews critically the work of another group.

**Revise/Revision.** Further proof of printing, corrections having been made. For articles, it may be rewritten with additional facts or information.

**Rewrite.** An adaptation of a news report.

**RF Carrier Wave.** Radio frequency energy which carries a video and/or audio signal in broadcasting.

**RF Interference.** An unwanted radio frequency signal that interferes with an audio or video signal.

**RF Mics.** Wireless mic. Radio frequency mic. A combination microphone and miniature broadcast transmitter which eliminates the need for mic cables.

**RF Modulator.** An electronic circuit that converts the audio and video into a single radio frequency TV signal. When part of a videotape machine the resulting signal can be viewed on a standard TV set, generally on either channel 3 or 4.

**RF.** Radio frequency. A specific portion of the electromagnetic spectrum used by carrier waves in broadcasting.

**RGB.** (red, green and blue) The primary colours of light used to create a colour TV image. CMYK is the four primary colours.

**RGB encoder.** Device that converts composite video into RGB video.

**RGB monitor.** A type of colour monitor with separate inputs for red, green and blue. Normally associated with high-resolution display systems. See also RGB video.

**RGB Video.** A video (generally computer) viewing system that uses discrete red, green and blue signals in separate wires.

**Rhetoric.** See Media influence.

**Rhythm, Law of.** In layouts, pictures or other artwork, the eye should be encouraged to travel naturally through elements of design.

**Ribbon Mike.** A type of microphone that makes use of a metal ribbon suspended in a magnetic field. When sound waves strike the ribbon, the resulting vibratory movement of the ribbon creates a minute voltage. See Microphone.

**Ride Gain.** To manually keep the audio or video levels within acceptable limits.

**Riding the Showing.** Either viewing outdoor advertising sites for a proposed poster campaign, or inspecting such sites.

**Right of Reply.** The idea that persons who feel that they have been misrepresented should have the right to challenge media producers on air in a newspaper.

**Rim.** The copy editors, collectively. Dates back to the days when the copy desk was a horseshoe-shaped piece of furniture with rim editors around the outside and slot editors on the inside, doling out and checking work.

**Ring Papers.** In continental Europe, newspapers like the German Bild or in Africa, the former Zik Group of newspapers with regional editions.

**River.** White space running across text, made by spaces between words, which looks unsightly.

**Road Show.** A film, video, exhibition or sales presentation taken from town to town, perhaps using a purpose-built vehicle. Shows like this has been done by Gold Circle, Coca Cola, and Indomie.

**Roadblock or Roadblocking.** Slang term for placing television announcements at the same time on two or more networks, or at the same time on several stations in a single market; used as a remedy to channel switching during a commercial break.

**Roadside Poster.** As distinct from transport sites. Historically, outdoor advertising is divided into two forms, transportation extending to advertising on and in vehicles, and on premises. Various contractors offer packages of roadside poster campaigns, covering size, number of panels, areas, periods, average weekly Oscar audience per panel, package cost and comments on special characteristics.

**Role Playing.** Acting a part in a simulated face-to-face interview, usually at an editorial meeting or training session.

**Roll.** A lack of vertical synchronisation which causes a complete TV picture to appear to rotate upward or downward.

**Roll Film.** Any type of photographic film which is wound on a spool with paper backing, as opposed to film which is wound in a cartridge.

Roll-off.

Confusingly, roll film was originally often referred to as "cartridge" film because of its resemblance to a shotgun cartridge. The opaque backing paper allows roll film to be loaded in daylight and is typically printed with frame number markings which can be viewed through a small red window at the rear of the camera. A spool of rollfilm is usually loaded on one side of the camera and pulled across to an identical takeup spool on the other side of the shutter as pictures are taken. When the roll is fully exposed, the takeup spool is removed for processing and the spool on which the film was originally wound becomes the takeup spool for the next loading.

**Roll-off.** Preset attenuation in electronic equipment of a predetermined range of lower frequencies. Used by microphone manufacturers to reduce the proximity effect.

**Roman Letters.** Upright type as distinct from slopping Italics.

**Roman Numerals.** As written I for one, V for five, X for 10, C for 100, D for 500 and M for 1,000.

**Romance.** Fiction genre in which intimate personal relationships related to love and marriage are the central focus.

**ROP.** See Run of Paper.

**ROP Colour.** Colour printing that is done during the regular press run.

**ROS.** See Run of Station.

**Rosenzweig Picture Frustration Test.** Motivational research test consisting of cartoons in which one character is frustrated by another. A balloon has to be completed to show what the respondent imagines the frustrated character would say in the pictured situation. Reveals respondent's attitudes and motives regarding a particular topic which would be the subject of the survey.

**Roses Creative Awards.** Annual advertising awards sponsored by Adline. Categories include TV, radio, trade and consumer press, posters. Gold, silver, bronze trophies.

**Rostrum Camera.** In TV, a film camera fixed in position over a table and used to take still photographs.

**Rostrum Shooting.** Not live shooting, but camera work inside studio using camera on adjustable device with subjects such as stills or scale models on adjustable table.

**Rotary.** Printing machine having rotating place cylinder. Opposite to Flatbed.

**Rotary Fader.** As opposed to a linear fader, a volume control regulated by rotation.

**Rotary Plan.** Movable outdoor bulletins are moved from one fixed location to another one in the market at regular intervals.

**Rotasign.** Illuminated light-box displaying a sequence of up to 40 advertisements on continuous reel. Found in supermarkets and shopping precincts.

**Rotoscope.** Method of trying to simulate reality when producing animated (films) cartoons, by tracing directly from live-action film footage.

**Rough.** Illustration or design of a layout for an advertisement or other print work in rough form.

**Rough Cut.** Early stage in editing a programme or film.

**Rough Out.** First edited assembly of film shots in correct order and sequence according to script instructions.

**Roundel.** Circular Logotype similar to that of ICI.

**Rounding Off.** Mathematical procedure for eliminating small insignificant numbers or decimals of numbers, by taking the nearest significant value.

**Round-up.** Detailed study of single subject by several reporters.

**Royalty.** The payment made to an author of a book published and marketed by a commissioned publisher.

**RTNDA.** Radio Television News Directors Association. A membership organisation of radio, television and online news directors, producers, executives and educators with about 3,000 members. It was founded in 1946 as an industry group to set standards for the nascent field of broadcast journalism, and to defend the First Amendment in instances where broadcast media was being threatened. It is probably best known for the Edward R. Murrow Award, given annually since 1971 for excellence in electronic journalism. Murrow famously gave a speech at an RTNDA event held in his honour in 1958, harshly critical of the network television establishment of the day, and its emphasis on popular entertainment rather than news and public affairs programming. This speech was the cornerstone of the plot of the 2005 motion picture *Good Night, and Good Luck*.

**RTS.** Contax's term for Real time system.

**Rule.** Thick, thin, wavy, dotted or any other special design of line used in print, as in rule separating a column of text, or outlining a coupon. It is usually expressed with its width as in, "a 1-point rule." Do not call them lines, except in hairline.

**Rule of Thirds.** A composition guideline that suggests putting the centre of interest at the crosspoints of two vertical and two horizontal lines that divide the frame into three equal segments.

**Rumble Filter.** Audio filter that eliminates low frequencies associated with such things as wind, hum, and other types of low frequency noise.

**Rumour.** Communication that takes place mainly by word of mouth in the absence of reliable or complete information about events of great concern to those involved. Mass media can feed rumour (e.g. early reports of some disaster) or replace rumour. Rumour develops where mass media are generally inadequate or unreliable (as in totalitarian societies or under condition of war). Networks of personal relations facilitate rumour, but under extreme conditions are not necessary.

**Run.** (1) Period of printing an edition or publishing a story. (2) Quantity to be printed.

**Run-around.** Type surrounding a picture or other shape. Artistic but often detrimental to readability of text. Best avoided in advertisements and sales letters.

**Run of Day/Period/Week/Month Spots.** TV commercials, usually at cheaper rate, which a station can use at its discretion.

**Run of Paper (ROP).** Instruction to a publisher indicating that no special position is sought for an advertisement, It is positioned anywhere in a publication, with no choice of a specific place for it to appear. i.e. it can be placed in any convenient part of the advertising space of the publication. A lower charge is usually payable in such circumstances than where a specific position is demanded.

**Run of Schedule (ROS).** Broadcast commercial announcements that can be scheduled at the station's discretion anytime; in some cases, the advertiser can specify or request certain time periods; for example, ROS 10:00 a.m. - 4:00 p.m. Monday - Friday.

**Run-of-week.** In publishing, advertisement inserted at publisher's discretion in one issue of a daily, during a week.

**Run-of-week Spot.** An arrangement whereby a TV contractor undertakes to transmit a commercial during a particular week but since a discount is allowable, will not specify the exact time of transmission.

**Run-of-year.** In publishing, advertisement which publisher may insert at his discretion and at lower rate, in any month's issue of a magazine. In TV, low filler rate for commercials shown at discretion of station.

**Run-on.** (1) In printing and publishing, type which is set continuously as in a classified advertisement. (2) Additional copies of a piece of print. (3) Take copy from one page to another, as when extra words are inserted. To join up two paragraphs.

**Running Head, Headlines.** In a book or magazine, repetition of title at top of each page.

**Running Story.** A story which changes rapidly between editions, as in a plane crash or a story which develops over several days like the Okija shrine saga.

**Running Titles.** The title of a publication written in all pages of the book.

# S

**S/s.** Same size: instruction to process, to make engraving the same size as the original.

**Sacred Cow.** News or promotional material which a publisher or editor demands must be published, often for personal reasons.

**Saddle-stitch.** Popular method of binding magazines with wire stitching from spine to centre-spread so that pages lie flat when magazines are opened.

**Safe Action Area.** Also called essential area. The inner 90 percent of the video frame. Since the outer 10 percent of a broadcast picture is typically cut off by over-scanning, this area is considered safe for most subject matter. See also safe title area.

**Safe Title Area.** The inner 80 percent of the video raster or frame. Since the outer 20 percent of a broadcast picture is cut off by some home receivers, this is considered safe for essential subject matter such as titles and text. See also safe action area.

**Safelight.** An enclosed darkroom lamp fitted with a filter to screen out light rays to which film and paper are sensitive. Light source consisting of housing, lamp and screen of a colour that will not affect the photographic material in use. Safelight screens are available in various colours and sizes for specific applications.

**Safety Chain.** A metal chain (sometimes a cable) attached to both a light and a lighting grid, designed to keep a light from falling if it's clamp comes loose.

**Safety Interlock.** A feature on all Kodak Advantix cameras that prevents the film door from opening mid-roll and exposing film to light.

**SAG.** Screen Actors Guild. Trade union for motion picture and television actors. The union represents over 120,000 film actors in the United States. It guarantees members safe working conditions, a minimum wage on union productions ("scale", currently $1,620 per week), and handles payment of residuals. Since 1995 the guild has also selected members for the Screen Actors Guild Award.

**Sales Calls.** Visits to customers or prospective customers by a sales person.

**Sales Costs.** Costs of field selling effort.

**Sales Drive.** Particularly active selling campaign.

**Sales Effort.** Extent of selling activity.

**Sales Feature.** Aspect of a product which can be shown as a customer benefit.

**Sales Kit.** Sales presentation, communicational selling aids and administrative stationery and equipment carried by the salesman for the transaction of business.

**Sales Lead.** Good enquiry resulting from advertising which a salesman can follow up. Advertisements must give a reader the opportunity to refuse or invite a representative's call.

**Sales Literature.** Pamphlets, leaflets, point-of-sale showcards, etc. which give product information to potential customers.

**Sales Meeting.** Gathering of salesmen usually led by a field supervisor, for a training session or for dissemination of information.

**Sales Mix.** Breakdown of sales revenue by product groups and normally expressed in percentage terms.

**Sales Networks.** A group of broadcasting stations linked together by a financial agreement to benefit all member stations by offering advertisers a joint rate.

**Sales Penetration.** Extent to which total market potential has been realised, i.e. the proportion of people in that market who have become users or consumers of a product or service.

**Sales Planning.** Determining sales objectives and selling activity quotas in an effort to achieve pre-set sales targets.

**Sales Platform.** Main selling proposition upon which a particular campaign is to be based.

**Sales Promotion.** Any non-face-to-face activity concerned with the promotion of sales, but often taken also to include advertising. In consumer marketing, frequently used to denote any below-the-line advertising expenditure and having close connections with in-store merchandising.

**Sales Representative.** Sales person usually associated with technical or professional selling, although often acknowledged as a facade created by sales people and their managers in an effort to embellish their function.

**Sales Research.** Study of field and office activities in an effort to discover means of improving sales force productivity.

**Sales Territory.** Geographical area, market segment, or product group within which individual sales people are responsible for developing sales.

**Sales Tools.** Synonym for sales aids.

**Sales Volume.** Sales achievement expressed in quantitative, physical or volume terms.

**Salutation.** Personal greeting at beginning of a letter, which may be personalised by insertion of name by word processor or Laser printing. Dear Sir/Madam should never be used.

**Sample(s).** (1) Representative item or portion used by salesmen to assist in convincing buyers of product's quality. (2) Representative microcosm of the entire population or universe taken to represent the characteristics of the whole. Accuracy of resultant information may be calculated according to sample size and sampling technique used. (3) In digital audio production, sounds or sequence of sounds captured by a computer for use in future productions.

**Sample Frame.** Specified make-up of population data on which marketing research sample is to be based. It could be membership lists, census returns, types of dwellings. Primary sampling area can be chosen areas, secondary sampling frame can be selected people in these areas. This is the source of the sample; the list of population members from which the sample is chosen. For instance, all people listed in a telephone book, or all registered voters, or all families with children enrolled in a particular school might be chosen as the sampling frame.

**Sampling Distribution of Means.** Distribution of all possible means that might have been obtained if successive samples of the same size had been drawn. Even where data are not normally distributed, this distribution is usually normal.

**Sampling Points.** Places where interviews are conducted. The more sampling points, the more representative the sample.

**Sandwich Board.** Advertising poster carried by a person in public, usually in the form of two displays, one at the front and one at the back, suspended over the shoulder and thus 'sandwiching' the carrier.

**Sandwich-board Advertising.** Outdoor advertising medium, person carrying placards on chest and back. Restaurants like McDonalds often use this method to assist customers locate the store; directing them to the closest.

**Sans Serif.** Typeface without serifs at ends of strokes. Generally a low-contrast design. Sans serif faces lend a clean, simple appearance to documents. Good for bold displays. Bad for text in small type. Less easy to read on shiny paper than on newsprint or matt surface paper e.g. **This sentence is set in sans serif.**

**Satellite.** Device placed in space by a rocket and orbiting earth. In television, it permits the relay of live programmes including news events worldwide. Enables newspapers to be transmitted for international publication. Also used for cross-frontier TV programmes such as Sky, received either by individual dish or via cable television.

**Satellite Station.** A broadcast station in a fringe reception area, to boost the effective range of the main station's signal.

**Satirical Advertising.** Advertising which contains ironical comment on the advertiser, product or service. Kind of wry humour, laughing at itself to make sales point.

**Saturated Colour.** A pure colour, one that does not have significant amounts of white or black.

**Saturation.** The percentage of the total number of households that subscribe to a given medium. Also the purity of a colour, its freedom from black or white. An attribute of perceived colour, or the percentage of hue in the colour. Saturated colours are called vivid, strong, or deep. Desaturated colours are called dull, weak, or washed out. See flight.

**Saturation Advertising.** Excessive advertising to make impact on the market. Once used by detergent advertisers on TV, provoking public criticism. Replaced by advertising aimed at achieving certain percentage coverage of market or a given volume of audience ratings, after which the commercial is withdrawn for a while. Some commercials have been used for up to 18 months because they were never shown for too long to bore.

**Saturation Campaign.** Intensive use of mass media in a single campaign.

**Saturation Distribution.** As occurs with Free Newspapers delivered door-to-door, street-by-street throughout circulation area.

**Saturation Point.** Level at which any further expansion of distribution in a market is unlikely to be achieved and where further sales are restricted to the potential arising from replacement needs or population growth.

**SCA.** Subsidiary Communications Authorisation. A broadcast signal contained within a normal FM broadcast transmission. For example, background music at many department stores is transmitted via SCA. Most banks in the UK and restaurants broadcast through this means. A special receiver is required to receive the SCA signals.

**Scale.** Focusing method consisting of set of marks to indicate distances at which a lens is focused. May be engraved around the lens barrel, on the focusing control or on the camera body.

**Scale, Law of.** Large bold type contrasts with small light type. Dark colours advance, pale colours recede as with red versus pale blue.

**Scamp, Scribble.** Rough visual or sketch of an advertisement which is not measured exactly like a Layout.

**Scan Mark.** Control mark on pre-printed colours WEBS which is read on an electronic scanner to obtain correct register with black and white pages when newspaper is printed.

**Scanachrome.** Way of producing full-colour displays and posters on any flexible material.

**Scanner.** A device for converting photographs and graphics to disk for the computer to read.

**Scantex 2000.** Machine capable or producing complete setting and artwork of an advertisement or other print. Retouches halftones; scans, retouches and enhances tone or line illustrations; reverses black to white, solid or tinted; produces areas of clean, even tints (including vignettes) in percentage and screen ruling required; rotates type; modifies; sets automatic run rounds; produces logos as type; links up with IBM compatible PCs. Sets pin sharp type 1 to 90mm cap height. Combinations of these features can be imposed together and viewed on 17" interactive graphic monitor and output via Image Setter on film or paper, right or wrong reading, up to a full 20' 24 image area.

**Scattergraph.** Graph with a scale for each two variables; values of variables are plotted in pairs, one for the X-axis and one for the Y-axis. When a line is drawn to pass through the centre of the points, it indicates the line of best fit. Once drawn, it can then be used to estimate the most likely level of expenditure necessary to achieve the return shown against the matching points on the other axis.

**Scatter Plan.** Commercial announcements that are scheduled during a variety of times in broadcast media; usually, the advertiser is permitted to specify general time periods during which the commercials will be scheduled; also called "scatter package."

**Scatter Proofs.** Used for checking quality of illustrations in photomechanical reproduction, several pictures being proofed together.

**SCC.** Single column centimetre.

**Schafline High-definition System.** Graphic system in which photographs are retouched to produce a very clear dot screen, line screen or special effect halftones so that halftones reproduce sharply on newsprint.

**Schedule.** A list of advertisements or media to be used in a campaign; a chart of the advertisements that have been planned.

**Schedule and Estimate**. A data form submitted by an advertising agency to the advertiser prior to a firm media purchase; it contains price and audience goals and a proposed schedule.

**Scheduling.** Normally refers specifically to detailed arrangements for commercials or advertisements appearing in the media.

**Schema.** A diagrammatic representation; an outline or model. In psychology, a pattern imposed on complex reality or experience to assist in explaining it, mediate perception, or guide response.

**Scheme Advertising.** Advertising normally of a below-the-line character.

**Scoop.** (1) An exclusive or first published news report. It earns by lines. Often, a news item itself is called a scoop when no one else has that news item. Its an advantage gained by the publisher over competitors. Usually when an event like a coup occurs or is imminent, if a newspaper or publisher gets hold of this info far ahead others, it could become a scoop worth reading. (2) A floodlight, often used as a fill light, which has a deep, diffuse, and generally elliptical reflector.

**Score.** Crease or fold, as with board covers.

**Scotchprint.** Proof taken on plastic material from letterpress plate or form, to convert colour plate from letterpress to offset-litho.

**Scratch and Sniff.** Scented printed inks as used for sales promotion gimmicks.

**Scratch Cards.** Sales promotion cards with latex patches which can be scratched off to reveal a lucky number, value of voucher, or fruit machine symbols.

**Scratch Track.** An audio track containing production cues or information. Used only as a guideline or reference during production or editing.

**Screamer.** Exclamation mark.

**Screen.** The number of dots to the square inch in a half-tone block. The correct screen varies according to the quality of paper which will be used for printing. In a camera, this means the surface upon which the lens projects an image for view-finding and, usually, focusing purposes in SLR cameras. Almost universally a Fresnel screen is used with a fine-ground surface. It often incorporates a microprism or split-image rangefinder.

**Screen Clash.** Distortion due to two or more halftone screens (as in colour work) having been positioned at wrong angles, resulting in a blurred dot pattern.

**Screen Dump.** A printout taken directly from the screen.

**Screened Line Art.** Line drawings, screened in either negative or positive form, and possibly including graduated screens; can achieve a softer halftone effect. Screened line art can also be set on screen backgrounds.

**Screened Type.** Laying a screen on type which can produce a ghostly or grey effect. Produced with digital typesetting.

**Screening.** Procedure by which new or modified product ideas are assessed in a methodical way against key factors for success. Products not meeting the essential criteria are thus eliminated at an early stage in their development. This is a discipline which should be imposed early on in the concept development stage in order to eliminate unnecessary wastage of resources on ideas which are unlikely to be successful.

**Script.** (1) Manuscript or typescript for publication. (2) Synonym for broadsheet. (3) Text of a commercial film or broadcast- usually contains dialogue and production directions for radio, film or television production. (4) Typeface resembling handwriting. (5) Arrangement of sounds, images and effects placed in sequence on a computer for presentation.

**SDC System Developing Companies.** Kodak and four other photo industry leaders who jointly developed the Advanced Photo System standards.

**Search.** A mode in a video editor used to locate a specific video frame.

**Search Engine.** Computer software used to find a specific word or phrase in a database or across a network such as the internet. Google and Yahoo are very popular search engines used via the Internet.

**Search Mode.** An editing system control that switches a VCR into a shuttle mode so that tape can move forward or backward at varying speeds so that needed segments can be located and cued.

**Seasonal Concentration.** Limiting sales or promotional campaigns to appropriate segments of the year.

**Seasonal Discount.** Discount offered by media owners to encourage business during what are considered to be slack periods in the year.

**Seasonal Rate.** Rates in advertising which vary according to the time of year.

**Seasoned Colour.** Usually a colour additional to black, unless another colour is the main colour.

**Secondary Audience.** The members of a print media audience who do not subscribe to or purchase the publication. See Pass-along readers.

**Secondary Colour.** Product of mixing two primary colours, e.g. blue and yellow to make green.

**Secondary Coverage.** Area in which reception of radio or television channels is subject to variation; usually the area concerned is catered for by another channel but is within the outer area of another.

**Secondary Data.** Information which already exists, e.g. internal company records, government and other official statistics.

**Secondary Listening Area.** The outlying area in which broadcast transmissions are subject to fading or static; in television, the Grade 3 signal contour.

**Secondary Market.** An area with a potential broadcast audience of between 200,000 and 1,00,000 listeners.

**Secondary Media.** Support media for primary. Choice and relevance of primary and secondary media may be the opposite for different advertisers. Should not therefore be confused with Above-the-line and Below-the-line media. An fmcg company might choose press and TV as primary media, exhibitions and Point of Sale material as secondary; a Direct Response company might use Direct Mail and catalogues as primary media and press as secondary.

**Secondary Readership.** (1) Others who read a publication in addition to the original buyers, e.g. members of family, neighbours, friends, pass-round readership at workplaces, those in waiting and reception rooms, etc. (2) Indicates readership of a publication by location, e.g. by the members of a household whose head buys the publication or by people in an organisation which subscribes to it, sometimes referred to as 'pass-on readership'.

**Secondary Research, Sources.** Already published or existing material. Not original primary research.

**Sedition/Seditious Libel.** Sedition is a term of law to refer to covert conduct such as speech and organisation that is deemed by the legal authority as tending toward insurrection against the established order, usually government. Sedition often included subversion of a constitution and incitement of discontent (or resistance) to lawful authority. It may include any commotion, though not aimed at direct and open violence against the laws. Because sedition is typically considered the subvert act, the overt acts that may be prosecutable under sedition laws vary from one legal code to another. Where those legal codes have a traceable history, there is also a record of the change of definition for what constituted sedition at certain points in history. This overview has served to develop a sociological definition of sedition as well, within study of persecution. The difference between sedition and treason consists primarily in the subjective ultimate object of the violation to the public peace. Sedition does not consist of levying war against a government nor of adhering to its enemies, giving enemies aid, and giving enemies comfort. Nor does it consist, in most representative democracies, of peaceful protest against a government, nor of attempting to change the government by democratic means (such as direct democracy or constitutional convention). Also seditious libel criticism of public persons, the government, or King. Truth was not a defense against seditious libel. The Alien and Sedition Acts of 1798 (English) broke with common law precedent in that it allowed for truth as a defense, though Judges were not consistent in their rulings. The phrase "seditious libel" and "blasphemous libel" are used interchangeably.

**Segmentation.** Breakdown of a market into discrete and identifiable elements, each of which may have its own special requirements of a product and each of which is likely to exhibit different habits affecting its exposure to advertising media. Other marketing factors such as optimum price, quality, packaging and distribution are likely to differ as between one segment and another. Typical breakdowns are based upon age, social standing, income, sex, geographical location, leisure pursuits.

**Segmented Publication.** Small circulation journal aimed at minority or special interest readership.

**Segments.** (1) Sections in a newspaper, magazine or publication, e.g. leisure, agriculture, environment, woman, education, society, etc pages. (2) Division of time on television in which advertisements appear, rates varying according to whether they are peak or off-peak segments. This could also mean a part of a broadcast programme.

**Selective Focus.** Choosing a lens opening that produces a shallow depth of field. Usually this is used to isolate a subject by causing most other elements in the scene to be blurred.

**Selective Positioning.** Choice and continuity of a special position within a type of advertising medium, aimed at a specific target audience.

**Selenium.** Light-sensitive substance which, when used in a barrier-layer construction, generates electrical current when exposed to light. Used in exposure metres. Needs no external power supply.

**Self-completion Panel.** Research panel in which respondents complete pre-coded diaries and return them to the research company each week, usually recording purchases.

**Self Cover.** Cover pages of a brochure or catalogue being of the same paper as inside pages.

**Self-liquidating Point-of-Purchase**. Display for which the retailer pays part or all of the costs.

**Self-liquidating Premium.** An item for which the cost is paid by the customer; the price that the consumer pays covers the manufacturing cost of the premium.

**Self-mailer.** A direct mail item that is mailed without an envelope.

**Self-reflective.** Applied to texts which display an awareness or a comment on their own artificial status as texts.

**Self-regulation.** Cinema and the press are regulated by bodies set up by the industries themselves.

**Self-timer.** Mechanism delaying the opening of the shutter for some seconds after the release has been operated. Also known as delayed action.

**Selling.** Process of persuasion leading to a continuing trading arrangement, initiated and perpetuated at either a personal or impersonal level but commonly confined to oral representation supported by visual aids.

**Semantic Differential.** Choice from an arrangement of pre-selected phrases to enable informant to register one with the closet affinity to his/her own opinion. Often expressed in a complete spectrum, e.g. bad, very poor, poor, fairly good, good, excellent, using numerical ratings like –3, -2, -1, 1, 2, 3, from which respondent chooses the description most nearly corresponding with his/her own views.

**Semantic Noise.** Interference with the communication process because of a misunderstanding caused by a cliché or slang.

**Semi-automatic Iris.** Diaphragm mechanism which closes down to the taking aperture when the shutter is released, but must be manually re-opened to full aperture.

**Semi-display.** In classified advertisement section of a newspaper those advertisements in which the copy is not run on but set in a variety of type sizes and displayed.

**Semiology.** The 'science of sign systems' or 'signification'. Originally founded on the study of general linguistics by Ferdinand de Saussure, it was developed into a method for the systematic analysis and interpretation of all symbolic texts. Systems of signs are organised within larger cultural and ideological systems that ultimately determine meaning. A key element of Semiology is the idea that any (meaningful) sign (of any kind) has a conceptual element that carries meaning as well as a physical manifestation (word, image, etc.).

**Semi-solus.** Advertisement that appears on a page containing another advertisement but which is not positioned adjacent to it.

**Semi-structured.** Research conduced by interviewer with guidelines but in which certain key questions may need to be answered.

**Sender/Receiver.** General term used in linear models of communication to denote the beginning and the end of a communication process.

**Sensationalism.** At one level an everyday word for all aspects of media content that is likely to attract attention, excite or inflame emotions. In this sense it is related to commercialisation and tabliodisation. It has also been deployed as a concept in content analysis, defined in terms of some 'indicators' for measuring the degree of sensationalism. The reason for doing so is a concern at the inconsistency between sensational and objective news reporting.

**Sensitivity.** Expression of the nature of a photographic emulsion's response to light. Can be concerned with the degree of sensitivity as expressed by film speed or response to light of various colours (spectral sensitivity).

**Sentence Completion.** Establishing attitudes or opinions by providing incomplete questions that the respondent may answer in any fashion he/she chooses. Often portrays the irrational areas of motivation that are difficult to elicit summary from a conventional interviewing situation.

**Sequential.** Taking events one at a time in an orderly fashion, usually to some agreed procedure.

**Serial.** Broadcasting, publishing, or filming of continuing story in sections, usually without a predictable end.

**Serial Association.** Way of post-testing advertisements by asking members of a discussion group to associate ideas with it. Result can show what desirable, undesirable, predictable, unexpected responses are provoked by the advertisement being tested.

**Series.** (1) Broadcasting, publishing, or filming of similar or related stories usually for a limited season. (2) Term in statistics for orderly arrangement of numerical data, usually in a sequence.

**Series Discount.** Discount given by advertising media owner in consideration of an undertaking by an advertiser to book a series of insertions within a given minimum number of issues.

**Serif.** Tail or cross stroke in a typeface, at one or both ends of a main stroke, decorative and are added to the end of a letter's main strokes. Serifs improve readability by leading the eye along the line of type.

**Service Department.** Part of an organisation concerned with providing after-sales service to customers; frequently involved with the handling of complaints which require tactful replacement or rectification to avoid temporary or permanent loss of goodwill.

**Service Fee.** Charge made, usually on a predetermined annual basis, by an advertising or public relations agency for the service it provides. Increasingly used instead of, or in addition to, the earlier convention of commission income.

**Servo Controlled.** An electronically controlled mechanical device, generally within a tape machine, that uses electronic feedback to maintain a desired and accurately controlled speed.

**Servo Zoom.** A lens which uses a motor-driven mechanism to alter focal length.

**SESAC, Society of European Stage Actors and Composers.** An agency that licenses copyrighted music.

**Set.** (1) Collection or groups of people, item, numbers or ideas. Each object in the set is a member or element of the set. Set theory is the branch of mathematics concerned with sets, their operations, and the properties concerned with their operations. (2) Where filming takes place. (3) Two or more songs played back to back without interfering commentary by the DJ.

**Set Solid.** Lines of type which are set close up to one another, without way spacing.

**Setmetre.** Electronic device used for TV audience measurement as part of system to produce BARB figures. Records on heat sensitive paper details of when TV receiver was switched on or off and to which station it is turned.

**Sets in Use**. The percentage of households that have broadcast receiving sets that are operating at one time within a market area; because many households have more than one receiving set, "households using television" and "households using radio" are the current common terms.

**Set-top Box.** Computer which sits on top of a television set and controls the variety of possible incoming signals.

**Set-ups.** Term used for the separate camera, lighting and sound positions necessary for shooting a feature film.

**Seven-point Formula.** The SOLAADS for news releases: 1. Subject. 2. Organisation. 3. Location. 4. Advantages. 5. Applications. 6. Details. 7. Source.

**SFX, SPFX.** Special audio or video effects used in the film, television, and entertainment industry to visualise scenes that cannot be achieved by normal means, such as space travel. They are also used when creating the effect by normal means is prohibitively expensive, such as an enormous explosion. They are also used to enhance previously filmed elements, by adding, removing or enhancing objects within the scene. Many different visual special effects techniques exist, ranging from traditional theatre effects or elaborately staged as in the "machine plays" of the Restoration spectacular, through classic film techniques invented in the early 20th century, such as aerial image photography and optical printers, to modern computer graphics techniques (CGI). Often several different techniques are used together in a single scene or shot to achieve the desired effect. Special effects are often "invisible." That is to say that the audience is unaware that what they are seeing is a special effect. This is often the case in historical movies, where the architecture and other surroundings of previous eras are created using special effects. Special Effects are traditionally divided into two domains : Optical Effects, that

SHF.

rely on manipulation of a photographed image, and Mechanical Effects - effects which take place during the live-action shooting.

**Shank.** Body of a metal type character.

**Share of Audience.** A percentage of households using television or people listening to radio(and thus of HUT or of HUR) who are tuned to a particular station or programme during a certain period. A stations 'share' is its percentage of households using television or people listening to radio. Not to be confused with rating (slang "share").

**Share of Market.** The percentage of the overall market's expenditure for a product or service garnered by ones (or a competitor's) product or service.

**Share of Voice (SOV).** The proportion of advertising expenditures that are made for a brand versus competitive brands.

**Sharpness.** A term used to describe the ability of a lens to render fine detail clearly; dependent on the contrast and resolution of a lens and varies with the f/stop. It depicts the clarity of the photographic image in terms of focus and contrast. In general, a lens is sharpest at the middle apertures. Largely subjective but can be measured to some extent by assessing adjacency effects, that is, the abruptness of the change in density between adjoining areas of different tone value.

**Sheet (Prefixed 4, 8, 16, 32 etc.).** Whole size of a piece of paper before cutting or folding.

**Sheet-fed.** Printing from separate sheets of paper, not from reels or webs.

**Shelf Edging.** As seen on edges of shelves behind shop or bar counter, narrow adhesive strips or paper bearing advertising messages.

**Shell Scheme.** Simple ready-made exhibition stands supplied at a cheap rate by exhibition promoters. Virtually cube-shaped with one end open to aisle and public.

**SHF.** Super high frequency. The frequencies ranging from 3 GHz to 30 GHz. These include communications satellite signals and most microwave transmissions.

**Shield Law.** A law protecting the confidentiality of reporter's sources. It exists in most countries and keeps a news reporter from having to reveal confidential sources of information.

**Ship Cinemas, TV.** Medium for advertising duty free and other goods on sale on cruise ships, ferries and other vessels.

**Ship Exhibitions.** Floating exhibitions on ships fitted out for the purpose, which either sail from port to port, or remain in one dock.

**Shock Mount.** A rubber or spring-based mic holder which reduces or eliminates the transfer of sound or vibration to the mic.

**Shock Value.** An element in news value based on the amount of amazement, surprise, horror or scandal represented by a story.

**Shoot.** (1) To take a photograph, or take pictures for a film or video. (2) Single mailing of Direct Mail piece.

**Shooting.** Term used in photoset newspaper. When the bromides of type are assembled in position on the page; the page goes to the camera room for shooting- it goes into negative form ready for plate making.

**Shooting Script.** The cameras script as distinct from the actor's script for a film or video. Sets out scenes with directions, and may be arranged out of sequence to provide convenient plan of actions, especially regarding on-location shots.

**Shopping.** Looking for a new advertising agency, as in 'shopping around'.

**Shopping Newspaper.** A newspaper-like publication that is devoted mainly to advertising, often distributed free to shoppers or to households (slang "shopper").

**Short Rate.** Higher rate charged for fewer insertions when advertiser does not take up full volume of advertising for which he had contracted originally. The money is thus owed to a media vehicle by an advertiser to offset the rate differential between the earned rate and the lower contracted rate.

**Shot.** The smallest element in any film sequence, a single take during shooting which may be further shortened during editing.

**Shot/Reverse Shot.** Term used for the conventional way of shooting an exchange between two characters in a film or television programme.

**Shotgun Mic.** A highly directional microphone capable of picking up sound over a great distance.

**Shoulder Time.** Time immediately preceding or following peak-time.

**Showcase.** Cabinet made of glass or clear plastic to display products protected against deterioration and pilferage. Though extensively used at point-of-sale, showcases are widely used at publics and private exhibitions, e.g. book showcase, when an indication will be given of where displayed articles may be purchased.

**Show Through.** Dark areas of print on reverse side showing through a light-toned picture or area of white space, giving dirty effect to an advertisement. Problem with some Tabloids that have long print-runs and are printed at high speed on poor quality paper.

**Showcard.** Point of Sale price strutted to stand or pierced to hang, printed on card, metal or plastic. Used for shop window, and shelf displays.

**Showing.** The number of outdoor posters that are necessary to reach a certain percentage of the mobile population in a market within a specified time; many outdoor markets are now purchased by gross rating points. See full showing and gross rating points.

**Shutter.** Blades, a curtain, plate, or some other movable cover in a camera that controls the time during which light reaches the film.

**Shutter Priority.** An exposure mode on an automatic or autofocus camera that lets one select the desired shutter speed; the camera sets the aperture for proper exposure. If the shutter speed is changed, or the light level changes, the camera adjusts the aperture automatically.

**Shuttle Speed.** How quickly a tape recorder can move a tape forward and backward.

**Sibilance.** A splattering, hissing vocal sound commonly caused by the combination of "S" sounds and poor audio equipment.

**Sidebar.** A column of copy and/or graphics which appears on the page of a magazine or newspaper to communicate information about the story or contents of the paper. It accompanies the main story, detailing with a particular angle or aspect, such as the hero's early childhood.

**Sidehead.** Crosshead. Sub-heading between paragraphs of text, usually flushed to the left hand edge of the column.

**Sidelighting.** Light striking a subject from the side relative to the position of the camera. It produces shadows and highlights to create modelling on the subject.

**Sidestitch or Stab Stitch.** Form of wire binding, stitching pages from front to back. Used for thicker magazines when saddle stitching is unsuitable. Covers are drawn on, giving a flat spine. While pages are less easy to open than with saddle stitching they do not burst free as with perfect binding.

**Sign/Signified/Signifier.** The sign, in semiotics, is divided into the signifier or physical form taken by the sign, and the signified, which is the concept it stands in for.

**Signals.** These are sounds of radio messages such as echo and other sounds which come under electro magnetic pulses. It gives rise to electronic communication such as radio, TV, fax, telephone, radio phone, computer, cablegram, satellite, cinema, internet, etc.

**Signal-to-noise Ratio; S/N.** The degree to which a desired signal stands out from background noise or interference. The higher the signal-to-noise ratio, the better the quality of the resulting sound or picture.

**Signature Slogan.** Strapline or pay-off slogan at the foot of an advertisement. May repeat a TV jingle. Creates corporate image such as Standard Trust Bank's (now United Bank for Africa) Always Within Reach or LG's Life's Good.

**Signatures.** In bookbinding, sets of 16 or 32 pages gathered for binding. Originates from printer's signature marking sets of pages. In a 16-page section of a yearbook, eight pages are printed on one side, eight on another.

**Significs.** Enquiry into questions of meaning, expression and interpretation, and the influence of language upon thought.

**Significance.** (1) Generally used to suggest relevance. (2) Statistical term with similar meaning but with more precise implication. Statistical tests are used to establish the significance level, e.g. T-tests (taking difference between average values) and Chi-tests (testing differences between distributions).

**Signs.** Visual outdoor advertising with a very long history, e.g. inn signs, apothecary's bottles, barber's red and white pole, wheelwright's wheel, and so on up to modern day signs such as those of petrol pumps and lighted signs including Newscasters in city centres.

**Silence.** The condition or quality of being or keeping still and silent. Silences are a natural and fundamental aspect of communication, often ignored because misconceived.

**Silicon.** Light-sensitive substance which generates a minute current when exposed to light.

**Silk Screening.** Method of printing by which ink is forced through a fine mesh on which have been superimposed opaque areas, representing the reverse of the design, through which ink will not pass. Much used in the production of high quality point-of-sale material.

**Silk Screen Printing.** Serigraphic printing process of Chinese origin which used a mesh of human hair. Stencils are made of the printing design, and ink squeezed through the screen made of silk, nylon, organdie or metal mesh. Much used for printing posters such as window bills, but versatile because many materials and non-flat surfaces can be printed. Can be applied to paper, board, wood, plastics, metal, glass. Used to print dials, book jackets, pens, ties, T-Shirts, ashtrays, bottles.

**Simple Camera.** A camera that has few or no adjustments to be made by the photographer. Usually, simple cameras have only one size of lens opening and one or two shutter speeds and do not require focusing by the photographer.

**Simulation.** The idea that media age changes the relationship between fabrication and reality, and image and truth. The development of new technologies produce their own worlds and different reality

Simulcast.

effects that can no longer be contradicted by pointing to brute data.

**Simulcast.** Playing a program over an AM and FM station at the same time.

**Single Column Centimetre (SCC).** Standard unit of measurement for print advertisements; one centimetre in a column.

**Single-copy Sales.** Newsstands, store sales. Anything not home delivered.

**Single Key Stroking.** Process of keying in copy in computerised newsrooms and newspaper advertisement offices where there is no foundry and no hot metal typesetting.

**Single-Lens-Reflex (SLR) Camera.** A type of camera that allows one to see through the camera's lens as one look in the camera's viewfinder. Other camera functions, such as light metering and flash control, also operate through the camera's lens.

**Single Servo AF (Nikon's term).** Once the subject is in focus, focus is locked. Useful for recomposing the picture.

**Single Source.** Information or data received or compiled from one origin alone, most often in connection with a research study.

**Site.** Poster location.

**Site Classification.** Grading of sites, with different rentals, according to location and, as in the case of major market areas, traffic volume.

**Situation Report.** Report on the current situation or circumstances, often shortened to 'sitrep.'

**Sixteen Sheets.** Most popular size of poster consisting of eight double crown sizes.

**Sixty.** Slang for a one-minute broadcast commercial announcement.

**Size Up.** Instruction to printer to set type a size-larger, when proofreading.

**Skew Control.** A playback control on a videotape machine which adjusts videotape tension and the length of the video tracks read from the videotape. Improper skew adjustment results in various picture aberrations.

**Skewness.** Distribution of data that differs from a normal distribution in that the mean and the mode are located at different points.

**Skip Instructions.** In a communication research questionnaire some questions may not be relevant to certain respondents, and the interviewer is instructed to move on to the next relevant question.

**Skybox.** A term for promotional boxes that are usually above the nameplate of the newspaper. Also known as a teaser.

**Skyscraper.** A vertical banner ad, usually at one side of a web page, usually 60 x 468 pixels in size.

**Slab Serif.** Kind of typeface with series of the same thickness as stems and arms of characters. Egyptian typefaces, e.g. Cairo, Karnack, Rockwell. Useful as display faces, but also legible as text type. Used for ITT logo.

**Slander.** A spoken defamatory statement or such a statement in any other transient form like significant looks, signs, etc.

**Slang.** A kind of language occurring chiefly in casual and playful speech, made up typically of short-lived coinages and figures of speech that are deliberately used in place of standard terms for added raciness, humour, irreverence, or other effect. See Jargon.

**Slant.** Central theme adopted by writer on a particular issue.

**Slash.** The oblique stroke (/).

**Slate.** Film industry term for the list of major features to be produced during a production period.

**Slave Unit.** Accessory flash 'slave' units are available to fire multiple flash units without multiple electrical connections to the camera. These units sense the light output of the first flash, which is mounted in the camera hot shoe, or cord-connected to the camera. When the light output is sensed, the slave unit triggers a second flash unit that is connected only to the slave. Additional slaves and flash units can be used, if needed.

**Sleeper Effect.** Studies which have shown that, even after the purely factual information within it has been forgotten, attitudes may still have shifted in favour of an advertisement, indicating that an attitude change has been effected- this is known as the sleeper effect.

**Sleeve.** In photogravure printing, cylindrical printing plate with recessed image. Cells of carrying depths hold ink according to the required tonal effect. Surface has grid which is scraped by a doctor's blade to remove excess ink. See Photogravure Klischograph Hard-dot Gravure.

**Slide.** A photographic transparency (positive) mounted for projection. Represents first generation production of an image. Most agencies and photo editors demands slides than prints. It has a very tight tolerance on exposure latitudes.

**Slip Edition.** A recast page or pages in which some but not all of the contents of the original edition are amalgamated with new material.

**Slipping.** Pasting an amendment on a poster.

**Slogan.** Rather like a TV Jingle, a catchy phrase that helps people to remember a product. Some persist long after original use, like Beer 'Ahead on Taste'. A very good slogan is Vigeo's 'Sometime, somehow, somewhere... you'll need us'.

**Slot.** (1) Commercial break in TV or radio programme. (2) One of the people on the copy desk who checks over the copy editors' work before committing it to type. Also used as a verb: "Hey, Charlie, slot me on this, will you?"

**Slow Sync.** A flash technique for using the flash at a slow shutter speed. Flash shooting in dim light or at night at a fast shutter speed often result in a flash-illuminated subject against a dark background. Using a slower shutter speed with the flash brings out the background details in the picture. Use of a slow shutter speed with Rear-Curtain Sync is particularly effective for illustrating the movement of a stream of light. Can be very creative if put to good use.

**Slug.** An internal name for a story, usually just one word. Elex might be the slug for a story on school elections.

**Small Ads.** Smalls or Classified Advertisements.

**SMATV.** Satellite Master Antenna Television. A type of parabolic antenna designed with the specific purpose of transmitting signals to and/or receiving from satellites. A satellite dish is a particular type of microwave antenna. Satellite dishes come in varying sizes and designs, and are most commonly used to receive satellite television. Modern dishes intended for home television use are generally 43 cm (18") to 80 cm (31") in diameter, and are fixed in one position, for Ku-band reception from one orbital position. Prior to the existence of DBS services, home users would generally have a motorised C-band satellite dish of up to 3 metres in diameter for reception of channels from different satellites. Overly small dishes can still cause problems, however, including rain fade and interference from adjacent satellites.

**Snipe.** Overlay or strip of copy added to poster.

**Snow.** A rapidly moving grainy effect in video caused by little or no picture information.

**Soaps, Soap Opera.** Slang for a continuing broadcast dramatic serial, usually a daytime and early evening program. Originating from American radio series sponsored by soap companies, now applied to popular TV series such as Ripples, Passions, Super Story, Checkmate, Papa Ajasco, Everyday People and Izozo.

**Social Anthropology.** The study of the evolution of human communities and cultures.

**Social Construction.** Generation of a shared reality through communication and other social interaction. Sometimes called constructivism, this term refers to a theoretical position that emphasises how social life influences our perception.

**Social Institutions.** Organisations in society that endure despite the departure of individuals. School systems, large corporations, and religious organisations are examples of institutions as are families, sororities, social clubs, and media organisations.

**Social Psychology.** The study of human behaviour. This is a branch of either sociology or psychology that is concerned with the psychology of human social groups, including the ways in which group membership affects individual thought and action.

**Social Responsibility.** Theory espousing privately owned media 'unless the government has to take over to ensure public service.' This is attributed to the mass media in certain normative theories of the press and based on propositions about the needs of (democratic) society, the unwritten obligations implicit in the freedom of publication as well as general ethical and moral principles relating to truth and justice.

**Social Responsibility Advertising.** Ads sponsored by organisations or companies admonishing us to act responsibly when consuming products or participating in activities. Responsibility in drinking, safe driving, and similar ads fall under this type of advertising.

**Social Role.** Prescribed way for someone in a given social relationship to act. Father, secretary, teacher and girlfriend are all examples of social roles; norms for individuals acting in these roles are different from the general norms of the society.

**Social Setting.** Particular social situation used as the object of a research study; these are usually social institutions, whether a large organisation, an individual family living together, or a media institution.

**Socialisation.** The general process of social formation of the young under the influence of so-called agencies of socialisation-traditionally the family, the school, religion and now mass media.

**Socialist Realism.** The prescribed realist form forced on soviet film-makers by the Stalin regime in the 1930s- featuring romanticised heroic workers.

**Socio-economic Groups.** Breakdown of population into sections to represent main subsections of a community according to selected economic and social criteria. The groups are designated by a letter series, namely, A, B, C1, C2, D, E, in which A and B represent the minority of higher income receivers in the scale, D and E the lower skilled, lower earners and C1 and C2 occupying a position midway between these extremes. Introduced by the IPA in 1962, as an aid to media distribution analysis, the scale has been the subject of the wide contention, since it is felt to be inadequate to reflect the facts of market segmentation in an era of rapid social changes. On the other hand, complex, problems of social measurement are involved in any attempt to set up any superior alternative.

**Sociology.** The study of human social behaviour, especially the study of the origins, organisation, institutions, and development of human society.

**SOF.** Sound-on-film. A film that includes a soundtrack. A good instance is the Lion King movie with the sound track of Angélique Kidjo

**Soft Focus.** Special photographic effect which is not sharp. It is produced by use of a special lens that creates soft outlines. Filters are more popular than lens as it is more economical and flexible.

**Soft News.** Articles in newspapers and magazines within element of news but mainly expressing the opinions of publications or a contributor. They are interesting but less important than hard news, focusing on people as well as facts and information and including interviews, reviews, articles, and editorials. It lacks the immediacy and urgency of hard news.

**Soft Selling.** Couching the selling message in a subtle or oblique way, as against a blatant or hard selling approach. Sometimes known as 'low pressure selling'.

**Soft Wipe.** A video wipe in which the demarcation line between the two sources blends into a soft line.

**Softlight.** A floodlight producing an extremely soft and virtually shadowless light. It is low or moderate in contrast, such as on an overcast day.

**Software.** The programs written for computers, or the films, music etc. which could be played on them.

**Solid.** Type is set solid when there is no leading or white space between lines.

**Solomon Four-group Design.** Experiment using four groups: a control group receiving no testing, a control group receiving a past-test only, a treatment group receiving a post-test only, and a treatment group receiving both a pre-test and post-test.

**Solus.** (1) An advertisement which stands alone on the page. (2) A solus poster site (e.g. a Bulleting Board or Super site). (3) An exhibition stand which occupies an island site, and has all four sides open to aisles and visitors.

**Solus Distribution.** In door-to-door delivery, a single mail drop. May be targeted to a defined geographical area such as by use of ACRON.

**Solus Position.** Position of isolation (i.e. separated from any immediate, especially competitive, announcements) of poster or press advertisement, for instance.

**Solus Spots.** TV commercials unaccompanied by other commercials.

**Sortation.** Database system used for Direct Mail which allows stored information to be selected according to specified characteristics, e.g. name, within date, media code, region. Also, as in the sortation plan of the Mailsort system of sorting direct mail shots on the basis of 1,520 direct selections of postcodes whereby mail goes direct to delivery offices, and 80 are residue selections to post offices where mail is sorted to delivery offices.

**SOT.** Sound-on-tape, videotape that includes a sound track.

**Sound Effect.** Frequently used to refer to artificially created sounds produced for audiovisual texts; also can be extended to refer to all aural material in a production apart form dialogue and music.

**Sound Image.** Term used to emphasise the possibility of analysing or reading sounds in the same way as pictures.

**Sound Recording.** First fixation of sound that can be aurally perceived or reproduced but not excluding sound track associated with cinema.

**Sound Stages.** Term describing the individual buildings available for shooting in a film studio- the name implies that they can be used for recording sound.

**Sound Track.** Narrow area running alongside the film which carries the sound recording. Is often used to refer to the actual sound recording itself.

**Sound Bite.** "Event" audio used during news or programming. For example, a 20 second segment recorded from the mayor's speech and used in the evening's news would be a sound bite.

**Source.** A person who gives information to a reporter or editor, for attribution in a news story. A source is normally not to be revealed in case of later problems. It is unethical in mass communications to reveal a source, even at gunpoint.

**Source Credibility.** The believability of a sender.

**Source Machine(s).** In videotape editing, the machine(s) that contain the original footage that will be edited onto the edited master.

**Soviet Communist Theory.** System of state owned media functioning as a propaganda instrument of the government.

**Sp.** In typesetting, spacing between type characters.

**Space.** Term used to describe pages available for advertising purposes in a publication; constitutes the product available for sale after text matter has been recommended.

**Space Buyer.** Person in an advertising agency responsible for purchasing advertisement in newspapers, magazine, and business publications, and sometimes outdoor and transit. See Media buyer.

**Space Position Value.** A measure of the effectiveness of an outdoor poster location.

**Spaghetti Westerns.** A circle of films made in Italy and Spain in the 1960s and 1970s, drawing on the Hollywood westerns for inspiration.

**Span of Control.** Breadth of control, measured in numbers of personnel and the rigour of their duties, which a manager or executive supervise effectively.

**SPD.** Silicon Photo Diode. Battery powered light sensitive cells - the most common light reading cells for cameras, external metering devices.

**Special Feature.** Part of a publication, or a separate publication, devoted to particular event or interest, ostensibly for readers' benefit but often to attract associated advertising expenditure.

**Specialogs.** Smaller issues of larger catalogues publicising a limited amount of merchandise and mailed to a highly specialised audience.

**Special or Preferred Position.** Advertisement position in a publication which is rated higher because of its special or higher readership. Insertion of an advertisement in what is regarded as a distinctive position in a publication, e.g. outside or inside covers, or facing matter. Such as selection frequently involves a higher charge being made to the advertiser and advance action on his part to secure it.

**Spectacular.** (1) Large, outdoor, electrically illuminated sign. (2) Unusual direct mail piece. (3) Elaborate special TV programme, irregularly scheduled. (4) Very large poster sites.

**Spectrum.** Full range of colours from violent to red.

**Speech Bubble.** As used in cartoons or with other pictures, spoken words written in balloons.

**Spend.** The advertising budget or Appropriation.

**Spike.** A tall steel spike on which unwanted copy is put. To kill something or disregard a news item. At one time, when editors were finished with a piece of paper, such as a story, headline or page proof, they would slam it down on an upright nail on their desk. Then, they would know they were done with it, but could go back to it later if they needed to. Today, many newsroom computers have a "spike" key for killing a story or file.

**Spin.** The activities of press or PR officers usually called spin doctors. See Spin Doctor.

**Spin Doctor.** Contemporary expression to refer to all those who have the job of managing (or massaging) the public presentation of information or ideas (especially on behalf of politicians) to maximum advantage. Their work results in the manipulation of news and is related to public relations and propaganda. The term 'flak' has also been used in this connection. The role of spin doctor has been greatly enhanced in a time of political marketing and professional management of campaigns. Its prominence also reflects the media's own attraction to 'horse-race' or 'strategic' rather than substantive reporting of politics.

**Spine.** Backbone or back edge of a book. Often carries information on the title of a book and the author's name.

**Spiral of Silence.** Concept that describes one version of the 'third-party' effect in opinion formation – the tendency for people to be influenced in what they think (or say they do) or by what they think other people think. The term was first applied by Elisabeth Noelle-Neumann to refer to the tendency for those who think they hold a minority or deviant view to refrain from expressing it in public, thus accelerating the dominance of the supposed consensus (the spiralling effect). The hypothesis is based on a presumed 'fear of isolation'. The main thrust of the theory is to attribute to the (leftist) media a powerful effect, since they are the main source of what people think is the dominant opinion of the moment. Also related to the better known 'bandwagon effect' whereby apparent front runners pick up support on this basis alone.

**Splash.** Main news story, associated with front page of newspapers but not exclusively.

**Split-image.** Form of rangefinder image, bisected so that the two halves of the image are aligned only when the correct object distance is set on the instrument or in the case of a coupled rangefinder, when the lens is correctly focused. SLR cameras may have a prismatic split-image system in their viewing screen. Works on the same principle as a microprism, and is restricted to apertures of f5.6 or greater.

**Split Run.** When the identical publication is printed and distributed in two or more separate production runs and deliveries to facilitate the insertion of different advertisements in each part run. The arrangement is often used to compare the measured effects of alternative pieces of advertising copy.

**Split Transmissions.** TV transmissions from different transmitters which permit advertisers to test alternative commercials.

**Sponsor.** Organisation financing sporting or other activities in order to gain coverage and prestige from its association with them. This could be an advertiser who buys the exclusive right to the time available for commercial announcements in a given broadcast program or segment.

**Sponsored Book.** Book specially produced for an organisation which undertakes to meet all or most of the production cost to the publisher, such publications are being produced for public relations' purposes.

**Sponsored Events.** In marketing, part of a public relations programme to emphasise the name of an organisation or product in a favourable light by paying all or some of the cost of a public sport or spectacle, e.g. cricket or motor-racing. The technique can be used in relation to any event which is likely to be patronised or otherwise come to the attention of the particular public the organisation desire to influence.

**Sponsored Project.** Project that receives funding from governmental, academic, industry, or private sources. Both human subjects procedures and intellectual property right issues can become more complex for sponsored projects.

**Sponsored Television.** Television broadcasting method where time periods are bought by companies, who then provide their own producer, director, and artists for a show and during broadcasting advertise their company products.

**Sponsorship.** Financial support by commercial organisations for arts, books, sports, events, expeditions, education and so on. May be for advertising, marketing or public relations purposes, or combination of these. Often dependent on subject being televised, but independent of TV programmes and not to be confused with sponsorship of whole programmes which is common in some parts of the world.

**Sport.** Another term for "commercial".

**Spot**. The purchase of broadcast slots by geographic or station breakdowns; the purchase of slots at certain times, usually during station breaks; the term "spot" can refer to the time used for the commercial announcement or it can refer to the announcement itself.

**Spot Colour.** The technique of colouring for emphasis of some areas of basic black and whit advertisements, usually with a single colour. Use in press advertisement of a single second colour for, say, brand name or Logotype.

**Spot Lengths.** Standard times for television commercials, e.g. 7, 15, 30, 45 and 60 seconds; 30 seconds being the base time.

**Spotlight.** Lighting instrument that produces a focused, relatively undiffused light.

**Spotlight Effect.** Video effect resulting in a circular section of the screen appearing brighter in order to highlight a particular element.

**Spot News.** Unexpected and unplanned news events such as natural disasters, air crashes, murders or assassinations.

**Spotting.** Retouching a processed print with a pencil or brush (with watercolours or dyes) to eliminate spots left by dust or scratches on the negative.

**Spot Radio or TV.** A market-by-market, station-by-station purchase of broadcasting time rather than purchasing time on a broadcast network.

**Spot Rate.** Rate for single TV commercial as distinct from packages.

**Spot Story.** A small story that is usually more specific, as opposed to a bigger story like a feature story. See Spot news.

**Spread.** (1) A double page spread, i.e. a pair of facing pages. (2) Two facing pages in a publication over which one advertisement may be printed.

**Spread Pasting Date.** Spacing out of dates for pasting of posters so that they appear at stated intervals.

**Spread Traffic.** Form of media readership research to measure the proportion of readers of an issue, who read or looked at each spread in a magazine producing a score for an average spread.

**Sputnik.** First artificial satellite launched into space, by the Russians in 1957.

**SQF.** Subjective Quality Factor. Essentially a lens rating system.

**SRA Sizes.** For offset printing machines, SRA paper sizes are slightly over similar sizes to allow for bleed or to allow trimming of grip edges.

**SRDS.** Standard Rate and Data Service. A source book listing current published rates for media.

**SSFDC.** For solid-state floppy disk, a type of alternative source of storage medium employed by Apple's Quick-Take digital camera as opposed to ATA standard Flash Memory card.

**Stabiliser.** In photography, alternative to fixer where permanence is not required. Used in automatic processing machines and can now provide prints that will not deteriorate noticeably over many months if kept away from strong light.

**Stain.** Discoloured areas on film or paper, usually caused by contaminated developing solutions or by insufficient fixing, washing, or agitation.

**Standard Advertising.** Ads paid for by the company or organisation that has products to sell or services to render.

**Standard Deviation.** Square root of the variance of a distribution; linear measure of dispersion. For known distribution shapes, the number of sources falling within a certain number of standard deviations from the mean is also known.

**Standard Error.** Measurement of accuracy of statistical measurements of sample. Expressed in two dimensions; the parameters of accuracy and the confidence level at which the study was undertaken.

**Standard Metropolitan Statistical Area (SMSA).** See Metropolitan area.

**Standardisation.** Has a double meaning: it can signify 'sameness'; but can also denote the maintenance of standards, in the sense of quality.

**Standby Space.** Low cost advertisement space filled at publisher's direction.

**Standout Test.** Method of researching the ability of a pack to stand out from existing competitors. The new pack is photographed among others on a shelf. Respondents are then shown picture on a screen and invited to identify the pack being tested. The time taken to find pack is then measured to show how quickly or slowly it is spotted.

**Stand-up.** A reporter's appearance in a TV news story. This is usually a head and shoulders shot which features the reporter talking into a microphone at the scene of the news event, often used as a transition, or at the beginning or ending.

**Star.** Actor whose image, via accumulated publicity, debate etc., is strong enough to be valued as an added component of any performance, and which acts as a specific attraction for audiences.

**Star Image.** The constructed image of the star, usually in relation to film and associated secondary circulation.

**Station Break.** The time between broadcast programs to permit station identification and spot announcements; slang for a 20-second broadcast announcement.

**Station Clearance.** See Clear Time.

**Station Identification.** The announcement of station call letters, usually with broadcast frequency or channel, and station location.

**Station Option Time.** A broadcast time for which the station has the option of selling advertising.

**Station Posters.** Advertisements consisting of posters in transit stations.

**Station Programme Cooperative (SPC).** Concept in public broadcasting that utilises direct feedback in the form of financial commitment from affiliate stations to determine which programmes will compose about one-third of the programming distributed by PBS.

**Station Representative.** Person or firm representing a number of different radio and television stations and selling time on those stations to advertisers. Could also mean time brokers.

**Statistical Analysis.** Application of statistical techniques or methods to a particular data set. Statistical analysis can be descriptive, exploratory, or hypothesis testing.

**Statistical Test.** Technique for determining whether a set of data do or do not support a particular hypothesis. Based on a particular confidence level, a statistical test asks whether observed results might have occurred by chance.

**Statistical Significance.** Confidence level achieved by a particular test. Normally, an acceptable confidence level is chosen in advance; test results then either do or not achieve statistical significance at the chosen level.

**Statutory Regulation.** Regulatory powers established by law (e.g. the Broadcasting acts of 1990 and 1996).

**Steadicam.** Trade name for a stabilising device allowing a camera operator to move freely without jerking the image.

**Stem.** Upright stroke in a type character.

**Stereotype, Stereotyping.** (1) Rigid set of attitudes or expectations. Although this term commonly refers to negative expectations about a group of people, such as ethnic group, it can also refer to expectations about a single individual or a thing and can be positive. (2) Printing plate cast in one piece from a matrix or mould. Also a representation of a type of person, without fine detail.

**Stereotype Photographs.** Use of stock pictures of different types of people in group depth interviewing. The respondents are asked which products they think would be bought by each person pictured.

**Stet.** Let it stand: a proofreading symbol on a copy that a correction or deletion has been made in error and should be ignored. The words affected are underlined with dots and the word 'stet' written in the margin. When stet is used it simply implies "leave it the way it is".

**Sticker.** Label, poster or other printed sheet intended for sticking on window, letter, envelope or other medium for display purposes.

This is one of the main means of spreading the news for the fight against HIV/AIDS.

**Still.** Single frame printed from photograph used in a continuous film. Generally refers to a photograph rather than the movie-film as such.

**Stimulus.** Initiating step or incentive intended to provoke a predictable response. Stimulus-response is a psychological process by which an experimental subject learns to perform some action in response to a message stimulus that has become associated with the action in question. It underlies a large body of learning theory that was applied in early research into the effects of communication and media. It has not however, proved a very good guide to reality.

**Stochastic Model.** A contrived, simulated situation where chance or random variables are used. Involves the use of conditions of uncertainty, and is an advanced form of linear programming.

**Stock.** Quality or type of paper or film to be used in a production or publication, e.g. 35mm stock.

**Stock Footage.** Film footage which may be hired for use in films, videos, commercials, either archival or old movie.

**Stone.** The table in the printing works where the newspaper pages are made up. A sub-editor making last minute preparation on the stone is said to be stone subbing. Originally the stone was made of stone or marble. Hence, Stone Editor or Stone Sub. In recent time, it is made of steel.

**Stop Bath.** Darkroom material. An acid rinse, usually a weak solution of acetic acid, used as a second step when developing black-and-white film or paper. It stops development and makes the hypo (fixing bath) last longer.

**Stop Motion.** Technique often used in TV commercials such as packs which unwrap themselves, move independently, faces that come to life on packs, and other 'trick' effects.

**Stopping Down.** Changing the lens aperture to a smaller opening; for example, from f/8 to f/11. For some lenses, like PC lens or attachment with none dedicated bellow on macro photography, stop down exposure metering is required for correct reading.

**Stop-down Metering.** TTL metering in which the light is measured at the picture-taking aperture. As the metre measures the light passing through the lens, there is no need for any lens-camera interconnections.

**Story.** General term applied to editorial matter in newspapers other than leading articles or features- compare with plot.

**Storyboard.** Visual of a TV commercial expressed in cartoon form, each sequence drawn in a shape like a TV screen. The blueprint is drawn to portray copy, dialogue and action, with caption notes regarding filming, audio components and script.

**Strap.** Sub-heading appearing above headline. For instance "Cabinet crisis" or "Bride trial" tell the reader at once that this is today's instalment and the heading itself brings out the new angle.

**Strapline.** Slogan or signature slogan usually placed at the foot of an advertisement.

**Strategic Research.** Research aimed at defining what a new advertising campaign should say.

**Strategy.** Plan, sometimes in outline only, for reaching certain objectives, usually quantified and more often on a relatively long time base.

**Stratification.** Structuring requirements or procedure laid down within a research survey questionnaire for the uniform control of interviews in such a way as to permit reliable summaries and comparisons of results to be drawn up.

**Stratification Sample.** Means of reducing the size of a national sample or number of Sampling Points, as in a large Random Sample. The population is divided into parts or strata. It can also mean the division of a sample according to proportion of men and women indicated by census.

**Strawboard.** Paperboard manufactured from straw rather than wood pulp. Used mainly in box making and book covers due to high rigidity.

**Streamer.** Banner headline spreading across the page.

**Streaming.** Watching or listening to video or audio in real time, rather than downloading files.

**Strikethrough.** Print on reverse side of a sheet showing through.

**Stringer.** Local freelance correspondent of a national media. Could work on a local newspaper. This writer or photographer is not a full-time employee, but is paid by the job. The term comes from the days when a writer would get paid by the column inch and would measure his or her contribution by holding a string along the story to measure its length, knot it, measure the next column or story, and so on, reporting the final length for pay.

**Strip.** A story that goes all the way across the top of the page -- or nearly so. Some people will call it a strip if it goes almost all the way across. Others will say it's not a true strip if there is anything above it, but will grudgingly concede the point.

**Strip Programming.** A broadcast program or commercial that is scheduled at the same time of day on successive days of the week, either Monday through Friday or Monday through Sunday. In press advertising, advertisement of shallow depth extending across all columns at the foot of a page. See across the board.

**Structuralism.** An approach to critical analysis which emphasises universal structures underlying the surface differences and apparent randomness of cultures, stories, media texts etc.

**Studio.** A place from which radio or TV programmes is transmitted. Could be the workroom of an artiste, photographer, musician, etc.

**Studio Lamps (3200K).** Tungsten or tungsten halogen lamps designed for studio use. It has a longer life than photo lamps, but a lower specific output and colour temperature. Are used with type B films.

**Studio System.** Hollywood production system from about 1930 to 1950, in which vertically integrated film companies produced, distributed and exhibited a constant stream of new films.

**Stuffer.** Piece of publicity matter intended for general distribution with other material such as outgoing mail or goods, e.g. 'envelope stuffer'.

**Style.** Rules concerning spelling, grammar, punctuation, and layout in publishing or broadcasting material.

**Stylebook.** Manual setting out corporate style, such as colour with number, logo, typeface, stationery design, and vehicle livery. Can also include everything from spelling of local streets to policy for handling profanities and juvenile crime victims.

**Sub.** (1) Preparing copy of publication. (2) Abbreviation of sub-editor.

**Subculture.** Specialised culture that exists within a larger, more complex one. The existence of ethnic subcultures, professional subcultures, and so on is characteristic of modern pluralistic societies and complicates communication.

**Sub-editing.** Simply late process in the production of a newspaper in which stories are shortened or rewritten to fit the space available and headlines and picture captions are written.

**Sub-editor.** The gatekeeper of a media house who acts as the last link between the editorial department and the production unit. Usually responsible for whatever mistakes or lapses that go through the sub-desk which eventually appear in the paper unless the editor detects them in the proofs.

**Subgroups.** The 'mass within a mass' on which the concept of mass audience is based.

**Sub-head.** Bold type in or preceding a line of printing but inferior or secondary to a main heading.

**Subject.** Participant in an experiment. Use of this term is consistent with an experimental approach in which the researcher strives to achieve maximum objectivity and to control conditions to the greatest extent possible.

**Subject-object Distinction.** Division between the social scientist as a researcher and the people he or she is studying. The significance of this distinction is a matter of some debate among philosophers of social science.

**Subject to Non-Renewal (SNR).** Commercial time that is available for purchase if the current advertiser does not renew.

**Subliminal Projection.** Delivery of an advertising message below receiver's level of awareness, but which registers in the subconscious. May be visual or audio or both.

**Subsample.** Subsection of a sample.

**Subscribed Circulation.** The part of a publisher's circulation which is paid for, as opposed to being distributed free of charge.

**Subscript.** Characters that drop below the baseline.

**Subtrunk.** Secondary cables branching out from the main trunk in a cable TV system to carry the signal to outlying areas.

**Summary Lead.** The traditional journalism tool used to start off most hard news stories. Normally thought of as the first few sentences of a news story which usually summarises the event and answers the questions: Who? What? When? Where? Why? How?

**Sunday Supplement.** A newspaper section in magazine format; also called "magazine supplement" or "magazine section" or simply "supplement." The style part of This Day newspapers published during weekends may be considered a Sunday supplement.

**Supers.** Words superimposed on TV commercials. Super is also a video effect that allows the television station to print and place over the name of a news source over his or her image when the source is shown talking in a news story.

**Superscript.** Characters that rise above the x-height.

**Supersite.** Large tailor-made posters or displays, often hand printed or cut out so as to give a three dimensional effect.

**Superstructure.** Ideological structures built on an economic base according to Marxist theory.

**Supertype Headline Fonts.** Special digital typesetting headline faces which have four letters with integrated accents instead of basic mathematical signs. Supertype fonts make it unnecessary to use the same drawing for both text and headline setting. Permit compressed headline settings.

**Supplement.** Special feature section of a publication. See sunday supplement.

**Supplementary Lens.** Generally a simple positive (converging) lens used in front of the camera lens to enable it to focus at close range. The effect is to provide a lens of shorter focal length without altering the lens-film separation, thus giving the extra extension required for close focusing.

**Surveillance.** New media technologies are increasingly being used to make visible the activities of citizens within public and private contexts. These activities are usually connected to powerful agencies that attempt to normalise and thereby control the behaviour of ordinary people.

**Survey.** Study based on sampling techniques. It employs series of questions asked of a relatively large number of people believed to be representative of an even larger population. Surveys may be in person, by telephone, or by mail; a variety of sampling techniques are used to chose the respondent.

**Sustaining Period**. A period of time during an advertising campaign when advertisements are used to remind the audience of the product or service or of the campaign; often, a time of reduced advertising expenditures following the introductory flight.

**Sustaining Show.** A program broadcast at the expense of the station and not supported by the sale of commercial time.

**S-VHS.** (Super Video Home System) A videotape format based on VHS, but with wider luminance bandwidth, which has a potential horizontal resolution of more than 400 lines. Allows component recording and playback without cross-luminance or cross-colour artefacts. Clearer than the conventional VHS because it separates chrominance and luminance transmission.

**Swash Letter.** Ornamental type character.

**Swatch.** Sample of ink, paint, plastic, fabric or other material for purposes of colour matching.

**Sweep.** The period of the year when a ratings service measures the broadcast audience in the majority of the markets throughout the country; for example, surveys that are scheduled for November 2-24 would be referred to as the "November sweep."

**Symbol.** Distinctive sign or graphic design denoting a company or product. Often a pictorial presentation of a company or product name.

**Symbolic Interaction.** A branch of sociology that is concerned with the roots of both self-identity and social meaning in the symbolic communication and other interaction that occurs between two or more individuals.

**Sync.** Synchronisation, the coordination of occurrences to operate in unison with respect to time. This process can be a premeditated arrangement set forth on a parallel time scape, or it can be an observable coincidence in eventuality. Systems operating with all their parts in synchrony are said to be synchronous or in sync. Some systems may be only approximately synchronised, or plesiochronous. For some applications relative offsets between events need to be determined, for others only the order of the event is important. The idea of simultaneity has many difficulties, both in practice and theory. Whilst well-designed time synchronisation is an important tool for creating reliable systems, excessive use of synchronisation where it is not necessary can make systems less fault-tolerant, and hence less reliable. This basic synchronising pulse in video keeps the various pieces of the video equipment electronically coordinated.

**Sync Buzz.** An undesirable noise containing harmonics of 59.94 Hz. Heard on television audio under certain signal and transmission conditions as, for example, when the transmission of electronically-generated characters are of high level or have a resolution greater than the NTSC broadcast capability.

**Sync Cords.** See PC cords.

**Sync Delay.** All electronic flash units require X sync, but flashbulbs require a time delay between firing the flash and opening the camera shutter. The optimum delay varies among flashbulb types, but one will get much of the flashbulb light through the shutter and onto the film even if delay is not exactly correct. Firing delay for flashbulbs is indicated by code letters: "F"- fast; "M"- medium; "MF" - medium fast; "S" – slow.

**Sync Generator.** An electronic device that generates the variety of timing pulses needed to keep the video equipment synchronised.

**Sync Roll.** The momentary or continuous vertical rolling of a television picture due to loss of sync.

**Sync Socket.** PC terminal/PC Socket.

**Synchronisation License.** A step in obtaining clearance to use a copyrighted work which grants a producer permission to use the music for a specific period.

**Synchronous.** A satellite that travels at the same speed in proportion to earth's rotation and thus appears to remain stationary over one point of the earth. Also called geostationary.

**Syndicated Article.** Feature article for publication in more than one journal. Best negotiated with editors of non-competing circulation journals rather than dispatched like news releases.

**Syndicated Programming.** Programming distributed directly to stations instead of through network distribution channels. The group of stations airing the programmes sometimes is collectively called a 'network'.

**Syndicates.** Companies whose business it is to promote and sell comics, columns, and other special features to newspaper.

**Syndicator.** Television program distributor who works with reruns or new programs on a market-to-market basis. See packager.

**Synergy.** The combined marketing of products across different media and other products (in music, toys, internet and television programmes, T-shirts, theme park rides and so on) which are often owned by the same corporation, such that the total effect is greater than the sum of the different parts.

**Syntagmatic.** See paradigm, with which it is often used in combination.

**Syntactics.** The branch of semiotics that deals with the formal properties of signs and symbols.

**Syntax.** The combination of words or other elements of sentence structure to form grammatical sentences.

**Systematic Error.** In communication research, an error caused by bias.

**Systematic Random Sampling.** Sampling in which the first element is chosen randomly, a specific number of elements are then skipped over before the second element is chosen, and so on; used usually where sampling frame is a list, such as a telephone book.

**Syuzhet.** Term in specialist narrative theory-Russian for plot.

# T

**3D Colour Matrix Metre.** Basically, a Nikon pioneered technology first featured on its flagship model, the F5. 3D Colour Matrix Metre evaluates not only each scene's brightness and contrast but, using a special Red Green Blue (RGB) sensor, it also evaluates the scene's colours. Then its powerful micro-computer and database together guide it to unequalled exposure control. Currently, 3D Colour Matrix Metre will work only with F5 and with D-type Nikkor lenses.

**25 Per Cent Production Quota.** Requirement for British broadcasters to commission 25 per cent of programmes from 'independents'.

**T-1 line.** A high-speed internet connection available from the phone companies.

**T-Grain Technology.** Trademark for patented Kodak film emulsion technology used in all Kodak Advanced Photo System films; uniquely shaped grains that align better than conventional silver crystals, absorbing and transmitting light more effectively to produce sharper images.

**T (setting).** Setting that holds the camera shuttle open until the shuttle dial is turned or release and hit the second time. This setting differs from 'B' (Bulb) that it usually a stand alone setting and never drains the battery power and thus ideal for really long time exposures.

**t Test.** Statistical test for comparing two means. Although special tests are available for other situations, a simple t test should only be used to make a single comparison.

**Tab.** Short for tabloid. Refers to any newspaper or section folded to that size. See Tabloid.

**Table of Random Numbers.** Tabulation of numbers where the numbers have no repetitive order or pattern, usually listed in rows and columns of five digits. Used for selecting people or items at random for sampling purposes.

**Tabloid.** Small page newspaper like Nigeria's king of tabloids, The Sun. Although often used in derogatory sense to describe popular press, the term has been used to describe small format newspapers since 1093. Derived from chemist Henry Wellcom's combination of 'tablet' and 'alkaloid' for his medicinal product in 1884. (slang "tab").

**Tabloid TV Programming.** a form of talk-show programming that resembles tabloid newspapers in the exploitation of sensational events, personalities or topics. The shows cover provocative subjects and aggressively schedule controversial guests who discuss once-taboo topics.

**Tabliodisation.** A term derived from the common tabloid format for sensationalist (i.e. gossip and scandal-mongering) newspapers, to refer to the alleged process of 'dumbing down' or going 'down-market' of the more serious press in many countries. The main believed cause was commercialisation and intense competition for readers. The process has also affected television news and 'actuality' formats in general, especially in the United States, and caused alarm at the decline of journalistic standards, rise in public ignorance and risk of confusion between fiction and reality (e.g. 'infotainment').

**Tabulation.** Putting data into tables, usually of a numerical order.

**Tachistoscope.** (1) In advertising research, a projection device used to measure the thresholds at which the features of an advertisement are registered. Is also used for measuring visual impact of an advertisement when exposed for only a short time. (2) In research, instrument which makes visual presentations of subjects for very short spells so that respondents only have time to glance at them.

**Tag.** To make closing comments at the end of a program segment. Tags like "Court told" or "Police claim" or "says OBJ" can make a half finished court story much safer or throw far more onus on a speaker who makes wild charges in a speech which you sense may be exaggerated. Also dealer identification, usually added to the end of a broadcast commercial announcement to indicate where the product or service being advertised can be purchased in the local market.

Tail.

**Tail.** Bottom margin of a page.

**Take.** (1) A portion of copy given to a linotype operator. Stories can be given out in 'short takes'. (2) A single shot. In single-camera production a specific shot often requires several takes before it meets the approval of the director.

**Take a Level.** To speak into a microphone prior to broadcast or recording so that an audio engineer can adjust the volume control.

**Take-one Cards.** Cards attached to posters and taken by passers-by.

**Takeout.** A longer story that takes a step back from daily, breaking news stories to put a running story with frequent developments into context and perspective.

**Talbot, William Henry Fox.** (February 11, 1800 - September 17, 1877) He was one of the first photographers and made major contributions to the photographic process. He is also remembered as the holder of a patent which affected the early development of photography in England. See Calotype.

**Talent.** Individuals who perform in front of a camera or microphone, the performers.

**Talent Release.** Model release. A form signed by a person appearing in a videotape which grants legal permission to a production agency to broadcast the segment under specified terms.

**Talk-show Programming.** A basic TV format involving a host and a sidekick/foil, a small band and a number of guests (whichever way the producer designed the set) who either perform or are interviewed in front of a studio audience. They come together to discuss various topics put forth by the talk show host. The stage setting is usually a desk and couch or the reproduction of an informal living room, and viewers are encouraged to feel as if they are eavesdropping on conversations in the host's own personal domain. Popular talk-show programmes include The Oprah Winfrey Show, Tyra Show- with Tyra Banks- in the U.S.; Patito's Gang with Pat Utomi, Inside Out with Agatha Amata- in Nigeria; Good Morning America and the Larry King Live on CNN.

**Talking Head.** Slang for the typical (and not too exciting) head-and-shoulders shot of actors seen on talk shows and newscasts.

**Tally Light.** The red light on a video camera that indicates the camera is on the air or that videotape is recording.

**Target Audience.** Any group of persons who have a common bond, such as shared demographic and/or psychographic characteristics that specific programming attempts to attract into the audience.

**Target Group.** Those persons to whom a campaign is directed; those individuals with similar characteristics who are prospects for a product or service; also called "consumer profile."

**Target Group Index.** Source of market data owned by BMRB. Based on questionnaires answered by 24,000 adults a year, covering 400 products fields, their demographic characteristics and media exposure.

**Target Market.** The geographic area or areas to which a campaign is directed; the areas where a product is being sold or introduced; also called "market profile."

**Target Profile.** A demographic description of the target groups, often including the geographic target markets.

**Target Sum Method.** Also called cost of exposure, task approach or objective method of arriving at the advertising appropriation. Once the market objective is decided the cost of advertising to achieve target is estimated.

**Targeting.** Aiming advertising at specific audience and selecting media which do so most effectively and economically. In direct mail and door-to-door distribution, geodemographic systems such as Acrn, Mosaic, Pin and Super Profiles can be used to select neighbourhoods containing required target market characteristics.

**Target Weight.** Used for weighing advertising expenditure; a means of varying expenditure according to the influence of demographic factors.

**Task Method.** Variation on Target Sum Method of assessing advertising Appropriation the budget being planned for particular purposes or campaigns such as a new product launch.

**Taste Culture.** A more or less organised and semi-autonomous set of cultural preferences based on certain shared tastes, although independent of actual social organisation. In this the concept differs from the earlier approaches to taste patterns that were mainly explained in terms of social background, class or milieu. Related to life-style.

**TAT.** Thematic Apperception Test. Historically, this has been amongst the most widely used, researched, and taught projective psychological tests. Its adherents claim that it taps a subject's unconscious to reveal repressed aspects of personality, motives and needs for achievement, power and intimacy, and problem-solving abilities. It is popularly known as the picture interpretation technique because it uses a standard series of 31 provocative yet ambiguous pictures about which the subject must tell a story. In the case of adults and adolescents of average intelligence, a subject is asked to tell as dramatic a story as they can for each picture, including:(a) what has led up to the event shown, (b) what is happening at the moment, (c) what the characters are feeling and thinking, and (d) what the outcome of the story was. For children or individuals of limited cognitive abilities, instructions ask that the subject tell a story including what happened before and what is happening now, what the people are feeling and thinking and how it will come out. The 31 cards are meant to be split into two "series" of ten pictures each, with the pictures of the second series being purposely more unusual, dramatic, and bizarre than those of the first. Suggested administration involves one full hour being devoted to a series, with the two sessions being separated by a day or more. Several cards in the test are present in order to ensure that the subject is able to be provided with cards picturing individuals of the same gender. Eleven cards including the black card have been found suitable for both sexes, by portraying no human figures, an individual of each sex, or an individual of ambiguous gender. Each story created by a subject is carefully analysed to uncover underlying needs, attitudes, and patterns of reaction. The TAT is a projective test in that and its assessment of the subject is based on what he or she projects onto the ambiguous images.

**Taxi-cab Advertising.** Advertisements in the passenger section, either fixed to panel facing passengers or on under parts of tip-up seats. Also on exterior panel fitted to nearside cab driver's panel.

**TBA.** Short for To Be Announced, To Be Ascertained or To Be Advised. These terms are almost always used in their abbreviated forms- denoting that a datum for which the abbreviation is a stand-in is yet to be announced/ascertained/advised as of the time of writing

**TBC.** Time Base Corrector. An electronic device that stabilises the scanning and timing pulses in video. The timebase correction technique is used with this corrector to reduce or eliminate errors present in all analogue recordings on mechanical media, including video tape recorders and videocassette recorders, caused by mechanical instability. If the mechanism ran at an absolutely constant speed, and never varied from moment to moment, or from the time of recording to the time of playback, then the timing of the playback signal would be exactly the same as the input. However, due to inevitable mechanical imperfections, the timing of the playback always differs from the original signal. The discrete nature of video signals - division into lines and fields - means that any such timing distortion must appear as timebase errors.

**TC.** Till countermanded or cancelled. Stipulation in contract that it will run until stopped by the advertiser.

**TCA.** (1) Television Consumer Audit. (2) Television Critics Association - a group of approximately 200 United States and Canadian journalists and columnists who cover television programming. They meet in the Los Angeles area twice a year, in January and July. The organisation sponsors the TCA Awards, honouring television excellence in 11 categories, which are presented every summer.

**TEA.** Terminal Education Age. (As used in media studies).

**Tear Sheet.** Serving as a file or voucher copy of an advertisement, specimen page or advertisement torn from a publication and usually sent to the advertiser for approval or for checking.

**Tease.** Small headline, usually underscored, placed above and to the left of main headline.

**Teaser.** Advertisement which by withholding information about the product and/or sponsor, is designed to arouse widespread attention through the operation of curiosity. Often takes the form of a poster or series of posters. It precedes the major portion of an advertising campaign. Also intriguing scenes or a montage from a forthcoming show, sometimes shown before the opening credits of a TV programme to arouse viewer interest and curiosity. It encourages the audience to stay tuned and see more. Also shows what is in the inside of the paper or previews a story or series.

**Technical Director; TD.** The individual who operates the control room switcher and is in charge of various technical aspects of a production.

**Technical Press.** Periodicals dealing with technical subjects. Usually grouped together as 'trade & technical', referring in effect to all publications directed to a non-consumer public.

**Technicolor.** Colour film process developed for cinema in the 1930s.

**Technique.** Procedure that is part of or that contributes to a method. The term is more specific than method or methodology. For example, most statistical procedures are more accurately described as techniques rather than methods.

**Technobabble.** Confusing technical jargon. A portmanteau of technology and babble, this is a form of prose using jargon, buzzwords and highly esoteric language to give an impression of plausibility through mystification and misdirection. This is not to be confused with jargon itself, but rather technobabble is a conscious attempt to deliver jargon to outsiders, without insight or comprehensive explanation, to make unsound or unprovable arguments appear to have merit. The primary function of technobabble is to obscure the truth of a situation by overdressing the words and concepts.

**Technophobia.** Fear of machines or technology, especially in science fiction narratives.

**Telecast.** A term sometimes applied to the transmission of a TV programme.

**Telecine.** An area of a production facility with equipment for converting film and slides to video.

**Telecommunication.** The science and technology of communication at a distance by electronic transmission of impulses, as by telegraph, cable, telephone, radio, or television.

**Teleconferencing.** Communication between individuals or groups using two-way video and audio systems.

**Teledemocracy.** Term used to describe theories that telecommunications serve to advance democracy by extending information and widening access to information.

**Telegenic.** Characteristics of a person whose features will appear attractive on television.

**Telegrafnoe Agentstvo Sovetskogo Soyuza (TASS).** The Telegraph Agency of the Soviet Union. Founded in 1925 by the defunct Soviet Union, with headquarters in Moscow. Its origin, according to wikepedia, is in a letter sent by Finance Minister Vladimir Kokovtsov to foreign minister on March 26, 1904 writing that 'our trade and industrial circles, as well as the Finance Ministry, are ever more in need of an independent exchange of information with foreign countries by telegraph and of a way to make internal business developments widely-known'. In July 1904 a meeting was held about setting up an official telegraph agency, St. Petersburg Telegraph Agency (SPTA). Its purpose was 'to distribute political, financial, economic, trade, and other information of public interest within the country and abroad...'. SPTA began work as Russia's official news agency on September 1, 1904. On August 19, 1914, one day after St. Petersburg was renamed Petrograd, SPTA was renamed the Petrograd Telegraph Agency (PTA). It was seized by Bolsheviks on November 7, 1917; on December 1, PTA is decreed to be the central information agency of the RSFSR Sovnarkom. On September 7, 1918, PTA and Sovnarkom Press Bureau were merged into the Russian Telegraph Agency (ROSTA). On 25 July 1925 it became the Telegraph Agency of the Soviet Union or Telegrafnoe Agentstvo Sovetskogo Soyuza (TASS) by decree of the USSR Central Executive Committee Presidium. In 1992, following the dissolution of the Soviet Union, it officially became the Information Telegraph Agency of Russia; due to its long past as TASS, it has operated as ITAR-TASS ever since. As of May 2006, while the main press agency is still called ITAR-TASS, it prefers TASS as a brand; its slogan on its English website is "Every time in real time. TASS", and most of its other businesses use only TASS in their names. It is still state-funded, and according to its website, it now produces about 700 newspaper pages per day, just under its Soviet peak. It has 74 bureaus and offices in Russia and other CIS countries and 65 bureaus in 62 foreign countries. See Associated Press and Reuters.

**Telegram.** A communication by telegraph; now only available for international purposes.

**Telemarketing.** Selling by use of telephones, either initiating the calls or receiving orders.

**Telematics.** The integrated use of telecommunications and informatics, also known as Information and Communications Technology. More specifically it is the science of sending, receiving and storing information via telecommunication devices.

**Telephoto Lens.** A lens that seemingly brings a subject matter closer to the camera than a normal lens at the same camera-to-subject distance. A telephoto lens has a longer focal length and narrower field of view than a normal lens and has a shallower depth of field than wide angle lenses. But it can do isolation of subject and have a longer reach without going near to the subject. Life can be very difficult in sports and wildlife photography. Telephoto lens whose focal length is longer than the diagonal of the film frame; in 35mm photography, lenses longer than 50-5Bmm; is also referred to as a "long" lens.

**Telephone Answering Service.** Mechanical or manual servicing of calls or inquiries through the telephone network.

**Teleports.** Engineering complexes that contain on-line technical capabilities primarily related to satellite communications. It provides uplink and downlink services for audio, video, and data and voice transmission on ku-band and c-band satellites. They normally have microwave relay and fibre optic capabilities for technical interconnections to and from producers, stations, syndicators and satellite news gathering operations and can provide scrambling services. Some teleports have production and postproduction facilities.

**Teleprompter**. Originally, a brand name for a camera prompter. A device used by on-air talent that rolls an image of a script across a screen near the camera lens.

**Teletext**. One-way over-the-air transmission system using the vertical blanking interval of television to send textual information.

**Telethon**. A lengthy television program to raise funds for a charity.

**Television.** The transmission of visual images by means of electromagnetic waves. The television camera scans the field of view and activates a photoelectric cell, the impulses from which, propagated as electromagnetic waves, cause the electron beam of a cathode-ray tube in the receiver (television set) to scan the viewing screen in steps identical with those of the scanning camera, thus reproducing the field of view on the screen. It has merits of a multi-million audience, vision, sound, movement and colour. The word is derived from mixed Latin and Greek roots, meaning "far seeing"- Greek "tele," meaning far, and Latin "visus," meaning seeing.

**Television/Radio Age.** A bi-monthly trade publication of general interest with a stronger emphasis on advertising than Broadcasting Magazine.

**Television Household.** A broadcast rating term used to describe any home with a television set, as distinguished from a household using television.

**Television Producer.** One who produces programmes by bringing them to life on air via the TV.

**Television Rating. TVR.** Way of measuring exposure/impacts of individual TV spots according to recorded audience figure for programme in which the spot appears. A TV campaign can aim to achieve a certain volume of TVRs, after which it may be withdrawn.

**Television Register, The.** Monitors TV/radio commercials for advertisers/agencies. Part of Advertising Research Services group which includes the Media Register.

**Television Response Handling.** As with holiday advertising, TV programme companies accept enquires produced by commercials and supply names and addresses to advertisers.

Telidon.

> They also place orders phoned in to a computer service which supplies advertisers with printouts of orders within 24 hours. Has been used by record companies.

**Telidon.** A teletext and videotext system for digital character coding that can be transmitted over broadcast, telephone or cable systems.

**Template.** Shape or sheet with cut-outs used as drawing aid, or for printing solid panels, perhaps of a second colour on which text is printed in black.

**Ten.** Slang for a ten-second broadcast commercial announcement.

**Tent Pole.** A TV programming term describing a show that sits in the middle of the prime time schedule. It supports the evening programming on a network and the other shows are scheduled around it.

**Tentpole Movie.** A major film which a studio hopes will provide the support for its annual slate and almost guarantee box-office returns.

**Termination.** The resistance or load that marks the end of coaxial video conductors usually 75 ohms. A lack of termination generally causes video level problems.

**Terrain Shielding.** A broadcasting situation in which mountainous or other irregular terrain blocks or weakens the transmitted signals of a radio or television facility. Such topographical shielding sometimes prevents interference with the signals of other nearby broadcast operations.

**Terrestrial Interference.** Electrical noise from earth-based RF that interferes with satellite reception.

**Territories.** Geographical areas for which the rights to a media product are negotiated.

**Tertiary Readership.** Indicates readerships of a publication seen casually during or while waiting for some other activity, normally outside the home, e.g. at hairdressers or surgery.

**Test Area or Town.** Area used in Test-marketing which is representative of the broad scale market, having similar customers shops and media such as regional TV.

**Test Marketing.** Method of testing a marketing plan on a limited scale, simulating as nearly as possible all the factors involved in a national campaign; usually carried out in a restricted but representative location, often a particular TV region. This procedure enables a marketing company to obtain an indication of likely market acceptance without the full commitment and expense of a national launch. It also exposes the product and the plan to competitors, and consequently the results of the test can seldom be regarded as absolutely conclusive.

**Test Patterns.** An optical chart used to calibrate and align electronic equipment. It contains geometric patterns in circles and squares to allow technicians to align cameras and the output of the signals of other equipment for optimum resolution, focus, contrast, linearity and framing in monitors and home receivers. It is intended to evaluate specific video qualities such as linearity and resolution.

**Testimonial.** Any reference made by an advertiser to the favourable opinion of another in circumstances in which the consumer is likely to give added credence to that opinion because of the ostensible independence of the person or institution said to hold it. Users often offer surprising testimonials. Some testimonials are by users, others are endorsements by celebrities who are paid a fee. In the history of advertising the most famous testimonials are probably those of the society ladies who were delighted in allowing their portraits to appear in Pond's face cream, advertisements (originating in Ireland) with the statement 'I always use Pond's'.

**Testimonial Advertisement.** Piece of promotion that uses the implied or explicit patronage of a product by a well-known person, or organisation.

**Text.** The body of undisplayed copy forming the reading matter as in newspaper columns or book. It could be a poster, photograph, haircut etc.

**Text Mark.** In print instructions or corrections, mark made within the text itself (e.g. underlining word to be set in italics) in addition to marks made in the margin.

**Text Type.** Type used for setting body matter, usually smaller than 12pt, and preferably serifed for easy reading, such as Times, Plantin, Garamond.

**Thematic Appreciation Test.** Projective test used in Motivational Research. The respondent is shown a set of pictures, such as press cuttings or advertisements, and asked to invent a story about each one in turn. Some of the pictures could feature in advertising. The test reveals what respondent reads into pictures, his reactions and his personality.

**Theme Advertising.** Advertising, normally of an above-the-line character.

**Themed Break.** In TV advertising, two or more spots booked to appear in same break for different products made by the same advertiser.

**Theory.** Explanatory idea that helps to account for empirical data. Although the types of theories used in qualitative versus quantitative work and the ways in which these theories are tested differ, explanation is always the goal.

**Thermography.** Printed process that produces a raised surface resembling Die-stamping as often used for letterheads. Printed sheets are dusted with resinous powder which, under heat, fuses with ink, swells and gives print a raised, glazed appearance.

**Thesis Hunting.** Tendency to choose only those pieces of data that support a theoretical idea and ignore the rest. Most commonly a criticism of quantitative research, thesis hunting can be a failing of quantitative researchers.

**Thin Negative.** A negative that is underexposed or underdeveloped, or both. A thin negative appears less dense than a normal negative.

**Thirty.** Slang for a 30-second broadcast commercial announcement.

**Three-chip Camera.** A video camera that uses three CCDs, one devoted to each of the primary colours.

**Three-shot.** A video picture containing three individuals.

**Threshold Effects.** Stage in advertising expenditure when advertising proves effective in producing desired results.

**Threshold Goals.** Minimum level of achievement acceptable.

**Through-the-lens (TTL).** Type of exposure metre built into the camera body and reading through the camera lens. May measure either at full aperture or at picture taking aperture.

**Through-The-Lens Focusing.** Viewing a scene to be photographed through the same lens that admits light to the film. Through-the-lens viewing, as in a single-lens-reflex (SLR) camera, while focusing and composing a picture, eliminates parallax.

**Through-The-Lens Metering.** Metre built into the camera that determines exposure for the scene by reading light that passes through the lens during picture-taking. Most SLR cameras have built-in metres which measure light after it has passed through the lens, a feature that enables exposure readings to be taken from the actual image about to be recorded on film, whatever the lens angle of view and regardless of whether a filter is used or not.

**Through-the-line Agency.** Advertising agency which provides strategy planning service, combining Above-the line and Below-the-line media on a one-stop shopping basis. Such agencies existed in the 1960s.

**Throwaways.** Free shopping newspapers.

**Thumb Corner.** The upper, outside corner of pages. So-called because that's where a reader might grab them to turn to the next page.

**Thumbnail.** Miniature sketch, a reduced printout of a page that is particularly useful for checking the overall layout.

**Ticketboard.** Pasteboard.

**Tie Ins.** (1) In advertising, used to describe a marketing strategy, frequently used in book publishing, where different advertising media 'tie-in' or 'tie together' a common message about a product. An example would be TV commercials, floor displays, and billboards promoting a book. (2) In journalism, placing the facts of a new story within the context of past events. Also known as a tie back. See Cooperative advertising and Dealer tie-in.

**Tiering (Programme).** A method of buying a first-run programme. Stations negotiate deals in which they obtain the option of running the programme in any programme tier, such as early fringe or late night. The station then pays an appropriate negotiated price based on where the show actually runs in the schedule.

**TIFF.** (tagged-image file format) A data format standard associated with one type of computer graphics.

**Tighten Up.** To zoom in or dolly in on a subject.

**Till Ancelled.** Outdoor advertising instruction to show posters, or keep a site, until due notice of cancellation is given.

**Till Forbidden (TF).** A newspaper insertion order abbreviation; run the advertisement until told to stop.

**Tilt.** The rotation of a stationary camera on its vertical y-axis. The operator moves the camera up or down to follow the action, such as when people stand up or sit down.

**Tilting.** The process of creating the opening and closing credits of a production. Sometimes refers to process of creating subtitles for dialogue.

**Timber.** Sound characteristics, including overtones, which differentiate musical instruments.

**Time-base.** The timing component of a video signal, particularly the horizontal and vertical sync pulses.

**Time Base Corrector / TBC.** Electronic device that corrects the minute timing errors generally associated with VCRs and small video cameras.

**Time Broker.** A person or company that sells large blocks of time to advertisers.

**Time Buyer.** The person who is responsible for purchasing advertising on radio and television. See media buyer.

**Time Code.** SMPTE/EBU time code. A series of eight numbers identifying the hours, minutes, seconds and frames related to a specific video frame on a tape.

**Time-code Generator.** A device which supplies an electronic SMPTE/EBU time-code signal to recording equipment.

**Time Compressor.** Electronic signal processing system allowing a recorded videotape to be replayed somewhat faster or slower than normal without noticeable effects.

**Time Exposure.** A comparatively long exposure made in seconds or minutes.

**Time-lapse Photography.** Significantly slowing down the frame rate of motion photography so that events which may take minutes, hours, or even days, can be shown and observed within seconds.

**Timelenght.** Time of a commercial spot in television or radio.

**Time Period Rating (TPR).** the rating for a particular broadcast time period, regardless of the program that was broadcast during that slot.

**Time Segment.** Period of time in television or radio broadcasting during which commercials are booked. Often, each time segment has a different charging rate as audiences are constantly changing during broadcasting periods.

**Time-series Analysis.** set of techniques for attempting to determine the relative order of items in a complex sequence. For example, content analysis might ask whether a particular theme was more common before or after certain historical events.

**Time Sheet.** A form used by a time buyer to keep track of the data on a media buy; also called a "buy sheet": the form used to keep track of how advertising agency personnel use their time, for application in billing purposes.

**Time-shift Broadcasts.** Phenomenon of VCRs whereby programmes are videotaped and watched at a later time, to the exclusion of programmes then being broadcast.

**Time-space Compression.** The idea that new technologies have made it possible to go travelling without leaving home. The arrival of real time media experiences mean that we are able to view an event irrespective of our geographical location and without any noticeable time delay. Within the economy this has introduced the possibility of 'just in time' forms of production, and within urban contexts the 24-hour city.

**Tint.** Shades of white in a finished print, controlled by the colour of the paper, varying from white to buff.

**Tip.** A lead or piece of new information about a new story.

**Tip-in.** Loose single tip sheet inserted in a newspaper between folded pages, or a single sheet of two pages gummed and not bound into a magazine or book.

**Tip-on.** A detachable item glued to an advertisement or direct mail shot.

**Title or Credit Title.** List of executives and performers in a television or film programme.

**Title Corner.** Advertisement space on either side of the title or masthead of a newspaper. Pairs are called ears.

**Title Page.** A page that contains very useful information about a book. The author's full name, the publisher, place and date of publication may be found on this page.

**TK.** Proof-reader's insertion mark for data to come. Sometimes written as TKTK.

**TLR.** Twin lens reflex camera that have separate viewing and actual exposure lens. Rollei still have one in production.

**To Be Announced (TBA).** Used as a notification in broadcast program schedules.

**Tone.** The degree of lightness or darkness in any given area of a print; also referred to as value. Cold tones (bluish) and warm tones (reddish) refer to the colour of the image in both black-and-white and colour photographs.

**Tone Generator.** Electronic circuit which can create an even, standardised reference tone for test and set-up purposes.

**Tone Step Reproduction.** With digital design, a generation of graphic variations to a single stored picture. Halftone can be displayed in numerous grey steps, all of which can be assessed and changed. Various background effects can be created for monochrome, real colours or process colour printing.

**Toning.** Intensifying or changing the tone of a photographic print after processing. Solutions called toners are used to produce various shades of colours.

**Top 40.** A radio format that feature the top "rock" songs of the day and maintains a playlist of 40 titles at one time.

**Top heads.** Headlines at the top of a column.

**Toronto School.** Describes a body of work mainly derived from theories of Marshall McLuhan, and in turn derived from an earlier scholar at the University of Toronto, the economic historian Harold Innis. At the core is a form of communication technology determinism that attributes distinctive social and cultural effects to the dominant form and vehicle of communication, independent of the actual content.

**Total Audience.** The number of all the different homes or individuals who are tuned to a broadcast program for six minutes or longer.

**Total Audience Package (TAP).** Commercial spots spread across time segments, usually at discretion of media owner, throughout broadcasting hours.

**Total Effective Exposure.** Measure of reader, viewer or listener exposure to an advertisement or a medium.

**Total Hours.** In commercial radio research, total length of time listened to radio, or to a station, by the population group being measured, calculated by summing every 15 minutes listened.

**Track Kerning.** Where a whole line of text characters is uniformly spaced closer or further apart from normal.

**Tracking.** (1) The average space between characters in a block of text. Sometimes also referred to as letter spacing. (2) An electronic process causing the heads in a videotape playback device to exactly follow the tracks laid down in an original recording. Most often used in playing back a tape that has been re-recorded on a different but same videotape format machine, a tracking control device electronically compensates for the minor differences in the alignment of the recording heads between different videotape machines and corrects jitter and skewing.

**Tracking Shot.** A dolly shot that follows a moving subject or moves with respect to a stationary subject. Advertisement for a number of a manufacturer's brands.

**Traction.** A programming term describing the condition of a show that has established itself with a small but regular audience. It attracts the same demographics each week and has the possibility of growth, having established some traction.

**Trade Advertising.** Advertising aimed at distributors to encourage them to stock goods, using trade press, direct mail and exhibitions. It is designed to increase sales specifically for retailers and wholesalers.

**Trade Characters.** Two types. (1) Characters used to personalise and characterise products. They may be ones specially to do with the product; animals associated with the product or licensed characters from, say, cartoons. (2) Live characters, as when an advertiser is represented by a customed character.

**Trade Fairs.** Fairs held in a selected national market to show and promote goods made in another country or made under license or other arrangements in the country concerned.

**Trade Magazines.** Subcategory of business magazines.

**Trade Mark.** Mark used in relation to goods so as to indicate a connection in the course of trade between the goods and the proprietor or registered supplier registration under the appropriate Act provides exclusive right or usage.

**Trade Name.** A name for a product as distinct from a registered trade mark or name, e.g. instant coffee or aspirin.

**Trade-out.** An exchange of merchandise for a service: for example, in advertising, a merchant will trade the use of a product for an equivalent amount of advertising in print or broadcast media.

**Trade Paper.** A specialised publication for a specific profession, trade, or industry; another term for some business publications.

**Trade Press.** Strictly referring to periodicals dealing with particular trades.

**Trade Price.** Discounted price for the benefit of another in a trading position and not usually open to a consumer.

**Trade Promotion.** Mounting a marketing campaign to the retail trade in an effort to persuade retailers to stock and display the company's products.

**Trade Propaganda.** Misuse of terminology, but sometimes used to describe trade advertising, which is not propaganda.

**Trade Publication.** See Trade Paper.

**Trade Setting.** Typesetting by a trade house on direct instructions from a client or agency, usually working to tight specifications and resulting in higher quality output.

**Trade Show.** Synonym for exhibition, but often used to describe an exhibition for non-consumer markets.

**Traditional Media.** (1) Local mass media like metal gongs and flutes used in developing countries like Nigeria to communicate mainly in rural areas. See Oramedia. (2) Media advertising, or the above-the-line media of press, TV, radio, cinema and outdoor.

**Traffic.** (1) Progressing and scheduling of activities in an advertising agency to ensure events take place on time and are completed according to requirement. Also scheduling commercial announcements at a broadcast station. (2) Pattern of movement of news stories in a medium.

**Traffic Count.** Count of persons (or vehicles) passing a particular point, usually an outdoor panel location, during a specified period of time.

Traffic Department.

**Traffic Department.** Responsible for distribution of instructions and progress chasing in advertising agency.

**Trailers.** Short videos used to promote a film or programme on videocassette. Similar and often identical to the brief promotional films shown in motion picture theatres, they feature highlights of the title, including snapping dialogue, exciting sequences and intriguing shots. They take their name from such motion picture promos.

**Train Exhibitions.** Exhibitions mounted on special trains and toured to stations, placed in bay or siding, and attended by invited guests.

**Trainnie.** Colour transparency.

**Transcribe.** To copy out in manuscript or type. Usually when an interview is conducted with a tape recorder it is transcribed for easy analysis.

**Transient Medium.** Fleeting advertising medium in which a message cannot be retained (except by taping) such as radio, cinema, TV, loudspeaker van, telecaster, as distinct from press or direct mail advertising.

**Transistor.** A tiny device that provides the same oscillation, switching and amplification functions of the vacuum tube, but is much smaller, more reliable and requires less power. Consisting of semiconductors, the term was devised by combining the two words transfer and resistor.

**Transition.** A rhetorical device used in writing to move the story smoothly from one set of ideas to the next by finding a way to connect the ideas logically.

**Translators.** Television transmitting antennas, usually located on high natural terrain.

**Transmission.** (1) The passage of radio waves in the space between the transmitting and receiving stations. (2) The mechanism of broadcasting radio or TV programmes.

**Transmission Standard.** The broadcast standard used for transmitting signals to the home.

**Transmitter.** A broadcast instrument usually mounted on a mast, which radiates radio frequency or signal. It uses the audio/video signal to modulate a carrier wave at the station's assigned frequency.

**Transparency.** (1) Trainnie. Full colour photographic positive on transparent film. (2) Also the way in which media texts present themselves as natural; their construction is invisible to casual readers.

**Transparent Magnetic Layer.** Information storage layer built into Advanced Photo System film that enables enhanced information exchange capabilities, improving print quality by capturing lighting and scene information and other picture-taking data; basis for future information exchange features.

**Transponder.** An electronic component of a communication satellite that receives and translates the audio and video signal from an uplink to another frequency and transmits the signal back to earth. It is a combination of transmitter and receiver. Satellites contain up to 24 transponders, each capable of receiving and transmitting one channel.

**Transport Advertising.** Special form of poster advertising sited on or inside buses, main line and tube railway trains, or other forms of transportation, e.g. taxicabs and trucks. Also refers to posters exhibited at railway stations, bus stops, airline terminals, seaports and the like.

**Transportation Advertising.** Although sometimes included with outdoor advertising, can be regarded as a separate medium as the public is often in closer contact and able to absorb longer messages than in possible with, for instance, street posters and signs. Includes all advertising inside and outside public service vehicles and premises and on transportation properties. In Nigeria, companies like Dangote Industries and V-Mobile build bus stops with their name and message inscribed on the shades.

**Transpose.** Marked on proof as 'trs' meaning change position of setting, as when letters are set in wrong sequence.

**Travelling Shot.** A moving camera shot.

**Treatment.** (1) Sequential descriptive document in film making, giving a detailed outline of the form a film is likely to take. Used generally with same meaning in relation to any form of planned communication. (2) A written description of proposals for making a film or video. When this has been approved or amended, the shooting script is created.

**Treatment Group.** In an experiment, the people on whom an influence is being measured. The 'treatment' can result from the experimenter's manipulation of any independent variable, such as exposure to different types of sources of information.

**Tree Network.** A cable distribution system in which one origination point transmits a signal that, through various branches, finally reaches subscribers in their homes. The design resembles a tree in as much as the signals from the headend (the root) are carried to trunk lines (major limbs) and then through feeder cables (large branches) to cable drops (small branches) and finally to the individual converter (leaf) in the home.

**Trend Analysis.** Extrapolation of historical figures for the purpose of studying their significance.

**Trend Story.** A feature story that focuses on the current fads, directions, tendencies, and inclinations of society.

**Trends.** Report on direct response campaigns produced by Nationwide Marketing Research for precision marketing and supplied as an insert in that magazine. Reports on advertisers, brands, media, including non couponed page space, couponed page space, inserts, use of colour, and special aspects such as back-to-back coupons, and coupon details such as keying, telephone ordering facility, premium incentives and whether payment requested with order.

**Triadic Test.** Research test to distinguish the odd one out when respondent is presented with three objects.

**Triangulation.** Using substantially different methods to study the same problem, such as a combination of qualitative and quantitative approaches. Achieving parallel results with different methods vastly increases the researcher's confidence in those results.

**Trim Marks.** Hairline marks that are produced on a final print out to specify where cutting or folding is to take place.

**Trimmed Size.** Final size of a print job when sheets have been trimmed. The amount that has to be cut off is called 'trim'.

**Tripartite.** Three-sided representations as occurs with media research committees when advertisers, advertising agency and media owners' organisations are represented.

**Triple Spotting.** Broadcasting of three TV commercials in succession or back to back.

**Tripod.** A three legged mounting device that supports a head on which a camera is mounted. Most tripods have an adjustable middle vertical pedestal, which can be cranked up or down to raise or lower the camera mounting head and thus the camera. The tripod legs also often telescope so that the camera can be raised or lowered by as much as three feet. Sometimes wheels are attached to facilitate camera movement. Another is the monopod, single leg tripod.

**Trolley Ads.** Advertisements on trolleys in supermarkets.

**Truck.** A camera movement along with its mount in which the camera mount is moved left or right at the command of the director to 'truck right (or left).' The effect is a sideways parallel motion, past the subject. It is sometimes called a 'crab.' The term is also used in television to refer to a remote truck.

**Trunk.** Main line or highways of a cable system in a tree network.

**T/S.** The tilt and shift lens, Canon's version of the PC (perspective control) lens.

**TSA.** Total survey area, as used in commercial radio research.

**T-side.** Advertising space in shape of T on double-decked bus sides.

**T-stop.** As contrasting to relying on a simple mathematical ratio, an iris setting that designates the actual amount of light going through a lens. T-stops are more accurate than f-stops, which do not take into consideration light losses within the lens.

**T-Test.** Statistical test to measure differences between two average values.

**TTL Auto Flash.** The camera's light sensor measures flash illumination, as reflected by the subject on the film and shuts off the flash where measurement indicates a correct exposure. Because the sensor that controls the flash receives light through the lens, TTL auto flash can be used for bounce flash photography, fill flash, multiple flash photography, etc. An additional advantage of TTL auto flash is that it enables one to use a wide range of aperture settings, while ensuring correct exposure.

**Tube Cards.** Advertisements inside railway compartments, particularly associated with Greater London Tube train network.

**Tuckboxes.** Cardboard containers, bearing customer's name, logo or advertisement, for custom playing cards.

**Tungsten Light.** Light from regular room lamps and ceiling fixtures, not fluorescent. Images produced under this light source can be extremely warm. Need some colour balance filtration or flash to neutralize that.

**Tungsten-halogen Light.** Quartz light. The most-used type of studio and on-location light. They get their name from the tungsten element that is encased within a quartz filled with halogen gas.

**Turn.** Continuation of a news item in another column or page.

**Turn-around.** Film industry term for a script dropped by one studio and waiting for another to pick it up.

**Turnline.** Tells you to go to the next page where the article continues.

**Turnover.** The frequency with which the audience for a broadcast program changes over a period of time. Could also mean the measurable profit of a media organisation which could be calculated daily, weekly, monthly, quarterly or annually as determined by the organisation. See audience turnover.

**TVR.** Television rating; indicates coverage of target audiences by individual programmes or advertisements on commercial television.

**Tweak.** To accurately align electronic equipment.

**Tweeter.** A small speaker designed to reproduce high audio frequencies, typically from around 2,000 Hertz to 20,000 Hertz (20,000 Hz is generally considered to be the upper limit of the human ear). Some tweeters can reach up to 30-35kHz.

**Twenty.** Slang for a 20-second broadcast commercial announcement also called a "chain break" or "station break."

**Twisted Pair.** A standard telephone wire.

**Two-colour.** Number of colours used in printing an advertisement or publication. Usually black plus another colour.

**Two-page Spread.** A single print advertisement that crosses two facing pages; also called "double spread" or "double truck". See centre spread and double truck.

**Two-shot.** A picture showing two individuals.

**Two-stage Sell.** In direct response marketing, two-stage mailing campaign, first seeking enquiry, and second converting enquiry into sale. Can also apply to off-the page offers.

**Two-step Flow.** Process by which information disseminated by mass media is (1) received by a direct audience and then (2) relayed to other persons second- hand.

**Two-tailed Test.** Statistical test that tests a nondirectional hypothesis, such as a hypothesis of difference. In a two-tailed test, extreme values in either direction will result in rejection of the null hypothesis.

**Two-way ANOVA.** Analysis of the independent and interactive effects of two independent variables on a single dependent variable.

**Type.** Characters made of metal or plastics and used in printing.

**Type I Error.** Rejection of a null hypothesis that is actually true; the acceptance of a hypothesis that should not have been accepted. The probability of Type I error is set by the researcher; it is the complement of the confidence level.

**Type II Error.** Acceptance of a null hypothesis that is actually false; the rejection of a hypothesis that should have been accepted. The probability of Type II error is related to the statistical power of the test used and the confidence level.

**Type A film.** Colour film balanced for use with photolamps (3400K).

**Type B film.** Colour film balanced for use with studio lamps (3200K).

**Type Area.** The printed area of a page surrounded by margins, or that part of an advertisement layout devoted to text.

**Type Family.** All varieties of a typeface, e.g. roman, italic, light, medium, bold, extra bold, condensed, expanded.

**Type-high.** In relief printing (letterpress) common height of all printing metal such as type, rules, line and halftone blocks, this being 0.918 of an inch.

**Type Mark-up.** Copy ready for printer with instructions given regarding typefaces and type sizes.

**Type Modification.** In digital typesetting, ability to condense or expand type widths.

**Type Series.** All sizes in one typeface.

**Typeface.** A design of type such as Garamond, Helvetica, Times New Roman, Arial, Rockwell, Plantin or Times.

**Typesetter.** Person who sets type. Originally the hand compositor, then the operator of a typesetting machine, and now the keyboard operator of a computerised typesetting machine.

**Typesetting.** Now completely computerised, the process of arranging text in precise positions on the page. The PageMaker software and similar applications are well known tools for typesetting.

**Typographer.** Person who selects type and instructs typesetter regarding typefaces, type sizes, and measure of type areas or column widths. Products Type Mark-up.

**Typographic Errors.** Literals made by typesetter. With computerised typesetting these errors can be different from those produced with metal typesetting. Word breaks can occur badly because of justification of lines; a key may be pressed for italics and not released correctly so that unintended italics are set. Mostly occurs with litho printing. Proof reading has to be extra vigilant to spot such typographical errors.

**Typography.** Art of selecting typefaces, and of marking up copy for typesetting.

**Typological Analysis.** Combination of households into 'generic' classifications. The aim is to establish distinct profiles for given families or households.

# U

**UD.** Ultra Low dispersion lens.

**UHF.** Ultra High Frequency. Ultra high frequency (UHF) designates a range (band) of electromagnetic waves whose frequency is between 300 MHz and 3.0 GHz. Waves whose frequency is above the UHF band fall into the microwave or higher bands, while lower frequency signals fall into the VHF or lower bands. UHF and VHF are the most common frequency bands for television. Modern mobile phones also transmit and receive within the UHF spectrum, and UHF is widely used for two-way radio communication (usually using narrowband frequency modulation, but digital services are on the rise) by both public service agencies and the general public. Though television broadcasting is common on UHF, there has traditionally been very little radio broadcasting in this band until fairly recently. One rare use of UHF waves is in the detection of partial discharges. These discharges occur due to the sharp geometries created in high voltage insulated equipment. The advantage is that this method can be used to localise the source of the discharge, but it is extremely sensitive to external noise. Nonetheless, such detection methods are used in the field especially for large distribution transformers. See VHF.

**U-matic.** Trade name for the 3/4-inch tape format invented by Sony. It was among the first video formats to contain the videotape inside a cassette, as opposed to the various open-reel formats of the time. Because of its 3/4" wideness, it is often known as 'three-quarter-inch' or simply 'three-quarter'. U-matic was named after the shape of the tape path when it was threaded around the helical video head drum, which resembled the letter U. Betamax used this same type of "U-load" as well.

**Ultradirectional.** A mic with a highly directional response pattern. See microphone.

**Ultra-wide Angle Lens.** Extra-wide angle lens, usually those with an angle of view greater than 90°. For 35 mm cameras the description usually applies to lenses of shorter focal length than about 24 mm.

**Umbrella Advertising.** A single advertisement for a number of a manufacturer's brands.

**Umbrella Reflector.** A white or silver umbrella with a bright light placed near the centre used for creating soft light.

**Unaided Recall.** In communication research, asking questions without identifying what is being researched.

**Unbalanced Line.** Audio sources associated with non-professional equipment which rely on two-conductors. Unbalanced lines tend to be susceptible to hum and electronic interference.

**Underexposure.** A condition in which too little light reaches the film, producing a thin negative, a dark slide, or a muddy-looking print.

**Underground Press.** A radical newspaper or production which seeks to fulfil a certain course via the medium.

**Underscan.** Video display scanning technique in which the entire video signal, including black parameter retrace portions, is displayed on the CRT.

**Unduplicated Audience.** The total number of different people who are exposed to an advertisement or campaign through multiple insertions in more than one media vehicle. See cumulative audience.

**Ungathered.** Loose printed sheets not collated in numbered page other.

**Unicam.** Camcorder. A combination all-in-one camera and recorder.

**Unidimensional.** A characteristic, such as an attitude or personality variable, that is best represented as a single factor, as opposed to one that is actually a composite of two or more interrelated factors.

**Unidirectional Microphone.** An extremely sensitive microphone with a pickup pattern in the one direction in which it is pointed. It is relatively insensitive to sounds coming from the sides or rear or a specific direction. See Microphone.

**Unipod.** Also refer as monopod. A camera support consisting of a single, adjustable leg, used to support or hold the camera steady. See tripod.

**Unit.** Advertising unit; the form and context in which an advertisement appears in a media vehicle; for example, full-page, half-page vertical, centre spread, black and white, back cover, two colours; thirty-second commercial, ten-second ID, and so on.

**Unit Production System, Unit-Based Production.** Way of organising production under Hollywood studio system.

**United Press International (UPI).** A global news agency founded in 1958 and headquartered in the United States of America. It files its news stories in English, Spanish and Arabic. With roots dating back to 1907, it was once one of the three biggest news agencies in the world, along with the Associated Press and Reuters, but has dwindled in size and continues to redefine itself. Today, it is owned by News World Communications, which is owned by the Unification Church.

**Unity, Law of.** Blending the elements of a design, such as an advertisement layout, to form a unified whole. A unified advertisement thus seen as a whole, and not as a number of individual and perhaps distracting bits.

**Universal Service.** In relation to public service broadcasting, a service available to everyone at the same price.

**Universe.** In communication research, the population, or the whole from which a random or quota sample is chosen. In broadcast rating this can be the sample area, metro area, or rating area. It is the total population or audience that may have some interest in a programme, product or service.

**Unjustified.** Typesetting with a free or ragged right-hand edge. May suit simulation of readers' letters, or for small areas of copy. Tiresome and difficult to read if applied to long runs of copy. Generally best avoided if legibility is to be maximised.

**Unobtrusive Observation.** Observation in which those being observed are not aware of the researcher's presence. Unobtrusive observation in public places is generally considered legal but always poses ethical questions.

**Unscrambling.** Changing electronic signal into picture and sound, as with satellite TV.

**Unshift.** Keyboard name for lower case type, i.e. small characters.

**Unsolicited Home Visits.** Under the BCAP unsolicited calls should not be made on those who reply to advertisements. An adequate opportunity should be given to refuse a representative's visit. Coupons are best worded so that an enquirer can state whether or not a follow up call is welcomed. To ask for an enquirer to state his telephone number is tantamount to inviting a follow up phone call.

**Unwired Network.** A temporary assemblage of television stations airing the same commercials.

**Up-cut.** Switching to a videotape late, resulting in momentary loss of video or audio at the start.

**Upfront Buying.** Initial purchasing of network television advertising by firms wishing to have optimal selection of available programs; reserving advertising time on network television programs when the seasonal schedule is first announced; this tactic often requires longer schedules and higher prices.

**Uplink.** A ground-to-satellite transmitter link that sends a signal to a satellite and is often part of the mobile van. It is the entire ground to sky satellite system, including the transmitter and antenna and associated electronic equipment of the earth station as well as the receiving transponders on the satellites.

**Upper Case.** Capital letters in printing or typescript.

**Uppie.** Unpretentious, privately individualistic egoist.

**Upscale.** People at the top end of a demographic scale or products of class and distinction. People with high levels of income or members of the big professions are considered to be upscale and become target audience for expensive products and services. Programmes, products and commercials are then developed to appeal to their tastes. The opposite term 'downscale,' is rarely used in advertising or programming circles because of its negative connotation.

**Upward Communication.** Communication from staff to management as seen with speak-up schemes, quality circles, open door policies, works councils, co-partnership and house journals with candid reader comments.

**URL.** Uniform Resource Locator, the technical name for a web address.

**Usage Level**. Classifying media audiences by the amount of the product or service they use.

**Usage Pull.** Technique ascribed to Roser Reeves in USA, to discern the proportionate change in usage of a product as between those who are familiar with its advertising and those who are not.

**Uses and Gratification Approach.** A version of individualist functional theory and research that seeks to explain media use and the satisfaction derived from them in terms of the motives and self-perceived needs of audience members. This is also one version of 'active audience' theory and has been applied in the study of media effects on the grounds that any effect has to be consistent with the needs of the audience.

**Utopian.** Utopia, in its most common and general positive meaning, refers to the human efforts to create a better, or perhaps perfect society. It is associated with an ideal, if not impossible, social world. Ideas which could be/are considered able to radically change our world are often called utopian ideas. 'Utopian' in a negative meaning is used to discredit ideas as too advanced, too optimistic or unrealistic, impossible to realise. Hence, for example, the use by Marxists, of such expressions as "utopian socialism". It has also been used to describe actual communities founded in attempts to create such a society. Although some authors have described their utopias in detail, and with an effort to show a level of practicality, the term "utopia" has come to be applied to notions that are (supposedly) too optimistic and idealistic for practical application.

**UV.** The ultra violet ray. This is beyond the visible spectrum that is its invisible electromagnetic radiation of the sunlight. UV lenses are very expensive, only Nikon has an offering in its Nikkor lens line.

**UV Filter (ultraviolet filter).** Transparent filter that absorbs UV wavelengths. Used to help penetrate haze and give clearer video of distant views. Also used over a lens simply to protect the surface of the lens.

**UV Varnishing.** Application of varnish to covers of brochures, or emphasis to certain areas of print such as illustrations.

# V

**Valence.** Aspects, such as colour and brightness, which attract or repel, so that they can be said to have positive or negative valence.

**Validity.** Whether the researcher is measuring or observing what he or she thinks is being measured or observed. Misleading survey questions, initial observations of a poorly understood culture, or experiments based on erroneous reasoning all lack validity.

**Value.** Lightness or darkness of tone of picture.

**Value Judgment.** Subjective expression of opinion unsupported by fact or available data.

**Value Structures.** A normative, conceptual standard of the desirable that predispositionally influences individuals in choosing among personally perceived alternatives of behaviour.

**Value System.** What is thought to be important or valuable in a particular culture; what is considered worth pursuing and preserving; what gives life its meaning.

**Vandal Proof.** Protection of posters against damage by vandals, especially by printing posters (such as 4 sheets for shopping precincts) on vandal proof material.

**Variable.** Characteristic that can be measured or assessed empirically; an abstract quality that can take on any one of two or more values in a given instance.

**Variable-Contrast Paper.** Photographic paper that provides different grades of contrast when exposed through special filters.

**Variable Focus Lens.** Lens of which the focal length can be continuously varied between set limits. The lens must be refocused with each change in focal length.

**Variable Space.** Spacing inserted between words to justify line and achieve an even right hand edge.

**Variance.** (1) Statistical term for the arithmetic mean of the square deviations of the values from the mean. (2) Management accounting term indicating the difference between a budgeted item and its actual cost or performance. (3) In a dispute, disagreement between executives on questions of policy or strategy.

**Variety, Law of.** In design, avoidance of monotony by use of variety of elements such as variations in typography, use of illustrations and colour.

**Variometre.** Instrument for measuring visual impact of an advertisement by varying amount of light available to view test subjects. Illumination is gradually increased to reveal more of the test elements. The aim is to show which elements are more legible at low level of illumination. Also called shadow box.

**VCR.** Videocassette recorder.

**VCR Plus.** A small, remote-controlled battery-operated device that triggers the recording of a programme off the air or from a cable system on a videocassette recorder (VCR) when the viewer punches in a specific code on its keypad. The code corresponds to a given programme and is published in a TV Guide or local newspaper, next to the programme listing. The hand-held 4-by-6-by-1-inch gadget is designed to simplify the off-air recording of programmes.

**VCR-2.** A dual deck videocassette machine consisting of two videocassette recorders. It allows convenient dubbing and videotape editing for the home video buff. It has two loading slots, side by side on the front panel. A blank tape is inserted in one slot and the tape to be copied in the other. When the button marked 'Copy Tape' is pushed it starts both cassettes rolling.

**VDT.** Visual Display Terminals. Data from electronic keyboards and computers appear on a device similar to a television screen.

**Vectorscope.** A specialised, stand alone, electronic testing device that measures the purity of a colour signal's hue and chrominance. Like an oscilloscope or waveform monitor, the apparatus takes a

Vehicle.

small portion of the colour signal generated by a camera or test generator and graphically displays the colour bars continuously on a small round screen. The bars are represented, however, by six small boxes on the screen rather than by vertical bars. The vectorscope is more accurate than the human eye in measuring the correct balance in a colour picture. It is used to align cameras and equipment.

**Vehicle.** (1) In an ink, liquid component containing the pigment. (2) An individual outlet of an advertising medium, such as a certain magazine or a specific broadcast station or program.

**Velocity Mike.** See ribbon mike.

**Vendor.** Person or organisation with products or services to sell. Those who sell newspapers, magazines or other publications are called vendors.

**Verisimilitude.** Quality of seeming like what is taken to be the real world of a particular text; see realism.

**Vernacular Newspapers.** In third world countries with many languages, vernacular newspapers, sometimes sponsored by government, are means of reaching ethnic groups. Vernacular newspapers or publications are written in vernacular to communicate to a wider audience, especially to illiterates who cant read or write or to those who do not understand English language. Some vernacular newspapers in Nigeria include: "Irohin Yoruba" - Yoruba, Gaskiya Tafi Kwabo" -Hausa, "Gboningbonhon", "Isokan" - Yoruba, "Amana" - Hausa, "Udola"- Igbo, and "Ogene" also Igbo

**Verso.** Left hand page, or back of a page in a book. The opposite side of recto.

**Vertical Advertising.** Co-operative advertising, publication reaching different levels of a specific business or profession.

**Vertical Blanking Interval.** A period in which the electron beam in display is blanked out while it travels from the bottom of the screen to the top.

**Vertical Circulation/Publications.** Business publication edited for persons at all levels in a specific industry or profession.

**Vertical Cume.** The total number of different people who are tuned to successive broadcast programs.

**Vertical Integration.** Business activity involving one company acquiring others elsewhere in the production process.

**Vertical Journals.** Those journals read by people of varying status from operators to top management in the same industry.

**Vertical Publication.** A business or trade publication that is of interest to all levels or job functions within a single business or profession.

**Vertical Saturation.** Many broadcast commercial announcements scheduled throughout the course of a single day, generally designed to reach many different people, in an attempt to reach a high percentage of the broadcast audience.

**Vet.** Study for inaccuracies.

**VH-1.** A basic cable service that programmes music videos that appeal to the youths from 25-35 years. Programming to an older audience than the adolescents who view MTV and channel O, the channel features comedy routines, artists' specials and some original musical programmes.

**VHF.** Very High Frequency. A term that designate the bandwidth in the electromagnetic spectrum. Commonly, is the radio frequency range from 30 MHz to 300 MHz. Frequencies immediately below VHF is HF, and the next higher frequencies are known as Ultra high frequency (UHF). Common uses for VHF are FM radio broadcast at 88–108 MHz and television broadcast (together with UHF). VHF is also commonly used for terrestrial navigation systems (VOR in particular) and aircraft communications. VHF frequencies' propagation characteristics are ideal for short-distance terrestrial communication, with a range generally somewhat farther than line-of-sight from the transmitter. Unlike high frequencies (HF), the ionosphere does not usually reflect VHF radio and thus transmissions are restricted to the local area (and does not interfere with transmissions thousands of kilometres away). VHF is also less affected by atmospheric noise and interference from electrical equipment than low frequencies. Whilst it is more easily blocked by land features than HF and lower frequencies, it is less bothered by buildings and other less substantial objects than higher frequencies. See UHF.

**VHS.** (video home system) A consumer oriented videotape format using 1/2-inch tape housed in a cassette. *VHS-C* smaller version.

**Video.** Any visual image that can normally be seen by the human eye. Derived from Latin 'to see', it is that portion in television engineering that appears on the screen from the camera pick-up tube and sends it to the cathode ray tube which finally displays it.

**Video Cassette Recording.** Process in which electronic signals representing sound and vision are superimposed upon a magnetic tape contained in a cassette for easy handling. The signals so stored are subsequently available for playback via a television monitor or screen as when required.

**Video Magazines.** Magazine- type information on a videocassette, periodically released to customers on a subscription basis.

**Video News Release.** Usually offered to broadcast stations rather than distributed like printed news release. Means of providing topical background information for news and other broadcast programmes.

**Video Vampire.** Any visual element that detracts from selling thrust of TV commercial.

**Videocassette.** Videotape recording contained in a cassette for playing on a VCR connected to a TV set. VHS is most popular but also on Betamax and Sony Umatic commercial format. Blank tapes for recording off-air. Largely replaced films, but films can be transferred to video, as can slides. By means of post-production techniques many computer graphics effects can be introduced. Used for documentaries, house magazines, etc. more portable than cans of film.

**Videocassette Recorder.** Playback devise for both recording on blank tape and for playing pre-recorded tapes via connection with TV set.

**Videophiles.** Sometimes called prosumers, these are people who are devoted to video cameras and production gear, and they purchase the latest equipment for use in amateur productions.

**Videophonics.** The technique of sending and receiving pictures by telephone wire.

**Videotape.** Magnetic tape counterpart of sound film. In various widths for commercial/domestic, reel-to-reel and cassette formats. Most TV programmes, TV commercials and documentaries are now on videotape. Computer graphics special effects can be applied.

**Videotape Editing.** The assembling of television shots into sequences, sequences into segments, and segments into a finished programme. In the process, good portions replace poor and are moved around into a final structured organisation. The shots, segments and sequences are joined electronically. There are two strategies of doing this: insert editing and assemble editing. Insert editing involves the replacement of an already existing shot, segment or sequence with another. Insert edits are made to correct mistakes or to improve the programme by inserting new and better material over old. Assemble edits are accomplished in chronological order from beginning to end by assembling the title, then first scene, second scene, third scene, etc., on a blank tape. Most editing projects begin with assemble editing in offline editing mode and progress to insert editing using online editing techniques.

**Video Tape Recording (VTR).** Pictures and sound recorded magnetically on tape which can then be reproduced upon a cathode ray tube. Often used for television commercials and programmes but also suitable for many forms of instructional training and evaluation of personnel.

**Videotext.** Generic term for two-way transmission systems, primarily of graphic and textual information. The system's two way capacity permits the consumer to perform such task as shopping and banking using the system.

**Videowalls.** A number of large television monitors arranged in vertical and horizontal rows, forming a rectangle or a square. The monitors are separated by thin borders and display the same or different crisp, bright high quality images. The total size and shape of the multi-screen unit is dependent on the number of picture modules used and their assembled configuration.

**Vidicon Tube.** A common pickup tube used in cameras for corporate television and audiovisual communications. It consists of a cylinder six inches in length and one-half inch in diameter and is cheap. It produces a slightly grainy picture; though it is not sensitive as the saticon tube.

Viewdata.

**Viewdata.** Post Office variant of ceefax and Oracle data. A type of videotext system.

**Viewer Response Service.** Most media organisations especially broadcast, offer telephone service so that viewers may respond to programmes, commercials, or any topical issue. Through this medium they could also request for a particular music or literature.

**Viewfinder.** See finder.

**Viewing Pattern.** Time of the day when certain viewers watch programmes. TV commercials can be targeted accordingly.

**Vignetting.** Underexposure of image corners produced deliberately by shading or unintentionally by inappropriate equipment, such as unsuitable lens hood or badly designed lens. A common fault of wide-angle lenses, owing to reflection cut-off, etc. of some of the very oblique rays. May be caused in some long-focus lenses by the length of the lens barrel.

**Vinyl.** Removable self-adhesive vinyl used for bus advertisement, especially for external positions. Preferred to paper posters which fade and saturate.

**Vinylite.** Plastic matrix.

**Violence Debate.** Recurring debates over assumed audience behaviour, focusing on the possible effects of representations of violence.

**VIPS Formula.** David Bernstein's formula for an effective advertisement. Visibility, Identity, Promise, Single-mindedness. The advertisement should be seen, there should be no doubt whose advertisement it is or its subject, a benefit should be offered, and the ad should stick to the point.

**Virtual.** Something which is a representation rather than the real thing, thus virtual reality.

**Virtual Community.** This describes the group or close personal associations formed on-line by participants in Internet exchanges and discussions. A virtual community is thought to have many of the features of a real community, including identification, bonding, shared norms and outlook, even without any physical contact or real personal knowledge of other members.

**Virtual Reality.** The development of new human experiences- involving all the senses- through the use of computer technology.

**Virtual Vision.** A production device that allows the cameraperson to see behind, above, or to the left or right without turning the head. A pair of goggles attached to a camera includes a tiny colour TV with a small mirror in front of it. The picture is projected from the mirror onto a visor. The user can view the picture, or if the visor is clear, can see the live action on the set.

**Visual.** Rough, scamp or scribble. Rough layout of an advertisement.

**Visual Display Unit.** Resembling a TV set, the monitor which gives visual presentation to computerised or keyed information.

**Visualiser.** Designer responsible for producing visual ideas for the interpretation and execution of an advertising brief. Usually, but not necessarily, an employee of an advertising agency.

**VLS.** A script designation for very long shot.

**VO.** See Voice Over.

**VOA.** Voice of America. This is the official international broadcasting service of the Government of the United States of America. It is similar to other international broadcasters such as the BBC World Service, Voice of Nigeria, Deutsche Welle, Radio Netherlands, Radio France Internationale and Voice of Russia. Its oversight bureau is the International Broadcasting Bureau which is committed to 'public diplomacy'. There are also many affiliate stations and contracted stations which carry VOA programs. VOA programs in many, if not most, of its broadcast languages are also available on the Internet in both streaming media and downloadable formats.

**Voice.** Extent of media coverage.

**Voice Over.** Narration with narrator not on screen, possibly with still photograph, used for documentaries. It is usually recorded and then played back over the visual portion of the production. The announcer's voice is heard over a spot or broadcast program.

**Voice Quality.** The way one's voice sound, including such characteristics as resonance, thinness, timbre, nasality, huskiness and tone.

**Volatile Memory.** Digitised information stored in a computer or microprocessor that remains only as long as there is electrical power.

**Volt, V.** A measure of electrical pressure. It is the SI derived unit of electric potential difference or electromotive force and is named in honour of the Italian physicist Alessandro Volta (1745–1827), who invented the voltaic pile, the first chemical battery. It is defined as the potential difference across a conductor when a current of one ampere dissipates one watt of power. Hence, it is the base SI representation $m^2 \cdot kg \cdot s^{-3} \cdot A^{-1}$, which can be equally represented as one joule of energy per coulomb of charge, J/C. 120 volts is the standard in the United States and many other countries.

**Volume Discount.** In radio or TV airtime buying, discount to agency on large expenditures, but volume and discount varies from one station to another.

**Voluntary Controls (Advertising).** System of self control adopted by UK advertising practitioners to ensure that advertisements conform to a defined code of practice.

**VON.** Voice of Nigeria. The Voice of Nigeria went on air on January 1, 1962 as part of the Nigeria Broadcasting Corporation. The Corporation is a parastatal of the Federal Ministry of Information and National Orientation. It has five directorates- Directorates of News, Programmes, Engineering, Finance and Supplies and Personnel. The news and programmes originating from the VON reflects views of Nigeria as a Federation and give adequate expression to the diverse culture and characteristics of the different peoples within the country. The news, views and comments from the station are geared towards strengthening Nigeria's policy and image. The station broadcasts in six languages for at least 18 hours a day in the following frequencies - 725KHZ, 41m; 1177KHZ, 25m; 1512KHZ, 19m; 9690KHZ, 31m. The languages include English, Hausa, French, Arabic, Swahili and Fulfude.

**Voucher Copy.** Free copy of publication containing advertisement, sent to agency or advertiser. The agency voucher clerk checks insertions, positions, colour and reproduction quality before payment is made.

**Voyeurism.** The pleasure of looking while unseen; used in thinking about male pleasure in the ways cinema, especially, constructs women as objects of the male gaze.

**VTR.** Videotape recorder.

**VU Metre.** A metre calibrated in volume units and in percentage of modulation. VU metres indicate "loudness."

**VU (volume unit).** Unit of measure for audio level or signal strength.

# W

**W's and an H, Five.** The five primary questions used in reporting or news writing; Who? What? When? Where? Why? How? A news story normally answers these questions.

**Wait Order.** An instruction or request to delay publication of a print advertisement; also, but seldom, used in broadcast. On another hand, paper set advertisement, usually for insertion in local newspaper, awaiting advertiser's instruction to print it.

**Walk-Through.** A rough rehearsal in which no cameras are used. Generally the actors walk from place to place and check their actions without speaking any dialogue.

**Wallpaper.** Way of pre-printing full colour whole page advertisements for black and white newspapers, using photogravure, and printing on a web without break. When the web is fed into the newspaper press it is cut irrespective of match. Generally replaced by litho-printed pre-printed colour pages, or colour is printed on the run.

**Warm.** A colour picture that contains a noticeable amount of red or yellow.

**Warm Colours.** Red and yellow shades, which also appear to advance whereas pale or cold colours like blue and mauve, tend to recede.

**Warm-Up.** A brief bit of business with a studio audience that combines casual chat with jokes and questions and answers. Commonly used in game shows, the star, one of the leads, or the producer warms up the audience by appearing on stage and chatting informally with them. This period prior to the show is designed to get the audience in a mood that is receptive to watching or participating in the programme.

**Wash Drawing.** Drawing painted in grey and black.

**Waste Circulation.** Parts of a circulation that are of no value to the advertiser but which he nevertheless have to pay for its campaign. The readers of this publication are not prospects for the product or service being advertised; the advertisement is disseminated in an area where the product or service is not distributed.

**Watchdog.** Watchdog journalism is at the heart of a media's commitment to public service. It refers to forms of activist journalism aimed at holding accountable public personalities and institutions whose functions impact on the social and political life. The term lapdog journalism is sometimes used as a conceptual opposite to watchdog journalism.

**Watermark.** Made by wire design during papermaking, and impressed by dandy roll, to produce papermaker's trademark or to distinguish a particular paper.

**Watt.** A unit of electrical power equal to the voltage times the amperage.

**Wave Posting.** In outdoor advertising, and especially when local promotions are being held, concentration of poster showings in a succession of areas.

**Waveform Monitor.** An electronic device that measures the black and white information in a colour picture and the synchronisation of a television signal. A waveform monitor is also used to determine the luminance of a colour signal and strength of the video level of that signal. The monitor measures the signal balance of colour cameras, videotape recorders and other electronic units. It is a type of oscilloscope or CRT.

**Weasel Words.** Imprecise words which evade definite statements, e.g. may be for yes, seldom for never, but bad for good. Words which avoid admitting too much.

**Web.** Large reel of paper, or other material, used when printing by rotary press.

**Web-fed.** Printing from web or reel of paper instead of sheets.

**Web-offset.** Method of offset-litho printing in which paper is fed into the press from a reel as compared with a sheet feed.

**Web-offset-litho.** Rotary lithographic printing process, plate cylinder first printing onto blanket which offsets onto paper, and using webs or reels of paper instead of flat sheets. High-speed process as used for most newspaper printing.

**Weight.** (1) The relative lightness or boldness of the characters in the various typefaces within a type family. Weight is indicated by relative terms such as thin, light, medium bold, extra-bold and black.(2) Volume of advertising.

**Weighted Average.** Individual group averages multiplied by values assigned to each group. Weighting is a statistical technique for adjusting averages according to their significance in the total.

**Weight of Viewing.** Division of ITV audiences into heavy, light and regular viewers, approximately one third each.

**Weightings.** In communication research, adjustment of figures to overcome imbalance.

**Wet-on-wet.** Printing colours in sequence before drying, which can cause loss of register if paper stretches.

**Wf.** Wrong fount. Proof reader's mark if any wrong type fount has been set.

**White Balancing.** Electronically adjusting a camera's chroma channels for a light source so that white will be reproduced as true white. Most cameras can automatically white balance when the operator fills the screen with a white card and pushes a white balance button.

**White Line.** Spacing between lines of typesetting, formerly known as leading when strips of non-type high metal are inserted between lines of metal type.

**White Out.** Reverse out or printing white on another colour.

**White Space.** The blank spaces on a printed page- considered to be an important component in the overall design and look of the page.

**Wholesaler.** A company or individual serving as a middleman between a programme supplier and the retail video store.

**Wide.** Transition in video editing in which one image replaces another according to a specific pattern such as the appearance of a page being turned.

**Wide-Angle Lens.** A lens or a scene that represents an angle of view significantly wider than normal. A wide-angle lens or shot is either a prime lens with a focal length significantly less (at least 25 percent less) than a normal lens, or a zoom lens used at a focal length significantly less than normal- can lead to distortion of objects very close to the camera. Also can be explained as a lens whose focal length is shorter than the diagonal of the film frame; in 35mm photography, lenses shorter than 50mm; also referred to as a short lens.

**Widow.** Lonely single word on last line of paragraph. Should appear at top of a column or page. The worst: single words. Computerised typesetting makes them far more common than a fussy page makeup person would have tolerated. Some people use this term to refer to any short line at the end of a paragraph and trim stories deftly by eliminating just enough words to eliminate the widows. Text should be edited to eliminate widow if possible by shortening sentence.

**Wild Sound; Wild Track.** Sound, generally background sound, recorded independently of the video and added during postproduction. Does not need to be synchronised with the video.

**Wild Spots.** Radio commercials guaranteed by a station to be played at some point within a designated block of time.

**Window.** In litho film, space where halftones are to be stripped in.

**Windows.** The periods of availability in the various media for theatrical films.

**Windscreen.** A small fabric or foam rubber cover for the top of a microphone that reduces or eliminates the sound of moving air or wind.

**Wipe.** A sophisticated visual effect and form of dissolve that gradually replaces one moving image with another. The effect is of one picture wiping out the preceding one. As one picture disappears another is revealed.

**Wire Stand.** Point of sale display piece for counter or floor. Should have a plate identifying the supplier.

**Wire Stitching.** As in magazines.

**Wireless Microphone.** A microphone that has a built-in, low-power transmitter, or that is connected to a transmitter. Wireless mikes are commonly used when a mike cord would create a problem.

**Wood Free.** paper made of wood pulp or chemical pulp, and free from mechanical pulp, which has been cooked to dissolve lignin which otherwise causes browning effect. Better quality than newsprint. Typical white papers that stay white are coated wood free and wood free opaque.

**Woodshedding.** The careful study, making and rehearsing of broadcast copy before performance.

**Woofer.** A loudspeaker driver designed to produce low-frequency sounds, typically from around 40 Hertz up to a few hundred Hertz. The name, derived from one of the words for a dog's bark, contrasts with the name used for speakers designed to reproduce high-frequency sounds, tweeters.

**Word Break.** Division of word at the end of line, which should enable words to be read easily.

**Word of Mouth.** Informal way in which media products become known about audiences.

**Working Master.** A final edited master tape which is kept in pristine condition after making copies. These copies are then used for subsequent copies.

**Work Print.** Film footage that is assembled into a general order and sequence without sound or any optional effects, such as dissolves or superimpositions. Sometimes known as a rough cut, this print usually undergoes many editing changes before the separate audio, video and optical portions are sent back to the film laboratory to be combined into a composite or answer print. Used in off-line editing.

**Work-up Drawing.** Preliminary sketch before finished artwork is produced.

**Workings.** Number of times a piece of print has to pass through the machine before it is finished.

**World Wide Web.** The network of pages of images, texts and sounds on the Internet which can be viewed using browser software.

**WORM.** (write once read many [times]) A type of CD-ROM videodisc that allows the user to create data. The initials stand for write once, read many times. Using a personal computer, an operator can input digital data such as office records or archival information onto a blank disc. Once entered, the data cannot be changed. This limits flexibility but ensures a permanent record for the data, which can rapidly and easily be summoned at any time by using the CD-ROM device.

**Wowing.** The audible, undesirable, distorted sound when a record or tape is run at an incorrect or inconsistent speed. This is often as a result of starting a record before a turntable has reached full speed.

**Wrap.** The finish of a show or programme. The term is used to describe the conclusion of the day's work or, more often, the ending of the production for the entire project or completion of a film shoot. The term was borrowed from the idea of wrapping up an object to encase and secure it for transportation, in this case, to put a programme 'in the can.'

**Wraparound Programming.** Programming that is sometimes scheduled to appear before and after a major non-fiction programme that addresses the same theme or topic. Like bread in a sandwich, the shows wrap around the meat of the main programme.

**WS.** (1) Script designation for wide shot. (2) Watt per second. For flash mode, the measurement of electrical energy in the flash.

**WX.** Script symbol for "weather report".

**WYSIWYG.** An acronym (pronounced "wizzywig") for what-you-see-is-what-you-get. Refers to a computer screen representation of text or graphics being the same as the subsequent hardcopy printout.

# X

**X (X Bar).** Statistical symbol for average.

**X-axis.** The horizontal line (axis) of a graph or chart.

**X-certificate.** See certification of films.

**XCU.** Script designation for extreme close-up

**X-height (XH).** Standard height of a lower case letter in typography, usually measured by referring to the letter 'x'.

**X-height and Line.** Height of small letters without ascenders or descenders, e.g. a, e, i, o, u. Letters with low x-heights are difficult to read as text type. Some display faces have low x-heights which is acceptable in large sizes, but makes type unsuitable for body matter- a fault sometimes overlooked. Also called the mean line.

**X- letters.** Letters that are by formation characteristically self contained. It neither points top nor inclines down. Examples are a, e, c, o, u, v, x, z.

**X (setting).** Electronic flash units fire virtually instantaneously and reach full brightness immediately. Thus no time delay is required. Real time setting that causes the flash to burst in synchronises or instantaneously as the shuttle open up. For older manual camera, the X synch speed usually refers to the maximum speed that the camera can have its shuttle curtain open long enough to synchronise with the flash. In fact, if there is a time delay, the electronic flash may be all over before the shutter gets open. To fire electronic flash with a focal-plane shutter, the switch in the camera is closed at the instant the first curtain of the focal-plane shutter reaches fully open, this is called X synchronisation.

**XLR Connector.** Canon connector. A standard, three-prong professional audio connector.

**XLS.** A script designation for extra long shot.

**X-ray.** Electromagnetic waves at the upper end of the electromagnetic spectrum.

**X Sync Terminal.** Electronic flash units which mount on the hot shoe and are triggered by the electrical contact in the shoe. Other types use sync cord which connects to the sync terminal on the camera. Also referred to PC Terminal section.

**Xenon Flash.** Powerful swift light source used in photosetting.

**Xerography.** Photocopying process in which an image is reproduced when toner adheres to paper by means of light-sensitive electrostatic charge. In the process a photoelectric surface converts light into an electronic charge. Documents can be reproduced in black and white and in colour to a very high standard, reduced in size or enlarged. The electrostatic image of a document attracts charged ink powder which in turn is attracted to charged paper. A visible image is formed and fixed permanently by heating.

# Y

**Yagi.** A specific design for an outdoor TV antenna.

**Yamoussoukro Declaration.** Issued by African leaders in 1985, the declaration states 'One of the main keys to solving Africa's development problems lies in mastering the national management of information in all its forms'. The text of the declaration argued that information management and control are 'not only a positive force for regional and continental integration but also an essential condition for the survival of Africa within the community of nations in the 21st century'.

**Yapp.** Edges of a binding that exceeds pages of a book, as with covers of some bibles.

**Yates' Correction.** In communication research, adjustments necessary for a chi-square calculation when there is only one degree of freedom, that is, when a two-row by two-column table is being analysed.

**Yellow Journalism.** This is a pejorative reference to journalism that features scandal-mongering sensationalism, jingoism or other unethical or unprofessional practices by news media organisations or individual journalists. It involves the use of cheaply sensational or unscrupulous methods in reporting to attract and influence the readers. The term originated during the circulation battles between Joseph Pulitzer's New York World and William Randolph Hearst's New York Journal from 1895 to about 1898, and can refer specifically to this period. Both papers were accused by more established publishers of sensationalising the news in order to drive up circulation, although the newspapers did serious reporting as well. The New York Press coined the term "Yellow Journalism" in early 1897 to describe the work of Pulitzer and Hearst. The newspaper did not define the term, and in 1898 simply elaborated, "We called them Yellow because they are Yellow."

**Yo-Yo Shots.** Repeated zooming in and out on subjects. An annoying effect associated with amateur productions.

# Z

**Zahn, Johann.** (1631—1707) The seventeenth century German author of *Oculus Artificialis Teledioptricus Sive Telescopium* (Würzburg, 1685). This work contains many descriptions and diagrams, illustrations and sketches of both the camera obscura and magic lantern, along with various other lanterns, slides, projection types, and peepshow boxes. As a student of light, Zahn is considered the most prolific writer and illustrator of the camera obscura. See Camera.

**Zapping.** Flicking from one TV channel to another by use of remote control, as when viewer does not wish to watch a programme or a commercial. It is the physical manifestation of the process of grazing. They zap rapidly from one channel to another until a programme catches the viewer's attention. Others zap the channels or turn off the sound during commercials in the programme they are watching.

**Zebra Stripes.** Black lines superimposed over specific areas of an image in the viewfinders of some cameras used as an aid in making video level adjustments.

**Zipper.** Special perforated seal applied to mail shots.

**Zipping.** The process of using a remote control device to fast-forward a pre-recorded videocassette to a new segment, scene or spot. It is similar to zapping. It sometimes become a form of grazing, although it is necessarily confined to one programme or film at a time, rather than many channels and programmes, as is the case with zapping.

**Zone.** Part of a newspaper's circulation area. If the newspaper divides its circulation area into zones, advertisers may buy ads in just their local areas. Often, news coverage is zoned to complement zoned advertising.

**Zoned Campaigns/Plan.** Advertising campaigns restricted to certain geographical areas, ether to boost sales in a weak-selling area, or to launch a product area by area as when Glo Mobile launched her GPRS and MMS in Nigeria. Also know as local plan.

**Zoom/Zooming.** The process of varying the focal length, using the lens on a camera, to bring picture into close-up or the reverse. This arrangement or zooming allows the operator to change the focal length and move between telephoto and wide angle settings.

**Zoom Lens.** Simply a lens with a continuously variable focal length and angle of acceptance. It is a convenient and versatile TV device that is actually a combination of lenses. It has a variable, rather than fixed focal length and can operate in a range from wide angle to a telephoto lens without losing focus. The lens can be used to change angles between shots or to zoom in on or away from a subject during a shot. Numerous cameras now come with automatic zoom lenses. A fall-off in brightness at the edges of an image, slide, or print can be caused by poor lens design, using a lens hood not matched to the lens, or attaching too many filters to the front of the lens.

**Zoom Ratio.** Numbers indicating zoom range for a lens. The mathematical ratio for a zoom lens derived by dividing its shortest focal length into its longest focal length.

**Zoopraxography.** A process developed by pioneer photographer Eadward Muybridge (1830-1904) who was not the inventor of cine-film but made the first photographic moving pictures. He called this Zoopraxography. Muybridge described his Zoopraxiscope as being 'the first apparatus ever used, or constructed, for synthetically demonstrating movements analytically photo graphed from life'. In 1878 he set up an experiment at Palo Alto, California, to ascertain by photography, whether all four hooves of a galloping horse were ever simultaneously clear of the ground. 24 cameras were aligned along the running track, each triggered off by the horse as it galloped past. The Zoopraxiscope comprised basically of a spinning glass disc bearing the photographs in sequence of movement. The disc, when attached to a central shaft, resolved in front of the condensing lens of a projecting lantern parallel to end close to another disc fixed to a tabular shaft which encircled the other, and round which it rotated in the reverse direction. However, by 1885 Muybridge had produced an encyclopaedia of motion: men and women, clothed and unclothed, performed simple actions such as running, drinking cups of tea or shoeing horses; and a massive and varied study of animals and birds in movement. Essentially the first movie projector, the stop-motion images were initially painted onto the glass, as silhouettes. A second series of discs, made in 1892-4, used outline drawings printed onto the discs photographically, then coloured by hand. Some of the animated images are very complex, featuring multiple combinations of sequences of animal and human movement. His carefully catalogued work was published in 1887. Also images from all of the known 71 surviving discs have recently been reproduced in the book *Eadweard Muybridge: The Kingston Museum Bequest* (The Projection Box, 2004). See Muybridge, Eadward.

# Bibliography

Allen, Robert C. (1992). *Channels of Discourse Reassembled*. Chapel Hill, NC: University of North Carolina Press.

Andersen, Neil. (1989). *Media Works*. Toronto: Oxford University Press.

Baggaley, Jon and Duck, Steve. (1976). *Dynamics of Television*, England: Saxon House.

Barwise, Patrick and Ehrenberg, Andrew. (1988). *Television and its Audience*, London: Sage Publication.

Barman, Sandra and Sreberny-Mohammadi, Annabelle. (eds.) (1996). *Globalisation, Communication, and Transnational Civil Society*, Cresskill: Hampton Press.

Berger, Asa. (1982). *Media Analysis Techniques*. London: Sage Publication.

Berger, Arthur Asa. (1995). *Essentials of Mass Communication Theory*, London: Sage Publication.

Bianculli, David. (1992). *Teleliteracy: Taking Television Seriously*. New York: Continuum.

Bower, Robert T. (1985). *The Changing Television Audience in America*. New York: Columbia University Press.

Branston, Gill and Stafford, Roy. (2003). *The Media Student's Book*, (Third Edition), London: Routledge.

Brown, Ray. (1993). *Characteristics of Local Media Audiences*, England: Glower Publishing.

Buckingham, David (Editor). (1993). *Reading Audiences: Young People and The Media*. Manchester: Manchester University Press.

Cantor, Muriel G. and Cantor, Joel M. (1992). *Prime-Time Television: Content and Control*, (Second Edition), London: Sage Publications.

Carey, James W. (Editor). (1988). *Media, Myths and Narratives: Television and the Press*. London: Sage Publication.

Cashmore, Ellis (1994). *... and there was television*, London: Routledge.

Cobley, Paul. (ed.) (1996). *The Communication Theory Reader*, London: Routledge.

Collins, Richard. (1990). *Television: Policy and Culture*, London: Unwin Hyman.

Crisell, Andrew. (1986). *Understanding Radio*. London: Methuen.

Crisell, Andrew. (2002). *An Introductory History of British Broadcasting*, (Second Edition) London: Routledge.

Cubitt, Sean. (1991). *Timeshift: On Video Culture*, London: Routledge.

Cutlip, Scott. (1994). *The Unseen Power: Public Relations*, A History. Hillsdale, N.J.: Erlbaum Associates.

Dimbleby, Nick; Dimbleby, Richard; and Whittington, Ken. (1994). *Practical Media: A Guide to Production Techniques*, London: Hodder & Stoughton.

Dominick, Joseph, R. (1993). *The Dynamics of Mass Communication*, (Fourth Edition) New York: McGraw-Hill.

Duncan, Barry. (1988). *Mass Media and Popular Culture*. Toronto: Harcourt, Brace, Jovanovich.

Durham, Meenakshi Gigi and Kellner, Douglas. M. (eds.) (2006). *Media and Cultural Studies: Keyworks*. Oxford: Blackwell.

Elliott, Deni (Editor). (1986). *Responsible Journalism*. London: Sage Publication.

Farrah, Joseph. (1998). *Dictionary of Marketing and Advertising*, Malaysia: Golden Books.

Fedler, Fred, Bender, John R., Davenport, Lucinda D. and Drager, Michael W. (2001). *Reporting for the Media*, (Second Edition), Orlando: Harcourt College Publishers.

Fiske, John. (1987). *Television Culture*. London: Methuen.

Fiske, John. (1990). *Introduction to Communication Studies* (2nd Edition). London: Routledge.

Fiske, John and Hartley, John. (1992). *Reading Television*, London: Routledge.

Gauntlett, David and Hill, Annette. (1999). *TV Living: Television, Culture and Everyday Life*, London: Routledge and British Film Institute.

Goodhardt, G. J., Ehrenberg, A. S. C., and Collins, M.A. (1975). *The Television Audience: Patterns of Viewing*, England: Saxon House.

Grunig, James E. and Hunt, Todd. (1984). *Managing Public Relations*, New York: Holt, Rinehart and Winston.

Hansen, Anders; Cottle, Simon; Negrine, Ralph and Newbold, Chris. (1998). *Mass Communication Research Methods*, New York: Palgrave.

Hartley, John. (1982). *Understanding News*. New York: Routledge.

Jefkins, Frank. (1994). *Advertising*, (Third Edition), London: Macmillan.

Jefkins, Frank. (1998). *Public Relations*, (Revised by Yadin, Daniel), Essex: Pearson Education.

Levinson, Paul. (1999). *Digital McLuhan: A guide to the Information Millennium*, London: Routledge.

Lull, James. (1990). *Inside Family Viewing: Ethnographic Research on Television's Audiences*. New York: Routledge.

Lull, James. (1995). *Media, Communication, Culture: A Global Approach*, Cambridge: Polity Press.

MacBride Commission, The. (2004). *Many Voices, One World: Towards a New, More Just, and More Efficient World Information and Communication Order*, (Report by the International Commission for the Study of Communication Problems), USA: Rowman & Littlefield.

Macnamara, Jim (2005). *Jim Macnamara's Public Relations Handbook*, (5th ed.), Melbourne: Information Australia.

Marchand, Phillip. (1998). *Marshall McLuhan- The Medium and the Messenger: A Biography*, Cambridge: The MIT Press, Massachusetts.

McLuhan, Marshall. (2001). *Understanding Media: The Extensions of Man*, London: Routledge.

Mc Quail, Denis and Windahl, Sven. (1993). *Communication Models for the Study of Mass Communications*, (2nd Edition), London: Longman.

Mc Quail, Denis. (2005). *Mc Quail's Mass Communication Theory*, (5th Edition), London: Sage Publication.

Moores, Shaun. (1993). *Interpreting Audiences: The Ethnography of Media Consumption*, London: Sage Publication.

Myers, David G. (2001). *Psychology*, (6th ed) New York: Worth.

Okunna, Chinyere (ed.). (2002). *Teaching Mass Communication: A Multi-Dimensional Approach*, Enugu: New Generation Books.

Patterson, Freeman. (1989). *Photography and The Art of Seeing*, Toronto: Key Porter Books.

Phillips, David (2001). *Online Public Relations*, London: Kogan Page.

Postman, Neil and Powers, Steve. (1992). *How To Watch TV News*. New York: Penguin.

Priest, Susanna Hornig. (1996). *Doing Media Research: An Introduction*, London: Sage Publication.

Reed, Robert M. and Reed, Maxine K. (1994) *The Facts on File Dictionary of Television, Cable, and Video*, New York: Facts on File.

Rushkoff, Douglas. (1994). *Media Virus: Hidden Agendas in Popular Culture*. New York: Ballantine.

Schneider, Cynthia and Wallis, Brian (eds.). (1998). *Global Television*, New York: Wedge Press.

Starr, Paul (2004). *The Creation of the Media: Political Origins of Modern Communications*, New York: Basic Books.

Stevenson, Nick. (2004). *Understanding Media Cultures: Social Theory and Mass Communication*, (Second Edition), London: Sage Publication.

Stevenson, Hilliard L. (1991). *Writing for Television and Radio*, (Fifth Edition), Calif: Wadsworths.

Storey, John. (1993). *An Introductory Guide to Cultural Theory and Popular Culture*. Athens, Georgia: University of Georgia Press.

Thomas, Roger. (2001). *What's At Issue? Media and Censorship*, Oxford: Heinemann Library.

Watney, Simon. (1987). *Policing Desire: Pornography. Aids and The Media*. London: Methuen.

Watson, James and Hill, Anne. (2000). *Dictionary of Communication and Media Studies*, (5th Edition), London: Arnold.

Watson, James. (2003). *Media Communication: A Introduction to Theory and Process*, (Second Edition), New York: Palgrave Macmillan.